MARV LEVY

Where Else Would You Rather Be?

MARV LEVY
FOREWORD BY JIM KELLY

www.SportsPublishingLLC.com

ISBN: 1-58261-797-X

Publisher: Peter L. Bannon and Joseph J. Bannon Sr.
Senior managing editor: Susan M. Moyer
Acquisitions editor: Bob Snodgrass
Developmental editor: Elisa Bock Laird
Art director: K. Jeffrey Higgerson
Dust jacket/photo spread design, imaging: Heidi Norsen
Project manager: Greg Hickman
Copy editor: Cynthia L. McNew
Photo editor: Erin Linden-Levy
Vice president of sales and marketing: Kevin King
Media and promotions managers: Michael Hagan (regional), Randy Fouts (national), Maurey Williamson (print)

Printed in the United States of America

Sports Publishing L.L.C.
804 North Neil Street
Champaign, IL 61820

Phone: 1-877-424-2665
Fax: 217-363-2073
Web site: www.SportsPublishingLLC.com

To the wonderful women in My Life:

My dear mother, Ida
My beautiful wife, Frannie
My lovely sister, Marilyn
My darling daughter, Kimberly

None of them (and that includes my former wife, Dorothy, who was with me during my earlier years) ever gained a yard or made a tackle, but without their love and support I wouldn't be RIGHT HERE! RIGHT NOW!

CONTENTS

FOREWORD

In 1986, Marv Levy arrived in Buffalo to establish a new and exciting era in Buffalo Bills history. He came to the team nine games into the season, and we couldn't have been more ready for his leadership and passion about the game.

When discussions were taking place about his coming to our team, I was curious about the type of coach he would be. Of course, he had a good reputation in the NFL, but how would he fit with our group of personalities? I arrived at the start of that season and understood we needed someone who could communicate well and lead by example.

We went 4-12 that first year under Marv, and it didn't take long for him to determine that more talent was needed for us to succeed. He has the ability to see the whole picture as well as the details, and he was going to secure the talent necessary for us to get on the right path to success. Not many coaches in the NFL can compare to Marv.

Marv was well respected by the players on our team because he knew what to say and when to say it. He didn't waste words or use them loosely. His "Marvisms," as we referred to them, would impact all of us in some manner because they were humorous or insightful. He expected the players to listen and then determine for ourselves his message. Here are just a couple of my favorites:

"Where would you rather be than right here, right now?"

"When it's too tough for them, it's just right for us."

"Keep your eye on the target."

"Once you get a reputation as an early riser, you can sleep until noon."

The reason I'm in the Pro Football Hall of Fame and the reason we made it to four Super Bowls was because of the confidence Marv had in my teammates and me. We went to the no-huddle offense in 1990, and he put it all on the line by letting me call my own plays. How many coaches would put it all on the line with one person? His attitude was, "If you screw up, it's my job. But it's your job, too."

Marv's confidence in the no-huddle offense was important to our team and our future. He believed in my ability to use the talent of Thurman Thomas, Andre Reed, Kent Hull, and many others. How exciting it was that Marv and I were on the same page and working toward the same goals. We are both perfectionists when it comes to getting things done and doing it the right way.

Marv maintained a low profile as our coach, but inside the locker room he stood out as our leader. He didn't care if he received recognition, and with our group of superstars, he didn't mind. That approach allowed him to focus on preparing for game day, and once he was on the field, it was all business. I know that he seemed to be mild-mannered, but when he was ticked off, it was obvious to everyone. This is where he showed his passion for the game. He stood up for his team—his group of guys that he would go to battle with.

We fought and won many battles together. On the days when things would turn for the worse, Marv helped understand that in life you turn negatives into positives. When we lost four straight Super Bowls, he always found a way to be positive, always made us look at the next journey. He got us focused on the next season and how we would reach our goals. He was an inspiration to all of us.

His outlook stayed with me and inspired me, especially when my son was born in 1997. I thought what every daddy thinks—the football games in the backyard, going fishing with your son, and sharing recreational activities. Throughout the course of your life, you take so many things for granted.

Hunter was born on Valentine's Day, my birthday. He has Krabbe's disease, a disorder of the nervous system, and most children don't survive more than two years. Now I know some of those tough times in my career made me able to handle having a special-needs child. Now I'm totally prepared to spend my life looking for a cure. I have been blessed in so many ways, and one of them is that Hunter was there when I was inducted into the Pro Football Hall of Fame in 2002 with Marv as my presenter.

Marv always had a way with words, but there was one thing that I still think of today. At my induction, he said, "Never mind about his arm. It was great, but what Jim Kelly really had, physically, was his heart. His heart was as stout as a nose tackle's butt." I was honored to have Marv present me, and I couldn't think of anybody else I'd rather have as a coach and a friend.

And it's an honor to know your coach is in the Hall of Fame, too. He deserves it.

—Jim Kelly

PREFACE

"Football doesn't build character; it reveals character."

I can't recall who first wrote that line, but I am convinced that he was correct. I believe, also, that there are many other activities and events that occur in a person's life to provide such revelation. Be aware, therefore, that this is a book about much more than touchdowns and interceptions. True, I will delve into the impact of victories and defeats, but such experiences for all of us happen frequently far outside the restrictive stripes of the gridiron.

Do you love football? So do I! Football stories will appear often in these pages, but this is not another "football book." It is a story about lessons learned—for me, and I fervently hope for you as well.

I have told my story as I remember it, not as I researched it. Every detail (time, score, location, yard line, exact quote, barometric pressure, etc.) will not always be precise, but any oversights of that nature will be inconsequential. They will be accurate enough so that "you get the idea."

There are times, I freely admit, when I purposely exaggerate, sometimes to a considerable extent. Doing so helps me portray a situation or someone's personality more forcefully. That is my intention. In those instances when I parody someone's peculiarities, I am not seeking to be mean or petty. If fun is being made, it was because of my intent to provide some good-natured ribbing. You will find that I often make myself the subject of such tongue-in-cheek ridicule.

The astute reader may even uncover some of those rare paragraphs wherein I have resorted to the employment of unabashed fiction. Why? So that I can depict, with high humor I hope, an event, an era, or even a poignant moment in time, that's why. My careful calculations have helped me determine that the contents of this book are composed of 95.7 percent fact and 4.3 percent fiction. (The previous sentence serves as a sterling example of that "4.3 percent" fiction *and* my renowned mathematical acumen.)

Also I hereby confess that upon occasion, in order to emphasize a sentiment, I chose to call upon some timeworn cliché. Such literary transgressions were not due to laziness on my part. Heavens, no! They were selected because, after exhaustive mental exercise, I finally conceded that in utilizing such recognizably familiar phraseologies I was able to best convey the wisdom I wished to impart. (But let's keep that just between you and me and the lamppost.)

I have sought to reflect, as I wrote, the mindset I had at a specific time in my life when the experiences I write about actually took place. If, for example, you detect an adolescent tone when I relate my activities in the 1940s, then I will have succeeded.

There will be instances in this book when I have used the vernacular of the playing field, the locker room, of the army barracks, and occasionally that of the times during which an event truly occurred. I apologize for any offense caused by language a reader might find crude, with the hope that this forewarning helps to mitigate any inclinations to gasp. Likewise, whenever I dredge up some dated term or phrase from the 1940s that you might feel is trite, go ahead and roll your eyes. That would be "just swell" with me.

Football is fun, and life should be fun, too. Consistent with that premise I have sought to highlight the humor and light-heartedness inherent in many of the episodes of my life whenever doing so is not in bad taste or inappropriate.

Life is not all frivolity, however, and so in this book I also recount many serious moments, some frought with drama or even pathos. In writing it I was often revisited by the emotions I had experienced at the time of the actual event I was recalling.

One final caveat: Despite the overwhelming sense of gratitude I feel toward all of the people who have enriched my life, there is a story and a message I hope to provide for many of you readers whom I have never met. I will, therefore, refrain from making this narrative a list of "thank yous" directed toward the numerous people—players, coaches, friends, family, loved ones—who have contributed so much in making my life a blessed one. I am indeed grateful and indebted to all of them, but to treat that subject sufficiently would require an entire book in itself. Someday I'll write it.

SECTION I

"WHEN YOU ARE GOING THROUGH HELL,
KEEP ON GOING."

—WINSTON CHURCHILL

CHAPTER 1

Tampa Stadium, January 27, 1991

The ball rose, twirling end over end into the balmy Florida night sky. Forty-seven yards away from where it had been launched, the goalposts beckoned. An eerie silence descended on the packed stadium as the eyes of more than 70,000 people followed the solitary missile on its lonely journey. Elsewhere, in front of television sets throughout the world, millions of enthralled viewers joined in the vigil.

Standing just outside the perimeter of the playing field, I too, mouth agape, gazed transfixed as the ball's flight reached its apex and then continued hurtling toward the uprights' outstretched arms.

The seven-month odyssey we had begun on a hot, humid July day at our training camp site in Fredonia, New York, was split seconds away from its culmination. The New York Giants were leading our Buffalo Bills 20-19.

At stake? The Super Bowl championship!

Just a minute and 26 seconds earlier—it had seemed like ages ago—we had taken possession of the football on our own 15-yard line with a minute and 30 seconds remaining to be played in the game. We would have this one final opportunity to achieve the most coveted of all football triumphs.

We went to work.

No huddle. Jim Kelly to Andre Reed; a screen pass to Thurman Thomas; and then Thurman again, this time on a draw play. Another completion to Andre. The clock kept running. Spike the ball. Kill the clock. Now it was Jim to James Lofton, who caught the pass inches inside the left sideline stripe. Quickly, James stepped out of bounds at the Giants' 29-yard line. There were four seconds left to play.

I sent our field goal team out onto the field.

Snap! Hold! Kick! The ball leapt into the sky and soared toward the beseeching arms of the goalposts. Closer and closer it came. And then—it fluttered on by, a scant two feet outside of the right upright.

The game was over. The Giants were Super Bowl champions. Imagine their jubilation. Imagine our desolation.

♦♦♦♦♦♦♦♦

When you are a coach in the National Football League, there always comes one specific moment on game day when you are going to experience one of two intense emotions. Either a wave of ethereal serenity will wash over you, or—at the other end of the spectrum—you will become the victim of a despair so gripping that you can feel it physically. It is when you have lost the game, of course, that the latter sensation takes hold, and if that loss represents your outcome in the Super Bowl, the impact of what you are feeling is multiplied by infinity.

It starts with a throbbing in your temples; then you feel it creeping tightly up the back of your neck. You sense a weakening in all your joints and an invisible constriction clutching at your throat. You feel it in the shallowness of your breathing and in the absence of your appetite. There is a knot in your gut and a clenching of your jaws, which numbs your molars. You feel the heat behind your eyes, and you become aware of an unpleasant taste in your mouth.

Most of all you feel the energy from that despicable frustration flowing from your torso down your arms into your balled-up fists while your psyche screams at you to pound those fists against any inanimate object in the area.

Every coach knows when that exact moment is going to come. Surprisingly, it does not occur as the final gun sounds and the certainty of victory or defeat has been determined. The game may have ended, but there are still many tasks that need immediate attention.

In leaving the field a coach must be gracious in victory and able to maintain his dignity in defeat. In the locker room there are tired, bruised, and often injured players. They, along with the assistant coaches and everyone else who had been so immersed in that week's effort, need a head coach who is in charge and who can provide a sense of perspective. Very soon after the game the coach will meet with the media. His words and his demeanor will come under close scrutiny.

In talking with the media it is essential that the coach be honest and forthcoming, but he must also be keenly aware of the impact his words will have on his players, on the organization, and on the members of his staff. Most of all he must remain in control even in those instances when he feels and wishes to convey anger. The time to allow his emotions to take over has not yet arrived.

It is only when he returns very late at night to the lonely quiet of his bedroom or hotel room that the coach realizes there is nothing more to be done until the following day when he begins preparations for the next game. (WHAT NEXT GAME? WE JUST LOST THE SUPER BOWL, DAMN IT!)

That's when it really hit me.

I spent most of that tormented night trying to refrain, sometimes unsuccessfully, from kicking away my blankets and from pummeling my mattress. In the darkness I winced as I listened to an occasional sob from my dear wife, Frannie. She had dried the tears from the cheeks of our daughter, Kimberly, just before we finally returned to our room that night, and now it was Frannie's turn to weep.

A few hours earlier I had been in a stadium rocking with noise, music, fireworks, and fanfare. I had stood along the sideline when Whitney Houston sang the most beautiful and stirring rendition of "The Star Spangled Banner" I had ever heard. The spirit of patriotism that permeated our nation, then in the throes of the Gulf War, showed in the faces of the capacity crowd and of the players and coaches near me as fighter planes from the United States Air Force roared low over the stadium during the pregame ceremonies.

I recalled the pride that had welled up inside of me as our Buffalo Bills, AFC champions, were introduced to the welcoming accompaniment of thunderous cheers just prior to the kickoff. The excitement, the adrenaline rush, and, yes, the confidence I felt while having to make 200 or more split-second decisions during the course of the game had been exhilarating and consuming.

Now, just a few hours later, I lay there in the darkness, disconsolate. As I tossed about, occasionally grunting in anger, I kept replaying the game in my mind, but it always came out the same. We had lost.

At about 5:00 a.m. I was exhausted, but still awake, when some words, in the form of a question, invaded my consciousness. I sat up in bed, startled, and then, whimsically, I gave voice to those words by whispering their challenge into the quiet of the night: "What are you going to do about it?"

My mind was racing now, and faster than any damn Internet hookup ever it went directly back to a day I hadn't thought about for more than 47 years. It was December 13, 1943, and I was riding on a troop train full of recent enlistees heading from Chicago to Greensboro, North Carolina, where we were to begin basic training as members of the Army Air Corps. Just before I departed from Union Station in

Chicago, my mother had given me a slim volume of English poetry, and as the train chugged southward, I opened the book and began to read.

As farmland slipped by outside my window, I became engrossed in the pages in front of me. There was one poem I reread several times because its message fascinated me. In its entirety it was composed of just four simple, poignant lines. An unknown English writer had composed it in tribute to some 16th-century Scottish warrior.

I did not recall having read those lines again since that forgotten day during World War II, but as I sat in bed and as this tortured night neared its end, the words sprang at me again, pristine and clear:

"Fight on, my men," Sir Andrew said.
"A little I'm hurt but not yet slain.
"I'll just lie down and bleed awhile,
"And then I'll rise and fight again."

I repeated the question to myself, "What are you going to do about it?"

This time, however, I spoke it firmly and resolutely because I now knew exactly what I was going to do (Thank you, Sir Andrew! Thank you, Mother dear!), and I'd begin first thing in the morning. I glanced over at Frannie, finally sleeping peacefully. Less than 60 seconds later I was, too.

After all, I had to be fresh for tomorrow.

I settled into my seat for the airplane trip back to Buffalo on the morning after we had played in Super Bowl XXV. The airline had provided a stack of newspapers for us at the entry door. No one picked one up.

As they came onto our charter flight, our players were more subdued than I could ever recall having seen them. They were somber, but they came aboard—coats, ties, clean shirts, clean-shaven, their heads held high. There was no "angry with someone else" attitude about any of them. Quietly they filed back to their seats.

In just a few hours we would be back home in the midwinter cold of upstate New York, and our players were all carrying mittens. No one needed regular gloves, I would learn, because no one would be pointing fingers.

Once the plane was airborne, I made my way back down the aisle, something I did, win or lose, on the journey home after every road game. I didn't say much, and neither did any of the players. It wasn't the time for that, and we all knew it. I could feel their pain, and they could feel mine, too. Most of the players looked up as I came by, and when they did, we would exchange a reassuring glimmer of a smile.

However, as I continued moving toward the back of the airplane, I became aware that it wasn't the faint smiles tugging at the corners of their mouths that struck me. It was the look in their eyes. What I saw reflected was not defeat. I saw resolve. And do you know what? That's what I had expected. How could I not have been proud to coach men such as these?

I had expressed that exact sentiment to our team as soon as I could after the game the night before.

♦♦♦♦♦♦♦♦

When I had returned to the locker room after congratulating the Giants' coach, Bill Parcells, most of them were sitting on the stools in front of their lockers gazing vacantly at a far wall or at the floor. You could hear the fan as it whirred overhead, but not much else. The only other sound was an occasional ripping of tape as a few of them absent-mindedly pulled the wrappings from their wrists.

I knew they didn't want to listen to some long-winded speech at that grieving moment. There are occasions when a coach's words—and even his eloquence—are meaningful to his players. This was not one of those times. Any lengthy oration by me now would be nothing more than irritating noise. Yet I knew that to refrain from all communication would have been a gesture that they could rightly interpret as a display of anger and disdain toward them. No feelings were further from my heart than those. And so I spoke, briefly and sincerely.

"There is not a loser in this room," I said.

I told them I was proud of them and proud to be their coach.

I injected no pep talk rhetoric, nor were my words tinged with remorse. I told them that I'd reserve making any further remarks until the next day after we had returned to Buffalo, where we would hold our final team meeting at our stadium complex in Orchard Park.

That was it for our team as a group, but there was still one player with whom I wanted to visit personally. It was our place kicker, Scott Norwood.

Scott was a quiet, somewhat introspective person. He was conscientious, dependable, and respected by his teammates and coaches. On several occasions during our march to the AFC championship Scott had delivered the game-winning kick in the game's final moments. There would also be contests in the following season when Scott's last-minute heroics would once again propel our Bills to a crucial victory.

His outward appearance now as he sat with his teammates in the almost silent locker room didn't seem much different from any of theirs, but I could only imagine the torment he felt inside. I found a stool, pulled it over, and sat down next to Scott. While I was searching my mind seeking the right words to say, some other stalwarts did it for me.

Linebacker Darryl Talley and defensive back Nate Odomes stopped by, and Darryl spoke.

"Hey, Scott, if Nate and I had tackled their receiver on that third and 14 during their touchdown drive, it wouldn't have come down to one last kick."

Nate nodded his assent.

Then our great wide receiver, Andre Reed, drifted over.

"You know, Scott," he said, "if I'd have hung on to that pass on their 15-yard line in the first half, we probably would have come away with seven points instead of three."

Defensive lineman Jeff Wright also approached Scott.

"Doggone it, Scott, when Bruce Smith sacked Hostetler in the end zone and forced him to fumble, we could have had a touchdown instead of just a safety if I'd been able to recover it."

They kept on coming. Carlton Bailey, Pete Metzelaars, Kirby Jackson, Cornelius Bennett, Kent Hull, Frank Reich, Mark Kelso, Kenny Davis, Steve Tasker, Jim Kelly, Shane Conlan, Dwight Drane, Keith McKeller, Mark Pike, and others. Each with his own mea culpa.

I knew by that time that Scott didn't need a "me too" from his coach. I patted him on the shoulder, and as I walked away, I couldn't tell whether that film of moisture I saw was in his eyes or in mine.

When our plane arrived at Greater Buffalo International Airport, we boarded the team buses expecting to go directly to Rich Stadium. Instead, we headed toward City Hall in downtown Buffalo. Why, I wondered. We had lost. We had let our fans down! What was there to celebrate?

In the next hour or so we found out.

The buses parked behind City Hall, and we were shepherded in through the back entrance. Then we proceeded down the long, quiet hallways to the foot of a winding stairway at the front of the building. We ascended several floors and emerged onto a spacious, old stone balcony that overlooked historic Niagara Square. Assembled below in the biting January cold and snow were 30,000 Buffalo Bills fans.

How long had they been waiting? I didn't know; and they didn't care.

As our party moved out onto the balcony, a tumultuous welcome erupted from the assembled throng. They sustained the clamor. On and on it reverberated. When finally the noise began to subside, several of the fans started a chant. Quickly, others joined in. Soon they were bellowing in unison, "We want Scott! We want Scott! We want Scott!"

The crescendo mounted, and at last Scott Norwood, urged forward by several nudges from his teammates, stepped forth to speak.

His voice was cracking, but he spoke for us all when he said, "I know I've never felt more loved than right now. We will be back. You can count on it, and we are dedicating next season to the fans of Buffalo."

Scott Norwood, a shy young man, less than 24 hours removed from his greatest professional disappointment, had given voice to the passion that would drive the Bills players and our fans in the seasons to come.

We learned a great deal about those Bills fans on that day and in the weeks that followed. Their support, their healthy ardor, and their warm-heartedness were always there to uplift our team whenever we needed it most. The resilience and admirable qualities of character that were to mark our Bills teams were inspired in great measure by the people of Buffalo. There are no fans anywhere like Bills fans. Their loyalty and their hardiness are unparalleled. We are so proud to have represented them on the field of play.

After the reception in Niagara Square, we returned to our complex at Rich Stadium, where we held our final team meeting before the players would disperse for the off season. The bulletin board immediately outside the entrance to our meeting room displayed just one item that I had posted. It was that four-line poem—typed up and considerably enlarged—about Sir Andrew. After the meeting several of the players asked me if they could have a copy of the poem, and I was pleased to honor their requests. In the years that followed, someone—I don't know who—would post that verse on the bulletin board whenever we had suffered a disheartening setback.

The season-ending meeting was primarily for the purpose of orientation relative to off-season activities. We secured mailing addresses, arranged for needed follow-up medical attention, and talked about the importance and nature of our off-season conditioning program. At the meeting I informed our players about the periodic newsletters that I would be sending, and I gave them a heads-up regarding the dates for our off-season minicamp. In other words, it was all business—except for one final comment that I felt it was now appropriate to offer.

It was up to them, I said, whether—disappointed and exhausted—they would merely lie there in the fetal position and admit defeat or whether they would "rise and fight again."

When the meeting ended and the players had all departed, I sat alone in the empty classroom reflecting on the challenge I had just issued, not only to them but to myself as well. How would they respond?

How about me? I had been coaching football for more than 40 years, and I was now approaching my 66th birthday. So what! I stared at those now vacant chairs, and I thought about the men who would fill them when our team assembled once again for the next season. I knew that they weren't about to surrender. And neither was I.

Ahead of us still lay a saga that would include some scenes of ecstatic exhilaration, moments of crushing disappointment, and some unbelievable comebacks. But most of all, our story would be about resilience, about the renewal of spirit.

As I write this now more than a decade later, I am aware that when that ball sailed outside the right goalpost late on the night of January 27, 1991, my story could have ended there.

It didn't.

And it didn't start there either.

SECTION II

FROM SOUTH CHICAGO TO HARVARD

CHAPTER 2

Sowt Chick-ahgo in da Nineteen Toitees

There is a cavernous dark red brick building located at 70th Street and East End Avenue on the South Side of Chicago. It was built by the city long before Gus Dorais and Knute Rockne ever hooked up for a completed forward pass. When it was constructed, they were probably calling "Pop" Warner "Skippy." Benjamin Harrison was president when they laid the cornerstone. Some long-forgotten Board of Education official, sporting ponderous, bushy sideburns and a walrus mustache, had named it Parkside School. He got it half right. It was a school, kindergarten through eighth grade, but during the years I attended, I searched in vain, on all sides, and I never did find that park.

Park? That's one of those places with grass and trees, isn't it? In my neighborhood we had only cement, asphalt, gravel, and dirt. In our part of Chicago we all thought the word *tree* was what you said after "one" and "two."

On one side of our school there was an alley. On the other three sides there were city streets. Across from the school, two of those streets were crowded with tenements. On the other one, small dilapidated wooden stores, with living quarters upstairs or in the back, beckoned the neighborhood kids to come get their haircuts, school supplies, licorice whips, jawbreakers, Mary Janes, and other two-for-a-penny delights.

It was at Parkside School where most of the kids I knew learned to speak and write English. They sure didn't hear it at home. Almost all the kids at Parkside, just like my sister, Marilyn, and me, were children of immigrant parents. In visiting my pals I had heard spoken, at various times, Polish, Italian, Yiddish, Greek, Lithuanian, and Russian. In many homes you heard several languages spoken, and sometimes not one of them was English.

In that respect I was more fortunate. Although my mother, Ida, the oldest of five, had come to America in 1908 from a small village in Russia, her command of English was magnificent. As the years passed, despite never having gone to school, she became a prodigious reader, eventually devouring the works of Shakespeare, other literary giants, and many lesser writers. Poets who wondered if their creations were ever read need not have worried—Ida was at the library.

My father, Sam, had been born in England and came to this country when he was six years old. He spoke the language as I knew it, although several of his older brothers and sisters (there were 13 in all) sure did talk funny. It was easier for me to understand Vinnie Serena's mother during an Italian tirade than it was to understand some of the oh-so-British repartee from my aunts and uncles.

My father spent his young boyhood years growing up in the Maxwell Street area of Chicago, where his father was a garment peddler. My dad had always loved animals, and so it was only natural that he took over caring for the horse that pulled his father's rickety wagon. Dad had a closer relationship with that horse than he did with some of his siblings. Because he was to be the primary caretaker of the horse, he was also given the responsibility for naming her, and even though she was a mare, in youthful innocence, he named her Dick. Many years later, one of Dad's brothers commented to me that perhaps it would have been more appropriate to have named her "No Dick."

Appreciation of the English language came to me from my Russian-born mother, but a love of sports and competition came from my dad. His friends told me that he had been the best basketball player at Medill High School on Chicago's West Side in 1916, but he never stayed to play his senior year. When the United States entered World War I in 1917, he left home and school at 16, fibbed about his age, and enlisted in the Marine Corps.

A year later, Corporal Sam Levy, as a member of the Fourth Marine Brigade, fought in the Battle of Belleau Wood. There, just 25 miles from Paris, the last advance of the German army in World War I was repulsed. A grateful French government, in acknowledgment of the brigade's gallantry, decreed that Belleau Wood was to be renamed. Henceforth, it was to be called "The Woods of the United States Marines." It is still known by that name today.

The victory had not come easily. Of the 4,000 marines engaged in the 11-day battle, 2,500 had been casualties. My dad was one of them, having been struck in the back, arm, and hand by shrapnel fragments and then gassed. He recovered at a hospital in France, but for many years after the war he would have recurring attacks from the effects of the gassing.

One time, in 1936, when he had to go back into the Veterans Hospital for a short stay, my mother took me to visit him there. At that age I had little concept of time, but I recall asking my father how long ago his current stay there had begun. He told me that he had been there for four days. After hearing that I turned to the World War I veteran in the bed next to my father's and asked him the same question. Never in my life have I been less prepared for the answer I received.

"Son, I've been here since 1918," he said.

I grew up a lot that day.

There wasn't much that could keep my father down, however. As the years passed, the effects of the mustard gas diminished and finally desisted completely. He was a robust, husky man of medium height, and he always stood straight as the flagpole in the schoolyard at Parkside, shoulders back and chest thrust out, ever the marine. Although his bearing was military, his nature was not. He was a happy, energetic, gregarious man who loved his work and who loved his play.

He was in the wholesale produce business. Dad and his partner, Bill Dikatoulos, owned and ran the Commonwealth Produce Company located in Chicago's bustling South Water Street Market. When you "owned" in those days, the name of the company might sound imposing, but you were the employer *and* the employee. My father was out of bed at 3:00 a.m. six days a week (seven during the wine grape season) and on his way to work long before my sister and I were awake for our one-block walk to Parkside School.

The work was hard, as I was to learn after reaching my 13th birthday, because after that I was required to spend my Saturdays working at his produce house. Those luxurious Saturday mornings of sleeping late and then rushing off to play softball or football in the gravel schoolyard right under the "No Ball Playing Allowed" signs were over. The work was not fun, but it was fun to be with my dad, watching him smiling as he carried 100-pound sacks of potatoes—one on each shoulder—all the while maintaining a constant banter with the customers and other workers in the market.

It seemed as though he enjoyed working there even during Chicago's biting winters, and if he did, I can assure you I did not share that feeling with him. Not that I didn't learn a lot. Perhaps the most valuable lesson I learned was that I'd do almost anything to keep from having to continue working at the market for the rest of my life. He must have read my thoughts long before they had crystallized for me, because on one autumn Saturday, at about 10:00 a.m., when I was 14 years old, I sensed him studying me as I was desultorily sweeping the cold concrete floor. He clamped his hand—thick fingers nicked and scraped from heaving crates of fruit—onto the handle of my broom. We both hesitated for an instant, and then he cocked his head to one side and spoke.

"Marv, go on home and play football."

That's what I did, and that is what I would continue to do on countless Saturdays and Sundays for years to come.

Only once since that time have I returned to the South Water Market. Forty-four years later I came back there with my father one day when he visited his friends for the last time. He was 84 years old and not in good health. Yet there wasn't a line in his face or a wrinkle in his clothes, and he still carried himself as erect and as proud as he had back in 1917 on the boot camp parade ground at Parris Island.

He had retired nine years earlier, but as we walked along the dock that stretched in front of a seemingly endless string of produce houses, the men poured out to shake his hand, to muss his hair, and, in the case of some, to clasp him in a bear hug. One elderly man from one of the largest produce houses called me aside and told me how my dad, during the Depression, had given him the money, with a "pay me back when you can," so that the man could make the payment he needed to make in order to keep from having his small delivery truck repossessed. Whenever I reflect back on some of the many games I have coached and the pride I have felt after some of our most meaningful victories, I realize that I have never known a prouder moment than that one.

One month later my father died of cancer.

All the guys I knew at Parkside School thought they were great athletes. You had to be a ballplayer then; there was no money around to do anything else because the Great Depression lay heavy on the land. If you were lucky, like I was, you got 15 cents a week from your parents, 10 cents of which gained you admission to the Jeffrey Theater, where you could revel in the antics of Laurel and Hardy or in the heroics of Errol Flynn. The big decision came in how you elected to spend that other precious nickel. Once you have had to agonize over whether to have a "slider" at the White Castle Hamburger House or to invest instead in one of those individually wrapped, single-portion Dolly Madison cherry pies at Mr. Cook's School Store, you'll never have a problem when it comes to deciding between punting or going for it on fourth down.

At Parkside we played our games in the sunshine or in rain, snow, and wind, whatever nature offered, and although we all thought we were great athletes, there were really very few who had superior ability.

Two of the older guys, Sandy Bunsen and Bob Prout (the latter's name had been shortened from its original and more exotic Polish version), were the idols of the neighborhood.

Sandy had been the best pitcher in the Chicago prep league. At Hyde Park High School, where he was averaging more than 15 strikeouts a game, his fastball had earned a nickname of its own: "The Bunsen Burner." There was one fellow in our neighborhood who had fantasized that the ultimate in achievement for any of us would be to one day become President of the United States. He was alone in that misguided view. For the rest of us, playing baseball for the Chicago Cubs was the station in life that had no equal. Come on, now! Who would you really like to be: Franklin Delano Roosevelt or Gabby Hartnett?

The Cubs signed Sandy Bunsen right out of high school and assigned him to its farm club in Janesville of the Wisconsin State League. In Sandy's third game with the Janesville Cubs, the Eau Claire cleanup man put out the flame in "The Bunsen Burner" when he lashed one of Sandy's offerings straight back at the mound. The ball struck Sandy flush on the left cheekbone, fracturing it and badly injuring his left eye. It took a long while, but Sandy recovered. Not well enough to pitch again, however. Less than a year later Sandy went to work for the Illinois Central Railroad.

Bob Prout was big, blond, curly-haired, good looking, and left handed. What an outfielder he was! He could catch any ball he could get to, and he could get to any ball. If he was in the outfield, there was no way you were ever going to take an extra base on Lefty Prout, and if he was on the base paths, there was no way you were going to keep him from getting an extra base when he determined to go for it. Best of all, he hit nothing but line drives. In our neighborhood we felt the only difference between Bob Prout and Joe DiMaggio was that Bob batted left handed and preferred pierogi to spaghetti.

On the ball field, no one was smarter than Bob. He never made a mistake. Except once! That was when he signed with the St. Louis Cardinals. Among the players on their roster who could play in the outfield were Joe Medwick, Terry Moore, Enos Slaughter, Stan Musial, and Pepper Martin. Bob couldn't have known he was signing a Cardinals contract. When they told him he'd be joining those fellows, he must have thought he was being inducted into the Hall of Fame.

The Cardinals sent Bob to their Albany, Georgia, farm club, where he led the team in batting average, runs batted in, and home runs. The following year, he went to training camp with the Cardinals, but by opening day he was back in Albany, where once again he led the team in all three categories. In 1941 the Cardinals moved Bob up to their top minor league club, the Columbus Redbirds of the American Association. When that season finished—even though he had posted a .330 batting average—it was apparent to Bob that there still wasn't a place for him in the talent-laden Cardinals outfield.

It was late September 1941, and the United States had not yet entered World War II. Even so, the Selective Service System (a contemporary euphemism for the military draft) had been instituted with the proviso that selectees were to serve for one year, after which time their obligation would have been fulfilled. Bob decided to get his one year out of the way quickly while some of the aging Cardinals could grow a year older. He asked that his number be called, and it was. On an October day, less than two months before the Japanese attack on Pearl Harbor, he left for Fort Sheridan.

Lefty Prout came home from the war four and a half years later. When he returned, his baseball skills were as rusty as the 1934 Ford he had left behind.

In the spring of 1946, Bob Prout headed south once again, but this time he didn't take his baseball mitt. Instead, he took his G.I. Bill and traveled downstate to Champaign, where he enrolled at the University of Illinois. For several decades, until he retired a few years ago, Bob was a successful businessman in Chicago, but I still remember Lefty Prout as the best baseball player who ever came out of Parkside School.

When it came to athletics, the thing I did best was run fast. When I first made this discovery, it surprised the hell out of me, but it sure must have made a strong impression, because even though I was only five years old at the time, I still have a vivid recollection of the incident that brought this realization to me.

At the end of my first day in kindergarten, as the members of our class exited onto the outer sidewalk, some kid yelled, "Race you to the corner," and away he sped.

Most of the rest of us, myself included, sprinted in pursuit. Within a few seconds I had left the pack behind and was closing in quickly on "Mr. Head Start." Fifteen yards from the corner I zipped by him, winning easily. The "Race to the Corner" became a daily ritual, and without exception I always got there first. Judging who came in second became a more difficult task for me than winning the race itself. As I passed from one grade to the next, I continued to be the fastest runner in my class.

It was the practice of the South Shore YMCA to organize athletic competitions in various sports between students at the six public grammar schools clustered in our section on the city. I always won the sprints for my age group, and I truly began to believe that it would be impossible for anyone to ever beat me. That was until Bobby Marek moved from the West Side of Chicago into our neighborhood and enrolled at Parkside School, entering the same seventh grade class that I attended. After that I won a lot of silver medals. He got all the gold ones.

Bobby and I became good pals, but after we graduated from Parkside, we didn't have the opportunity to continue our friendship because his home was in the Hyde Park High School district and mine was located in South Shore High School area. Once we got to high school, I concentrated on other sports and ran in just one track meet.

Bobby became quite a track star at Hyde Park, however. In the city of Chicago there was only one better sprinter, a little cannonball from Wendell Phillips High School named Buddy Young. Bobby was a modest, honest, courteous person. He was a better-than-average student, more conscientious than bright, and he had a terrific sense of humor. Everyone admired Bobby, and I really wish I could have gotten to know him better. Yes, sir, he really could run. But one spring day in 1944 at Monte Cassino he ran into some German army machine gun bullets. They buried my friend in the American Military Cemetery on an Italian hillside just a few days after he had reached his 19th birthday.

You got a darn good education at Parkside School. The teachers there knew their subject matter, their students, and their discipline. Most of our teachers were imposing Irish ladies—Miss McCracken, Mrs. Dalton, Mrs. Horrigan, Miss McCullough, Mrs. Forsythe, and Miss Callahan. My favorite was my sixth grade teacher, Amanda C. Gaudette. She was young and pretty and lively, and although she made learning fun, you sure couldn't push her around. Try doing that and she'd send you on that most dreaded of all journeys—the trip to the principal's office for a conversation with Mrs. McInerney. Compared to her, Warren Sapp is a pansy.

Another thing we liked about Miss Gaudette was the way she was interested in the teams at Parkside that played in the YMCA-sponsored grammar school league. We had competition with five other schools in softball, basketball, and track.

My favorite was basketball, but that was because we had the best team in the league. It sure wasn't because I was the best player on our team. Even though I was a starter, the other four players were all better than I was. Marlin Johnson was our playmaker. The Giannopoulos brothers, Marco and Tiky, whose family lived in the apartment upstairs from ours, could play rings around me. (Their sister, Sophie, was better than either of them, but she wasn't eligible to play in the all-boys competition.) Our best player by far, however, was Paul Schnackenberg. He is the reason we won every game. Paul went on to South Shore High School, and he was selected as the outstanding player in the city in 1944 when South Shore won the city championship. Paul later starred at the University of Illinois.

Participation on the grammar school basketball team at Parkside exposed me for the first time to that mystic figure known as "The Coach." That, however, was not the appellation we used when talking to or about our coach. We knew him simply as "Yanno." To this day I still do not know if that was his first name, his last name, his nickname, or his only name. Yanno was three or four years older than those of us on the team, and he had been a good player at Parkside several years earlier. Apparently, he hadn't been quite talented enough to make the varsity in high school, and so he applied what knowledge he had to coaching the sport. That expertise consisted of how to hold and how to use your elbows.

Yanno's philosophy was simple: Intimidate your opponent. And he set the pattern for employing those tactics by intimidating the hell out of us. When it came to learning our names, Yanno had very little difficulty since he had apparently decided to call us all by the exact same name. It was "Hey You!"

We knew immediately which one of us he meant, because he always accompanied these endearing words by extending his clenched fist, pointing his thumb directly at the specific "Hey You!" he was addressing. When he did this, he would lower his chin and peer at you through his eyebrows. As soon as the desired hush had fallen over the gym, he would utter a barely audible, "C'meah!" while rotating his fist backward until his thumb finally pointed straight down at the toes of his highly polished Flagg Brothers cordovan wingtip shoes.

Yanno was the only coach I have ever known who didn't even need a whistle. By curling his lips into a singularly grotesque configuration, he could emit a chilling blast, shrill enough to blow a Chicago traffic cop right off the corner of State and Madison.

Yanno was a successful coach. He had the right ingredient for being one—a player named Paul Schnackenberg. As a result we won all the games Yanno coached. Whether he was a good teacher of basketball, I don't know. I was too frightened of him to think about anything but survival.

It wasn't all sports at Parkside, however. While I was there, I really enjoyed the classroom work, although I never would have admitted it publicly. As a result I got very good grades, a condition that I am sorry to say I did not carry over to high school. I must have been pretty popular, also, because I was elected president of my graduating class. My mother was as proud of that as I was of the punt I blocked in the first high school football game I played.

On graduation day at Parkside, I wore a suit for the first time in my life. I had my first brush with heart palpitations when I learned that it had cost my parents almost $20.

♦♦♦♦♦♦♦♦

During my final year in grammar school, the dominant topic of discussion in our neighborhood centered upon the magnificent new high school that was being constructed just a few blocks from where I lived. Most of my friends and I would be members of the first class entering South Shore High School. The words of the new school's alma mater capture best how we all felt about enrolling there:

> School of our dreams, thy children we
> Pledge now our hearts and hands to thee.
> Our love shall grow as years roll by,
> Strengthened by friendship's golden tie.
> School of our dreams: South Shore, South Shore,
> Thy name we'll praise forever more.

My first year at South Shore High School was not a dream; it was pure hell. During my grammar school days, everything had seemed to come so easily. When I graduated at 13, I was one of the tallest kids in the class standing five feet, nine inches. After examining me and gazing at my size 12 feet, a doctor had told my mother that I would probably grow to be six feet, six inches tall and weigh 240 pounds. Jimmy the Greek he wasn't. I grew another inch and a half (don't forget that half-inch) and never weighed more than 180 pounds.

The demands in both the classroom and in athletics at South Shore were much more fierce than any I had known before, and although I am not happy to admit it, I did not respond well. Instead of trying harder to meet these more intense challenges, I goofed off. My grades were awful. Although I didn't flunk any courses as a freshman, I received a D in every one of my academic classes.

In the Chicago Prep League at that time, a student was allowed to participate in one "bladder sport" (football *or* basketball) a school year. Don't ask me why; that was the rule. I selected freshman basketball, attacked it without verve or confidence, and didn't make the final cut.

Worst of all, because of these traumas, my personality took a definite turn for the obnoxious. I withdrew from friendships and became belligerently introspective. Soon I began missing a lot of school days, sometimes by feigning illness but more often through good, honest truancy. My mother was at school more than I was, and I undoubtedly caused my parents a considerable amount of heartache. The guilt and frustration I felt as a result of their anguish eroded my disposition and outlook still further. All I needed at that time to complete the picture was a real good case of acne—and I got that, too.

I was looking forward to my sophomore year in high school with the same enthusiasm I might have today for attending a rock concert by that "song artist," Enema M. (Oh, it's Eminem? What's the difference?) If it had not been for the intercession of two people—one a teacher, the other a fellow student—I would most likely have continued on my path toward self-degradation.

Alice B. Conlan was my homeroom teacher. (She had the perfect initials for a schoolteacher: A.B.C.) Her talents and qualifications went far beyond the ABCs, however. Mrs. Conlan was a gray-haired lady, well groomed and very proper. Her face reflected composure and seriousness, but her eyes always smiled.

How she was capable of seeing even a glimmer of promise in me at that time is something I shall never be able to fathom, but she did. She possessed that golden touch, knowing exactly when to encourage and exactly when to give you a psychological kick in the butt (my term, not hers). She was a big-league teacher, and the reason I know she was so good is that she reached even me.

Mrs. Conlan was more successful in getting her students to set realistic goals than any person I have ever known. When it came to zeroing in on the target, the only competition she had in those days was the Norden Bombsight.[1] Sometimes she made you really stretch, but always for something that was in your reach if gave an extra grunt.

---

1. The Norden Bombsight, named after the man who had invented it, was standard equipment aboard the U.S. Eighth Air Force heavy bombers stationed in England during World War II. These B-17s and B-24s flew countless missions over Germany, and the Norden Bombsight helped direct their bomb loads at the Nazi industrial and military facilities thousands of feet below.

I learned quickly that there was no way you were ever going to "BS" Mrs. Conlan. She would know that was happening before you even realized you were trying to do it. Excuses and copouts never got you off the hook with her, but she had a way, even though you might have come up short, of getting you to redirect your energies so that your bruised confidence recovered and then gained strength. Building confidence, in fact, was her specialty. If I could call upon just one person from the past to come back and minister to the mindsets of my players before a momentous game some day, Vince Lombardi and Knute Rockne would have to wait out in the hall. I'd choose Alice B. Conlan.

With her help, my grades started to improve. More importantly, I began to like attending school. Once she had gotten hold of me, the truant officer might as well have taken an extended sabbatical. During my final three years in high school, I never missed another day.

Although her challenges were realistic, she also had a great feel for exactly when to throw down the gauntlet. I remember one occasion when she adroitly maneuvered me into boastfully proclaiming, "I can get an A any time I want." When she scoffed, I told her to keep an eye on my performance in my English class that semester. Up to that point I had never registered any grade higher than a C, and so I would be battling not just bad habits but a dismal scholastic reputation, as well. Talk about working hard; I could have used a week in Acapulco when that semester ended.

When the final grades came out I had gotten my A in English. It became all the more gratifying when I showed that A to Mrs. Conlan and saw that her sense of satisfaction exceeded even mine.

Unfortunately, that was the only A I received during my four years in high school. There was an occasional B in courses that captured my interest, but most of the time I received Cs. Those grades, combined with my terrible performance as a freshman, meant that I graduated in the lower half of my class, but if it hadn't been for Mrs. Conlan, I wouldn't have made it at all. Although I never did see Mrs. Conlan again after I graduated, there was one occasion, several years later while I was a senior in college, when she was very much on my mind and in my heart. It was the day I was awarded my Phi Beta Kappa key.

Quite a different story was my friendship with Howie Erzinger. Howie, and another student named Herb Melnick, became the closest pals I had in high school. When my sophomore year began, I didn't associate with Howie, but I sure did know who he was. Everyone at South Shore knew Howie Erzinger.

In order for a young person to be someone of importance at South Shore High School, he or she had to be one of the following: an outstanding student, an outstanding athlete, or fortunate enough to be physically attractive. Lucky the soul who might possess even one of those attributes. Howie Erzinger enjoyed all three.

Although it seemed as if he never cracked a book, he always finished a semester with a report card full of As. As early as his sophomore year, he was a starting forward on the school basketball team, and if Tyrone Power had ever seen Howie, he might have experienced a twinge of envy. A typical sequence of activity for Howie would include his scoring 22 points, with every hair on his head remaining perfectly in place, during an afternoon basketball game victory by the South Shore Seahawks; taking the school's Yearbook Queen to a movie that evening while foregoing all study; and then, the next day at 8:00 a.m., breezing through a geometry exam on the way to yet another A.

Normally, you could really learn to hate a guy like that if only he'd been a little bit egotistical or somewhat of a horse's ass, but he didn't give the rest of us even that satisfaction. You couldn't help but like Howie Erzinger. There wasn't a phony bone in his body. He was friendly but never condescending. Howie worked hard, but he never strained. He also had a remarkable knack for being aware of another person's feelings and for another person's need for self-respect.

That must have been the reason why, one day when we passed each other in the hallway, he turned around, caught up with me, and began talking. This was to be the first time we ever spoke to each other.

"You're not going out for basketball this year?" he asked.

"No," I told him. "I've decided to try football."

I'd already been at football practices for several days, and I guessed that Howie must have known or he wouldn't have asked about basketball tryouts. It surprised me that Howie was aware of what might be happening so far as football practice was concerned. That he knew I even existed surprised me more.

"I've seen you play basketball in gym class," he said, "and you sure impressed me. I thought you might try out for the team again, but if you've decided to play football, I bet you'll do a great job there."

With that we parted, each of us heading for our next scheduled class. For the rest of the day I didn't concentrate very well on my classroom work, but later that afternoon I had one hell of an outstanding day on the football practice field. During the course of the next two months, Howie and I became close friends, and I emerged as one of the top sophomore players on the football team.

All sophomores on the squad, along with several of the juniors who weren't talented enough for the varsity, participated in a junior varsity schedule. With my natural speed and a fairly good ability to catch the ball, I was a starting end on the JV team. The only trouble was that we rarely threw the ball. We operated from the short punt formation, a system that predated the Industrial Revolution. My few moments of minor stardom occurred while I was playing on defense. In our first JV game, I blocked a punt on the last play of the first half, scoring a safety for our team, because the ball had ricocheted out the back of our opponents' end zone. That bit of heroics was directly responsible for our 2-0 rout of the Calumet High JVs that day.

In subsequent JV games that season, I blocked three more punts, and I developed quite a reputation as a master of that skill. Given the choice, my mother would have preferred a more reputable performance from me in my biology class. What did she know?

In those days you played football with no facemask and with no mouth guard (which accounts for my good looks today). When our coach explained to us that the proper technique for blocking kicks included crossing your arms in front of your face as you extended your hands at the ball, believe me, I listened! Still very much open to debate is the contention that perhaps a more important area of the anatomy had been left precariously vulnerable, but as a famous general once said, as he sent *other guys* into battle, "No guts, no glory."

It was extremely rare for a sophomore to get to play in the varsity contests, but along with two of my other classmates, I at least suited up for all those games. Our coach, Nate Wasserman, never so much as looked at us.

Nate was a lovable tyrant. The lovable part I learned about after I had graduated. While we were at South Shore, he was an unrelenting taskmaster. In later years we would all learn how much he cared about his former players. He followed us with interest and concern, always ready to help us in any way he could.

Among Wasserman's many eccentricities was his penchant for forgetting names. In the locker room, immediately prior to the kickoff on game day, his announcement of our starting lineup usually went something like this: "Okay, lemme see here. We'll start with Nott at left end, Farber at left tackle, Whosis at left guard, and Doyle at center. We'll have Addante at right guard, Whatchamacallit at right tackle, and O'Donnell at right end. In the backfield we've got Whatsisname at blocking back, Finnegan at fullback, Kardaras at tailback, and—uh—uh—You Know at wingback. Any questions?

No one ever asked Nate Wasserman a question! Not unless he wanted to hear bells until the following Wednesday. Nate had a cute habit of showing his displeasure by rapping a player vigorously on the side of his helmet, accompanying that action by vocally directing his favorite epithet, "Numb nuts!" at the recipient of his ire. We started many games at South Shore High School with anywhere from eight to 13 guys lining up for the opening kickoff.

One Saturday, seven games into the varsity's season, I was sitting on the bench minding my own business when I suddenly felt the blood drain from my head. Nate's authority-laden voice had called out my name. While peering out onto the field with one those Donald Rumsfeld "I know best" squints on his face, he grabbed me by the arm and growled, "Go in there for Whosis and tell them to run 138 Counter Crisscross." The play was a reverse, and I first began to realize that I had given the thumb to the wrong "Whosis" when I lined up for the play and figured out who was going to wind up carrying the ball. Yep, that's right!

I honestly believe that I would not have fumbled if my palms hadn't been so clammy from the stark fear that gripped me. I had already high-stepped my way 15 yards downfield when the ball slithered out of my grasp, and our opponents recovered it.

At halftime, as I sat dejectedly on the bench in the locker room, helmet in my lap, looking down, I received one of Nate's patented ear-boxings and went tumbling to the floor. As I struggled to regain my bearings, I noticed that all of the veteran varsity players had been sitting there with their helmets on. You're never too young to learn.

Later that evening when I recounted the entire incident to my father, his face grew solemn as he listened intently. When I finished speaking, he weighed the facts carefully, and finally he spoke.

"You know what I think?" he prodded.

I gave him an imploring "What? What?" look as I waited breathlessly for him to continue.

"I think you better learn not to fumble," he said.

Nate did not hold it against me for having fumbled. In fact, the very next week he sent me into the varsity game again. We were playing Bowen High School, and they were a powerhouse that year. Five of the players on their team went on to play collegiate football in the Big Ten.

All of the players on the Bowen team were huge Polish fellows. They worked in the steel mills during the summers, and they had the arms and the chests to prove it. Two out of every three of them had come straight from the womb with tattoos on their forearms. The Bowen student body was tremendously excited about their team, and they would whip themselves and their players into a frenzy by chanting that famed Bowen cheer: "Oo-sa-sa, Oo-sa-sa; hit 'em in the head with a kielbasa."[2]

We were hanging in there pretty well against them, and we had them backed up deep in their own territory when Nate sent me in to try blocking a punt. Damned if I didn't do it, and just as in my first JV game, the ball went out of the end zone and we had scored a safety.

Nate was so pleased with my performance on that play that he decided to keep me in the game. The rules require that after the safety Bowen would have to kick off to us. I still remember the guy I was assigned to block on our kickoff return. He was six foot, five inches, weighed 245 pounds, and could run like Seabiscuit. I can't recall his last name exactly, but it had more Zs in it than a Nytol commercial.

He came thundering downfield, and I took off at him in anticipation of hurling my entire 150 pounds (155, tops) directly at that naïve unsuspecting sucker. When he got so close that I could smell the garlic on his breath, I remember telling myself, "That poor sumbitch still doesn't see me coming." He didn't have to.

As the "Polish Express" went rolling over me, I heard (and felt, believe me!) the bones just above my right ankle crack, but what really teed me off was that as I lay there writhing on the ground, I caught a glimpse of that same damn yo-yo making the tackle deep in our territory. Talk about "the thrill of victory and the agony of defeat!" On one play I blocked a punt for a score, and on the next play I broke my leg. It just goes to prove what they say: "You can't win them all!"

My sophomore season had ended abruptly, but it wasn't all that bad. A lot of pretty girls who smelled real nice wanted to sign my cast.

As a junior and senior I started most of the football games for dear old South Shore, and although it was a big deal to me at the time, I have to admit that I was just an average player on a mediocre team. At the end of the season, when the newspapers published the prep league All-Star teams, there might be one or two guys from South Shore listed in the small print section titled: "Other Players Receiving Mention."

High school wasn't all classrooms and sports. There was social life, for instance. Social life meant girls, and it was because of a girl that my

---

2. For the benefit of those readers who indeed never have been hit on the head by a kielbasa, it should be explained that a kielbasa (pronounced KEEL-baa-saa) is a long, very hard Polish sausage of considerable heft. The kielbasa should be treated with extreme caution because it has proven to be lethal when: 1. used to deliver a blow to a person's head or 2. eaten.

friendship with Howie Erzinger was sorely tested. Not that we ever competed over the same girl. I may not have been very smart, but I damn well knew enough not to climb into the ring with "Joe Louis."

Almost half of my junior year had passed, and I still hadn't mustered enough courage to ask a girl out on a date. This was a condition that proved to be anathema in Howie's eyes, and he bugged me about it unmercifully. When neither he nor I could stand the railing any longer, I relented, and his girlfriend arranged for a friend of hers to go with me so that we could all be together on a double date. Howie's girlfriend was gorgeous. I wish I could say that her friend was plain. Truth is she looked like she had been backing up a weak line.

It was not only my first date, but as dates go, it also established a mark for brevity, which still claims a prominent line or two in *The Guinness Book of Records*. By 9:30 p.m. I was back home, listening in solitude as my radio brought me *The Music of Art Kassell and His Castles in the Air from the Romantic Aragon Ballroom on Chicago's Glamorous North Side.*

Incensed as I was at Howie, I had to admit that I came away with a lesson for the ages: Make your own choices! With the swift realization that there were pretty and personable young dolls bubbling through the halls at South Shore High School, and in order to insulate myself from any future misbegotten generosity on Howie's part, I forthwith adopted that philosophy for all matters involving romantic potential. Howie Erzinger had won again, but he had engineered it so that I was the beneficiary of his victory. What a guy, huh?

Now that the barrier had been breached, I tried to date every good-looking girl in the junior and senior class.[3] I might have succeeded, too, except that my career was cut short by graduation.

By today's standards, our mixed-gender social activities must have seemed very insipid, although we didn't think so. Unless something very unusual came up, our hot night on the town consisted of going to a neighborhood movie theater, following that with a visit to either Cunis' or Mitchells' ice cream parlor (really tough decision!), all culminating with a passionate grand finale when you kissed your date goodnight at her front door. During this climactic scene I always experienced a sense of inhibition sweeping over me as a consequence of my gut feeling that a silent audience within the darkened house was according us mixed reviews—stern disapproval from my date's parents counterbalanced by voyeuristic accolades from her younger sisters and brothers.

---

3. I realize that you, dear reader, are undoubtedly seeing me as being very shallow, but please remember, that was then and this is now.

When it came to being dissolute, I have to acknowledge that our cholesterol intake from all those weekend milkshakes was shameful, but that was the extent of it. The only guy we knew who ever had an experience with drugs was Augie Gorski. That happened once when he put his arm through a window and had to have a needle full of penicillin stuck into his rear end. I'd rather have to read the annotated works of Chaucer than do that.

So far as use of alcohol was concerned, it just never occurred to us. First of all it cost money, which was the main thing none of us had. Secondly, I had tasted a beer once, and next to liver, I had never put anything that vile into my mouth. Finally, if any of our parents ever found out we had been drinking, we would have wound up having an extended stay on the Injured Reserve List.

How about automobiles? Are you kidding? Only about one family in five even owned one. Besides, the built-in copout for parents at that time was: "Don't you know there's a war going on?" We were in high school during the early part of World War II, and gas was very tightly rationed. No sane father was going to allow his meager gasoline supply to be dissipated so that a bunch of kids could drive to the Avalon Theater in order to watch the Three Stooges. Only one guy at our high school, Danny Feeney, had his own automobile, and he was usually in more trouble than a Watergate defendant.

If you wanted to go to the Jeffrey Theater, you walked. When you had a date and really wanted to impress her, however, there was a problem with the Jeffrey. The films they showed there did not qualify as recent releases by a span of about eight years. In order to treat your girlfriend like she was really uptown, you took her to the Avalon. That meant an additional 10 cents (each!) for admission plus the cost of a streetcar ride, but hey, what the hell!

The streetcars in Chicago were antique red trolley cars that hurtled along at precarious speeds, jouncing their passengers around on slippery, woven straw seats. I remember once coming home after an evening at the Avalon watching Claude Raines "round up the usual suspects." The girl I was with had gotten real cozy with me, and while traveling home aboard the 79th Street trolley, we tried to exchange a few kisses. When I arrived home my father looked at me, and then he became rather upset.

"Who the devil were you out with tonight?" he demanded.

"Violet Neal," I replied.

"Well, young man," he said, "I think you better not see her any more. She's too much of a hot number for you."

When I gazed into the mirror a few moments later I understood his consternation. I had one beautiful lipstick implant, which ran at a rakish diagonal angle from the bridge of my nose through my right eyebrow, eventually disappearing into my hairline. There was another tattooed just below my Adam's apple, and a third bright red smudge that started on the left bicep of my white shirt and curved in a garish arc around to the elbow. But, shoot! If my dad thought I looked bad, he should have seen Violet's bloody nose.

On our dates there was always more than one couple. Frequently, there were as many as five or six, but it was only on rare occasions that Howie Erzinger, Herb Melnick, and I did not go out together. Herb was my other close pal in high school, and we still remain very good friends today, seeing each other several times a year although we live half a continent apart. How could a guy with a chum-friendly name like his not be a good friend? He is the only person I've ever known whose entire name is composed of four separate first names: HERB - BERT MEL - NICK.

Herb, like the rest of us, loved sports, but to say that he was an average athlete is being a mite charitable. He didn't play on any of the varsity teams, but he was a pretty good pickup player, and for several years in a row he led the playground leagues in getting injured. He was one helluva fan, however, and he could devour *The St. Louis Sporting News* faster than William "The Refrigerator" Perry could put away a Big Mac. You want to know who led the Sally League in stolen bases in 1940? Give Herb a call.

There is no one I have ever known who could keep me laughing longer and harder than Herb did. On numerous occasions he succeeded in bringing both Howie and me to our knees, partly from laughter and partly in our supplications to him to desist. He has had me so weak from laughing that my bout with mononucleosis in comparison seemed like a walk in the park. Herb was truly a born-again entertainer, and he performed the lead comic role in several school plays.

Herb also styled himself a songwriter. Among his most noteworthy efforts was a catchy number that he titled "I Kissed Her Gently on the Lips and Left Her Behind for You." There were numerous others of dubious merit, including a few he composed while he was in the army during the latter stages of World War II. One of those, which springs to my mind every now and then, was his spirited flag-waver entitled "Send My Absentee Vote to the Mayor of Terre Haute." Real-life experiences were often responsible for inspiring Herb's musical endeavors.

Fortunately, this review of Maestro Melnick's compositions spares you from having to listen to the music; it was worse than the words.

Herb was big on football fight songs, also. Within days after the Chicago Bears had introduced their now famous "Bear Down Chicago Bears," everyone in the city was singing it. The present-day Arizona Cardinals had not yet moved from Chicago to St. Louis and then on to Arizona, and so they were still known (not surprisingly) as the Chicago Cardinals. Herb went to work and came up with a real foot-stomper for them. He called it—are you ready?—"Stack Up Chicago Cards," and he mailed it in for their approval. When they returned the song to him along with their rejection letter, they also enclosed an application form for buying season tickets. Undismayed, he followed with "Keep a Stiff Upper Lip Pittsburgh Steelers" and "Stand Tall New York Giants," but neither of those efforts on his part met with critical acclaim either.

Among Herb's other numerous idiosyncrasies he had this uncomfortable (for the rest of us) habit of yelling outrageous things in public. Once, in the autumn of 1945, just a couple of months after the war had ended, Herb and I, still not discharged from service, were both home on furlough. Through some unbelievable good fortune we had managed to finagle two tickets for the seventh game of the World Series between the Detroit Tigers and the Chicago Cubs. That's right! The Chicago Cubs were in the World Series. You can look it up.

The Cubs had picked up a pitcher, waived by the New York Yankees at midseason, named Hank Borowy. Borowy had won 11 games while losing just one after joining the Cubbies, and he was the main reason the Cubs had won the pennant. Hank had also been the starting and winning pitcher in two of the three World Series victories that the Cubs had notched, and now, after just one day's rest, they had sent him to the mound again hoping that there might be one more miracle that this stouthearted man could perform.

It was obvious from the outset, however, that his tired arm had finally given out, and when the Tigers loaded the bases in the top of the first inning, the Cubs' manager, Phil Cavaretta, had to replace Hank with the only other capable hurler on the pitching staff. In from the bullpen came the wily veteran, "Oom Paul" Derringer. Oh, how the Wrigley Field faithful loved this guy. He had saved countless games for the Cubbies during their march to the National League title.

When Derringer's first pitch missed the outside corner for ball one, Herb did it again, shouting, "Get that bum outta there." He might as well have yelled that at Hitler during a Nazi Party rally at Nuremberg. It is the closest brush with sudden death that I ever have had. The dispositions of the agitated Cubs fans positioned in our vicinity were eroded still further when Paul Richards, the Tigers' catcher, hammered Derringer's next pitch off the right center field wall for a two-bagger, clearing the bases in the process. Thank God we were wearing American uniforms.

The Cubs, of course, lost the game and the World Series, to boot. As we were exiting the ballpark after the game, Herb was booming out a new cry: "Wait till next year!" We've been waiting, and waiting, and waiting, and—.

Herb Melnick also loved to argue—about anything—and he never lost an argument. This was not because of any facility he had for presenting his case; it was just that he never conceded. If he ever found himself in the position where the other fellow's evidence was irrefutably overwhelming, Herb would bring the discussion to an abrupt conclusion by snapping, "I refuse to listen to reason." In contending with Herb, I employed a technique of my own, which allowed me at least to fight him to a standoff. Whenever he might have me verbally pinned in the corner, I'd merely say, "Bullshit!" And then I'd leave the room.

During our final weeks in service, after the war had ended, Herb was stationed at Fort Campbell, Kentucky, where he was in charge of organizing the athletic programs for the soldiers on the base. One time, when we were speaking to each other on the telephone, he began bragging to me about all the great athletes at Fort Campbell, one superlative following the other. He was beginning to get under my skin, but the real topper came when he told me that they had a baseball pitcher stationed there who would someday become a star in the big leagues. When I let Herb know that his exaggerating was starting to play havoc with his credibility, he really became exercised.

"Oh yeah!' he said. "He'll not only pitch in the majors; he'll become one of the greatest of all time. Write his name down so that you'll be sure to remember it."

"Bullshit!" I said, and then I slammed the phone down.

I never did write down the guy's name, but I sure do remember it. It was Warren Spahn.

CHAPTER 3

Nothing Can Stop the Army Air Corps

The day after I graduated from high school I enlisted, along with 21 of my classmates, in the Army Air Corps. It would still be a couple of months, however, until I would be called up to active service because the rules required an enlistee to be 18. Frankly, I couldn't understand it one bit. We'd been screwing around with that war for two years now and still hadn't put it to bed. Why the hell didn't they take me in right away so that I could get the damned thing finished up for them?

It was apparent to me that the dum-dums in the Pentagon were not very alert. If they would have taken the time to go to a couple of Van Johnson or John Wayne movies, they would have learned in a New York minute how things ought to be handled.

I remember Van Johnson in one of those epics. He was returning in his B-24 Liberator from a mission on which he had completely destroyed the German ball bearing industry when his plane got jumped by 27 Messerschmitts. While piloting the plane with one hand, he shot down nine of the bastards before his plane took a mortal hit. After all surviving members of his crew had bailed out, he hauled ass out of there, too.

He floated to the ground with his hat still perfectly in place, and what a hat it was! After I had been in the Army Air Corps for a while I tried to get my hat to look like his, but, no matter what I did, mine never acquired a 50-mission crush anywhere near as authentic as his.

Somehow or other Van had gotten hold of a German army uniform, and this was proving to be a godsend during his harrowing efforts to make it back to England. He had one real close call when some Gestapo creeps became suspicious and subjected him to an intensive interrogation. Fortunately, Van was able to dispel their doubts by meeting every test. The clincher came when he reeled off the final score of the 1938 Reich Championship soccer match between Bremen and Leipzig, including his take on the officiating gaffe in the final moments of the game that resulted in the head referee being reprimanded and then stripped of his swastika.

As Van made his way westward across the continent he proved to be a real thorn in the side of the Nazis, blowing up bridges and ammunition dumps. He also succeeded in saving General Eisenhower's life when he skewered Obersturmbannfuehrer Wolfgang Schliepper, who was the mastermind of a sinister assassination plot against the supreme commander of our Allied forces.

By a stroke of luck Van had run into four brilliant German nuclear scientists who had become disenchanted by the Nazis' excesses and who wanted to defect. They joined Van on his perilous journey, disguising themselves as simple milkmaids after shaving off their goatees.

It wasn't all work and no play for Van, however. He found time to jump into the sack with more women than the entire Ninth Army even saw once they hit the continent. Those cuties may have had names such as Monique and Nicole, but they all looked like Ava Gardner to me. A few of the mademoiselles were members of the French resistance, but they sure didn't offer any resistance when Van turned on the charm.

After the seductions, Van, along with the four milkmaids/scientists, bolted over to the Eiffel Tower where, on a clandestine radio, he beamed an uplifting message back to London. He concluded this broadcast by singing, for the benefit of the heretofore dispirited British populace, "There'll Be Bluebirds over the White Cliffs of Dover." History records that on the very next day England's prime minister, his eyes still rimmed red from joyous weeping, delivered his immortal "Never in the course of human events has so much been owed by so many to so few" speech.

Van finally made it to the Channel coast where a motor launch, commanded by British naval officer Peter Lawford, was waiting in the choppy waters to take him and the four scientists back to England.

Just at that point, some Wehrmacht Pfc. named Heinke, the front edge of whose helmet paralleled his upper lip, hurled a hand grenade into the vessel. Quicker than you could say, "Holy moley!" Van threw his body onto the live grenade. He took the full force of the explosion right in the gut, saving the lives of all the others aboard. Through some fortuitous quirk of fate the boat remained undamaged, but Van, even though he had managed to survive, was in terrible shape. His hat, however, remained on his head at the same jaunty angle as always.

Peter managed to get his beleaguered craft back to London, however, and after three days in the hospital Van was ready for his next mission. Myself, I would have taken longer.

They tell me that when that movie had completed filming, Van took just three weeks off in order to rest up in Palm Springs and was right back on the set again to start shooting the sequel. Three weeks isn't much time to get it back together again, but dammit, you had to realize there was a war going on.

I'm not going to go into detail regarding John Wayne's movies, and so you're just going to have to take my word for it. His exploits would have made Van Johnson seem like a stay-at-home mom.

The GIs who were overseas must have really loved and idolized Van and the Duke, and they probably would have given away a week's C rations in order to have been even half as heroic.

In contrast to those two warriors of the big screen, I had seen newsreels of the klutzes we had over there doing the actual fighting, and it was plain to me why we were having such a tough go of it. These guys were all crouching behind the shelter of tanks as they inched forward, and on a lot of occasions some of the more faint-hearted ones were seen burrowing their noses into the ground behind mounds of earth simply because there were a few German artillery shells going off around them.

They showed a picture of one dogface who had been wounded, and all he did was just lie there carrying on something disgraceful. Do you think John Wayne would have stopped storming a pillbox just because he'd had his leg blown off above the knee?

Most of the soldiers I saw in those newsreels appeared frightened and very tired. You'd think if they were going to be on camera, they'd at least have enough self-esteem to put up a good front. In all the time Van Johnson had required to work his way out of German occupied territory he hadn't slept a wink. Even on those occasions when he had access to a bed, there was always some dolly in it who kept him awake all night, anyway. Despite his lack of sleep, you could always count on Van to be as fresh and lively as a puppy.

Also, the poor slobs in those newsreels had no sense of style whatever. They were unkempt as hell. Many of them had three or four days' growths of beard, and you could practically smell their B.O. Besides, it was appalling how careless so many of them were in dressing for the war; a lot of the items they wore were not even color coordinated.

If you wanted to know why they were advancing so slowly all you had to do was look at all the crap they were carrying around with them. I mean, there were gas masks, and rifles, and mess kits, and backpacks, and any number of other nondescript pieces of junk. All old Van had ever needed was his multipurpose knife and a bottle of Pouilly Fuisse.

It wasn't just their physical appearance that caught my attention, however; they seemed to have a lack of élan, as well. There wasn't one wimp who, like John Wayne, ever stood up in the face of withering machine gun fire and shouted, "Send me more Krauts!"

I could see the problem. How come those ding-dongs in Washington who were running the show couldn't?

◆◆◆◆◆◆◆◆

On a December day in 1943 I was finally called to active duty, and on the 13th I was riding a troop train south toward Greensboro, North Carolina, where I was to begin my basic training. It was on that trip that I became engrossed in the book of poetry my mother had given to me in Union Station just before I departed from Chicago. My father's birthday was only two days away, and, inspired by the contents of the book I had received from my mother, I decided to compose a few lines of verse to send to him. One night, more than 45 years later, after he had passed away, I was reviewing some items he had saved, and I came across a yellowing, fragile sheet of paper containing the poem I had sent to him on his birthday so many years before. It read as follows:

I was born a common man.
My father so was he.
But prouder not could be a king,
For we be men who are free.
Our nation has blessed us in many ways,
With liberty for all.
And as my father did many years ago
It's my time to answer the call.
Our cause is just; that I know,
And for that I'd bear a gun.
My father did many years ago,
And I'm so proud to be his son.

I was born a common man.
My father so was he.
But prouder not could be a king,
For we be men who are free.

◆◆◆◆◆◆◆◆

Everyone has a reason, I guess, why they pick one branch of service in preference to the others. Eddie Wiltshire, for instance, who graduated from high school with me, selected the navy for the sole reason that the swabbies didn't have to wear neckties. Good enough. My choice was the Army Air Corps. Sure I wanted to fly, but more than anything else, I was wild about their song. Not only that, I heard that 98 percent of the men coming into the Air Corps were being sent to Miami Beach for their basic training with their quarters located in the luxurious ocean-front hotels the government had taken over for the duration. Hot damn!

Trouble is they sent me to Greensboro Army Air Corps Base in North Carolina, and we moved into what must have been the same barracks that had been used by Stonewall Jackson's troops in 1861.

I had nothing to complain about, however, because I was very fortunate to have been accepted in the first place. It was required that you have 20/20 vision in order to get into the aviation cadet program, and when I had taken the enlistment physical, I tested 20/40 in both eyes. The sergeant who had administered the eye exam told me that would, of course, disqualify me. I was the last person being tested that day, and as the sergeant was gathering up his materials, we talked briefly. It turned out that his younger sister was dating Bob Finnegan, who had been the captain of our high school football team.

Upon learning that I was a friend and teammate of Bob, he asked me how badly I wanted to be in the Air Corps. The way I fell to my knees must have convinced him, because he told me that he would mark a 20/20 on my chart. He explained that in some subsequent physical exam during the nine-month pilot training program my visual defect would probably be discovered. But by that time, at least, I would already be in the Air Corps, and they would assign me to some other duty within the Corps.

When I left the examining station several minutes later whistling, "Off we go into the wild blue yonder," I had been accepted. During the next few months I ate more carrots than Bugs Bunny.

Basic training was a gas. It lasted through December, January, and February, and it was so cold down there in Dixie that I checked once or twice to be certain that I was in Greensboro and not Greenland. Memories of basic training are a distant blur to me now, except I remember thinking I had mistakenly been sent to an infantry outfit. We didn't see a single airplane; all we did during the entire 12 weeks was march and learn how to carry and handle a rifle.

In basic training you get no time off until the 10th and 11th weekends in camp. If, up to that time you've had a spotless record, you could then get those coveted weekend passes. It was Friday of the 10th week, and our squad was policing the grounds, picking up "anything that doesn't grow." I must have been daydreaming about that first weekend pass, because I walked past a small scrap of paper lying on the ground. From our drill instructor Sgt. Raymond Klopsch's reaction you would have thought that I had just passed along vital secrets to the enemy. He positioned himself two inches away from my face and screamed, "Soldier, do you see that piece of paper?"

"Yep," I said.

One instant later horror gripped me because, when I heard an explosion and saw Sgt. Klopsch fly into the air, I thought he had stepped on a land mine.

"Yep! Yep! What the hell do you mean 'Yep'?" Answer a question from a person of superior rank like a hell-for-leather, go-for-broke American soldier should answer it," he demanded.

"Yes, Sir!" I barked.

"Yes, Sir, what?" he still wanted to know.

By this time I was becoming very confused, not to mention scared shitless, but I did the best I could.

"Yes SirREE!" (I added a crisp little salute for good measure.)

When good ol' Sarge burst out laughing and then, with a smile on his face, put his arm around my shoulder, I speculated that he might invite me over to the PX with him later to have a couple of beers. In fact, when he started to speak it sounded fairly encouraging.

"You know, I like you, soldier," he said. "And because I like you, I am not going to take away your weekend pass—*next weekend.* But this weekend your ass is on cleanup duty in the latrines."

The world really isn't fair, you know. Gary Cooper says, "Yep," and then he rides off into the sunset with Grace Kelly. I say it and wind up spending 14 hours on my hands and knees with a bucket of Lysol.

That was it for basic training. When it finished, we were no longer PACs.[1] I was sent to Bergstrom Field near Austin, Texas, where I was to begin preflight training. Anatoly Scharansky couldn't have been any more eager to get out of Russia than I was to get into an airplane.

On our first full day at Bergstrom Field, we were all sitting in our barracks, full of nervous anticipation, as the morning hours slipped away.

At last some tech sergeant, with a real pair of wings pinned to the chest of his uniform, came through the door and snapped, "Which of you men want to be pilots?"

Theoretically, the men in the aviation cadet program could choose between training to become a pilot, a navigator, or a bombardier. Every one of us, however, visualized himself at the controls. In a move that could have been choreographed by Gower Champion, we leapt to our

1. PAC was a special rank designation meaning Pre-Aviation Cadet.

feet in unison emitting a husky cry of affirmation so resolute that it would have scared the bejesus out of a kamikaze pilot.

"Very well, follow me," the sergeant commanded.

At that point we would have followed him on a frontal attack against the Seigfreid Line. He marched us across the base, eventually reaching a huge warehouse. Outside that building, the most enormous quantity of lumber I had ever seen was scattered about.

On that very spot I had my first experience as a pilot in the U.S. Army Air Corps when the sergeant gave us our instructions:

"I want you men to take all the wood you see here and 'pile it' neatly inside the warehouse."

Unfortunately, everything we did in the preflight program didn't turn out to be as much fun as that had been. I was about to receive a devastating blow to my morale. Before beginning our instruction we were required to take another physical exam, and once again I flunked the eye test.

The officer in charge told me that under the circumstances I would not be allowed to continue in the Aviation Cadet program, and that within a few days' time I would be reassigned. This was the first time in my life that I was overwhelmed by such a deep and gnawing feeling of disappointment. Other than the times, many years later, when my parents died, I was not to know such desolation of spirit again until the day I was fired by the Kansas City Chiefs. At Bergstrom Field, at least, there was sound justification for not letting me continue with flight training. There was no similar justification when the Chiefs dismissed me.

Several days later I received orders to report to Laurinburg-Maxton Army Air Base in North Carolina, where I was to undergo eight weeks' training so that I could become a qualified weather observer.

Eight weeks! To become a weather observer? Hell, when I was five years old, I used to look out the window and be able to say to my mother, "It's raining." I didn't need to know anything about isobars and occluded fronts. Besides, if they didn't think I could see well enough to spot a German cross on the side of a Fokker 100 yards away, how in heaven's name did they expect me to identify some cirrus clouds that were 20,000 feet in the sky?

Laurinburg-Maxton AAB was named after the community located immediately outside the gate from the base. The name of the town was longer than its one paved street, and so whenever we had time off on the weekends, we would take the 110-mile bus ride to Charlotte. This was a stupid thing to do because there were more servicemen stationed in the various camps throughout North Carolina than we had in the entire South Pacific, and we all gravitated to Charlotte on the weekends. Panic-stricken mothers in Charlotte sequestered their daughters in bomb shelters from sundown on Fridays until dawn on Monday mornings.

One Sunday morning a buddy of mine, named Windy Bayless, and I were in the USO whiling away some time playing a rip-roaring game of Chinese checkers when a kindly, gray-haired lady approached us and asked if we'd like to come to her home that afternoon for Sunday dinner. It didn't sound very exciting to us, and so we declined politely.

We watched her move about the room asking others the same question. The paratroopers from Camp Mackall turned her down; so did the infantrymen from Fort Bragg. The leathernecks from Camp Lejeune and the marine flyers from the Cherry Point Air Station also begged off. Windy and I began to feel sorry for her, and so Windy finally said, "Come on, let's go with her. We don't have anything else to do."

We asked her if the offer was still good, and she was delighted. That was to be the first of several Sunday dinners for Windy and me at Mrs. Hersey's house. She was a very good cook, but I'd be lying if I said that it was the menu that kept us coming back every weekend.

When we arrived at her house there were 12—*count 'em, 12*— cuddlesome young Southern belles whom Mrs. Hersey had invited over to share the nourishment with us. We got to know them very well. I was still only 18 at the time, but there was one woman there named Lily Mobley, who was 25 years old, and who, I think, took a real shine to me. She was very pretty and built, but, because of the age difference, I was in such awe of her that I failed to employ Sgt. Klopsch's number one tenet—the one about having the killer instinct.

Windy and I swore a blood oath that under pain of torture neither of us would ever divulge a word about our discovery. The atom bomb secret was not as well kept. We'd hit Charlotte every weekend and disappear from sight. I wonder if the other guys thought we were sweet on each other.

On the last Sunday before finishing Weather Observers School, Windy and I stopped by Mrs. Hersey's house for the last time in order to say goodbye. We were to be shipped out to an unknown destinations right after graduation. The girls gathered in a circle around us, and it took me 45 minutes to kiss them all. And that was just the first lap.

I often think about Mrs. Hersey. She was a wonderful lady, and she contributed a great deal toward helping us win the war. I am not referring now to what she did for Windy and for me. On the mantle at her home there were pictures of her three sons, all in uniform. The one in the marines was later wounded badly on Okinawa.

♦♦♦♦♦♦♦♦

On our last day at Laurinburg-Maxton AAB they issued us some mean-looking equipment. I received everything except a cyanide pill to take in the event of being captured. Deep down I was hoping they would assign me to England, but whatever lay ahead I was spoiling for action, man! When I opened my orders and read that I was being sent to Apalachicola, I figured I was going to the Pacific until I found out that Apalachicola was in—*Florida*?

For 11 endless months I was a weather observer at the glider-training base at Apalachicola. Luckily I didn't die of malaria. It may seem to you that I had pretty soft duty, but let me tell you a thing or two. I didn't have a safe minute in all the time I was there. Between the glider pilot trainees who kept crashing into our barracks and the boredom, I feel fortunate to have survived. Besides, you never knew when one of those V-2 rockets the Germans were shooting at England might stray way off course and catch us unaware.

I haven't even told you yet about the hurricanes. Apalachicola is located up in the Florida panhandle on the Gulf of Mexico, and those damn hurricanes used to blow in every Monday, Wednesday, and Friday, except for holidays, of course. Probably my finest day during the war came one time when we were hit by a particularly fierce storm. I had been on duty for 17 hours straight, and conditions had been doing nothing but getting worse. I was dog-tired and was trying to do more things at once than a short-order cook. At one of the most chaotic moments of the ordeal some major with a riding crop bustled into the station and asked me if he could use the Jeep assigned to our weather station. Since entering service I had always fashioned myself to be uniquely cut out for leadership roles, but the only thing that I had charge of during my entire time in the Air Corps was that Jeep.

Inundated with work, I hurriedly told him, "Sure. Go ahead."

There was a 75 mile-an-hour wind out there; it was raining gliders, and he picked that instant to be chicken shit.

"Don't you say, 'Sir' when speaking to an officer?" he wanted to know.

I was extremely weary, but I still managed to respond, "Yes, Sir."

"That's better," he said. "Now, once again, may I use your Jeep?"

This time, invigorated, I could hardly wait to answer.

"No, Sir," I said and returned to my duties.

After the storm had abated, all the men in the weather station, including Lt. Madsen, carried me back to my barracks on their shoulders.

◆◆◆◆◆◆◆◆

There were some monumental figures on the world's stage during World War II. See if any of these names ring a bell: Churchill, Roosevelt, Hitler, Stalin, Hirohito, Mussolini, de Gaulle, Chiang Kai-shek, Eisenhower? A few others such as Zhukov, Rommel, Montgomery, Nimitz, and MacArthur were also acknowledged biggies, but the person I remember best was Clint Lowery.

Clint bunked directly across the aisle from me at Apalachicola. We had a very eclectic group of soldiers quartered in our building. Several of us were weather observers. Roll call also included a group of mechanics, some other guys assigned to the motor pool, one clerk, and a few of the most owl-like supply sergeants Uncle Sam had ever issued.

No one could tell you what responsibility Clint had, however, because he rarely left the barracks except at meal times. His records undoubtedly had been lost during some previous routine snafu, and he wasn't about to make any waves. Almost everyone in our barracks had a few stripes on his sleeve except for Clint. The only marks on his shirt came from gravy stains. He was a buck private.

Clint was older than all the rest of us—a lot older. Most of the guys were between 18 and 23 years old. Clint was 40, and he appeared to be 15 years older than that. He had been drafted two or three days before reaching the age that would have disqualified him for induction. Clint was more angry about that than my father had been the day I rearranged the front grill on his two-day-old Pontiac.

Sociability was not Clint's long suit, and he kept pretty much to himself except for joining in the poker games whenever payday rolled around. After losing all of his money, he'd then retire to his bunk, lying for hours on end, his hands clasped behind his head, staring at the beams overhead. From time to time I used to gaze up at the spot on the ceiling where his eyes were focused, but I never did figure out what it was up there that fascinated him so.

To Clint's credit, it should be noted that he set aside a time each day when he would do some reading. This wholesome activity was confined exclusively to scouring the local newspaper, *The Tallahassean,* for reports about the progress of the war. After reading the newspaper accounts he would offer an observation of his own, always pertaining to just one subject. If the day's news, for instance, dealt with a big advance on the eastern front by the Russians, Clint would say, "I'm 28 miles closer to home." Home for Clint was Chattanooga, Tennessee, where he had worked, in what capacity I do not know, for the Coca Cola Bottling Company. The job was waiting for him after the war.

Clint's personal hygiene habits were a little shaky, also. Once a week—maybe—he'd get around to taking a shower, and there were times when you could detect an industrial-strength odor in his general vicinity. The other guys in the barracks rode him about this, but Clint usually just ignored their comments.

There was one corporal, however, who often went above and beyond the call of duty in ragging Clint. This soldier was a cleanliness freak, the kind of guy who owned matching hairbrushes, shower clogs, and a huge bar of scented soap that hung from a pastel rope. There were 41 different brands of aftershave lotion on that man's shelf. All that tra-la-la was his business, I guess, but when he started throwing handfuls of talcum powder at himself, several of the GIs nearby who suffered from respiratory problems had to break out their gas masks.

One day Clint finally cracked under this fellow's unrelenting insults. The corporal had been insisting, once again, that Clint should shower every day, whereupon Clint confronted him, demanding to know, "Just how the hell often do you take a shower?"

Oozing pride and self-satisfaction, the corporal announced to Clint (and all other bystanders, as well), "I'll have you know that I shower twice every single day."

Clint was stymied briefly, but then he lighted up and said, "Yeah! Well, if you have to shower twice every day you sure must be a dirty bastard."

You would never know it from looking at Clint—because he was very slim—but he really loved to eat. About 30 minutes before the mess hall opened for a meal, Clint would head over that way so that he would be present and accounted for when they unlocked the doors. On those occasions when I wandered past the mess hall before it had opened, I'd spot Clint in a line with the rest of the regulars on the little walk that ran alongside the building.

Despite the differences between us, I liked Clint, and he liked me. One of the reasons we hit it off was because I'd give him whatever money he needed, after the fifth of each month, so that he could buy cigarettes. He didn't want a lump sum but insisted on taking it only when he wanted to get one or two packs. It never amounted to very much, and I didn't bother to keep track. He did, I guess, because on the first of every month he'd always pay me back.

The time I enjoyed spending most with Clint occurred on those occasions when I would come into the mess hall in the evenings toward the end of the serving period. He'd still be sitting at a table all by himself smoking a cigarette, coughing a little, and nursing a tepid, one-third-filled cup of coffee that had ashes floating around in it. I'd bring my tray over to his table, and he'd keep me company while I ate my meal. I really can't remember what we'd talk about; it wasn't sports or girls—the only two subjects where my conversation was guaranteed to dazzle—but we always found something to keep us entertained. After dinner we'd stroll over to the PX where Clint would pick up *The Tallahassean,* and then we'd head back to the barracks together.

During my last few months in service I was transferred to Morrison Field near Palm Beach, Florida, but Clint and I exchanged a letter or two. After the war had ended and we were both discharged, Clint returned to Chattanooga. We didn't continue our correspondence, but every year at Christmas, for a long time, we'd send cards to each other. His greeting always came on the company Christmas cards from the Coca Cola Bottling Company.

Usually I'd remember about the card at the last minute, and I'd ask one of the football secretaries to pick one up for me during her lunch hour. She'd bring back something with a picture on the front of Rudolph the Reindeer or of some kittens dressed up like Santa Claus. Most of the time I'd write a word or two inside the card. One Christmas, about 15 years after the war had ended, we both missed sending cards, and soon we had lost track of each other.

The long, fearsome, bloody struggle was drawing to its finish. With the conflict ended, our war department began very quickly to muster out the more than 15 million men who were in uniform. It took a while for them to get to me, because most of the men had been in service quite a bit longer than I had. Priority in qualifying for discharge was determined by the number of "points" a man had accumulated, and points were awarded on the basis of time in service, overseas duty, and exposure to combat. Compared to most of the others I was 0 for three.

By the end of February 1946, I was the only soldier left in our barracks. It was eerie. The ghosts of a lot of friends and of many unknown young men who were never going to go home kept me company in that deathly quiet big barn of a structure.

One day at about 5:00 a.m., I was awakened by someone tapping on my shoulder. When I opened my eyes, there was Major Davis standing over my bunk, and he told me to be prepared in one hour's time to leave for Camp Grant, Illinois, where I was to be discharged. Twenty minutes later I was showered, shaved, packed, and standing out in front of the barracks with all my gear wondering when in the hell that driver who was to take me to the train was going to show up.

At Camp Grant they offered us all kinds of inducements to reenlist, including a Japanese camera with its own carrying case, but I wanted out. At the rate I had been getting promoted—I was a corporal—I would be 87 years old by the time I made lieutenant.

I was discharged and heading for home, feeling sheepish about not having served any time overseas. In later years, when people would ask me what I had done during the war, I'd usually dance around the subject. When they'd finally come right out and ask, "Were you in the armed forces during the war?" I'd answer right back, "Well, hell yes; we won, didn't we?"

On the final leg of my trip home—from Camp Grant back to Chicago—I also was warmed by thoughts of what lay ahead for me, but those reflections were tempered by a sense of melancholy as I recalled the 21 classmates whom I had joined when we had enlisted in the Army Air Corps on that day after we graduated from high school. Nineteen of us were now coming home. The other three—Bob Bailey, Eddie Roth, and Ed Gilfoyle—remained forever young.

Upon receiving our discharges most of us found ourselves with a few free months at our disposal before we would enroll in college and we used that opportunity to do some prime time celebrating. The restaurants and bars were filled every night, and we didn't want to miss any of the revelry. Aah, Freedom!

Our favorite spot was Martin's Lounge on the corner of 71st Street and Jeffery Avenue where, during late 1945 and the early months of 1946, we would all congregate every night. On a man's first visit there upon returning from service and still in uniform, he'd walk in, and there he'd be treated to a raucous welcome home from everyone. On one night we would raise our glasses and sing a toast to Will Darch, a veteran of Iwo Jima. Two nights later Dudley Simpson, recovered from his wounds at Okinawa, rolled in, and our salute would resound again. Twenty minutes later it was Earl Johnson (82nd Airborne). Night after night they kept coming: Bob Peterson and Danny Trahey in their navy uniforms; Carmie Esposito (army engineers); Irv Oppenheim (China/Burma/India Theater); Hank Stein (3rd Army in Europe); Francis Patrick Aloysius McCarthy, in his perfectly tailored Marine Corps dress blues. The seemingly endless parade continued. And we always heralded each man's return home by belting out the same song, sung to the music of "The Battle Hymn of the Republic":

> "Now that the war is over we will all enlist again.
> Yes, the war is over, and we'll all enlist again.
> At last the war is over, and we'll all enlist again.
> We will; LIKE HELL WE WILL!"

Has America ever known a moment more sublime?

CHAPTER 4

What in the World Is a Kohawk?

As a young boy back in the 1930s I listened in fascination to one of President Franklin Delano Roosevelt's famous "fireside chats." Those radio broadcasts—heard by 80 percent of America's adult population—always began with his signature phrase: "My fellow Americans."

On that particular night, young as I was, I sensed that he was talking directly to me. I am certain that others my age felt the same, because as he spoke about the crushing economic burdens inflicted upon our nation by the Depression and about the growing military menace posed by the rise of Hitler and the Nazis in Germany, he uttered nine words that we have never forgotten.

There was a challenge in his voice when he spoke those words, but he also injected a rousing note of confidence in us when he said, "This generation of Americans has a rendezvous with destiny."

Now, it was 1946. The war was won. The factories were booming. The boys were home. We felt that "destiny" was still there ahead of us. Work. Challenges. Careers. Marriages. Children. Family. What fun! Many of us, myself included, were about to embark upon an experience we had dreamed about during our indeterminate time in service. At last, we were going to go to college.

After one semester at the University of Wyoming, where I found the demands imposed by the football program allowed insufficient time for pursuing my academic desires, I gave my cowboy hat, my snowshoes, and my earmuffs to my roommate, and I transferred to Coe College in Cedar Rapids, Iowa. Coe College is a small coed liberal arts institution. It had an enrollment of approximately 1,200 students when I arrived there, and during the course of the school year you would get to know just about all of them. Coe was a member of the Midwest Conference, and, like the other conference schools such as Grinnell, Carleton, Lawrence, and Knox, it had very high academic standards. I would not have been admitted to Coe on the basis of my high school transcript, but my strong performance during my semester at Wyoming made it possible.

Attending college there was a magnificent experience for me, and after having completed my undergraduate studies at Coe, I have often been perplexed about why anyone would want to attend one of those massive state universities. Our classes were small and stimulating. Also, I was able to participate in an intercollegiate athletic program that combined perspective with the idealism that sports are purported to embody. Every "student/athlete" who ever lined up for a kickoff or placed his feet in the starting blocks was a student, first and foremost.

Our athletic teams at Coe were known as "The Kohawks." No one I have ever met knows what a Kohawk is. Noteworthy among Coe College's attributes is its outstanding department of music, and there emerged a proliferation of songs extolling the college's many virtues. One of those ditties, seeks to explain what a Kohawk is:

> I'm a Kohawk; I'm a Kohawk,
> And my ears are made of leather;
> And they flap in windy weather.
> Gosh all hemlock; tough as a pine knot;
> I'm a Kohawk, can't you see?

Now you know.

While I was at Coe, I played varsity football and ran the quarter-mile on the track team. Midway through my senior year, when several players were dropped from the basketball team for training violations, I was recruited from the intramural league, and I played enough to earn a varsity basketball letter to go with the four I had in track and the three in football. We may not have been "big-league," but we had big fun.

At Coe there were opportunities to engage in a variety of school activities and sufficient time, as well, to gain an outstanding education—if you were willing to work for it. Although my grades were excellent, they came as a result of hard study and not because of any superior intellect. There was a fellow in my graduating class named Bill

Matoush who notched four years of straight As, and he graduated summa cum laude. At Coe, I too received straight As, but the one B that I had received during my only semester at Wyoming kept me from matching Bill's outstanding performance. Among the members of our graduating class my grade point was next highest, and I graduated magna cum laude. That orgy in Latin culminated with my induction toward the end of my senior year into Phi Beta Kappa.

My roommate during most of my time at Coe was a little fellow, also from Chicago, named Frank LaBarbara. Despite his small stature, Frank was the leading scorer on the basketball team, and he led the nation two years in a row in free throw shooting percentage. Frank provided a wonderful environment for studying. Not at first, however.

As a freshman Frank rarely opened a book. When he wasn't practicing his damn free throw shooting, he'd be in the student union playing cards until closing time. Then he would come back to the room, put a Vaughan Monroe album on his record player, and turn the volume up to level "Catastrophic Explosion." You try studying when old "Muscle Throat" is bellowing, "Dance, Ballerina, Dance."

One night at around 11:00, during final exams at the end of our freshman year, I was preparing for bed when Frank returned to our room, his basketball shoes hanging to his chest from the laces tied together behind his neck. After unburdening himself of the shoes, he removed his weighty economics textbook from the top shelf, where it had rested unmolested since the first day of the semester. He blew the dust off the cover, cracked the stiffness out of the binding, and sat down to begin studying for his next day's final exam. I went to sleep.

At about 4:00 a.m. I was jolted awake by the sound of Frank's book striking the wall, where he had thrown it in anger. He stared at me in silence for a few moments, and then he said, "How in the hell do they expect you to read a damn 967-page book in one night?"

Frank came very close to flunking out that first year. He was placed on intensive-care probation, but someone must have said the right things to him, because after that, he got academic religion. He became more conscientious and more organized than an Eagle Scout. At 7:00 p.m.—at the sound of the tone—every evening he would say to any visitors in our room, "Frank's my name, and Frank's my nature. Get out of here; it's time to study." He did extremely well in his educational pursuits from that time on, but I'll tell you something: I had a hard time getting used to all that quiet.

For three years I was a starting halfback on the football team at Coe, and although I had matured and become a darn good player, I probably wasn't quite as good as I thought. My love was football, but the sport in which I had the most ability was track. Although our football team was mediocre at best, we had a very strong track team. We won the Midwest Conference championship several times and set numerous relay team records while competing in the Drake Relays and in many of the lesser relay meets in Iowa, Illinois, and Wisconsin.

Our track coach was a wonderful man named Harris Lamb, who had been a legendary athlete at Coe 20 years earlier. Harris was one of three men I would come to know during my college years who had a profound influence on the course of my life. He was an eternal optimist, and he was the quintessential coach. He knew his business, and he knew and loved the young men who were in his charge. Harris Lamb was the embodiment of that sometimes overused phrase: "Sports builds character." It sure had built it into that man.

Just as with my own father, I never heard Harris speak a dirty word. If he ever would have read this book and seen some of the language I've used on occasion, I'm sure he would have shaken his head in disapproval. But then, he would have forgiven me.

Harris handled many hardships with grace and dignity and with a soaring spirit that uplifted those whose lives he touched. For many years Harris's wife, Thelma, had been a wheelchair-bound invalid whose health was slowly, but steadily, declining. Once, when we had some time trials scheduled on the Saturday prior to our first track meet of the season, Harris had a makeshift platform erected on the infield. He brought Thelma there in her wheelchair, and he lifted her and the chair up onto that platform. He then addressed all of us on the team by saying, "Okay, fellas, these are going to be authentic track meet conditions today. We've got the Queen of the Meet right here, and she is going to award ribbons to those of you who have the best time in each event."

Harris had prepared some homemade ribbons, and after we ran our trials in each event, the man with the best time would trot over to the platform, where Thelma would make the presentation. Among my life's most prized keepsakes, I still have one of those ribbons.

Very shortly after I graduated from Coe, Thelma died, and several years later Harris married another fine lady. Harris and Edna Lamb continued to live just a mile or so from the Coe campus for almost 50 years, until Harris, well into his 90s, passed away in 1997.

Both of Harris's children, Marv and Nancy, were students at Coe during my time there. Marv Lamb was a good trackman, and we were teammates. He was a handsome, wholesome young man, and he was the apple of Harris's eye. After Marv graduated he enlisted in the air force, and during a training flight near Tucumcari, New Mexico, his plane crashed and Marv perished in the accident. Harris somehow weathered that tragedy. Harris's daughter, Nancy, is married to a Coe alumnus, John Skogsbergh, and she still lives in Cedar Rapids today. She has her father's personality. Lucky girl!

For that day and age and for the level of competition we faced, I was a pretty good quarter-miler, running the distance in about 49 seconds flat. But the main man on our track team was a tireless whirlwind by the name of Charles "Chilly" Hopkins. Had he entered, he could have won the conference championship in every running event, from the 220-yard dash through the two-mile run. "Chilly" did win the conference crown all four years in the 880, and he also won titles in the 440 and in the one-mile run. The reason we set so may relay records is that the rest of us would always pass the baton to "Chilly" for the anchor leg.

In his final semester at Coe, "Chilly", in order to fulfill his graduation requirements, was carrying an extremely heavy class load. As a result, his conditioning and his performance levels were not up to what they had been in previous years. In the last dual meet of our senior year, "Chilly" and I were both entered in the 440-yard dash. I had never beaten "Chilly." In fact, he had never been beaten in any dual meet race during his entire time in college.

When we came off the last turn, we were running one-two, and no one else was close. "Chilly" had a three-yard lead on me when we both began our finishing kick, but I could sense immediately that I had a lot more left than he had. I closed the gap swiftly, and about 20 yards from the finish line, I was about to surge past him, but I just couldn't bring myself to do it. I decided to stay abreast of "Chilly" so that we would be co-winners. My timing wasn't delicate enough, however, and as we hit the tape, I was an eyelash length behind him. "Chilly" Hopkins finished his collegiate track career undefeated in dual meets. I still do not know today whether I am happy or angry that I did not pass him.

Forty years later it was my great honor to be asked by my old college teammate and pal, "Chilly" Hopkins, to be his presenter on the day he was inducted into the Coe College Athletic Hall of Fame.

Social life at Coe was primarily campus-oriented, and it was tame by any standards. All students were required to live in the college dorms, and women—discrimination be damned—had to be in by 10:00 p.m. on school nights. On weekends they could whoop it up until midnight.

Probably the most serious student escapade occurred during Homecoming one year when several fun-loving sorts commandeered a coffin from the "Bury Grinnell" Homecoming Parade float and put it to circumspect use. A fellow student, Don Malcheff, having imbibed so much celebratory liquid refreshment that deep slumber had overtaken him, was laid in the coffin on his back, hands folded peacefully on his chest. Then the jolly pranksters managed to spirit the open coffin, Don included, into the dimly illuminated lobby of the women's dormitory, and they placed it so that the single flickering light in the lobby would shine revealingly upon the somber casket. We (oops, "they") then retired for the night, allowing events to run their course.

History selected Christopher Columbus to discover the New World, but it was the Goddess of Fate who chose that unfortunate coed who discovered Don in repose. This frail and unsuspecting innocent, while on her way to answer a call of nature, was padding through the lobby, hair in curlers, cold cream slathered on her face, her rosebud-patterned quilted robe pulled about her, when she happened upon that ghoulish scene, and she reacted predictably.

The sounds of her shrieks have long ago faded away, but the debate still rages over whether her nervous breakdown or Don's was more spectacular.

Although more than half a century has passed since that memorable night in the foyer of Voorhees Hall, I take a great deal of pride in noting that, despite the unflagging efforts of the Blue Ribbon Faculty Panel commissioned to investigate this historic scandal, none of the deed's perpetrators has ever been apprehended.

While I was a student at Coe, there were a number of girls whose company I enjoyed, but for the first three years I was too busy with other activities to become serious about any of them.

On the first day of classes each semester, students frequently have difficulty finding the location of their classrooms, and it is not uncommon for several of them to show up a little late. At the beginning of the spring semester during my junior year I had arrived on time for one of my classes, and the session had just begun when a young coed I had never seen before came bustling into the classroom and sat in the only empty chair. It was the seat next to mine, and let me tell you that when Dorothy Prout turned to me and said, "Hello," I was gripped immediately by the realization that among matters of importance in the world, this class in nineteenth century English literature was going to rank right up there with the Chicago Cubs. I became an instant devotee of the subject matter, and we hadn't even opened our books yet.

Dorothy was a sparkling blond bundle of energy with the look of perpetual laughter in her eyes. Unfortunately, Dorothy had not been as enamored as I had with the subject matter, nor did she seem taken by my presence, because on the next day she dropped the class. Despairingly, I would have to plod through Thomas Carlyle's *Sartor Resartus* without her at my side. If, by the way, you are ever in a position to inflict cruel and unusual punishment upon your worst enemy, make the scoundrel read that baby.

Dorothy had transferred to Coe that semester, and it took me two weeks to find her again on campus. I attempted to fill the only free spot on my class schedule by enrolling for a subject she was taking, but the school authorities gave me a very strange look when I requested instruction in women's field hockey.

Eventually I found her, however, and my search was to be rewarded. Two and a half years later Dorothy and I were married.

There came a day, at last, during my senior year that I had been awaiting anxiously. I am not referring to Graduation Day. Bigger than that! I'm talking about the National Football League's draft of college players. Pro scouts had been coming through Cedar Rapids all spring. They consistently timed me at 4.4 seconds in the 40-yard dash, a good time even today. When those scouts talk with you, you become convinced that only a clerical error could cause you to be drafted any lower than mid-second round.

The big day arrived. I had flown in my agent, my tax accountant, my financial adviser, and my theatrical booking agent for the event. In order to handle the crush of anticipated calls, we arranged to have the telephone company install a switchboard in my room, manned (womaned?) by the school's six cheerleaders. I sent out to a local catering service and had them load up trays of food for the tables in the dorm lounge. We had reserved that space to function as headquarters for the local media, all of whom had been invited for the occasion.

Only one of their members was able to make it that day, however, because the state high school baseball quarterfinals were underway at the same time, and Cedar Rapids Roosevelt High was playing

Muscatine. Nevertheless, the lady was, I thought, on the brink of a career-making scoop.

The phone did not ring at all during the first day as rounds one through six were tolled off. I was feeling pretty low, but there were still six more rounds to be addressed the following day before the proceedings would conclude. When a mere two picks remained in the last round, I finally received a call. It turned out that it was just some poor guy who had dialed incorrectly in his frantic attempt to reach the Suicide Prevention Hotline. By the time we finished our conversation, he was trying to cheer me up.

The draft was over, and I hadn't been selected. I threw the lime Jell-O mold against the wall, splattering the poster of Rita Hayworth, and I stomped out of the room.

Four days later there was a call for me on the pay phone out in the hall. (I had had the switchboard removed so that my roommate would have a place to sleep.) The person on the other end of the line was some man up in Iron Mountain, Michigan, who said he owned a gas station and the semipro football team there and that he'd like to have me come play for his club. I hung up. Later that day I phoned all the networks and told them I'd like to announce my retirement.

The vignette about "Draft Day," which I have just recounted, is pure fiction (except that I truly did log 4.4 40-yard dash time). Why then would I include it among my "experiences?"

My purpose was to depict a scenario—in admittedly overblown form—that I have witnessed numerous times during my lifelong involvement with football. The misguided expectancies, the puffery, even the innocent misplacement of values provide a sometimes humorous and sometimes sad commentary on what the true rewards for playing the game ought to be. By painting myself as the unsuspecting dupe in the previous scene I have sought to personalize the experience, not only for myself, but for the observer, as well.

In actuality, I had known my football playing limitations, and my plans were directed toward continuing my education. Near the end of my senior year I received the thrilling news that I had been accepted for admission to Harvard Law School. It was a goal I had been seeking since that first day I had walked onto campus four years earlier.

There was an underlying problem stirring within me, however. During my years at Coe I had been exposed to intercollegiate athletics functioning within an idealistic and ennobling framework. Also, two of my coaches at Coe, Harris Lamb, of whom I have already written, and Dick Clausen, my football coach, loomed before me as compelling examples of what the coaching life could be.

Dick was a big bear of a man who had come to Coe at the beginning of my junior season. He had taken over a program that had been struggling, and under his leadership we had improved and had gained respectability swiftly.

Dick Clausen was the consummate teacher. His understanding of fundamentals, his ability to organize his staff and to present his subject matter, and his gift for motivating and developing confidence in his players were all qualities I didn't know football coaches possessed until I came under Dick's tutelage. He was firm but always approachable. He expected you to get the job done, and you damn well did.

From Dick Clausen I gleaned a coaching tenet that for me has remained the spring from which all my coaching philosophy flows: *What it takes to win is simple—but it isn't easy!*

Dick Clausen must have had 14 eyes, because no matter where he might be on the practice field, if you made a mistake he spotted it and had it corrected—*right then!* This tendency of his to descend on us from any direction in order to grab hold of our errors led us to refer to him as "The Claw." It was a name we used only among ourselves. When we talked directly with him, he was always "Coach Clausen."

Gnawing within me was the notion that coaching would be a wonderful way to spend one's life, but a sense of incongruity accompanied those feelings. Sports had been a bountiful diversion throughout my younger years, but ever since my days in the Army Air Corps, my sights had been set inexorably upon becoming a lawyer. I could not now turn back from a goal that had once seemed so distant and which was now soaring into view on the near horizon, and so I prepared to depart for Harvard.

During my senior year, my name was placed on the ballot as a candidate for the presidency of the Student Council. The platform on which I campaigned reflected genius at work. It embraced just two planks: No more creamed chipped beef on rusk in the dining hall *and* replacing some of the records in the jukebox at the student union, starting with "Rock of Ages" is out and something by the fabulous Ink Spots is in. Riding that bold, avant-garde platform I was elected in a landslide. What a celebration we had at the grille in the student union that evening! We danced until midnight to the newly installed mellow tones of "To Each His Own."

CHAPTER 5

Fair Harvard

On September 1, 1950, my father drove me to Union Station in Chicago, where I boarded a train. My immediate destination was New York City. In New York I changed to another train, this one bound for Boston, and upon arriving there I gathered my luggage, disembarked, and fought my way onto the subway, which departed downtown Boston for outlying areas.

At the Cambridge subway station, still laboring with my luggage, I climbed the long, steep stairway and exited into the middle of busy Harvard Square. Across the street, in staid grandeur, loomed the campus of Harvard University. I made my way through the traffic to the other side of the street, where an arched tunnel provided passage through the thick brick outer wall to the grounds inside. Chiseled into the concrete at the top of the entry arch an inscription caught my eye. It read: "Enter to Grow in Wisdom." I passed through the darkened tunnel and emerged into the sunlight.

It had been a long trip from 71st Street and East End Avenue on the South Side of Chicago to Harvard Yard.

Beginning my law school classes, I thought, would serve to get me firmly back on track and keep me headed unwaveringly toward that day when I would, indeed, graduate into the legal profession. That may have been what I thought, but it wasn't what I felt. Although my body was in the classrooms, my heart kept drifting out to the playing fields.

I gazed about at my classmates as they sat, raptly attentive, listening to the dissection of countless case studies. Perhaps among their number sat a man who, like several Harvard law students before him, might someday hold the highest office in the land. Did he fantasize even now of a future time when he might be in Washington hearing the flourishes and ruffles and then the playing of "Hail to the Chief"? My dreams had different accompaniment. Play for me, "Hail to the Redskins." Their visions were of black robes; mine were of flashy red and gold uniforms.

My roommate at Harvard was a fellow from Baltimore named Gerald Zelinski. After every case he studied, he'd expound on his legal interpretation before rendering his "ruling." His convoluted presentations soon led me and others in our dorm to calling him Oliver Wendell Zelinski, and by such name he was known during his three years at Harvard. His main adversary in those legal discussions was a student from Danville, Kentucky, named Jazz Davis, who lived in the room across the hall from us. He addressed everybody as "Hey Jazz," and so we all returned the favor. Twenty-five years later he became federal Judge Kenneth Davis. No one called him "Jazz" any more.

On a few occasions I tried to discuss my dilemma with Oliver Wendell, but he was far too engrossed with matters of state to offer any insights. Whenever I raised the issue about my desire to coach football, he'd just look at me as if I had prepared a very incomplete legal brief, and then he'd turn his attention back to more weighty subjects.

In the middle of my third week at Harvard Law School, I made the decision that I was going to be a football coach. Law classes had begun three weeks earlier than the scheduled beginning sessions for the Graduate School of Arts and Sciences, and I wanted very much to remain that year at Harvard. I petitioned the dean of the graduate school requesting admission for that fall term. With regret now, I must admit that I cannot recall the name of that caring educator. He listened compassionately to my plea for admission, he carefully studied my undergraduate record, and he granted my request for transfer to the graduate school effective immediately.

Now I had to inform my parents about the decision I had made, and I dreaded inflicting the disappointment I thought they would experience upon hearing that news. Wrong again! My father's words, as always, were simple: "If that is what you've decided you are going to do, just make damn sure you do a good job of it," he said. And then his voice softened, and he added, "I know you will."

My mother accepted it with even greater equanimity. I should have known she would. She always had an unfettered sense of values. A few days later, I received a letter from her. My mother's mailings frequently included a quotation from some writer or poet that she deemed to be appropriate for the occasion. In this letter she had enclosed a poem whose author I do not know, which finished with the following lines:

Oh, Youth, go forth and do!
You, too, to fame may rise;
You can be strong and wise.
Stand up to life and play the man
You can if you but think you can;
The great men were once as you.
You envy them their proud success?
'Twas won with gifts that you possess.

The first time I thought I might be in over my head at Harvard occurred at, of all places, the opening football game of the season between Harvard and Dartmouth. During the halftime performance by the Harvard Band, they moved from formation to formation with intriguing precision, but I became most confused when some of their alignments spelled out words that I could not understand.

My enthusiasm flagged noticeably, however, during the halftime ceremonies, where out on the field the band members had spelled out "Veritas."

"What the deuce does that say?" I asked the man sitting next to me.

He was wearing a never-pressed, nubby tweed jacket that had imitation leather patches on the elbows, and his uniquely styled gray hair looked as if he had forgotten to use a comb after having set his hair dryer on high.

He glanced up from the differential calculus book in which he had remained engrossed even during Dick Clasby's 86-yard touchdown run early in the second quarter, and he then studied me for a while over the top of his half-glasses.

"It says 'Veritas,'" he said. I could tell from the puzzlement on his face that he was considering whether to offer me use of his glasses so that I could verify that information for myself.

"V-E-R-I-T-A-S." I spelled it out, pointing my forefinger at each letter as I said it. "Yep, that's right," I continued. "What does it mean?"

"Veritas? It's the Harvard motto. It means 'truth.' It's in Latin," he told me incredulously.

"Dang!" I said. "Of course, slipped my mind for a second."

Geez! Latin! When I had taken high school Latin, I got as far as "puella est agricola," and everything after that became as chaotic as a goal line stand. Back then I thought "hic haec hoc" was the snap cadence for the football team at Chicago Vocational High School. Nevertheless, he seemed like a friendly enough gentleman to me, and so I asked him what he thought of Dartmouth's combination nickel pass coverage schemes in long-yardage situations. He said "Up yours" in Latin and then returned to studying his book.

At one time I had honestly believed that an academic experience could never be described as being exhilarating, but my year at Harvard cured me of that opinion. What a magnificent group of professors I encountered there. Their stimulating lectures made me hunger for those daily trips to Widener and Lamont libraries and kept me delving more deeply into the subject matter each night until my eyes would close involuntarily.

One of my professors, Dr. Owens, who taught a course in English history from 1815 to the present, stuttered considerably when he spoke, and whenever he became a bit excited, the frequency of his stuttering would increase. Although a person might think that this impediment would impair the good professor's ability to teach effectively, it actually served to enhance the impact of his presentations and often helped to add sumptuous drama to that day's lesson.

He made his points slowly, and he developed them with an artist's touch. All of us in the lecture hall could feel the excitement grow whenever Dr. Owens built toward a climactic statement, because his voice would begin to rise and his stuttering would become more pronounced. At the exact moment when we knew that the fateful word or phrase was about to be spoken, a paroxysm of stuttering would overcome him, leaving us all hanging in excruciating anticipation. Finally, the concluding utterance would explode from his mouth, and the lecture hall would erupt in applause. Dr. Owens left the lecture hall at the end of many of his soliloquies to the sounds of a thundering standing ovation.

My favorite recollection of a classroom performance by Dr. Owens is the one in which he spoke at great length about the provincialism and arrogance that prevailed in Victorian England at the beginning of the 20th century. As his fascinating account drew toward its conclusion, he used as an illustration a haughty headline that had appeared one day in the *London Times.* That headline, he said, read as follows: "S-S-St-S-Storm in the Eng-Eng-English Ch-Ch-Channel; C-C-C-C-C-C-Continent Isolated."

♦♦♦♦♦♦♦♦

It was my intention to fulfill all requirements for my master of arts degree during the one year I planned to be at Harvard, because I wanted to begin teaching and coaching by the following autumn. This meant that, in addition to a heavy course load, I would have to complete my master's thesis as well. My work was cut out for me, all right, but I was encouraged by the progress I was making. Encouraged, that is, until I received a blindside cross-body block that knocked me reeling. Ten weeks into my first semester, I learned that, during the examination period at the end of the school year, I would also be required to display a reading knowledge of French.

My only exposure to French language study had come during the first semester of my freshman year in high school. At the conclusion of that term, Mrs. Meinders, my high school French teacher, called me to her office for a conference. She told me that I was not sufficiently prepared to continue studying the subject. She was, however, a compassionate woman, and she said that if I would promise her that I would never enter a French classroom again, she would let me off the hook and give me a D in the course.

In grateful appreciation I said to her, "Mrs. Meinders, if I ever set foot in a French class again, may the Cubs never win another World Series!"

That did it. She was thoroughly convinced, and she gave me the D. I have honored that pact all the years of my life. I am sure that the sweet lady, when engaged in her daily review of the National League baseball standings, has cursed me many times for what she must perceive as my duplicity. But my conscience remains clear.

At Harvard we were too far into the semester for me to add a French class to my already overly ambitious course load, anyway, and so I decided that there was only one long-shot solution available for me. I purchased a French grammar book and some French vocabulary cards in order to study the subject in my spare time. *What spare time?*

Don't ask me how I did it, but when that year was over, I had received all As, had written my master's thesis, and would have been able to read bedtime stories to Brigitte Bardot should such a happy opportunity ever have presented itself.[1]

My time at Harvard was not all heavy sweat, however. On a few occasions, several of my classmates and I traveled to Wellesley in order to attend some of the Wellesley-Harvard dances that took place on the beautiful campus of that all women's university. One young woman there, with whom I was dancing, asked me what I planned to do after getting my degree, and when I told her I was going to be a football coach, she thought I was the wittiest devil at the gala.

One day I received a telephone call from a freshman student at Harvard whom I had known casually back in Cedar Rapids. His name was John Culver. John told me that he was having some difficulty adjusting to college life at Harvard and that he would appreciate an opportunity to visit with me. John had been an outstanding football player and trackman at Franklin High School in Cedar Rapids, and his Franklin High track team often worked out at Coe at the same time our college team practiced. I had become acquainted with him during those sessions.

When John and I talked at Harvard, he revealed to me that he was very homesick and was considering returning to Cedar Rapids, where he would enroll at Coe College. I urged him to stick it out for a while. He had a fine mind, and I felt that Harvard was the perfect place for him to be. It would have been near tragic for him to abandon his opportunity at Harvard at this early juncture.

I visited with John several more times, and once we attended a Boston Red Sox baseball game together. As time passed, John became very well adjusted to college life in Cambridge, and he began to love Harvard. Why not? He loved it so well, in fact, that after four years as an undergraduate, he entered Harvard Law School, eventually earning his law degree there.

---

1. For those of you who are either too young to remember her *or* who were so involved with other compelling matters that you were never aware of this lady, let me tell you two things: 1. Get with it, man! and 2. Brigitte Bardot became, during the 1950s and 1960s, the most famous French actress to grace the movie world. She was the icon of female sexuality. Also, she was directly responsible for inspiring many American men to speak their first words in French, when, upon seeing her, they would cry out, "Oo-la-la!"

As an undergraduate, John was the starting fullback for three years on the Harvard football team. Twenty-four years after we had had our first meeting at his room in Thayer Hall, John Culver was elected to the U.S. Senate. I'd vote for him any time.

As the school year drew closer to its finish, I registered at the graduate school placement office, telling them that I would be looking for a teaching and football coaching position. The girl with whom I had danced at Wellesley apparently had a more keenly attuned sense of humor than the placement office people, because they did not see anything funny in my request. One of the women working there said something snippy like, "We are not the Florida Gators." She informed me further that the last time there had been a request placed through that office for a football coach occurred in 1889 when Walter Camp at Yale was seeking an assistant who might be adept at defending against the Flying Wedge. Nevertheless, I persisted, and, reluctantly, they placed my information in their files under "N" for "No Hope."

When there were only about two weeks remaining in that final semester, however, I received a summons to come to the placement office. Robert N. Cunningham, the headmaster from St. Louis Country Day School in Missouri, had asked to interview me. Mr. Cunningham was seeking to fill a vacancy on the Country Day School faculty with someone who was qualified to teach both English and history. Those were my majors. In addition, he also wanted that person to take over as the head coach of the school's basketball team. When I told him of my great desire to coach football, he said that he would arrange to have me also serve as a member of the football coaching staff.

We had a deal. I accepted the job, telling myself that the lucky man from St. Louis had just hired himself the best assistant football coach in North America.

In mid-June I received my master of arts degree along with an impressively engraved and crested diploma from Harvard University. When I returned to Chicago, I presented the diploma to my mother, who was rather overwhelmed by the gesture. She had it framed, and she hung it in her bedroom, where it remained throughout her lifetime. On many occasions I have studied the display, which she had taken so much care in arranging, but I never was able to understand what it said. It was all in Latin.

During the few weeks between my graduation from Harvard and my move to St. Louis later that summer, I stayed with my parents in their apartment in Chicago. In those days many of the home telephones required that the users drop a nickel into the slot of a metal box attached to the phone, after having told the operator verbally (no automated programs, thank goodness) the number with which the caller wished to be connected. Once every two months the phone company would send an employee to your home in order for him to open, with a key available only to that person, the coin box and thereby collect the accumulated nickels.

One day, while we were all at home, the man from the telephone company visited us in order to make his scheduled pickup. The person who came was Phil Johnson, a high school friend of mine, whom my father had always liked. Upon graduation Phil had joined the navy, and we had not had contact with each other since then. Phil went about his assigned task and stayed awhile longer. We all engaged in some enjoyable reminiscences during his visit, but after he had departed for his next call, I made a very stupid remark.

"Can you imagine a guy doing that for a living?" I blurted.

All of the "Hahvahd" snob in me had risen to the surface. I might as well have thrown a cherry bomb under my father's chair.

"Listen, young man," he said, his voice rising dangerously. "Just who in the hell do you think you are? For five years, while you have been playing little boys' games and sitting on your butt in some air-conditioned library, that man has been doing an honest day's work."[2]

He told me a few more things as well, and, as usual, he was right. I learned as much in those few minutes with my father as I had learned in a year at Harvard. The next day when he came home from work, he found a hand-painted sign that I had prepared and then scotch-taped to the outside of the door to our apartment. It read: "Sam Levy Lives Here. Enter to Grow in Wisdom."

---

2. Phil Johnson continued to work for the telephone company, and he did so with distinction. As time passed he advanced, and eventually he served as a top-level executive for AT&T until he retired a few years ago.

SECTION III

TIME TO START EARNING A LIVING

CHAPTER 6

Just Call Me "Coach"

While I was attending Harvard, Dorothy Prout had remained in Iowa, continuing her undergraduate studies. We kept in close touch by an occasional long-distance telephone call and more frequently by letter. When breaks occurred, we would visit each other. The summer before my teaching duties in St. Louis began, I worked as the athletic director at Camp Interlaken for Boys in Eagle River, Wisconsin. Dorothy got a job at a nearby resort, and we spent all of our free time together. By the time the summer had ended, Dorothy and I planned to be married.

There was a big problem, however. I didn't have a cent to my name. We decided, therefore, that I'd work for a year and save. After all, I was looking forward to big bucks in my new job. Through some hard-nosed negotiating with Mr. Cunningham, he finally agreed to pay me $3,050 for my first year. Who knows how high it might go after that?

A year apart would have been unbearable, and so Dorothy got a job at the Scruggs, Vandervoort, and Barney department store in St. Louis. Great! We'd be able to see each other.

The football team at Country Day School was one of the powers of the Private School League, consistently winning about 85 percent of its games. The program was extremely well organized, and much of the success enjoyed by the varsity was the result of a unique developmental procedure that head coach Bob Hughes had instituted. The varsity was known as the A team. There was also a B team that comprised promising players who were too young or still not physically mature enough to play at the varsity level. At the feeblest end of the competitive ladder there was a C team made up of freshmen and undersized sophomores.

Mr. Cunningham had told me that he would find a place for me on the football coaching staff, and he was true to his word. I was appointed as an assistant—on the C team! And that is where I started my football coaching career.

The head coach of the C team was an admirable older man named Don Webb. Don gave me plenty of guidance, but he also allowed me a great deal of freedom in applying my own creative energies. We both attacked that C team schedule as if a good season might bring us a New Year's Day Rose Bowl bid. We won all of our games, but we never received any overtures from the bowl committees. At the outset of our second year together, they moved Don up to coach the B team, and I went with him as his assistant. We were on our way. Look out ahead!

It did not take long for Dorothy and me to realize that it was going to be very difficult to juggle the demands of that year. There were classes and athletic team practices for which I had to prepare. When I did manage to spend time with Dorothy, it was usually late in the evening, and I was likely to be very weary. The next day I would be even more tired, and I was distressed to think that my performance at work would suffer. Conversely, when Dorothy finished her work each day, she had time available, and I was not there to fill enough of it.

I became aware, also, that I was not going to be able to save as I had hoped. For the first time, I found out that rent and food cost money. Between us, we were paying two rents, a circumstance that can be detrimental to the health of a budget.

Following our first two games of the football season that year, our team had no scheduled game on the third Saturday. By that time I had become accustomed to big-time excitement on the weekends, and so, early in the week, I proposed to Dorothy that we get married on the Friday evening of that open date. How romantic can you get?

She thought it was a great idea, and so we called our parents. In a very small ceremony that Friday evening in St. Louis, with our parents, my sister, my aunt and uncle, and Herb Melnick and Herb Rothbart in attendance, Dorothy and I were married. Afterward we all went to the Chase Hotel to celebrate, and my dad danced almost every dance with her.

We had a fantastic honeymoon. It lasted all weekend. On Saturday morning we drove up to Champaign, Illinois, in order to take in the UCLA versus Illinois football game. For you purists—UCLA won 21-7. Immediately after the game we headed on over to Peoria and had a wild time that evening at the Western Tap. We came back to St. Louis on Sunday and spent the day moving into the new apartment we had rented. The street on which we were to live had to have been named with newlyweds in mind. It was Eager Road.

Monday found us both back at work. After all, we were going to be going up against Western Military Academy on the following Saturday, and they were no slouches.

♦♦♦♦♦♦♦♦

Finances were rather tight for Dorothy and me during that first year. Our initial purchase, when I'd get my paycheck, would always be a huge tub of peanut butter. That way we knew there would be some nourishment to get us through the last three or four days of the pay period. Although we may have had simple fare on the table, our entertainment menu was even sparser. Dinner out meant the Steak and Shake Drive-in. Other than that we made use of the free basketball tickets distributed to high school coaches by St. Louis University.

It wasn't for entertainment purposes alone, however, that I became a regular at Kiel Auditorium, where the Billikens (as they were known) played their home games. The St. Louis University basketball team, coached by a short, round man named Eddie Hickey, was one of the collegiate powers in the nation at that time. I went to the games more as a student than as a fan. Whenever Eddie Hickey conducted a coaching clinic, as he did on several weekends each year, you could wager that I'd be in the front row with a freshly sharpened pencil ready.

There was one occasion when Coach Hickey lectured about the essentials needed in teaching fundamental skills, and during that presentation he designated one of his favorite drills as being the single most effective teaching tool in his repertoire. It involved a crowd-pleasing and intricate three-man weave, which incorporated brilliantly all facets of dribbling, passing the ball, footwork, shooting, and teamwork into one cohesive structure. When I returned to coach our squad, I made them run that drill for endless hours. Thus was born, as a creation of the players I coached, the first nickname I had ever carried. To the hoopsters at Country Day School, I became known as "Weavy Levy."

The quality of our entertainment experienced an upturn on our first anniversary when my parents gave us a console black-and-white television as a gift. Dorothy, who had a penchant for rescuing stray dogs, had, just two days earlier, brought home a pathetic, but very lovable, puppy. The first day we left that pup at home by itself, we returned to find that it had chewed all of the knobs off the television set. After that we could get reception only on channel two. Thank goodness that was the channel that carried Sid Caesar and Imogene Coca.

The first year I coached the varsity basketball team at Country Day School, we had a good team. For the first time in many years, in any sport, our basketball team defeated archrival John Burroughs. In celebration of this victory, I sped to the supermarket, where I purchased a quart of grape jelly to go with our peanut butter supply.

Even though we had a good team, we were not good enough to win any championships that first year, but our prospects for the next year were glowing. It was likely that I would be sending the best team in the school's history onto the court, and we had a legitimate shot at making it to the state tournament. As the football season was drawing to a close, I could scarcely wait for the beginning of the basketball season.

The A team in football, on the next to the last weekend of their season, clinched the Private League championship, and after the game six of the players had broken training rules. Beer bust time! Head football coach Bob Hughes caught them in the act.

Bob was also the director of athletics at Country Day School. He had been coaching there for more than 25 years, and despite the strong teams he had fielded, he had enjoyed very few victories over John Burroughs. The final game of the season every year was against Burroughs, our traditional rival. They were not having a real good season, and Country Day would be a prohibitive favorite—*if* the six guilty players, all of them starters, played in the game.

The question of discipline was agonizingly weighed and discussed throughout the week. As the football game with John Burroughs approached, no decision as to their fate had as yet been rendered. On the eve of the game, Coach Hughes announced that any verdict regarding punishment would be delayed until calmer times.

The St. Louis Country Day School football team won its game, breaking the seven-year drought they had suffered at the hands of the John Burroughs gridders. On the following Monday, Bob announced that the students involved in the beer drinking incident would be ineligible to participate in interscholastic sports throughout the remainder of that semester.

Wait a minute! Those six players formed the heart of my basketball team. They hadn't broken any basketball rules. Nevertheless, the edict was irrevocable.

We labored through the first half of the season, but once the "ineligibles" rejoined the team in late January we went on a roll, winning the Private League championship in the last game of the regular season. We moved into tournament play, and we notched several victories in those tournaments. We had only to beat St. Louis University High School in order to win a berth in the state finals. University High, coached by Hank Raymond, who later in his career became the head basketball coach at Marquette University, defeated us, however, and it was they who moved on to the finals and eventually to the state title.

♦♦♦♦♦♦♦♦

One day, during the late fall of my second year at Country Day, my former college football coach, Dick Clausen, called. He asked me if I would drive down to Cape Girardeau, Missouri, in order to scout an opponent Coe would be facing the following week. Would I? I used the peanut butter money to fill my gas tank, and I headed south.

After attending the game, I arrived back home in St. Louis late Saturday night, and I went to work immediately on the scouting report. The master's thesis I had prepared at Harvard was a grocery list compared to the presentation I prepared for Dick. I worked on it all night and all day Sunday. That Sunday night I enjoyed the best night's sleep I had ever known. The first thing Monday morning I sent the packet to Dick, special delivery. In later years he told me that he had never seen another scouting report that could match the one I had sent him. With all due immodesty, I must admit, I believe it.

It must have impressed Dick even more than I had imagined, because, after my second year at Country Day, he called again. He had an opening on his staff for a backfield coach, and he wondered if I might be interested. From the yell I emitted, Dorothy must have thought that the short in our wiring had finally electrocuted me.

The job also entailed my taking over as head track coach, because my old coach, Harris Lamb, was resigning in order to become Coe's new director of alumni relations. I was also to serve as an assistant basketball coach. They could have thrown in cleaning up the john, and it would have made no difference to me. I accepted on the spot.

Dorothy was as thrilled as I was. Cedar Rapids was her hometown. Her parents, her two sisters, and countless friends also lived there.

At 3:00 a.m., when we had finally calmed down a bit, she asked me, "How much are they going to pay you?"

"I never asked him that," I responded.

What difference did that make, I wondered?

CHAPTER 7

I Gotta Go Back to Coe Again

Knock! Knock!
Who's there?
Avocado.
Avocado who?
Avocado go back to Coe again.
—From an old Coe College alumni joke

♦♦♦♦♦♦♦♦

The ultimate goal I had envisioned for myself was about to be fulfilled. Come to think of it, two impossible dreams had come true: I was a college football coach, *and* our 1941 Nash coupe had made it from St. Louis to Cedar Rapids.

Every opportunity that would ever come to me again stemmed from this one given to me by Dick Clausen shortly after I had reached my 28th birthday in the fall of 1953. I will always be grateful to Dick.

By the time I returned to Coe, Dick had the program rolling in high gear. During the next three years we lost just two games under his leadership, and twice Dick Clausen was named by the NCAA as the Small College Coach of the Year. We were simple, and we executed flawlessly, blowing the opposition off the field. A bad day for us was when we won by a modest 28-7. We did it without an athletic scholarship player on the team and with students who graduated in four years.

The way in which Dick had organized our staff duties, each of the assistant coaches was required to take his turn scouting an upcoming opponent. Twice a season a coach would have to miss the Coe game in order to carry out his scouting assignments. The first time I was to go on one of those trips, Dorothy pestered me about coming along.

"No way," I told her. "This is a business trip—100 percent."

"I'll help. I'll look at little things you tell me to watch for," she pleaded.

It sounded good to me, and so I relented.

When we arrived in Monmouth, Illinois, for the Monmouth College versus Lawrence College game, Dorothy said to me, "Why don't you just drop me off at that plushy new shopping center over there and pick me up after the game?"

I have always believed that Dorothy subscribed, in her own way, to a Will Rogers-type philosophy: She never saw a shopping mall she didn't like.

"Oh, no you don't," I told her. "You are going to help me scout, just like we agreed. I want you to tell me when Lawrence pulls their guards."

The game began, and as I looked downfield scrutinizing pass patterns, Dorothy used our binoculars in order to zero in on their guards. First quarter, no pulling guards. That was unusual, because Lawrence had been pulling their guards with considerable frequency in every game for several years. I glanced over at Dorothy and noticed that her binoculars were trained on the cheerleaders.

"Those guards pulled yet?" I asked.

"Not yet," she answered, swinging her head and the binoculars toward the concession stand. Late in the second quarter, I turned to ask the same question, but she had left for the ladies' room. During the third quarter, I posed that same inquiry four more times, and I always received the same negative answer. I became rather agitated early in the fourth quarter and demanded to know if she was watching the guards.

She put the binoculars aside and said to me testily, "Well, which ones are the guards?"

The next scouting trip I made, she stayed at home. Probably she went over to that new shopping mall on the west side.

As I have already noted, my responsibilities, in addition to coaching the backs in football, included serving as the assistant basketball coach and as the head coach of the track and cross-country teams. When it came to coaching, however, it was football that took full command of my heart.

Ever since an autumn Saturday afternoon in Chicago, when, as an 11-year-old, I had listened to Bill Stern's radio broadcast of the 1936 Ohio State versus Notre Dame game, I had been enthralled.[1] The Ohio State-Notre Dame game, often regarded as the most thrilling contest in collegiate football history, had been won by the Irish when they rallied from a 13-0 deficit by scoring three touchdowns in the final few minutes of the fourth quarter, thereby defeating the Buckeyes 18-13. Following Notre Dame's first two touchdowns, they had failed to convert the extra point attempts, and so, with just seconds remaining to be played, they had still trailed 13-12. The winning touchdown for the Irish came with only a tick or two left on the game clock when Notre Dame's Wayne Milner[2] caught a pass in the end zone from Bill Shakespeare (not *that* Bill Shakespeare), who had replaced the injured Adam Pilney moments earlier.

Wayne "Phiz" Phillips was the best running back we had at Coe. He was also the top sprinter on my track team. Good as he was in the dashes, Wayne could never win a race against a speedster from archrival Cornell College named Jerry Moore. In 22 consecutive matchups against Moore during Wayne Phillips's collegiate track career, Moore had been the victor every time. Wayne kept telling me, "Some day I am going to beat that guy."

Two of Wayne Phillips's greatest assets were his determination and his stamina. He would work for hours to correct a fault. I recall a time when he was having a problem getting a swift takeoff out of the starting blocks. Try as I might to help him, I was unable to come up with a solution. One day I asked my old track coach at Coe, Harris Lamb, to help me with Wayne's workout.

After very briefly studying some of the techniques Wayne was employing, Harris said to him, "Wayne, when you get into the starting blocks spread your fingers about an inch more."

---

1. No one in the 1930s did more to popularize collegiate football than announcer Bill Stern. And no one could capture the drama or stimulate your imagination as well as he could. He even made the timeouts seem exciting.

2. In 1971—35 years after that historic game—when I was an assistant coach with the Washington Redskins, I got to know Wayne Milner because he worked for our club as a game scout. One day he invited several of the coaches to his home, and, while we were there, he took us downstairs into his large family room. Covering one entire wall was a large blowup of a photograph taken just a few moments after Wayne had made that sainted catch. There, frozen in front of me, captured forever, was the sight of Wayne Milner running along the back of the end zone, triumphantly displaying the ball to Andy Pilney, who was being carried on a stretcher just outside the back stripe.

Wayne did as Harris had told him, and then he exploded out of the blocks. You could see the confidence surge back into him. Joyfully, we both thanked Harris for his sage observation.

Later, when Wayne had moved out of earshot, I said to Harris, "You never told me anything like that when I was on the track team. How come?"

Harris looked at me and smiled. "What I told him didn't mean a thing. He just thought it did, and that's what counts."

No wonder Harris Lamb had been such a successful track coach.

In Wayne's senior year, the Midwest Conference Track Meet was held at Ripon College in Wisconsin. In every one of the qualifying heats for the 100-yard dash and for the 220-yard dash, Jerry Moore finished first, and Wayne came in second. In the 100-yard dash finals it was the same story—Moore first and Phillips second.

By the time they lined up for the 220 finals, each of them had run nine races over the two-day period. This was to be Wayne's last race as a collegiate trackman. At about the 150-yard mark he drew even with Moore, and then, with that tremendous determination and conditioning working to his advantage, Wayne inched ahead and roared on to the only victory he ever gained over Moore.

Just one person ran those last 70 yards faster than Wayne Phillips—me! I sprinted alongside the track, papers and stopwatches falling out of my pockets, exhorting him on. At the end of the straightaway we jumped into each other's arms and went tumbling to the ground.

While we were rolling around in the cinders, Wayne shouted in my ear, "I told you I could beat that guy!"

From that day on, whenever I have seen Wayne Phillips, I have addressed him as "Mr. Champion."[3]

Early in September 1955, at the beginning of my third year of coaching at Coe, our head basketball coach, Tommy Thomsen, resigned in order to take a similar position at Creighton University. Dick

3. Eight years later I hired Wayne Phillips as an assistant football coach at the University of California, and a few years later he became the head football coach and the head track coach at Coe. During his 10-year Coe tenure, the football team won six conference titles, and the track team won eight consecutive Midwest Conference championships. I wonder if Coach Phillips ever told any of his sprinters to spread his fingers a little wider when taking his stance in the starting blocks.

Clausen, who was also the director of athletics, called me into his office and told me that I was the new head coach of the basketball team.

Two days later one of the history professors became very ill, and his doctor determined that the man should take the full year off. President Brooks informed me that the ailing professor's teaching load would be distributed among several faculty members, and he asked me to assume responsibility for one course in the history of Western Civilization.

I am grateful that one of the cooks in the dining hall didn't quit, too.

Beginning on October 15, I would handle my football coaching responsibilities in the afternoons and then return to the gym in the evenings to conduct basketball practice. When that was over, I'd stop by the library in order to prepare lesson plans and to grade papers. There were even a few occasions when I got some sleep. Fortunately, this load lessened slightly when the football season came to a close in mid-November.

As a basketball coach I applied that old "What it takes to win is simple! But it isn't easy!" dictum. I determined that we would work on just three areas of play:

1. Rebounding and rebound positioning.
2. Shooting.
3. Man-to-man defense.

When I say, "man-to-man defense" that is exactly what I mean. Our rules for this fundamental were very simple: There is your man. Put your nose up against his and stick with him. No switching. When he goes there, you go there. If he goes to the water fountain, you go to the water fountain. No excuses.

I worked our team hard. Too hard. After six games we had a 2-4 record. The best player on our team was a walking replica of Ichabod Crane named Al Purcell. He was a level-headed, team-oriented young man, and so when he asked to talk with me, I listened carefully. He told me that we were working too hard the day before and the day after a game, and that, as a result, the players were too bushed to perform well. After weighing what he had pointed out, I promised Al that on those days before and days after our games, we would limit any workouts to a maximum of 45 minutes.

After he had left my office, I pulled out a copy of our schedule in order to study it carefully. Oh, my gosh! For the remainder of the season we had games every Tuesday, Friday, and Saturday. At Coe, it was traditional that no athletic teams would play or practice on Sundays. That meant Monday was a day before a game; Wednesday was a day after a game; and Thursday was again a day before a game. If I was to keep the promise I had just made to Al Purcell, we would not have been able to practice for more than 45 minutes at any time during the remainder of the entire season!

I kept that promise—and we won the next 18 straight games! We also won the Midwest Conference championship, and we were selected to play in the NAIA National Invitational Tournament in Kansas City. Even though we were eliminated in the first round, it had been a wonderful experience.

At the conclusion of the 1954 football season, our coaching staff was ecstatic. We had received an invitation to participate in the Tangerine Bowl in Orlando, Florida. The faculty voted not to accept the bid. Dick Clausen was crushed, and I think that that may have been the reason he decided to listen more carefully to many of the coaching job offers he had been receiving from larger schools.

When the University of New Mexico came calling, he jumped at the opportunity.

It really was not my preference to leave Coe when I did. When Dick Clausen had been named as the new coach at New Mexico, he recommended to President Brooks that I be promoted to the head football coaching position at Coe. I wanted the job very badly, and I was interviewed and given serious consideration by the screening committee. When they informed me that they would be filling the vacancy by naming another candidate, they stated that, in their opinion, I was still too young to take over that responsibility. I was crushed, and so I determined to follow Dick Clausen and my football coaching dreams to Albuquerque.

Whether it applies to coaching football or any other endeavor, it seems as if only someone doing some shortsighted nitpicking feels a person is "too young" or "too old." In 1955, they said I was too young. Today they say I am too old. Both times, they are wrong.

Old? Young? Black? White? Man? Woman? Southerner? Easterner? Catholic? Jewish? Muslim? Wasp? Why confuse yourself? Consider just one question: How qualified is the person? Two years after my alma mater said I was too young, I was appointed head football coach at the University of New Mexico. Two years after that, I was hired as the new head coach at the University of California.

Upon accepting the position at New Mexico, Dick wanted all of us to accompany him as members of his coaching staff. There was some mild apprehension among several of the staff members and their wives because New Mexico seemed remote and foreboding. Dick sensed this uneasiness, and so he arranged to have a staff party at his house. To this get-together he invited a female friend of his family who had previously lived in Albuquerque.

Their friend—Mabel—arrived wearing a swirling fiesta dress. Her hands and wrists were adorned with beautiful turquoise and hammered steel jewelry. In her hair she wore some unique leather creations that had been painstakingly fashioned by Native Americans. She carried magnificently colored Indian blankets with her, as well. Photo albums, bulging with pictures of gorgeous mountain sunsets and prehistoric rock formations, were clasped to her sides beneath her arms.

"Once you get used to the lizards, you are going to absolutely love Albuquerque," she began. "They are not poisonous like the tarantulas are. And don't worry about the tarantulas. The rattlesnakes keep them pretty much at bay."

Wives paled at her words.

"Mabel! Mabel! Have some of these hors d'oeuvres!" Dick shouted, sprinting across the room with a tray in each hand.

Mabel waved him off, saying, "Not until I advise everyone about the best method for guarding against those Gila monsters."

When Dick finally managed to hustle Mabel—the half nelson helped—and her paraphernalia out the door, he turned back to all of us to see if he could pick up the pieces of his shattered dream. We were all so busy attending to our wives, who were in various states of emotional deterioration, that he had to tap a spoon against the side of a water glass in order to regain our attention.

"We open against the Air Force Academy," he said.

"Westward ho! On to Albuquerque!" the coaches all shouted as we leaped into the air, adding as a flourish some neatly turned airborne pirouettes. Two of the coaches, as they raised their fists exultantly toward the ceiling, released holds on their limp spouses, who went bouncing onto the carpet.

At the end of the school year, Dorothy and I loaded our car and headed for New Mexico. Included with the rest of our belongings, she had packed 40 yards of mosquito netting, two pith helmets, and an elephant gun.

CHAPTER 8

Where Else Would You Rather Be?

In late December 1955, Dick Clausen and the other members of the football coaching staff all departed for their new assignments at the University of New Mexico. I was the head basketball coach and head track coach at Coe that year, and so it was agreed that I would remain in Cedar Rapids to finish the school year.

When basketball season came to an end in March, I utilized what free time I had to recruit in Iowa on behalf of the New Mexico football program. My efforts yielded three players from the state: guard Bob Lozier from Des Moines, quarterback Chuck Roberts from Davenport, and a 150-pound halfback from Waterloo named Don Perkins. Don had been a unanimous All-State selection in high school, but the University of Iowa had felt he was too small. Iowa's head coach, Forrest Evashevski, fearing that Don might enroll at Iowa State and come back someday to haunt his Hawkeyes, encouraged him to accept the scholarship offer from New Mexico.

Once I arrived on the campus in Albuquerque that summer, Dick told me that Perkins was not going to be admitted to the university. That was difficult for me to understand, because Don had had good grades in high school and he was an alert, articulate young man with exemplary character qualities. Dick explained to me that Don had not taken some of the subjects required of out-of-state high school students in order to qualify for admission to the university.

I reflected again upon all the game films I had watched of Don in action. Convinced that he was the most exciting high school player I had ever seen, I asked Dick, "Do you know how good this fellow is?" Dick advised me that we were allowed just two admissions appeals a year, and he did not want to use one on a 150-pound halfback.

I was rather discouraged when I left Dick's office, and after walking about 50 feet down the hall, I spun about, retraced my steps, and went barging back in. "Do you know how *really* good this guy *really* is?"

My emotional appeal must have worked, because Dick sent me on over to see Dean Matheny in order to present an appeal on Don Perkins's behalf. My three weeks of law school training finally paid off, because the dean agreed to have Don admitted.

Four years later, Don Perkins, now a husky 185 pounds, graduated with honors from the University of New Mexico. They retired his football jersey—number 43. In 1960, the expansion Dallas Cowboys were allotted two pre-draft bonus picks from among that year's class of draft-eligible players. They named Don Perkins as one of them. Quarterback Don Meredith was the other player they chose. Don Perkins played seven seasons for the Cowboys, and he was the all-time leading rusher in Dallas history until Tony Dorsett broke that record many years after Don had retired. Don is a charter member of the Dallas Cowboys' Ring of Honor.

Don Perkins is the greatest all-around player I have ever coached. As a college player he was as dominant on defense as he was on offense. And, oh yes, as a collegian, he also led the nation on kickoff returns. After Don retired from professional football, he returned to New Mexico and worked as a special assistant to the governor.

The University of New Mexico football teams had experienced nine consecutive losing seasons prior to Dick Clausen's arrival in Albuquerque. Their previous year's record had been a dismal 1-9. Immediately upon Dick's assumption of the head coaching duties, a marked upturn in the fortunes took place. During his initial season the record improved to 4-6, but we had finished strong with two victories over a couple of perennial Skyline Conference powers, and we had recruited an excellent crop of freshmen. In the second season our record was nudged up to 5-5. Our sophomores had gained maturity, however, and we had added another sterling group of freshmen that would be joining the varsity in 1958.

Despite the team's improved performances, Dick was very unhappy with those losses when they occurred. He had seldom known any results other than winning, and in the past, with his championship teams, there had been lavish and deserved praise directed toward him. Now it was different. After some of our losses, there were some harsh newspaper commentaries, and they hurt Dick deeply. Dick had always been supportive of others during difficult times, and it was difficult for him to understand some of the venomous criticism he had to absorb over something so innocuous as a sporting event.

Shortly after Dick's second season at New Mexico had ended, he was offered the athletic directorship at the University of Arizona, and he accepted the position. It was the right job for the right man at the right time. Under Dick Clausen's stewardship, the program at Arizona grew and prospered, and they did it without violation of the rules. By the time he retired 20 years later, the weak teams and the second-rate facilities he inherited when he first came to Tucson were replaced with national championship contenders and a magnificent physical plant.

Upon leaving for Arizona, Dick once again recommended that I be named to fill the vacancy created by his departure, and New Mexico's director of athletics, Pete McDavid, agreed. One day later it was announced that I was to be the new head football coach at New Mexico. Not only that, I was going to be a very wealthy man. They were going to pay me $10,000 a year—*to coach football!*

Jubilation reigned in the Levy household. As I reflect back and realize that every promotion is a cause for celebration, I am still acutely aware that the exhilaration I experienced upon becoming head coach of the New Mexico Lobos was never equaled by any of my subsequent appointments. At last! I was a head football coach at a major college.

Happily, I was able to retain the other assistant coaches who had served with me on Dick Clausen's staff. They were a truly outstanding group. John Neumann was our line coach, Bill Weeks coached the backs, and Lou Cullen, a New Mexico alum, tutored the ends. I added a recent University of Iowa graduate, Don Chelf, to serve as coach of the freshman team. That was it—just four assistants. Please, don't confuse me with one of those 16-man staffs prevalent today that include "quality control" coaches, administrative assistants, computer coordinators, and a few other "what in the blazes does he really do" coaches.

With my first season at the helm approaching, our University of New Mexico staff went to work—spring practice, recruiting, off-season conditioning, getting ready for fall practice. We were scheduled to begin the season against our main rival—New Mexico State University. Our coaching staff spent the entire summer poring endlessly over every film in preparation for that initial contest.

We fashioned our game plan down to the most minute detail even before our team members showed up to begin two-a-day practices on September 1. After the players reported, they worked hard and so did the coaches. I could detect a sense of dedication and of optimism pervading us all. We labored, and we improved steadily as we practiced in the desert's searing late summer heat.

Finally, opening day arrived.

The players gathered around me along the sideline just prior to the kickoff, seeking some instruction that might help to alleviate the nervousness that afflicts all participants as they are about to enter intense competition. The band was playing the Lobos' fight song. Pretty cheerleaders were exhorting the crowd. The grandstands at Zimmerman Field were filled with people, noise, and color. In the distance, over the rim of the stadium, the setting sun reflected majestically off of the stately 5,000-foot-high Sandia Mountains. I looked into the eager faces of the young men who had prepared so diligently for this moment, and I was overcome by a sentiment so intense that the words welling up inside of me spilled out directly at them.

"Where else would you rather be than right here, right now?"

Those are the words I was to speak to my players just before the kickoff of every game I would ever coach throughout the next 40 years.

♦♦♦♦♦♦♦♦

Dick Clausen had been one of the outstanding teachers of the Split T formation in its purest form. It was a quick-striking system of offense originated in the late 1940s by coach Don Faurot at Missouri, adopted then utilized with great success by coach Jim Tatum at Maryland, and perfected by coach Bud Wilkinson at Oklahoma.

Every year Dick and his staff members at New Mexico had attended spring practices at the University of Oklahoma where Wilkinson's Sooners, operating from their Split T, had been the premier team in collegiate football throughout most of the 1950s. His teams set a record of 47 consecutive victories, a mark that has never been equaled.

The clarity of Wilkinson's thinking astounded me. With just a sentence or two on the practice field he was able to convey exactly how he wanted to have a maneuver executed, and even more importantly, his players, as a result of Bud's presentations, were able to translate his instructions immediately into successful action. In dissecting any aspect of the game, Bud Wilkinson would knife at once to the kernel of the matter, and though he never came across as pompous, his words bore the ring of universal truth.

I was not around when Knute Rockne, or Pop Warner, or Walter Camp, or Amos Alonzo Stagg, or Fritz Crisler, or Fielding "Hurry Up" Yost were coaching, and so I cannot comment on them. But during that portion of the 20th century when my life had been so closely tied to football, the best coach I have ever seen among the many titans who have paced the sidelines is Bud Wilkinson. That is how I felt in the 1950s, and that is what I still believe today.

In later years, when Wilkinson worked as an analyst on football telecasts, I continued to marvel at how well he presented exactly what was accurate and vital. As a football television analyst, also, Bud Wilkinson was the best I ever heard. He may not have been as much of a showman, but if it was "shtick" that I wanted with my sports I would have tuned in to *The Worst* (oops—*Best*) *Damn Sports Show Ever.*

By the late 1950s the defenses had caught up with the Split T, just as they always eventually do with every new and innovative style of attack. By that time, if a team attempted to stay with the Split T in its original form, they'd get stuffed. If a coach began to add this wrinkle and that wrinkle, the cohesiveness of the offense soon dissolved and he became a man without a philosophy, playing gridiron grab bag.

The idea of mixing a little bit of the best of several different styles of offense was unpalatable to me. There is an old saying that a man with two clocks never knows what time it is. (Sounds to me as if it must have been an old *Swiss* saying). I wanted an offense that was complete within itself, one in which all plays are complementary and each play helps to set up the other components of the offense. I wanted one that, although it had the facility to attack with balance and daring, was still limited enough so that we could teach our players to employ it flawlessly.

In instructing our players, I had often expounded one of my own philosophical tenets, "What it takes to win is simple, but it isn't easy!" Our offensive approach, I felt, had to be simple to understand, and it had to be founded on precise execution of fundamentals. When it came to the "not easy" part, I preferred it to be *not easy to defend.*

Back at the University of Delaware, in relative obscurity, coach Davey Nelson's teams had been running his Wing T formation for many years, steamrolling the small college competition they faced. Forrest Evashevski, Iowa's head coach and a former teammate of Nelson's when they had played at the University of Michigan, had also instituted this unusual form of attack in 1956, and his Hawkeyes had overwhelmed Big Ten opposition on their way to Rose Bowl victories.

Still, few other coaches understood the Wing T. It was a throwback to the ancient Single Wing formation, and no one wanted to be stigmatized by the dirtiest two words a coach can be called—"too conservative." The Split T, which had been in vogue during the 1950s, featured lightning-quick handoff plays with straight-ahead fire-out blocking and heart-stopping pitch or keep option plays in which the quarterback moved down the line of scrimmage just inches from the neutral zone. The Wing T, by contrast, seemed slower and more plodding, with massed interference and sledgehammer off tackle plays. However, that was just one part of the Wing T picture because it also included brilliantly conceived reverses and misdirection plays. It featured overpowering blocking at the point of attack and a bootleg passing game that burned hard supporting defensive secondaries with quick aerial touchdown strikes. Many coaches closed their eyes to the devastation that the Wing T could inflict on an opponent, primarily because they feared being labeled as old-fashioned.

At New Mexico we became the third team in the country to employ the Delaware Wing T formation. In both of the next two seasons, flying on the wings of that "T," we led the nation in rushing yardage. In 1959, we threw just 48 passes, 15 of them for touchdowns! Led by Don Perkins, our stable of fleet-footed running backs averaged 6.8 yards per carry, *and they all played defense, as well.*

We had an unusually small, but very quick, group of linemen. This was particularly true of our guards, who had to pull out on almost every play in order to lead our speedy backs through the hole and beyond. One of our best guards was a steel-tough five-foot, 10-inch 185-pounder named John Garber. I remember one game against Utah State when John played 60 minutes lined up opposite six-foot, five-inch, 270-pound Merlin Olsen. Merlin was to become a perennial All-Pro during his illustrious career with the Los Angeles Rams, and he was inducted into the Pro Football Hall of Fame. To John Garber's credit, let it be known that he was able to survive that ordeal and play again on future days. Not only that—we won the game!

After one game in which John had turned in a superb performance against the University of Montana, someone found a crumpled scouting report that one of the Montana players had carelessly left behind in their locker room at our stadium. In the personnel section where information on our players was detailed, there was a notation next to John's name, "He's a small potato." The person who found that report gave it to John. He took it good-naturedly, and, with a chuckle, he showed it to me. After reading it, I looked up, and then I said to him, "John, you may be a small potato, but you sure are hard to peel."

♦♦♦♦♦♦♦♦

In my first season as head coach of the Lobos, we got off to a slow start, winning our opener but dropping the next two games. I was beginning to feel the heat already. At the weekly Boosters Club meeting on the Monday following our second loss, a heavy contributor to the New Mexico athletic programs called me aside and said, "Marv, that black quarterback is going to get you fired."

Many people may not be aware that prior to the Supreme Court's *Brown v. Board of Education* decision in 1954 the educational system in the state of New Mexico was as segregated as any of those in the Deep South. When we recruited Don Perkins, Chuck Roberts, and another young man named Joe Gale, they became the first black players to ever play for the university. In the 1950s the word *black,* when used to describe a person's race, had derogatory connotations. Although that is not the way it is today, it certainly was back then. In making reference to a black person's race at that time, it was civil and proper to say "Negro."

Now, in 1958, Chuck was our starting quarterback. He was a junior, but during his previous season he had been a backup player and had seen little action on game days. Seeking to control my anger, I told the man at that Boosters Club event that Chuck was the best player we had at that position, and that we were going to continue starting him at quarterback.

"It's your funeral," he said, and he left me there, seething.

We won the next six games with Chuck as our signal caller. Then, in his senior year, he blossomed into an outstanding player and led us to a great season. There was one two-game span when, serving in his role on defense, he intercepted six of our opponents' pass attempts. His prowess as a defender led to his being drafted as a defensive back by the Rams. Chuck lasted just one full year with the Rams, and, when he was waived at the beginning of the following season, he enrolled in school again in order to begin work on a graduate degree.

Eighteen years after the incident at the Boosters Club meeting, I was driving through Albuquerque on vacation and decided to stop and renew some old acquaintances at the University of New Mexico. It was enjoyable for me to see athletic director Pete McDavid and some of my other friends who were still there. Before leaving the campus, I also paid a visit to the Dean of Men's office. When I arrived, the dean was in his office, busy with a student, but his secretary asked me to wait, saying that he would be free very soon. A few minutes later the student departed, and the secretary said to me, "Dean Roberts can see you now." That's right, it was Dr. Charles (just call me "Chuck") Roberts, the "black quarterback" who almost got me fired. I love America!

♦♦♦♦♦♦♦♦

In my first year as head coach at New Mexico, we finished with a 7-3 record, the first winning season the Lobos had posted in 12 years.

Even though we had defeated the University of Wyoming, they still won the Skyline Conference (the predecessor to today's Western Athletic Conference) title. Wyoming—coached by Bob Devaney, who later was the architect of national championship teams at Nebraska—suffered their only loss of the season when we upset them in Laramie. The two early-season defeats we had sustained, however, placed us behind the Cowboys in the final standings.

The win against Wyoming had been an emotional one for us. We trailed them 12-7 with just one minute to play, and we were facing a third down on our 47-yard line, when I ordered a draw play. As our team broke the huddle, my heart dropped when I heard all of the Wyoming coaches yelling from the sidelines, "Watch the draw!"

Fortunately, that is exactly what Wyoming did: they watched our fullback, Bo Bankston, streak 53 yards on a draw play for our winning touchdown. When we returned to the Albuquerque airport, a celebrating crowd of 20,000 New Mexico fans was there to welcome us home.

That first season finished on a very sour note, however. Our final game was against the Air Force Academy, and they were having a perfect season. They were undefeated and on their way to playing in the Sugar Bowl on New Year's Day. They crushed us 45-7 and in the process dampened what had otherwise been an excellent season. That game marked the first time since I had started my coaching career back at Country Day School that a team with which I had been associated was subjected to such an overwhelming thrashing. I wish I could say it was the last time. Under any circumstance, it was a very humbling experience.

On the Monday following our loss to the Air Force Academy, I called our staff together in order to outline the plan we would adopt in our preparations for our next scheduled game against the Air Force. In 1959, they were to be our final opponent once again.

We were a dominating team during my second year. We entered our final Skyline Conference game against Wyoming still undefeated in league play. They, too, were unbeaten, and so the winner of this matchup would emerge as the conference champion.

We trailed 19-13 at halftime, but when Don Perkins returned the kickoff 98 yards for a touchdown at the beginning of the second half, we took a tight-collared 20-19 lead. After Don's touchdown gallop, I glanced up at the scoreboard clock and noticed that only seven seconds had been required for him to negotiate that distance. I knew Don was swift of foot, but I made a mental note to request a thorough FBI checkup on that timekeeper anyway.

The gridiron battle continued at high pitch, and with just a little more than two minutes left to play, we were still clinging to our precarious one-point advantage. I noticed that we had a notoriously vulnerable defensive left halfback in the game and that Don was on our bench taking a brief rest from the action. The heck with that; he could rest all day—tomorrow! I told one of our assistants to get Don back into the game *tout de suite.*[1] I realize now that that poor coach was not up on his French, because when Don went sprinting out onto the field he replaced—Oh, no!—the *right* halfback!

On the next play, Wyoming's quarterback, Jim Walden, in later years the head football coach at Washington State University, lofted a 73-yard touchdown pass over the head of our still-on-the-field left halfback. The game and the title went to the Cowboys.

We had one game left, and we entered it intent on salvaging some pride as a reward for our season's long effort. Our finale would pit us once again against our nonconference nemesis, the Air Force Academy.

We went through an intense, arduous week of practice, and, at last, it was Saturday—New Mexico versus the Air Force Academy. At the half we were behind 21-7, but we were moving the ball well. In the second half we exploded for three touchdowns, and we held a 28-21 lead when the future airmen began their last-gasp drive. With only 20 seconds left to play they smashed into our end zone for a score, and then, boldly, they lined up for a two-point conversion attempt that, had it succeeded, would have given them a 29-28 triumph. Our plucky Lobos stopped them inches short, however, and we had won the game 28-27. In that contest we had thrown just three forward passes. Two of them, including a 75-yard romp on a Chuck Roberts-to-Don Perkins screen pass, went for touchdowns. During the course of my 47-year coaching career there have been three or four victories so memorable that they remain forever fresh in my mind. This was one of them.

---

1. For those readers who have spent more time studying the sports pages than your French grammar texts, let it be known that *tout de suite* means, "Right now, you jerk!" or something like that.

CHAPTER 9

California—Here I Come

At the NCAA Coaches Convention in January 1960 I found myself, at one of the social gatherings, standing next to Greg Engelhard, the director of athletics at the University of California. Pete Elliott, Cal's football coach, had recently resigned in order to take the job as head coach at the University of Illinois, and so I asked Greg about his plans for filling the vacancy. He told me that the university had a specific person in mind and that within the next few days he expected that they would be naming him as their new coach.

One day, six weeks later, when I was at work in our film review room, my secretary interrupted me so that I might take a call from a Mr. Engelhard in Berkeley, California. He asked me to fly to the Bay Area the next day in order to interview for the head football coaching position with California's Sturdy Golden Bears. Wow!

As I was to learn a couple of years later, the opportunity at the University of California had developed for me as the result of a very unusual chain of events. After Cal's talks with Navy's Eddie Erdelatz did not result in his being hired, the university conducted an exhaustive nationwide search for a coach. My name was not one of those under consideration. The screening committee finally concluded that they would offer the job to my old, friendly coaching adversary from Wyoming, Bob Devaney.

After a sufficient amount of soul-searching, Bob determined that the chances for winning at Cal were exceedingly slim (in retrospect, I wish that I, too, had been that clairvoyant). He told the people in Berkeley how grateful he was for their consideration, and he suggested to Adrian Kragen, the head of the screening committee, that they look at a young coach at the University of New Mexico (guess who?).

Professor Kragen relayed that information to Cal's chancellor, Glenn Seaborg, on the same day that the chancellor, a renowned atomic scientist, had spoken with a University of New Mexico science professor at the Los Alamos, New Mexico, Atomic Research Center. During their conversation, Dr. Seaborg had explained the difficulties Cal found in filling the football coaching vacancy, and the professor from New Mexico spoke favorably about me. Those two key recommendations led to my being interviewed at Cal.

Both Dorothy and I were excited about that upcoming interview, and she expressed her concern that I make the right impression.

"That San Francisco area is very sophisticated," she said. "You've got to look like you belong, and that means we are going downtown to buy you a hat."

The only hats I had worn since being discharged from the Army Air Corps had been the kind that had an adjustable strap in the back and had "Coach" written just above the peak on the front. We went to the finest men's shop in Albuquerque, where we spent three painstaking hours before arriving at the decision that she felt would decide my fate.

Armed with my new hat, my tweed topcoat with the velvet collar, and with my newly purchased leather briefcase that contained the latest issue of *Sports Illustrated* and a roll of Certs, I boarded the plane.

Engelhard and three members of the faculty screening committee met me at the airport and rushed me to the Claremont Hotel in Berkeley, where we engaged in an intensive four-hour long interview. Apparently, they were satisfied that I was their man, and they asked me to come with them the next morning to visit with Chancellor Seaborg. After telling me to get some rest, they got ready to leave.

Just before he exited the door of my room, Adrian Kragen turned to me and said, "Oh, by the way, Marv, when we go to see the chancellor tomorrow, leave that stupid hat here in the room."

The following morning, sans hat, I met with Chancellor Seaborg, and that afternoon I was named as the new head football coach.

I have often been asked if I felt badly about not having been Cal's first, or even their second, choice for the job, but I look at it this way: Catherine Parr was Henry VIII's sixth choice as his marriage partner. The first five were "fired," including the two who were beheaded.

♦♦♦♦♦♦♦♦

We were on our way to California, and we were going to conquer the world. Win the championship in this league, and you were in the Rose Bowl. All you other guys better run and hide. What difference did it make if all alumni, fans, and media in the Bay Area were all sniffing smelling salts instead of roses in disbelief at the news that the proud Golden Bears had selected as their coach some chap they had never heard of from the cactus country? Give us two weeks with those little teddy Bears, and we'd make them into ferocious grizzlies once again.

The headline in *San Francisco Chronicle* on the morning after my hiring read: "Marv Levy (Who?) Is Cal's New Coach." The *San Francisco Examiner* was equally unkind: "Cal Hires Egghead Coach." The alumni had been expecting Erdelatz, who had coached Navy to top 10 rankings for many years.

The first time I addressed the Golden Bears Booster Club, I tried to loosen them up a bit with this one: "I guess you were expecting Marilyn Monroe, and Ma Kettle showed up instead."

No one laughed.

One editorial page columnist named Charles McCabe, who billed himself as "The Fearless Spectator," was relentless and unmerciful. He devoted at least one column per week for months to butchering me. This was before he had ever met me or talked with me. Come to think of it, he still hasn't met or spoken with me.

McCabe's picture always appeared at the top of his column, showing him wearing authentic journalist's suspenders and a jauntily angled black derby hat. At one of the Bay Area's annual lighthearted football roasts a couple of years later, I was presented with a beautiful ribbon-bound hatbox. I opened it, lifted out a sparkling new derby that was nestled among the tissues within, and everyone enjoyed a knowing chuckle. Clever little joke. I wasted several more minutes of the audience's time, however, while I swished around with my hand through the papers in the hatbox, all the while reflecting a look of desirous anticipation at the prospect of finding the head that went with that derby. No such luck. I gave one of those "dang it" snaps of my fingers, and then, seemingly crestfallen, I returned to my seat.

I was a pretty nice fellow, and so I couldn't understand why everyone there was so disturbed about my arrival. I then realized that it wasn't me with whom they were angry. Their ire was directed primarily at the Cal administration, which was perceived as wanting to de-emphasize what had once been an outstanding football program at Berkeley. Lynn "Pappy" Waldorf's three consecutive Rose Bowl teams from 1948 to 1950 were distant memories. Pappy's teams had gone downhill quickly after 1950.

Sure we might have some tough obstacles to overcome, I felt, but we would surmount them. All we had to do was just out-coach the opposition. Oh, yeah! It didn't take me very long to learn that no matter how well you handle a bow and arrow, you aren't going to win many battles against armies that are using machine guns.

What a staff I put together. John Neumann and Lou Cullen had come with me from New Mexico, and they were as good as any coaches with whom I have ever worked. A graduate assistant from Pete Elliott's staff, named Jack Hart, who had been one of the cocaptains of the 1958 Rose Bowl team joined our staff. John Nikcevich, a former star at UCLA, came as our defensive line coach. He was tough; he was organized; and he was a superb teacher. Also on our staff was Dick Stanfel, who joined us after serving as Notre Dame's line coach. Dick had been a great NFL lineman, and even though he was with us at Cal for just one year, it would be my good fortune to work with him again when we both served as assistant coaches with the Philadelphia Eagles. As I mentioned earlier, Wayne Phillips, whom I had coached at Coe College, was also a member of our staff at Cal. Our backfield coach, Rocky Carzo, was a gem. He had played and coached at the University of Delaware and was, therefore, a prime authority on teaching and implementing our version of the Delaware Wing T formation. Rocky later served for many years as the head football coach at Tufts University. Eventually he moved up to become director of athletics there and continued in that role until his retirement a few years ago. There were also a couple of other men whose names, I am certain, will make all you football aficionados blink. I added a high school coach from Fremont, California, who had really impressed me during an interview. His name was Bill Walsh. Yes, it was *that* Bill Walsh, the one who went on to become a Hall of Fame NFL coach. A former Cal star football player, Mike White, working at that time in the alumni office, struck me as having a real talent for coaching. I hired him, and he later served in head coaching roles at Cal, at the University of Illinois, and with the Raiders.

Despite this impressive array of coaches, working at the highest level of intensity, in the climate that existed in the early 1960s at Cal, we were not able to win with any consistency.

Listening to, and then committing to memory, the words and music of college fight songs had always been a passion for me. I knew them all and often inflicted upon those people around me my usually off-key renditions. One of my favorites had always been the University of California's rousing "Fight for California." How could anyone not be inspired upon hearing those uplifting lyrics?

The sturdy Golden Bear,
Is watching from the skies;
Looks down upon our colors fair,
And guards us from his lair—air—air.
Our banner Gold and Blue,
The symbol on it too,
Means FIGHT! for Californ—ee—a,
For California, through and through!

Normally, there wouldn't be a word I would have changed, but after having been at Cal for a few weeks I realized that there had been a misprint when that song was published. They couldn't have meant "The *Sturdy* Golden Bear." I am certain they meant "The *Studious* Golden Bear."

Rising academic requirements and unbending admissions standards had become the norm at Berkeley. There were no equal opportunities or affirmative action admissions waivers in place at that time, and as a result, very few minority students were being admitted. During my four years as the coach, we were able to enroll only six black players. In order to be granted entry to Cal or UCLA, an applicant needed to be in the top 12 percent of his high school graduating class. The student also had to have carried a B average in four years of English, four years of a foreign language, four years of mathematics, and four years of science. Those were the entrance requirements for residents. They were even more stringent for out-of-state applicants. We had just two out-of-staters on the team during my four-year coaching tenure.

Was there any leeway? Well, yes, sort of—California's university system had a proviso that two percent of the entering freshman class could be composed of students who, even though they did not fully meet the base requirements, had been close to doing so, provided that they could also present some compelling redeeming qualification that merited their acceptance. At that time there were nine separate campuses functioning under these University of California guidelines. On each individual campus the director of admissions was allowed to interpret how the "redeeming qualifications" stipulation might be applied for his particular institution. At UCLA it was determined that athletic skill would be viewed favorably. At Berkeley, athletic prowess was specifically excluded from the list of "redeeming" considerations.

Billy Kilmer, Kermit Alexander, Gene Gaines, and Marv Luster all entered UCLA under the two-percent rule while I was coaching at Cal. Later, I was an assistant with the Redskins when Billy starred there at quarterback. I was an assistant with the Rams when Kermit sparkled as a defensive back there. I was head coach of the Montreal Alouettes when Gene Gaines and Marv Luster finished their 15-year careers in the Canadian Football League. Upon retirement, both Gene and Marv were inducted into the CFL Hall of Fame. Believe me, it was a lot more fun coaching teams for which these four men were playing than it was being on the side against which they were competing.

Those were not the only inequities that plagued us. By conference rule, all financial aid in the Pac-8 at that time was work aid. A student traded hours of work until his hourly wage earnings equaled the cost of his scholarship. At the other Pac-8 schools the athletes were logging their hours by showing recruits around the campus, by monitoring the dining hall (only while they were eating, of course), and by doing the same at the library (once again, only while they were there pursuing their study needs). At Cal, on the other hand, our players were required to report to the stadium every Sunday morning following a game where they would spend the full day cleaning it. Do you think our opposition used that one against us during the recruiting process?

To supporters of Cal football, I was viewed as the instrument by which these perceived administrative objectives were to be achieved. I came thinking I was going to take them to the Rose Bowl, and they thought I had come to take them to the Toilet Bowl. I've got a confession to make: Bob Devaney was a helluva lot smarter than I was.

When I saw our team on the first day of spring practice at Cal, I could not have been more startled had I seen Mother Theresa doing a Lenny Bruce routine. At New Mexico we had three backs on our team who had run 9.6 or faster in the 100-yard dash. We also had a 9.7 and a 9.8 sprinter, and they were substitutes. The one quality we did not lack at Cal was—slow! Our running backs at Cal were big, lumbering, willing lads who had the reactions of lava. I preferred calling them our "Pioneer Investor Savings" backfield. A large savings and loan association by that name, which was located in the Bay Area, had as its slogan, "Big! Safe! Friendly!" We fit the description.

You can count on it. There is one action every coach will take upon assuming a new job. With this one move he can establish that he is a man of decision and a doer of bold deeds. He can show his disdain for the ineptitude of his predecessor and can make it damn well known that from now on things are going to be different around here. What he must do is change those dreadful uniforms. I had high regard for the coaching of Pete Elliott, but I changed our uniforms anyway.

One week before our opening game the new jerseys we had ordered months earlier still had not arrived. I called the sporting goods company in order to express my concern.

"Don't worry about it," a man on the other end of the line told me.

"What does that mean? When are they going to be here?" I persisted.

"Don't worry about it," the man said again.

I hung up. And I worried about it.

Seventy-two hours until kickoff, and still—no delivery. On the day before the game, the salesman finally brought our new uniforms into the locker room. They were smashing. Rich colors. Handsome design. The finest material. And a big problem. The sleeves on the jerseys were huge, baggy monstrosities. They looked like the shirt Carl Hubbell had worn when he pitched the New York Giants to the World Series title in 1933. Beside myself, I complained bitterly to the salesman.

"Don't worry about it," he said.

Opening day at California Memorial Stadium had arrived. Nestled upon the slopes of picturesque Strawberry Canyon overlooking the full expanse of San Francisco Bay, it has to be the most beautiful setting for a football stadium anywhere in the country. Sixty thousand people were on hand to watch us play the heavily favored Green Wave from Tulane. (At Cal the other team was always favored.) The steeply inclined hill that rose 200 feet behind the east stands had 5,000 more spectators clinging to it, all of them opportunistic freebies. Appropriately, that piece of real estate has been known to generations of Cal students as Tightwad Hill.

With just one minute remaining, we trailed Tulane 7-3, but we had the ball, fourth down on the one-yard line. Our quarterback, Randy Gold, gave the ball to fullback George Pierovich, who slammed in over left tackle, but the Green Wave stopped George.

But wait! George didn't have the ball! Randy Gold, having executed a nifty fake, had kept it, and he was about to step into the left corner of the end zone, thereby setting off a celebration the likes of which hadn't been seen in Berkeley since VJ Day.

How cruel can fate be? A lone, desperate Tulane defender, reaching as far as sinew would allow, grabbed the superabundance of flapping material on the sleeve of Randy's jersey and was able to spin him out of bounds inches shy of the goal line. Now let me ask you something. Do you think I worried about it?

We lost the next two games, also, giving us an overall 0-3 record, and then we came precariously close to continuing that ugly streak. In our fourth game of the season, against Washington State, the score was tied 21-21, and the Cougars had the ball on their 35-yard line with time enough remaining in the game for just one more play. Their great All-America wide receiver, Hugh Campbell, raced past our secondary as their quarterback launched a mighty desperation heave. The ball appeared to have been thrown too far for any human to reach, but they say that Hugh Campbell could reach anything. They are right!

By virtue of a prodigious lunging, stretching effort, Hugh caught that pass on the tips of his fingers at our 15-yard line. As he struggled to regain his balance while traversing those excruciating final yards to our goal line, I twitched through more coaxing gyrations than a bowler trying to pickup a spare on a 7-10 split. I finally executed the correct snap of my hips, I guess, because Hugh went skidding to the turf a yard short. We hadn't lost number four, but we still hadn't won one, either.

The nightmare continued. Two more grimly contested defeats followed our tie game against Washington State. We battled Notre Dame and Southern Cal, and in both games we came close. But there had been no victory to reward us.

Next we traveled to Corvallis, Oregon, to play coach Tommy Prothro's high-flying Oregon State team. They were having an excellent winning year, with their sensational tailback, Terry Baker, leading the way. At the conclusion of the season, Baker was voted to be the recipient of the Heisman Trophy. On the first scrimmage play of the game, Terry hit in over his own right tackle and streaked 85 yards to a touchdown. It really wasn't a very smart thing for him to have done, however, because our players became very angry after that. They shut the Beavers out during the remainder of the afternoon, and we scored twice to win 14-6, our first victory of the season.

It would be nice to be able to say that it was the first of many that year, but the fact is we entered our final game of the schedule against Stanford still seeking our second win.

It had been a rough year for the Stanford team, as well. They were led by veteran coach "Cactus" Jack Curtice, a fine gentleman who was 15 years ahead of the times in his approach to offense. His teams operated from a magnificently conceived passing scheme in a day when no one else was throwing more than 10 times a game. He could score against anyone and quickly, too. His problem was that he did not have enough good players to keep his opponents from scoring more. Stanford, like Cal, had unbending, extremely high entrance requirements, and, again like our Golden Bears, they were playing a schedule against national powerhouse teams that did not grapple with academic restrictions similar to the ones that encumbered both of us.

The final game of the season every year between Cal and Stanford is THE BIG GAME.[1]

THE BIG GAME is always played before a capacity crowd, with the entire student body from each school sitting in a massive bloc on its respective side of the field, all of them wearing pure white shirts or blouses reflecting the sunshine (they hope) of the late November California afternoon. It is a convivial gathering, and there is seldom animosity during the struggle even after the winner has been determined.

There is one additional feature that helps to highlight the impact of THE BIG GAME. Regardless of how poorly your season may have been progressing up to the point when your team enters the field, a victory in this one redeems everything.

As in almost all other meetings between the two teams, our 1960 BIG GAME against Stanford was a classic struggle. We led at halftime 14-7, but a Stanford field goal early in the fourth quarter narrowed our lead to 14-10. When they kicked off to us, we mishandled the ball and we were very fortunate to take possession on our four-yard line.

For the next 13 and one-half minutes, utilizing 22 consecutive running plays, our Golden Bears stalwarts marched against Stanford. I do not know if records regarding that particular statistical category are kept, but it must have been the longest continuous drive in football history. The thunderous noise in old California Memorial Stadium, matched in only one other game I would ever coach, rose in crescendo with each first down we eked out. Inexorably, the clock kept running, and with fewer than 60 seconds remaining, Randy Gold, on a keeper from the two-yard line—the jerseys had been properly retailored—scored the clinching touchdown. We had won THE BIG GAME 21-10!

The next morning's banner in the *San Francisco Chronicle* told the story in just four words: "Cal Grinds to Victory." I had that headline framed, and it hangs in my den today, the only one I have ever dis-

1. It isn't just another big game for both schools in the sense that many colleges consider that their annual clash against their rival is a really big game. THE BIG GAME is the recognized title of the game between Cal and Stanford. No one calls it "the Cal-Stanford game." For many years the headlines in the Bay Area newspapers on the morning of that contest always screamed at you: "BIG GAME Today!" Then they would devote 12 pages to photos of the players, to a recounting of games gone by, and to human-interest sidebars such as "the fathers of the student managers in today's BIG GAME were student managers in THE BIG GAME of a generation ago."

played in this manner. The paper has grown yellow and brittle, but the scenes from that day remain as fresh in my mind as they were on that sparkling autumn afternoon in 1960 when the Sturdy Golden Bears drove relentlessly on toward the Stanford goal line.

The difficulties involved in recruiting and in winning at Cal were not confined exclusively to the stringent admissions standards. Many of you who are well versed in the history of country music are undoubtedly acquainted with the lyrics from a little number popularized by singer Barbara Mandrell in which she boasts, "I was country before country was even cool." Well, even before the onset of the activism that pulsated on campuses nationwide in the 1960s, the student body at Berkeley had thousands of radicals "before radical was even cool." How radical were they? Most of them thought Lenin was the founder of the John Birch Society.

Now, I have no objection to a person proclaiming a strongly held political conviction. It's part of the American way. All that is fine—until it begins to play havoc with my football team and with my rights, not to mention my livelihood.

Most parents of the player prospects we were trying to recruit did not want their sons in such an environment, and so, every time we visited a home to discuss a young man's possible enrollment, we stepped to the plate with two strikes and a nasty breaking ball on its way toward the outside corner.

More troublesome than that, however, were the sit-ins organized by those campus groups that were inclined to view intercollegiate athletics as a manifestation of rampant neo-fascism. When we sought to take the practice field during the week of preparations for our game against Southern California in 1961, we found the area completely covered with beads and beards and with the people wearing them. When they refused my courteous request that they get their asses out of there, I tried to move our drills to the stadium itself, but another "Red Army" was there holding maneuvers. One day of workouts was shot.

The next day we boarded buses in anticipation of conducting our practice session at one of the city high schools. Apparently, some KGB agent had infiltrated our ranks, because word of our plan had been leaked to the masses, and when we arrived at our destination, an unruly mob was there holding a rally calling for the storming of the Bank of America. Another day of practice down the drain.

On the third day I took no chances. No one was to know where we would be going except me. In this instance it was the bus driver who must have been compromised, because he didn't know where to go once I had apprised him of that day's planned practice site. For more than three hours he drove around searching vainly for our destination, which was located only a mile and a half from the campus. Finally, just as the sun was settling into the Pacific, he found it. Too late! No practice! The forces of evil had triumphed again.

Southern Cal won the game 28-14.

The ones who really bugged me, however, were those radical individuals who were members of our team. Not that I passed judgment on anyone's political beliefs. It's just that I can't stand *slow* radicals. You'd think that a guy who went around throwing Molotov cocktails would, at least, find it beneficial to learn how to run fast, wouldn't you?

During my second year we continued to struggle, although we did have a few bright moments. We opened the season facing the Texas Longhorns, the eventual national champions, and our 10-game schedule included seven of the top 10 teams in the final national rankings.

Coaches! Listen up! I'm going to tell you a magic secret, one that will ensure that your team will never become the victim of an upset. Do as we did at Cal—always be the underdog.

In our third game of that season we were the ones who almost pulled off a huge upset when we visited Columbia, Missouri, and fought coach Dan Devine's fifth-ranked Missouri Tigers to a 14-14 tie. When we arrived home after that near miss on the road, we began preparations for the following weekend's contest against the University of Washington, a team that had won the Rose Bowl at the conclusion of each of the two previous seasons. Once again, the Huskies were favored to win the Pac-8, and the results of their games so far gave every indication that they would succeed in getting back to Pasadena on New Year's Day for the third consecutive time.

We upset the Huskies 21-14, with the winning score coming in a most unusual manner. Going into the game our staff detected what we felt to be a flaw in their punt protection, and so we devised a special all-out 10-man rush to capitalize on that perceived weakness. From the outset our team played with great inspiration, and on seven of Washington's possessions, during the first 58 minutes, our defense forced them to punt. In every one of those situations we unleashed our 10-man stampede, but we did not succeed in blocking any of their kicks.

With two minutes left to play and the score tied 14-14, the Huskies once again lined up to punt the ball, this time from their 20-yard line. We hadn't been succeeding in our punt block attempts, and I didn't want to risk roughing their punter, thereby allowing them to keep the ball and affording to them the last opportunity either team would have to score. I decided, therefore, to call for a punt return, hoping that, after gaining possession, we could work our way into position for a winning field goal attempt before time might expire.

When I signaled the punt return call to the players out on the field, all of them got the message—except one. John Erby, our team captain, didn't catch it, and when the ball was snapped, he was the only man who rushed the punter. That's right! You guessed it! John blocked the punt, and we recovered the ball on Washington's three-yard line. Two plays later, halfback Jerry Scattini bulled over for the touchdown that led to the biggest upset of my career at California.

Certainly, I will always remember John Erby for that legendary moment on the grass at the south end of California Memorial Stadium. John, one of the few black players on our team, was to know other heroic times, as well, not all of them as happy as on this day in Berkeley. He later served as an army lieutenant in Vietnam, where, sadly, he lost a leg in combat. Several years after that, when Mike White had become the head football coach at Cal, he hired John to serve as an assistant on his staff. On an autumn day, more than a decade after he had blocked that kick, John Erby walked—not as nimbly as he once did—out onto the field where he had known that moment of gridiron glory.

During the celebration immediately following our victory against Washington, I awarded the game ball to the Cal Band. There is no more loyal and supportive group of students anywhere than those Golden Bears musicians. When they played "Palms of Victory" right after the game on that day, it had never sounded sweeter.

The Cal Band was always there to inspire us. I still recall one occasion when they were instrumental (excuse the play on words) in helping me teach our team how to execute a vital assignment. One day at practice, while we were working on field goal protection, one of the placekicks we attempted was blocked. I was irate, and I took the errant player to task for his laxity in protecting correctly. The player complained that the rushing unit had overloaded his area so heavily that it was impossible for him to execute his assignment effectively. I countered by advising him that, if a field goal unit protects as it should, it makes no difference how many opponents are rushing. To illustrate my point I called the entire 75-man squad out onto the field and had them all rush the kicker. They couldn't block it.

That should have sufficed as evidence enough to prove my case, but I decided to establish the merit of my message even more dramatically. The Cal Band, 180 strong, was practicing on the adjacent field, and I called them over and requested that they help me drive home an important coaching lesson. I asked them to join ranks with our 75 players in a concerted effort to block our next field goal try. With trombones, tubas, and drums flying, they too were unable to muster the pressure needed to block the kick. We may not have won a lot of games at Cal, but I'll tell you one thing. We never had a single damned field goal blocked in any game during the four years I coached there.

Prior to the beginning of my second year at Cal, I paid a visit to the admissions office. There was a quarterback at Campbell High School, 50 miles from campus, who was the nation's most coveted college football prospect. He was a good student, but, by a very narrow margin, he was going to fall shy of qualifying for admission to Cal. My plea to the director of admissions was a model of abject self-degradation, but I finally managed to gain mercy—and a concession—from that admissions officer. He agreed that he would accept the lad's application. That was the easy part. Now we had to go recruit him.

How we managed to get that done is material for a book in itself, but we succeeded, and in the fall of 1961 Craig Morton enrolled as a freshman at the University of California. At the end of his collegiate career Craig was a first-round draft choice, and he enjoyed an outstanding career in the NFL as the starting quarterback for three different teams—the New York Giants, the Dallas Cowboys, and the Denver Broncos. Only one other player, Jack Schraub, was drafted by the NFL in all the time I coached at Cal. Jack was an eleventh-round choice.

Craig Morton broke every Cal passing record that had existed prior to his taking the field for the Golden Bears, and in his senior season, he was the consensus All-America quarterback. Joe Namath and Roger Staubach both finished behind him in the balloting that year.

At the beginning of the 1962 season, my third at Cal, hopes were high. Craig Morton, after a sensational performance as quarterback for our freshman team the year before, would be eligible for varsity play, and he was the man who would lead us out of the wilderness. On the first day of practice Craig went down with a knee injury, and our team physician told me that he would most likely be out for the season.

Everybody believed that prognosis except Craig himself. In all my years of coaching I have never seen a player work with as much resolve and with as much confidence on his rehabilitation as Craig did. By the time we began preparations for our sixth game, he surprised us all by resuming light workouts, and the doctor told me that he might be ready to see a little action in a couple of weeks.

Our opponent in that sixth game was Penn State. Craig dressed for the game, but we did not plan to play him. By late in the second quarter we were getting clobbered by the Nittany Lions 23-0. Perhaps, while my attention was directed elsewhere, Craig tugged at our doctor's sleeve. I've never sought to unravel that mystery, but I have my suspicions, because the good doctor came to me along the sideline and said that, given Craig's continuing remarkable progress, it would be permissible for us to allow him to play for one series. Then, the doctor noted, he might be ready for a bit more action the following week.

I sent Craig into the game. On a swashbuckling six-play drive, he led our team to a touchdown just as time expired in the first half. At halftime I asked our doctor if we might play Craig for one more series, and the doctor consented. Six more plays. Another touchdown! I kept asking for and getting permission for "one more series."

We closed the gap to 23-21, and on a desperation fourth-down play late in the fourth quarter, one of our receivers could not hang on to a difficult catch in the end zone. In just a little more than two quarters against a strong team on a bad knee with hardly any practice in the first game of his college career, Craig set an all-time individual total offense record for a Cal football player. Still, we had lost the game.

The following week we played UCLA, the team that wound up winning the Pac-8 championship that year. A crowd of 45,000 had been expected, but after it was announced early in the week that Craig would be our starting quarterback, the stadium was packed to capacity by 82,000 fans. They got their money's worth. Craig played brilliantly, but the Bruins, led by Billy Kilmer and Kermit Alexander, won the game 26-16. Craig played well in the three remaining games, also, but we still weren't able to win enough to avoid registering our third consecutive losing season.

I wasn't happy with all those losses, and neither was anyone else. By the end of my third year there I began to see indications that my days at Cal might be numbered. There is a traditional cheer for the coach that the California student body renders toward the end of every game at California Memorial Stadium. The words employed in presenting that tribute depend specifically on the name of the person coaching the team. In my case the salute went as follows: "Coach! Coach Marv! Coach Marv Levy!" Near the conclusion of that year's BIG GAME, which we lost 30-13, they added a new twist. The chant, in this instance, was, "Coach! Coach Marv! Coach Marv *Leave!*"

Cal's athletic director, Pete Newell, would have liked to accommodate them. Pete had been named to his position just a month or so after I had been appointed as football coach. He had been Cal's head basketball coach during the several previous years and had enjoyed unparalleled success. In 1959, the Golden Bears had won the NCAA title, and in 1960 they had returned to the Final Four, losing to that year's national champion, Ohio State. Many of the game's outstanding coaches, even today, view Pete Newell as one of the greatest basketball teachers of all time, and I believe it a recognition well deserved.

Pete assumed his athletic directorship duties at an exceptionally difficult time for intercollegiate sports at Berkeley. Rising, rigid entrance requirements and the student activism on the campus were not the only problems with which he was confronted. His appointment coincided with a drastic change in the way athletics at Cal were to be supported financially. Funding for athletics was, at this time, removed from the liberal auspices of the Associated Students, where it had enjoyed luxurious fiscal nourishment for decades, and made entirely independent and self-sustaining. Pete started with the cupboard bare.

He needed to raise a lot of money, primarily from among older alumni contributors who expected Cal victories and not explanations about how difficult it had become to win. He also needed high-profile coaches in order to inspire confidence in the future among these potential financial supporters. I had come to the campus unheralded, and we hadn't won enough games to get anyone excited to the extent that they'd make any advance New Year's Day reservations for Pasadena.

I was to learn a few years later that, following my third season as coach, Pete had approached President Clark Kerr, telling President Kerr that he felt it would be beneficial to replace me. President Kerr was keenly aware of the difficult conditions under which our staff had been working, and he believed that given time we could bring the football program back to a respectable level. He told Pete that the only condition that would justify making a change would be if the players on the team had lost confidence in our staff, and he stated further that there was no evidence of that.

Unaware that all these maneuverings had been taking place, I looked forward to my fourth year at Cal with optimism. A healthy, seasoned Craig would be returning, and our intense recruiting efforts had brought several other solid players onto our team. One of them was a young speedster from St. Helena, California, named Tommy Blanchfield who, during his high school days, had scored a touchdown one out of every three times he had handled the ball.

At the end of the previous season I had made some changes on my coaching staff, and in the process of doing that, I was guilty of committing a grave injustice. It is one that I have always regretted. John Neumann and I had been together since we both began our college coaching careers in 1953 as members of Dick Clausen's staff at Coe. We had both gone on to New Mexico with Dick, and when I became the head coach of the Lobos, John remained there as my top assistant. When I moved on to Berkeley, John was the first coach I sought for my new staff, and I was delighted when he agreed to come west. He continued to do an outstanding job of coaching and of seeking to maintain equilibrium even as the pressures from losing at Cal mounted. Toward the latter part of our third year there, John and I were often in disagreement, and at times our private confrontations were extremely heated. Without question, John was always loyal, and whatever differences we had were never manifested in front of the squad.

When the season ended, I asked John to come to my office, where I told him that I felt we had become incompatible in our views about football. I told him that I believed it would be best if he were to leave our staff. In retrospect, I know that I acted too swiftly in the immediate aftermath of an emotion-packed season. Had I allowed a few weeks to pass, I am certain that our passions would have cooled and that we could have rationally resolved our differences. Had I been wise enough at the time to do that, I would also have retained an outstanding coach and a friendship that was very meaningful to me.

John was deeply hurt when he left, but he bounced back wonderfully. Later he became a successful head coach at a small college, and then he returned to coach and to become a member of the faculty at his alma mater, Springfield College in Massachusetts. He remained at Springfield throughout the remainder of his career, and his reputation as a coach, a teacher, and a man of high character is admired and respected by all who have worked with him or competed against him.

The rift that existed between John Neumann and me has long since healed. Several years after we had both departed from Cal, we met at an NCAA Coaches Convention, and I told him I had been wrong. Any bitterness John may have harbored had left him by that time, too, and he told me that he understood the pressures I had been subjected to. John and I still talk a few times a year on the telephone. Also, we have visited personally on some rare occasions, and I have been able to regain the friendship of a fine man.

John Neumann has forgiven me for the injustice I perpetrated, and I, in turn, no longer feel animosity toward Pete Newell for the treatment I was to receive—perhaps in fateful retribution for my releasing John—just one year later.

♦♦♦♦♦♦♦♦

We opened the 1963 campaign with a victory over Iowa State. Two weeks after that we traveled to Durham, North Carolina, where we fought the favored Duke Blue Devils to a tie. As the season progressed there were a few more Saturdays when we had reasons to celebrate. We trounced San Jose State, and we also defeated Utah on their home field in Provo. Our biggest triumph came late in the year in the Los Angeles Coliseum, where we trounced UCLA, the defending Pac-8 champion, 25-0. That was only the second time since 1950 that Cal had emerged victorious in a game against the Bruins. The Bears did not defeat them again until 1968, and in the next 26 games played following our win in 1963, when we shut out UCLA, the California Golden Bears won but twice while losing 24 times to their downstate rival.

We entered THE BIG GAME in 1963 with a 4-4-1 record. A victory against a resurgent Stanford team would allow us, for the first time during my tenure at Cal, to finish a season on the winning side of the ledger. THE BIG GAME was scheduled to be played in Stanford Stadium on November 23. We had been somewhat fortunate in that Stanford's best running back, Steve Thurlow, who would later become a star for the Giants, was still not recovered from a severe charley horse injury, and he would be unable to play.

On November 22, the day before the game, our coaching staff was gathered in our meeting room waiting for the players to finish showering. Rene Herrarias, Cal's basketball coach, came into the room with a stunned look on his face, and he told us the shocking news that President Kennedy had been shot. We all huddled around a radio listening to the grim news bulletins. After about an hour, one of the announcers ceased talking in mid-sentence, paused, and then, in a doleful voice, he said, "President Kennedy is dead."

Just one year earlier, the president had visited our University of California campus, and I had gotten to meet him. He was there to serve as the speaker for the Charter Day ceremonies held each year on the Berkeley campus. A throng of more than 90,000 people had jammed Memorial Stadium in order to hear his speech. When he had entered the stadium, he was part of an impressive academic procession that included all of Cal's distinguished faculty members bedecked in their varied colored caps and gowns.

Toward the conclusion of his remarks, the president reminisced about the time during World War II when he had been assigned by the navy to take some courses at Stanford. He recalled how he had come to this stadium to attend THE BIG GAME. He mused that back in those days it was filled for every football game, and he understood that that was no longer the case. Now, he noted, Cal filled it instead for an academic function such as the one we were enjoying this very day.

And then—I remember his exact words—he said, "This is a turn of events, I feel, which is not altogether healthy."

The president seemed considerably amused. So were all of the members of our coaching staff. I don't know about the faculty.

As the nation mourned the death of President Kennedy, all college football games for that Saturday were called off and were rescheduled for the following weekend. When we played Stanford a week later, Steve Thurlow had recovered, and he was in their starting lineup. Early in the fourth quarter we were trailing 14-10, when Tommy Blanchfield, on an electrifying punt return, raced 65 yards for the score that put us in front 17-14. Stanford countered with a grueling march, which featured some outstanding running by Thurlow, and they recaptured the lead 21-17. Very late in the game, they added an insurance touchdown.

Stanford won THE BIG GAME 28-17, and our winning season had eluded us. I didn't know it as I walked off the field, but it was the last game in which I would coach the Sturdy Golden Bears.

♦♦♦♦♦♦♦♦

When there had been about three games left in 1963, one of our most respected players came to see me. He told me that administrative officials within the athletic department had been making extensive inquiries into the players' feelings about me. At first, he said, he paid little attention to it, but when they persisted and became diligent in scheduling followup talks with any players who might have expressed negative sentiments about me, he began to take closer notice.

I thanked him for letting me know what was happening, but then I did nothing about it. I pushed the uneasiness I had felt as a result of my conversation with that player out of my mind, and soon I forgot about the matter altogether.

One day, two weeks after the season had ended, Pete Newell asked me to see him in his office. When I arrived, he told me that he had a petition from several of the players asking that I be replaced as football coach. Pete then requested that I tender my resignation.

I told him that I wanted to think about the situation, and I retired to the solitude of my office, where I spent several hours agonizing about what to do. Later in the day, I initiated another meeting with Pete. During this second meeting I told him that I did not want to give up the position. I pointed out to him that our team was on the upswing. I reminded him that Craig would be returning for his senior year; that we had added several more good players as the result of back-breaking recruiting efforts; that we had come very close to having a winning season; and that I sincerely believed we would be a strong, challenging team during the upcoming season. I talked about the many obstacles we had overcome and about how our current staff had paid their dues to get us to this point. I also knew, from having talked with several of our better players, whom I had called to my office, that my support among the great majority of our team members was solid.

Pete acknowledged all of these contentions as being accurate, but he also told me that with the prospects that prevailed for having a good team, he could now hire an outstanding established coach with a national reputation. He said that confidence in me among the alumni from whom he had to solicit financial support for the athletic program was almost nonexistent. He asked me once again to resign, and this time he said that if I did not, he would be compelled to fire me. This was to be the first time I heard specifically from Pete that he, personally, wanted me out, and upon becoming aware that the person to whom I must report directly no longer wished me to coach the team, I complied and submitted my resignation letter to him.

The drama that unfolded on that day in Pete Newell's office took place while President Kerr was out of town, and by the time he returned, my resignation was an accomplished fact. Any firing would have had to be okayed by the president. It was a few years later, when I was coaching at the College of William and Mary, that I learned from President Kerr that Pete probably would not have been authorized to fire me.

For the benefit of any coaches reading this book, please allow me to offer you some free advice. Don't ever resign under pressure. If it is a job into which you have poured everything in your being and one at which you know you can do better than someone with whom you might be replaced, fight like hell to keep it. Most likely you will be fired, anyway, but you'll feel a lot better when you walk away.

Pete Newell had been under great pressure himself. Perhaps his job would have been in jeopardy from rebellious alumni had he not taken bold action. The way it happened, however, involved an additional hurt for me, because I truly liked and admired him and I still do.

The year after I left Berkeley, Cal's record slipped to 3-7. Three years after I left it was still 3-7. They haven't been to the Rose Bowl since 1958.

Maybe, from my personal standpoint, it was best that I left when I did. It is the only job I have ever held where I must honestly admit that there was no chance to win in the foreseeable future. Had the situation been one where winning was possible, I would have wanted to remain there for the rest of my coaching days. I would gladly have become the West Coast version of Joe Paterno.

I departed as coach of the Golden Bears after the 1963 season, and 22 years would elapse before I would return to visit Berkeley. In the fall of 1985 I came back to Strawberry Canyon to serve as an analyst for the radio broadcasts of Cal's football games. Just before the kickoff, when that proud California Band came strutting out of the north tunnel at California Memorial Stadium and burst forth with the playing—as only they can—of "Fight for California," I felt the hair rise once again on the back of my neck. I leapt to my feet shouting, "Beat the Trojans!" and if our play-by-play announcer, Joe Starkey, hadn't grabbed me by my tie, I would have tumbled right out of the broadcast booth.

CHAPTER 10

The Overachievers

Three weeks passed after my firing, and nothing developed. One day, Dorothy asked me if maybe I ought to take another type of job in the meantime. I told her that I was too busy typing resumes to waste my time with something so mundane as honest employment.

Pappy Waldorf, Cal's coach during their glory days in the late 1940s, was a neighbor of mine in Berkeley. When he left the Cal job, the San Francisco 49ers hired him as their director of player personnel. One day, shortly after Christmas, Pappy invited me to come visit him at his home. When I arrived, he told me that the head football coaching position at the College of William and Mary was open, and he wondered if I might be interested in applying. William and Mary, established in 1693, was the second oldest U.S. college. Only Harvard, founded in 1636, had a longer history. Pappy told me that he had visited that beautiful campus in historic Williamsburg, Virginia, many times during his talent searches on behalf of the 49ers. He explained how impressed he had been by the atmosphere that prevailed there.

"How many football games have they won in the last 10 years?" I asked Pappy.

He conceded that he didn't know the exact answer to that one, but he did know that they had just concluded their ninth consecutive losing season. Oh! Oh! Another one of those, I thought. New Mexico had had 11 straight non-winning seasons when I became the coach there, and Cal hadn't won since Nostradamus had predicted that the Golden Bears were about to enter a very long dry spell.

Like the University of California, William and Mary also had very high academic standards, Pappy cautioned. But he said also that they would make some admissions concessions for outstanding athletes. The environment on the campus, he noted, was highly conducive to the nurturing of good teams. There was a small, spirited student body there that bordered on fanatic in their support of intercollegiate athletics.

Pappy informed me that he was friendly with Lester Hooker, the director of athletics at William and Mary, and that, if I so wished, Pappy would telephone him on my behalf.

When I said that I would appreciate his doing that, Pappy replied, "Good. I've already called him, and Les Hooker would like to have you contact him right away."

Three days later I was in Williamsburg, where I met with Les Hooker, and during that meeting we both agreed that I would be their new head football coach. All that needed to be done in order to make it official, Les told me, was to get the approval of the college president, Dr. Davis Y. Paschall. As Les and I strolled across that magnificent campus on our way to the President's House, I was unaware that I was about to meet the greatest educator I have ever had the privilege to know.

I met with Dr. Paschall and his wife, Agnes, in the two-and-a-half-century-old President's House, which had once been occupied by Thomas Jefferson when he had served as president of the college. Mrs. Paschall was an avid football fan, and she already knew all about me. Over the next five years I would come to know Dr. Paschall very well. We often traveled together to alumni meetings, where I would listen to this genteel Southern patrician weave his magic. More improvements were realized at William and Mary during his presidency than any other.

My meeting with Dr. and Mrs. Paschall went very well, but he told me that there was one problem that still needed to be addressed before we could reach the agreement that would result in my being officially named as their new football coach. That issue involved my contract. He told me that the compensation he was authorized to pay me was considerably lower than what I had been receiving at Cal, but that, in order to stay in line with other faculty salaries, it was essential for him to not go above the amount he was empowered to offer. He then mentioned that he had a contingency fund, to be used at his discretion for the good of the college. With some of these resources, he said, he would see to it that my moving expenses from Berkeley to Williamsburg would be reimbursed to me. It was standard procedure for colleges to pay moving expenses for newly hired members of the faculty and staff, and so that point seemed to be a negligible one to me.

I liked all of the people I had met at William and Mary, and I wanted to be a football coach. Salary had never meant that much to me before, and it didn't in this instance, either. I accepted the job and prepared to move to Virginia as soon as I could.

When I arrived to take up permanent residence in Williamsburg, President Paschall called me to his office and said he wished to pay me for the moving expenses I had incurred.

When I told him what my costs had been, he responded by saying, "Why, Mr. Levy, it's absolutely impossible to move from coast to coast for that slight amount. There are countless hidden expenses, also, which I am sure you must have overlooked in your haste to get here."

He then gave me a check for triple the amount I had presented to him. Despite my embarrassed protests, he continued to tell me how I had probably lost money on the move, and then, apologetically, he told me we'd have to conclude our conversation because he had a great deal of work to do on a speech he was scheduled to deliver to an alumni dinner in Roanoke that evening. (They'd better get their checkbooks ready.)

As I was leaving his office, Dr. Paschall asked me to remain a moment longer. On a sheet of paper he drew up a football play. It was a wild unbalanced line, triple reverse that evolved into a tackle-eligible throwing an across the field pass back to our quarterback.

"Here is a good play you might want to use someday," he said with a chuckle.

On future trips together, and at other times, also, when we had opportunities to visit with each other, he would frequently, just before we parted, remind me about that play and its merits. I'd always tell him that we were saving it for "just the right situation."

At the end of my first year at William and Mary I had a meeting with President Paschall, at which time we were to discuss my status for the following season. He offered me a substantial raise in salary, and I gladly accepted it.

Then he said, "Oh, by the way, Mr. Levy"—he always called me 'Mr. Levy'—"I want to pay you for those moving expenses you incurred when you came here last year."

"You paid me at that time," I reminded him.

He shuffled about among some papers on his desk, and with furrowed brow, he looked up and said, "Well, I don't have any record of having done that. I'll put a check for the proper amount in your next pay envelope."

Then he'd draw up that favorite trick play of his and hustle me out of his office. My "moving expenses," somewhat increased in amount over those of the previous year, accompanied my next paycheck.

At contract time, during each one of the subsequent three years that I coached at William and Mary, Dr. Paschall, after apologizing profusely for having waited so long in getting my moving expenses to me, would make certain that I received them "this time." He never lacked ingenuity for discovering methods to exhibit surprise, confusion, and disbelief when I tried to tell him that I could have moved to the moon with the reimbursements I had already received.

♦♦♦♦♦♦♦♦

The first and most vitally important priority any head coach should have when taking a new position is putting together his coaching staff. There was only one coach from the previous staff at William and Mary whom I knew. That was Augie Tammariello, the line coach. I liked him, and I liked his work, and so I invited him to stay. He accepted, and I was off to a good start. Now I had the unpleasant task of informing the other men who had been there that I would not be retaining them, because I had people in mind to fill the vacancies that existed. The athletic department agreed to provide a school automobile so that these men could travel to the NCAA Coaches Convention in New York City, which was just about to begin. While they were there, they would have opportunities to be in contact with hundreds of other coaches, thereby enhancing their chances of finding a new job.

Les Hooker and I drove to the convention in a different car. After two days of the scheduled four-day meetings, Les told me that there was nothing to do in New York City—I was too busy to try to figure that one out—and that he was going to be driving back to Williamsburg immediately. When I told him that I wished to stay till the conclusion of the meetings, he said that if I did that then I'd have to return in the same car with those other coaches. I dreaded the thought of having to travel 350 miles in a vehicle full of passengers whom I had, in essence, recently fired. It was leave early or ride with the unemployed coaches, and I opted for the latter.

While I was at the Coaches Convention, I worked assiduously at rounding out my staff. I filled all of the available slots.

On our trip back to Williamsburg, the men with whom I was riding understood that I had selected assistants whom I knew, or at least knew about, and they showed no resentment toward me. For the most part it was an enjoyable journey, and we all shared some interesting opinions about the coaching profession. During one segment of our trip, however, they talked among themselves about the head coach who had preceded me at William and Mary. He, of course, had been the man on whose staff they had served. Although I did not join in that conversation, they were aware that I, as a relative stranger, was able to hear everything that was being discussed. I did not know the man about whom they were speaking, but I became extremely uncomfortable in listening to some uncomplimentary comments they were making about him.

There was one of them, I noticed, who did not—and obviously was not—going to participate in a conversation of that nature. I sensed a look of displeasure on his face, and I was gratified to note that, at the first natural opportunity to do so, he jumped in with a remark that helped to steer the commentary in a different direction. Later, when the subject had changed, I was very favorably impressed by his knowledge and views regarding general coaching methods and techniques. I made up my mind to remember that man's name. It was Larry Peccatiello.

A few days later, one of the coaches I had lined up called and asked if I would release him from the commitment he had made to join our staff, and I agreed to his request. It was now my turn to place a telephone call. Mine was to Larry Peccatiello. I asked him to visit my office, and I offered him the job of defensive coordinator. Larry, a William and Mary alumnus, accepted immediately. I did it again! I found a young, relatively unknown coach who turned out to be a shining example of what a good coach should be.[1]

There were others on my staff at William and Mary whom I continue to remember fondly. I hired a graduate assistant from VMI named Bobby Ross.[2]

There was also an aspiring high school assistant coach from a small town in Virginia whose ability to teach his players caught my attention, and so I added him to the outstanding group that I was assembling in Williamsburg. His name was Larry Beightol, and today he is the offensive line coach for the Green Bay Packers.

There were other men whose coaching abilities were noteworthy even though they never went on to coach in the so-called "big time."

---

1. Before he retired a few years ago, his resume included more than 20 years as an NFL assistant. Most memorable was his extended stay with Joe Gibbs's Redskins teams. Today, Larry Peccatiello wears a Super Bowl ring on one of his fingers.

2. In later years he led Georgia Tech to a national championship. Bobby moved on from Georgia Tech to become the head coach of the Chargers, and later he assumed a similar role as head coach of the Lions. He guided San Diego to an AFC title and to a Super Bowl appearance.

Joe Downing, Jim Roe, Joe Teefey, Dick Harmison, and two of my former students at Coe College, Don Roby and Ralph Pucci, brought credit and dignity to the profession. I am so proud to have been able to work with these men.

♦♦♦♦♦♦♦♦

William and Mary has a jewel of a campus. It is located halfway between Jamestown, the New World's first permanent English colony, and the battlefield at Yorktown, where British General Cornwallis surrendered to George Washington at the end of the Revolutionary War in 1782. Both of those historic sites are fewer than 20 miles from Williamsburg.

The people in this colonial capital city, where the college stands majestically at the head of Duke of Gloucester Street, are friendly and hospitable, and it was in Williamsburg where I spent some of the happiest and most serene days of my coaching career.

Despite the beauties of the campus and the town, our football facilities left much to be desired. Our coaching staff spent our first summer vacation painting the locker room and the training quarters a bright green and gold—the school colors. Prior to our foray into interior decorating, the walls and floors had been a somber dark gray. Probably it had last been painted when Christopher Wren had been commissioned to do some touching up of the facilities back in the late 1600s.

America's most unique stadium graced our campus. It had been built during the Great Depression as a Work Projects Administration project. In order to have justified its construction, the government stipulated that the venue must also be used for livestock shows. So that the animals could be paraded into and out of the arena, a large entryway, which extended from one 35-yard line to the other, blighted the stadium's architectural integrity. This meant that there were no seats in that entire 30-yard swath. At least no season ticket buyers could complain that someone else was getting 50-yard line treatment when they weren't. By the time I was coaching at the college, the livestock extravaganzas had long since ceased, but they still hadn't filled in that barren opening between the 35-yard lines where prime seats would have been available.

Our equipment, also, was in a sad state of disrepair, and the press box-to-field telephone system we used on game days was reminiscent of two Dixie cups connected by a stretch of rusty piano wire. Our football offices were in a hovel. All of our coaches shared one large room that served as our staff meeting room, as our film room, and as our storage room. As one of the coaches might be trying to make his recruiting calls on the one telephone in the room, the other coaches would be reviewing film or trying to prepare practice plans.

Augie Tammariello was the hotshot recruiter on our staff, and it seemed that he was always doing some fast talking. After a while, the rest of us got used to it, and we just tuned him out. One day, Augie, in the midst of a conversation, clamped one hand over the mouthpiece of the phone and called out to us desperately, "Hey guys, do we offer a major in theology here?" We all shrugged, indicating that none of us really knew the answer. Without missing a beat, Augie was right back on the phone, and in a reassuringly authoritative voice, he spoke to the prospect on the other end of the line. "We rank fourth in the nation in theology," he said. I had a little talk with Augie later about that one. It was the closest we ever came to using misleading recruiting practices.

Yes, we had some problems confronting us, but as Pappy Waldorf had told me, there were numerous redeeming features that I would discover upon arriving in Williamsburg. Foremost among these were the fighting hearts of the young men who played on our teams at William and Mary. We were often out-scheduled, but we were never out-fought. We weren't out-scored that often either.

Our schedules were loaded with income-producing games against opponents whose recruiting resources and clout were far more potent than ours. Over the years we paid frequent visits to contest with teams such as Pitt, West Virginia, Navy, Syracuse, Virginia Tech, Boston College, and other Eastern heavy hitters. Amazingly, we were able to pull off a more than occasional upset against these formidable opponents, and when we played the teams at our own level, such as Davidson, VMI, Furman, the Citadel, or Richmond, we rarely lost a game.

At William and Mary we featured an attack that depended heavily on the forward pass. Wait a minute here! Is this the same coach whose New Mexico Lobos threw the ball *just three times in the entire game* when they pulled off their monumental upset of Air Force? Is this the Neanderthal who was in charge when California's Golden Bears kept it on the ground for *22 consecutive plays* on that late November day in 1960 when Cal marched to victory in THE BIG GAME? You betcha it was, because as I have often told the coaches with whom I've worked, "If you don't change with the times, the times are going to change you."

The style of attack we now adopted represented a sharp departure from the grind-it-out Wing T that we had employed at both New Mexico and California. The opponents we faced at William and Mary usually had players much larger and stronger than ours, and we had to acknowledge that there was no possibility that we were going to muscle our way to any victories. Also, our players' abilities and mental capacities were well suited to a more sophisticated and wide-open type of offense.

In order to make our pass-oriented approach effective, we needed to have good quarterbacks. Physical ability alone, at that position, is not enough. Mental sharpness, a high degree of motivation, and leadership qualities are all requirements, too. At William and Mary we had an abundance of young men who fit the description. Dan Darragh and Mike Madden were two outstanding quarterbacks who shared playing time during most of my days at the college. They did so without a semblance of one of those tiresome "quarterback controversies" that the media so often invents. (I'm curious. Has there ever been a "left guard controversy"?) After graduating, both men became successful lawyers. Darragh, a tall drop-back type, played several years as a starting quarterback for the Buffalo Bills during the 1970s. Madden was not as tall, but he was a dangerous run or pass threat who kept our opponents' defenses very unsettled.

Mike was also a classic competitor who played with such abandon that he injured himself frequently. I recall one game when he flew wildly into a melee populated mostly by burly linemen who were all lusting after a ball that had been fumbled. Miraculously, Mike wrested the ball away from all of the others and made the recovery. In the process of these heroics, he sustained a severe laceration on his eyelid that would require surgery to repair. By the time we got him to the hospital after the game, his face was so black from subcutaneous bleeding that he looked as if he had just emerged from three shifts in a bituminous coal mine.

Prior to entering the operating room, Mike telephoned his father, a judge in New Jersey, to inform him about the injury, about how it had occurred, and about the surgical procedure he was about to undergo. When he finally succeeded in allaying his father's concerns and was about to hang up, another very important thought occurred to Mike, and he shouted into the telephone, "Oh, Dad! Dad!" When his father acknowledged that he was still on the line, Mike continued. "I'm the guy who *recovered* that fumble," he said proudly. Fortunately, the operation was a complete success.

After Dan Darragh and Mike Madden graduated there were two more excellent quarterbacks, Wes Meteer and Jimmye Laycock, ready to move up from the freshman team. I had already departed by the time they did most of their playing, but they performed superbly when their turns came. For the past 20 years Jimmye has been the head football coach at William and Mary, and you can count me among the many Jimmye Laycock fans who pull for the Tribe to win.

Our real strength, however, lay in our exceptional receivers. One of the three legitimate first-team All-America players I tutored during my days as a college coach—Don Perkins and Craig Morton were the other two—was an end at William and Mary named George Pearce. George broke every pass receiving record, only to have many of those eclipsed two years later by his successor, Chuck Albertson.

Chuck was a meticulous practitioner of his craft, patterning himself after perfectionist Raymond Berry of the Baltimore Colts. He was an unemotional, ultra-studious player who was constantly asking questions about exactly how he should run his pass patterns. Ten years after Chuck had graduated (and I had moved on to the pro coaching ranks), I walked onto an elevator in a hotel in Los Angeles. There, dressed sharply in a tuxedo and apparently on his way to a formal function in the hotel, stood Chuck Albertson. With barely a flicker of surprise reflected on his face, and without a preliminary word of greeting, he said, "You know, Coach, when we used to face that inside-outside type of double coverage, don't you think I should have hooked up between them instead of continuing to carry out the called pattern?"

Our wide-open style of attack was conducive to the development of good receivers, and it also helped us in our efforts to recruit players who had such abilities. Tight end Ted Zychowski and wideout Jim Cavanaugh, both New York City area high school stars, came aboard, and they performed magnificently. Jim Cavanaugh has gone on to become a highly regarded college football coach, most recently as a member of the staff at Virginia Tech. We had another receiver named Ned Carr who is also worthy of mention. One season he caught 20 passes. What's so great about that, you ask? *Twelve of them were for touchdowns!*

I have never been associated with a more dedicated, more willing, more courageous group of young men than those whom I coached at William and Mary. During my first season there we had a varsity squad of just 24 players. Today, the athletic teams at the college are known as The Tribe. When I was there they were called The Indians, and thus that hardy band of 24 earned for itself a nickname of its own—one that shall remain forever in William and Mary lore. To this day they are still referred to as The Iron Indians. They won half their games, mostly against much stronger opponents, and they also won the hearts of everyone who knew them.

I have a designation of my own creation for them and for all the teams that performed during my five years at William and Mary. I will always think of them as the greatest bunch of overachievers ever assembled on a football field. They are, indeed, The Overachievers.

♦♦♦♦♦♦♦♦

As difficult as it was to gain admission to William and Mary, there were still some recruiting advantages that were unique to that institution. One of these stemmed from the cooperation we received from Bob Hughes, the director of admissions. We were able to request a review of qualifications for any prospective player who might not have been admitted through the normal admissions process. We never abused that privilege by presenting a plea for an obviously unworthy applicant. These young men were always of good character, and they always possessed good academic promise. We—and Bob—exercised proper judgment in selecting who would be the right candidates for consideration, and as a result, we were able to enroll many outstanding players and students who might otherwise not have been admitted. None of them ever embarrassed themselves, the college, or us.

Most noteworthy among those special admissions was a tough little linebacker from Monessen, Pennsylvania, named Terry O'Toole. Terry had very good grades in high school, but his College Board scores had been well below the normally acceptable level required for admission. There was a reason for that, however. Terry was almost totally deaf, and in addition, he stuttered noticeably, particularly when excited. To compensate for his hearing difficulties, however, he had learned to read lips very effectively.

In one game that we played against Boston College, the Eagles used an open huddle with their quarterback facing the line of scrimmage. Boston College used a signal system identical to ours, and so Terry was able, by virtue of reading the BC quarterback's lips, to know every play they were about to run. Terry became so excited that he began to stutter uncontrollably in his efforts to convey this information to his teammates. Although he never succeeded in letting the others in on his valuable information, Terry made 21 unassisted tackles that day in Chestnut Hill. His accomplishments went beyond that, however. Terry O'Toole was a first-team Southern Conference All-League selection two years in a row, and he graduated in the top 10 percent of his class.

There was a much more potent recruiting advantage that we enjoyed, however. William and Mary, at that time, was the only college in Virginia that was co-educational. The desire on the part of the female high school graduates in the state to attend college there was boundless. The number of female applicants for the incoming freshman class each year was vastly greater than the available number of vacancies that existed, and as a result, the admissions office was forced to be extremely selective. Every female admitted was a brilliant student, was most often from a well-to-do family that could afford the high cost of attending, and was a raving beauty.

Elitist? Undoubtedly. Did it make me feel a bit uncomfortable? Yes, it did. Did it help us recruit players? Hey! Was Newt Gingrich a politician? Every one of the young men we enticed to enroll knew that he had an opportunity to finish his undergraduate days with a degree from one of the nation's most renowned colleges and with a wife who was smart, rich, and beautiful. I told them that when I recruited them, and I wasn't telling any lies.

Once our targeted prospects began classes at William and Mary, we rarely lost any of them because of scholastic ineligibility. The classes were small; the faculty took pride in preparing the students to succeed; and there was a love of the college among the members of the student body that made it different from the environment that prevailed on so many campuses during the unsettled years of the 1960s.

♦♦♦♦♦♦♦♦

One team that was on our schedule every year was the Naval Academy. Perhaps it would be more accurate to say that we were on their schedule. For 50 consecutive years William and Mary's football teams had traveled to Annapolis in order to serve as the foil for Navy's Homecoming victory celebrations. That game was an almost sure win for the strong Midshipmen teams of that era. For us it was a big game, the highlight of our season, as we yearned for the thrill of a major upset victory over the Middies.

Every year, during the week that culminated with our game against Navy, we held highly charged, intensively focused practice sessions. I can recall an occasion, after one of those midweek practices, when I returned to the coaches' locker room and found defensive coordinator Larry Peccatiello sitting there looking pensive and downcast. When I inquired about what was bothering him, Larry complained that, despite his explicit instructions to our scout team signal caller, the young man was not doing a good enough job of impersonating the Navy quarterback. My response helped, at least, to alleviate some of Larry's consternation.

"You want the fourth-string quarterback at William and Mary to look like Roger Staubach?" I asked incredulously.

During my first three seasons we put forth valiant efforts in our battles against Navy, but we lost all of those games. That made it 25 consecutive times that William and Mary had been defeated by the Middies. The outlook in 1967, my fourth year, was very bleak. On successive weekends, prior to their upcoming game against us, the Navy gridders had triumphed over Penn State, Michigan, and Syracuse. They were undefeated, and coming into our game, Navy was the No. 1 team in the East. We took a vote, and we decided to show up anyway.

Navy-Marine Memorial Stadium is an impressive structure. It sits all alone on a flat plain about one-half mile from the Naval Academy's main campus. On game days, the Midshipmen, 4,400 strong, march from the central parade grounds to the stadium. Several large Navy bands accompany the meticulously uniformed and drilled sailors, and the brassy strains of "Anchors Aweigh" can be heard growing louder and louder as the marching men (and today, women too) draw closer. As that snappy group enters the stadium itself, they file, in seemingly endless procession, directly past the doorway of the visitor's locker room, at which time the sound of the music from those repetitive choruses of "Anchors Aweigh" reaches an intimidating level. When the game is over, the procedure is reversed, and many a William and Mary team, beaten and wearied from their futile exertions, has sat tight-lipped behind the closed doors of their locker room listening once again to the strains of that proud Navy anthem.

Inside the stadium, on the front wall of the upper deck, in bold black letters, strung in full circle far above the field, there is imprinted a linear list of the great and memorable battles in which the U.S. Navy and Marines have engaged during their long and glorious histories: Tripoli, Manila Bay, Belleau Wood, Chateau-Thierry, Midway, Guadalcanal, Bougainville, Tarawa, Iwo Jima, Coral Sea, Leyte Gulf, Saipan, Okinawa, Pork Chop Hill, Chosin Reservoir. When our team arrived at the stadium for our 1967 game against the Naval Academy, Les Hooker and I drifted out onto the field and gazed up in solemn reverence at the roll call of honor displayed upon the full circumference of that upper deck. As I stood there by Les's side, he continued to stare upward in awe, and then he commented, "Man, they sure do play one helluva tough schedule."

The game went badly for us from the outset. With a very stiff wind blowing, Navy elected to start the game with that strong breeze at its back, and their opening kickoff went deep into our end zone. We made the mistake of trying to run it out, and on the attempted return, one of our players was guilty of clipping in the end zone, resulting in a safety against us. Navy led 2-0 just five seconds into the game.

Following that safety, we were required to kick off—into the wind—from our own 20-yard line. Good luck! The Midshipmen took possession and began their drive at our 40-yard line, and two minutes later they scored a touchdown, upping their lead to 9-0. We still hadn't run a single play on offense. During the remainder of the first quarter, aided by that ever intensifying damned wind, they threatened to score several more times, but somehow we managed to stave them off without any further damage. In the second quarter, going into the wind, they could not move the ball, but we had little success gaining yardage, either, even with the elements now benefiting us. We went to the locker room at halftime still trailing 9-0.

In the third quarter, with the wind again in our favor, we knew that it was do-or-die time for us. We went to work, and we had a good drive going until one of their defensive backs intercepted a flat pass and streaked 75 yards for the touchdown that put Navy ahead 16-0. We came back at them again, however, and on the last play of the third quarter we finally went in for a touchdown. Our two-point attempt failed, and we now had to enter the final quarter fighting that strengthening blankety-blank gale *and* a 16-6 deficit against the strongest team in the East on their own battlefield.

Beginning early in the fourth quarter, the Midshipmen put together a long, time-consuming march, eventually reaching our 15-yard line. There they fumbled, and we pounced on the ball, taking possession with only six minutes remaining in the game. We struck quickly. Dan Darragh completed four straight passes, each one for sizeable yardage. The last one was a 27-yard touchdown strike to Chuck Albertson. This time our two-point conversion attempt was successful, and with three and one-half minutes left to play we had narrowed Navy's margin to 16-14.

On the next series, our defense stopped the Middies on three consecutive downs, forcing them to punt. Chip Young, our ace running back and an outstanding kick return man, brought that punt back from our 15-yard line to just across midfield, and on the first play from scrimmage, Darragh hit our diminutive halfback, Steve Slotnick, on an out and up pattern for the go-ahead touchdown. We tried for another two-pointer, failed, and led 20-16. The game clock showed less than a minute and one-half remaining.

Could we hold them?

On our ensuing kickoff, that *wonderful, delightful, lovable* wind played strange tricks with the ball, and one of our coverage men fell on it at the Navy 20-yard line. We stayed on the ground, milking the clock, and just a few seconds before the final gun sounded, halfback Terry Morton, behind a devastating block by tackle Joe Neilson banged into the end zone with a clinching touchdown, giving us a startling 27-16 upset victory. We had scored 21 points—going into the wind—in the final four minutes of the game.

Our jubilant players tumbled into the locker room, beside themselves with ecstasy. As the Corps of Midshipmen marched back out of the stadium, our athletic department business manager (also a former longtime assistant football coach at the college), Ed Derringe, who had sat in this same room following every one of the previous 25 defeats, shouted, "Open those doors! I want to hear 'Anchors Aweigh!'"

As the Midshipman and their bands passed by, our entire squad rose and joined together in singing the stirring words of that song. Admiral "Bull" Halsey never belted it out it any more lustily than my plucky little band of "Iron Indians" did on that day. It was one of those rare moments of bliss that none of us has ever forgotten.

It was also one of those seldom visited, but joyous, occasions that makes a coach forget all the endless late-night hours spent in a windowless 10-foot by 12-foot film room and all the weeks on the road away from home chasing recruiting prospects, most of whom go to school elsewhere. Forgotten are the injuries, the academic problems, the galling disappointment following games lost, the media criticism and second guessing, the boredom involved in the endless repetition of teaching fundamental skills, the stifling heat and humidity that attend the late summer two-a-day practices, and the frostbitten toes and fingers that plague you toward the end of the season.

The population of Williamsburg at that time was about 7,000, but when our team bus returned to the campus later that Saturday evening, 20,000 exuberant well-wishers were there to greet us. On the front steps of the Christopher Wren Building—the oldest college structure in America—I presented the game ball to President Paschall. He deserved it.

A few days later I received some mail from a retired naval officer, Admiral Gallery, who had attended the game at Annapolis. It was a gracious letter from this gentleman who admitted he had come to the game hoping for and expecting a victory by Navy. He wrote that his disappointment had been tempered considerably, however, by the realization that there were other men in this country, besides those who attended his alma mater, who had displayed, in the finest tradition of the navy, that they, too, knew you must "Never give up the ship!" Had I been in the navy, I would like to have served under that man.

More than 15 years later, while I was attending an NCAA Coaches Convention, I walked past one of the lobby displays, where a booklet published by the NCAA caught my eye. It was entitled: *The Ten Greatest Upsets in College Football History.* When I opened the book, there it was, prominently displayed at the top of the list. Standing there, I read again the thrilling account of our 1967 victory at Annapolis, and when I placed that volume back onto the table, I made certain that it was situated in the most prominent spot for passersby to see.

♦♦♦♦♦♦♦♦

My father was a frequent visitor to Williamsburg, and he tried to see as many of our games as he could. In 1967, he and my mother drove down from Chicago in order to visit us, and while they were on the last leg of their journey from Washington, D.C., to Williamsburg, he noticed a sign alongside the road that pointed toward the Quantico Marine Corps Base. In 1917, Quantico was the last stop his unit had made on their way to France during World War I, and now, moved by curiosity and nostalgia, he turned his car off the main highway so that he could set foot on that training site once again.

He was standing looking out at the parade ground, unaware that he had parked his vehicle in the space reserved for General Green, the base commandant of the Marine Corps. Just a few minutes later the general arrived in his automobile, and the MP on duty hurried over to my father in order to rectify the matter. When he told my father that he must move his car and why, my dad, who was somewhat embarrassed apologized, explaining that he had not known it was the general's reserved parking space. My dad did mention, also, that he had been a marine at Quantico 50 years before, and that this was the first time he had had an opportunity to return there.

When the MP relayed this information to General Green, the officer got out of his car, walked over to my father, and began to talk with him. Upon learning that my father had been with the Fourth Marine Brigade at Belleau Wood half a century before, the general paused, then saluted him and said, "Mister, you leave your automobile right where it is." I am telling you this story now. My dad has told it with a lump in his throat many times.

Following my second year at William and Mary, I was offered the head coaching position at the University of Arizona. Dick Clausen was the director of athletics at Arizona, and for that reason alone I came very close to accepting the job. We had seen definite progress taking place at William and Mary, however, and after some very serious soul-searching I finally made the decision to remain in Williamsburg.

We continued to improve during each of the next three seasons, also, and it is very likely that I could have continued to coach at William and Mary as long as I cared to do so. After five years, however, I was beginning to become restless. I could see that we would never become a team of national prominence, and although we could register some 7-3 and 6-4 records, there wasn't much chance of doing even that well very often, considering the strength of our schedules and the limited number of qualified applicants we could get into the school. Besides that, I had grown up in Chicago, and I missed all the taxicab fumes and concrete. I yearned once more for the big city.

The Philadelphia Eagles had just appointed a new head coach. It was Jerry Williams, a former star defensive back with the Eagles several years earlier. Jerry came to Philadelphia after a highly successful career as coach of the Calgary Stampeders of the Canadian Football League. During the years when I had been an assistant coach at the University of New Mexico, Jerry had been the head coach at the University of Montana, and I had come to know and admire him at that time. I telephoned him in Philadelphia in order to congratulate him upon his being named as the Eagles' new coach, and during our conversation he offered me a position on his coaching staff. The time had come, I felt, for me to move on, and because this opportunity also included working for Jerry, plus a move to professional football, I accepted his offer.

After all the arrangements had been made, I visited Dr. Paschall's office for the last time, in order to bid him farewell. We reminisced a bit and expressed to each other how much we had enjoyed our times together. We shook hands, and, as I was leaving, Dr. Paschall called out to me just before I reached the door. "Mr. Levy," he said, "You know, I wasn't kidding all those times I showed you that play of mine that I'd like to have seen you use."

When I closed the door behind me, he was still chuckling. I still do not know whether he was joking with me, but if someday, while I am once again coaching a football team, things aren't going right, and everything looks bleak, I am not going to ask my players to "win just one for the Gipper." What I am going to do is send that damn play into the game. And even if it doesn't work, I'll continue to revere Dr. Davis Y. Paschall to the end of my days.

SECTION IV

SPECIAL TEAMS ARE REALLY A KICK

CHAPTER 11

Pro Football! I Love It!

In one respect the Philadelphia Eagles coaching situation fit right in with the previous four jobs I had taken. The Eagles had experienced several consecutive losing seasons, and during the one immediately prior to the naming of Jerry Williams as head coach they had finished with a 2-12 record. The similarities ended there, however, because, despite a poor won-lost mark, the caliber of athletic ability and the intensity of play that I found on the professional level were in far greater contrast to the college game than I had anticipated.

In coming to Philadelphia I had expected that there would be a rather laid-back, I-know-it-all, "old pro" type of attitude among the players. Wrong! It was eye-opening for me to find how eager the professional players were for instruction in good playing techniques and how responsive they were to such coaching efforts directed toward them.

There was much for me to learn, also, and I received my first meaningful lesson about three days into our first training camp when Jerry scheduled a full-scale, all-out passing game scrimmage. With the other coaches—all veterans of several NFL coaching seasons—I took my place behind the offensive huddle to listen in on the play being called and to closely observe the action. On the first snap, all hell broke loose. The defensive linemen took off like four Titan missiles, and I stood there riveted in terror as bodies, grunts, sweat, obscenities, spit, chinstraps, flecks of blood, and hand pads filled the air. By virtue of some unexplained heavenly intervention I was not swept away with the avalanche.

When the din had quieted, I desperately surveyed the carnage to see if any of the other coaches might be in need of emergency medical attention, but I couldn't immediately locate any of them. When I finally did find them they were all safe, standing in a group 10 yards farther back from all that activity than I had been. Apparently, I had missed out on a real good joke, because they were all looking at me and laughing uproariously. They seemed to be a fun-loving bunch, and so I sidled over and hung around with them for the remainder of the scrimmage.

In becoming a coach in professional football I was introduced not only to better players, but also to another unique species as well—the team owner. The Eagles had been purchased that same year by a Philadelphia trucking magnate named Leonard Tose, and he was enjoying every minute of his new undertaking. Leonard (he preferred being called by his first name) was a convivial man, and he was a person I learned to like very much. He was *for* his team and *for* his coaches.

There is an atmosphere that prevails in your locker room after a game when your team has lost, and no one can react in a manner that will help you bounce back with confidence in preparing for the next game more effectively than the owner can. The exact words he chooses aren't really that important. Leonard Tose, in fact, rarely said anything after one of those defeats, but he projected the feeling that *we*—and that included *him*—had lost today. He, like the coaches, would pull up a stool and sit with his head in his hands, quietly sharing the agony we were all experiencing. He would then walk around and put his hand reassuringly on the shoulder of each of the staff members and then of the individual players in order to let us all know that he cared. Even after he silently exited the dressing room we all knew he was still with us.

In contrast, there are locker rooms where some owners engender the feeling that "You guys lost, and I am the one who has to suffer for it." This type of owner is doomed to fighting morale problems and to the frustration that results from repeated losing. I have heard from other coaches who have labored for owners of this nature. I am one lucky man, however, because all of the team owners for whom I have worked are men whose friendship I still treasure.

Someone once asked former Baltimore Colts player (and later, television commentator) Alex Hawkins who the most important person is in determining whether a professional team will be successful. Is it the quarterback? The head coach? The general manager? Is it the director of player personnel?

"None of these," Alex said. "It is the team owner."

At last! A TV commentator who knew what he was talking about.

The first week after our new Eagles staff had assembled in Philadelphia, Leonard arranged to take all our coaches out for dinner so that we might become better acquainted. Everyone enjoyed a sumptuous meal accompanied by liberal offerings of cocktails beforehand and by the constant refills of our wine glasses during the feast. All of us, with each additional sip and with Leonard leading the way, became increasingly bold in our predictions for the upcoming season. There was just one man, his name long forgotten, who refused to concur with the otherwise unanimous opinion that in our impending Super Bowl appearance, we would not only emerge victorious, but we would succeed in holding our unfortunate opponent scoreless, as well.

At one particularly expansive moment during the festivities, Leonard announced that any of us who might sometime desire use of his personal limousine and driver need only ask. Even with as much wine as I had enjoyed during the evening, I was still able to think with enough clarity to let that kind offer go on by.

The following day, as we were working in our offices on some playbook materials, I paid little attention when Dick Stanfel, the coach with whom I was sharing the room, picked up the telephone on his desk. As I continued diligently with my paperwork, I heard Dick's gruff voice speaking to the receptionist.

"Hello, Sally," he said. "This is Marv Levy. Would you please have Mr. Tose's limousine sent to the front door for me in 15 minutes."

(If they happen to be reading this, I'd like to apologize again to the two secretaries I knocked down on my frantic sprint to the front desk.)

When I returned to our office, Dick was not there. (Smart guy, that Dick.) It's just as well he wasn't, however. I needed to concentrate on redoing the notebook I had ruined when I upset that mug of coffee during Dick's phone call.

Dick Stanfel was another reason why I was so happy about joining the Eagles' coaching staff. Dick had been the line coach on my staff during my final year at Cal, and he had been serving with the Eagles ever since we had both departed Berkeley five years before. In later years he would work with distinction with other NFL teams, also, including his service with the Chicago Bears' 1985 Super Bowl championship team. You will never find a better line coach or a finer person.

When it came to teaching fundamental line techniques, Dick Stanfel had no peer. I've seen him terrorize more than one rookie as he pulled to trap the poor bumpkin in a demonstration of how it should be done. Many people who played or who closely observed professional football in the 1950s when Dick starred for the Detroit Lions and the Washington Redskins feel he is the best offensive lineman to have ever played the game. In 1954, as a member of the Lions' NFL championship team, Dick was selected as the NFL's Most Valuable Player, the only lineman ever to be so honored. It remains a mystery to me and to those who have seen Dick play that he has not yet been inducted into the Pro Football Hall of Fame. It is an injustice that should be rectified. Now, if he'll just grow up and forget those practical jokes.

Dick was fortunate in that he possessed a quality that I have observed in every outstanding football coach. He could get to the core of a matter quickly and simply. One evening, at our training camp during the summer of 1969, he offered an observation that made a lot of sense to me. It was the night that the first manned spacecraft to the moon was launched. Before our team meeting that evening, we had all clustered around a television set in order to watch the spectacular take-off. A few hours later, when we emerged from those meetings, we saw a full moon rising just above the horizon.

Dick turned to me and said, "Oh, my gosh! They are going to miss badly. The moon's way out there, and they were aiming that spaceship straight up into the air."

After hearing that, let me tell you, I was really relieved when I learned later that our astronauts had made it after all.

There is a considerable culture shock to which a coach is exposed when he makes the change from college to professional football, and not all of it is healthy. It does not take long until a newcomer becomes aware that the pro fans are a much more impatient and vociferous bunch than are their college counterparts. It takes very little provocation before their catcalls begin ringing down. When it came to booing and abuse, however, it is well to recognize that the Eagles fans had established an incomparable (and well-earned) reputation for their innovative methods of expressing their disdain. These zealots—from the "City of Brotherly Love"—begin revving up right in tune with the pregame introductions. Once they muster some momentum as the first couple of players are introduced, you are unable to hear the names of the other nine starters because the public address announcer's voice is drowned out by the swiftly rising crescendo of vituperation that rains down from the mean-spirited throng.

Perhaps those Philadelphia fans who introduced me to "Game Day in the NFL" were no more venomous than the rabid hordes elsewhere. It's just that the script for events at old Franklin Field, where we played our games back in that prehistoric era, always incorporated that ritual of lusty booing. Once, when we came back into the arena before the start of the second half, a perilous high-wire act, part of the halftime show, was in its most dangerous phase. The wire had been strung from the top of the upper deck on one side of the field to the other side. One lone performer, outlined against the cloudy sky, tottered in excruciating uncertainty along the hair-thin pathway to safety.

One of our young ball boys, his eyes wide in vicarious fear, his hands at his mouth, asked Joe Moss, the assistant coach standing next to him, "What would happen if he fell?"

Joe knew the answer to that one, "They'd boo like hell." Joe meant it.

There is also a marked adjustment a coach must make in how he handles the players. So often in college a coach finds himself in the role of cheerleader, seeking to inject into his charges the same high level of emotion that the coach himself is experiencing. In pro football the players are high strung as it is, and the season is a long one. If a coach tries to teach by the "Shout and Kick Ass" method, it won't take long for the players to regard him merely as a distracting noise. Besides that, the players have feet, and the coach has a rear end, and you never know when one of those earnest gridders might figure out that turnabout is fair play. This is an adjustment that a coach newly arrived from the collegiate ranks needs to make swiftly. He needs to recognize that if he wants his pupils to respond, he must become a patient and painstaking teacher. The good news is that it is a healthy change.

One other big difference is the players' lifestyles. The pros have money in their jeans, often lots of it. Some of them use it wisely; others proceed as if they will earn at that same level all their lives. With additional resources and much more free time on their hands—no classes to attend or to study for—the pros are exposed to many more temptations. Again, those with good judgment are able to cope.

The stay-out-late guys are easy to spot. They show up at practice at the last minute, and they often doze through the team meetings. A general listlessness begins to dull their performance. They never reach their potential, and only rarely does this type of player ever mend his ways. How do you motivate a person like this? *You don't!* I readily admit that there is a secret involved in how to motivate NFL players. It's simple. Bring only *intrinsically* motivated players onto your roster. They hunger for guidance. They'll observe, and they'll listen when you show them and when you tell them how they can get better. I have found that the high lifers enjoy short careers. As I have often told our players, "You can't hoot with the owls at night if you want to soar with the eagles during the day."

I found, also, that several aspects of coaching in the professional ranks were very refreshing. Foremost among these was the honesty with which the game was approached. You knew from the outset that the objective was to win. There was no mealy-mouthed talk about "student-athletes" when "*athlete*-student" would have been more accurate. True, there are many colleges where the *student* is the legitimate first part of that word combination, but unfortunately, those schools very often find themselves at a disadvantage when athletic competition is taking place. That leads me to a second desirable feature inherent to pro football.

Every professional team has the same "entrance requirements," and therefore, you immediately have a 50-50 chance to compete. The rules that govern one team's ability to acquire and to keep players are exactly the same as they are for all the other teams. Perhaps one team may be better coached or more effectively administered than most of the others, but those are attributes that were not attained through unfair advantage. Over the short haul, when a team in professional football does not show some improvement, you can make a case for laying the responsibility on the coach's shoulders, but when a franchise wallows in futility for an extended period of years, it is being poorly run from the top. In this latter instance, it is time for the owner to look beyond the coaching staff at higher echelons, himself included.

There is a third benefit that all dedicated coaches will embrace enthusiastically once they move from the college to the professional ranks. For the person who truly loves the act of coaching, professional football offers far greater year-round exposure to the game itself. I would estimate that a college football coach devotes 75 percent of his time to matters of recruiting and to coping with the impact that academics will have on his squad members. Many spend their free time seeking summer jobs for the players or devoting long hours buttering up potential financial backers of the school's athletic programs. All the time he is doing this, the true coach has his heart and his mind in the film room where he should be, in person, in order to study and to find improved techniques for teaching his sport. On the professional level a "coach" is exactly that—100 percent of the time, and for that reason alone the caliber of coaching is infinitely better.

My responsibility with the Eagles was to coach the special teams. *Special teams* is a designation I detest. It is a dance around the subject as if someone is trying to hide what he truly means. To me, there are no *special teams*; they are kicking teams. Later, when I became an NFL head coach and organized my own coaching staffs, I called them the kicking teams, and the man who coached them was *the kicking teams coach.*

At the time I coached the—get used to it, folks—*kicking teams* for the Philadelphia Eagles, we were one of only two clubs in the NFL to have a staff member assigned specifically to that responsibility, and as a result, we had outstanding performance from those units. The Los Angeles Rams, coached by innovative George Allen, had been the first, just one year earlier, to hire a full-time man to mentor the kicking teams, and George had picked a good one when he selected Dick Vermeil.

Toward the end of the 1969 season our Eagles played against the Rams, and during the two hours before the opening kickoff, Dick and I had an opportunity to renew our friendship. Most of our conversation revolved around our then-current main interest—the kicking game. As we chatted, I became envious when I learned about the amount of time and attention Dick was able to devote to his charges within the framework of George Allen's philosophy of the game. George believed, as I do, that kicking is exactly equal in importance to both offense and defense, and I yearned for a day when I might coach in such an environment.

Our Eagles didn't make it to the Super Bowl in 1969 as we had all predicted during those mellow moments at the dinner with Leonard. We did experience some modest improvement over the previous season's 2-12 record, however, by finishing 4-9-1, and we were in every game right up until the final gun.

A couple of weeks after the season had ended, I received a telephone call from Dick Vermeil. He told me that he was leaving his position with the Rams in order to become the offensive coordinator on Tommy Prothro's staff at UCLA. He wanted me to know that he had recommended to George Allen that I should be the person George should hire to take over as the Rams' new kicking teams coach. If I wished to express my interest, Dick suggested that I contact George directly.

After gaining permission from Jerry Williams to pursue the matter, I placed a call to George on a Sunday. He was cordial, and he asked enough questions to run my long distance phone bill up to a scandalous figure. Before hanging up he said that he'd like to talk with me further. Thank goodness he said that he'd initiate the next call. At dawn on Monday (What time was it in California!) he did call, and without any preliminaries, he launched immediately into the conversation by saying that if I could be there by the following Monday, the job was mine. It was an assignment I really wanted.

"I'll be there," I told him. (Marv, you idiot! Once again you forgot to ask what they were going to pay you.)

I spent Tuesday at the Eagles' offices winding up my affairs there. When I returned home that evening, Dorothy greeted me breathlessly at the door.

"George Allen just called," she said. "He told me to tell you that it is imperative for you to be in the Rams' office, ready to work, by 8 a.m. this Friday."

"This Friday!" I exclaimed. "That's impossible. What did you tell him?"

"I told him we'd be there," she said with a smile of satisfaction that begged for a compliment.

Dorothy wanted to return to California as badly as I did. I telephoned George, and he verified that it was very important for me to be there Friday because some urgent issues had to be addressed then.

On Wednesday morning we called the movers and talked them into coming for our belongings early the following day. We spent all day Wednesday packing at a breakneck tempo, wedging in trips to the bank and calls to the utilities companies. At 3 a.m. Thursday we fell into bed, and we were awake again at 6 a.m. in order to resume our feverish endeavors once again. The movers departed with the last of our furniture at 4 p.m. on Thursday.

Late Thursday night we boarded the last flight leaving Philadelphia for Los Angeles. Besides the heavy assortment of baggage, we were taking, I was also dragging around a dog kennel that housed the latest stray canine Dorothy had befriended.

When our plane arrived in Los Angeles we took a $50 cab ride (that was big bucks in 1970) from the airport to the Rams' practice and office complex in Long Beach, beating the 8 a.m. deadline by a breathless 10 minutes. No one else had as yet shown up for work, and so, surrounded by our piles of personal equipment and an irritable puppy, we camped outside the locked doors and waited for that 8 a.m. hour when that meeting of such vital portent was supposed to take place.

At 15 minutes until 10 a.m. a secretary finally arrived to open the office doors. She eyed our scruffy ensemble warily and was about to offer me a quarter as alms before I was able to convince her that I was the new assistant coach. She invited us all inside. I asked her what time she expected George to arrive.

"Coach Allen left for the Caribbean yesterday on a two-week vacation," she said.

Maybe it was all for the best. Dorothy and I checked into a motel across the street and slept the entire weekend. We'd need the rest, because I was about to embark on the most stimulating, exciting, and often bizarre experience I had ever known.

CHAPTER 12

California Dreamin' with George Allen

During the phone calls I had had with George Allen when I was in Philadelphia, he had told me that he would be able to offer me only a one-year contract. He advised me that unless the Rams made it to the Super Bowl in 1970, the entire staff would probably be fired. This was information he felt I should be aware of before accepting the job. It was common knowledge that George and team owner Dan Reeves were at odds with each other. Two years earlier, in fact, Reeves had actually fired him, but when the players had petitioned the owner to retain George, Reeves had acceded to their request.

I appreciated George's honesty, but if I had cared about security, I would have become an accountant instead of a football coach. I didn't hesitate in telling George that I wanted to come to work for him. I knew we would win, and I also knew that I wanted to work in the type of program that George ran. Even if he were fired, there would be many other teams clamoring to hire him, and if I did the kind of job I believed that I would do, George would very likely put me on his new staff.

George had many attributes, and not the least among them was his ability to find outstanding staff members and his willingness to utilize their creative thinking. (Oh! Oh! Did I just indulge in a bit of personal braggadocio? I apologize.) You would think that every head coach would have the appetite to capitalize fully on the talents of his assistant coaches, but too frequently they don't. Many are fearful of hiring men who might possess greater expertise in certain areas of the game than the head coach himself. That was an insecurity that did not plague George. In fact, I never saw him display any self-doubt.

When I came to Los Angeles, Ted Marchibroda was coaching the quarterbacks and the running backs, while longtime veteran Ray

Prohaska handled the offensive line. Tom Catlin, Laverne Torgeson, and George all collaborated in coaching the Rams' overpowering defense. As coach of the kicking teams, I was one of two newcomers in 1970. The other one was Boyd Dowler, beginning his first year in coaching after his outstanding career as a flanker on the Packers teams that had owned the 1960s. Boyd was the receivers coach, having replaced Howard Schnellenberger, who left to join Don Shula's staff in Miami.

The most valuable assistant George had, however, was a man who had no specific position assignment, but he was as important to George Allen as Gracie Allen (no relation) was to George Burns. Some people and some events just seem to go together. I take nothing away from George when I declare that he would not have been as successful as he was without Joe Sullivan. Who? He was George's "special assistant," that's who. So what, you say, all these big-time coaches have special assistants, don't they? Not like Joe Sullivan, they don't.

George was Mr. Ideas; Joe was Mr. Details. There has never been a more persistent, thorough, loyal, tireless presence in the game than Joe. George's teams didn't need a business manager, a traveling secretary, a film breakdown man, a manager of facilities, a trade negotiator, a waiver wire specialist, a contract negotiator, a legal expert, or any of the other impressively titled employees usually required for this myriad of responsibilities. Joe could handle all of those tasks before the morning coffee break.

One of our coaches once speculated that a typical instruction from George to Joe might be as follows: "Joe, I've got a great idea. I'm going to create the universe. You take care of the details."

Directing the kicking teams for the Rams and later for the Redskins was the most enjoyable coaching experience I have had in my career. Once George determined that he had confidence in a staff member, he allowed that man to handle his assigned responsibility without standing around peering over the guy's shoulder. It wasn't that George ever lost touch or interest in any department of play, because he remained fully abreast of what was happening. He'd inquire frequently about what you were doing, and it is to his credit that the most often asked question he directed at me was a positive one: "Marv, what can we do to make our kicking game better?"

He wasn't asking that question merely to appear interested. George listened intently to the answer, and he weighed carefully the validity of any proposals. Most importantly, he acted upon sound recommendations, pursuing implementation of good ideas to fulfillment.

George loved to assign projects to everyone in the organization. At the conclusion of each season, he always asked all the coaches to do research on many subjects. The long list for each coach differed from those he gave to the others, but three topics appeared on everyone's agenda every year:

1. What can we do to help us win that no one else in the NFL is doing?
2. What is it that we can do better in order to win?
3. Make up a reel of film that will be uniquely helpful for use as a teaching device.

George's idiosyncrasies often tempted us to mimic him, sometimes just to provide some lighthearted tension breakers. On one occasion, Boyd Dowler put a note on the desk of our film coordinator, Nate Fine, instructing Nate to make up a 400-foot reel of plays that no one had ever run before. (Huh?) At the bottom of that message Boyd had inscribed a masterfully forged George Allen signature. In this contrived missive, "George" explained that he was not currently in the office, but he stressed that he'd need the completed reel placed on his desk by the time he returned for the team meeting later that day. Although I do not know if Nate found a way to come up with those "plays that have never been run before," I do recall that, when I meandered by his studio at lunchtime, he seemed to be working at a more feverish pace than usual.

More than any other coach I have known, George was convinced that you could win several games a year with your kicking game, but only if you were willing to devote the time, attention, and commitment needed to be successful in this department. When he selected our 40-man roster (the maximum number allotted in the late 1960s and early 1970s), George always allowed the kicking teams coach to have the greatest impact in determining the last six men. The fifth running back we kept most likely would not have been among the five best running backs competing for a position with our team. The same was true for the last man kept among the wide receivers, the tight ends, the defensive linemen, the linebackers, and the defensive backs.

Why would we retain players like that? Because they were the best *hard core* kicking game players at their respective positions! The term *hard core* refers to players on the kick coverage units and to the blockers and rushers on the kick return teams. Two players who starred with the Washington Redskins during George's tenure as head coach, Bill Malinchak and Ted Vactor, made the team—and their mark—because they had an outstanding ability *and determination* to block punts and field goals.

George often contended that the outcome of at least three games every year would be determined by kicking game plays. Such plays would not be the result of happenstance or good fortune, he said. They would occur because of talent and preparation. He was right! In keeping those last six men on our roster primarily for their hard core kicking teams abilities, we were able to win enough games to make the difference between being or not being a championship-contending team every year under George's leadership.

In working for George, and because of his beliefs and cooperation, I was able to develop, for the first time in NFL history, a cohesive "Philosophy of the Kicking Game." Until that time there had been some coaches who believed in the importance of the kicking game to the extent that they paid more than normal attention to it, but no one had tried to define its role more specifically than that.

In Los Angeles I prepared a kicking game playbook—about 150 pages—similar to those playbooks being employed by the offensive and the defensive units. The first chapter in this playbook was devoted to defining our philosophy. In this segment I pointed out that 22 percent of all plays were kicking plays of some nature—punts, kickoffs, PATs, field goals, kicks after a safety, onside kickoffs, etc. Each kicking game play, I stressed, is more heavily weighted than almost any single offensive or defensive play from scrimmage because at least one of three game-altering elements is inherent to every kicking play:

1. A change of ball possession will occur as on a punt or a kickoff.
2. A large amount of yardage with heavy impact on field position is involved. A punt, for instance, usually means a 35- to 45-yard switch, and it includes the ominous potential for an all-the-way return by a dangerous runner in a broken field environment.
3. A clearly defined opportunity to score prevails, with success or failure to be determined on that specific play. This, of course, is the situation that exists on every PAT and field goal attempt.

An additional element of our philosophy emphasized that football is an energetic sport, and nowhere in the game is the opportunity for confirming the physical nature of your team more available than in the high-speed, high-momentum activity that takes place during a kicking game play. The pattern for aggressiveness that a team is going to display throughout the contest is established by its kicking units.

After a touchdown has been scored, the kickoff that follows is the single most important factor determining whether the scoring team will retain the momentum or whether the team that just surrendered that touchdown will be able to swing the pendulum back. If your coverage unit can drop the opponent inside its 25-yard line, statistics show that you will be the next team to score 75 percent of the time. If, however, the kickoff is brought back to their 40-yard line or beyond, it is the return team that scores next 80 percent of the time.

Being in charge of the kicking teams has other advantages for the coach who wishes to grow in his profession. The kicking game coach is, in essence, the *coordinator* for one of the three *equally important* departments of play—kicking, defense, and offense. He works directly with no other staff members, however, and on his shoulders rests the full responsibility for devising the system and the game planning. Because the several distinctly different kicking game units require a considerable variety of skills, the kicking game coach winds up working with almost every member of the playing roster. As a result, he is exposed to a responsibility more closely akin to that of the head coach than any of the other coordinators or position coaches are.

In my opinion, an outstanding opportunity to train for becoming an eventual head coach exists for the man in charge of the kicking teams. That was my first assignment in professional football, and it prepared me for the head coaching duties I was to assume with the Chiefs, the Montreal Alouettes, and the Bills. Dick Vermeil, later a head coach with the Eagles, the St. Louis Rams, and the Chiefs, was another man who began his NFL coaching career as a kicking game coach. So did head coaches Mike Ditka (Bears and Saints), Bill Cowher (Steelers), Bobby Ross (Chargers and Lions), Marty Schottenheimer (Browns, Chiefs, Redskins, and Chargers), and Dick LeBeau (Bengals). Between us, as head coaches, we have made nine Super Bowl appearances.

Many coaches today continue to pay lip service to the importance of the kicking game, but too few are willing to devote everything it requires to get maximum results. For that reason I believe that a coach can get a huge jump on his opponents by doing all it takes to excel in the kicking game. Such resolve would include apportioning one-third of his practice time to the kicking game. Most coaches will look for a different way to do it. I'd really look forward to playing against them.

After I arrived in Los Angeles in February 1970, there was a compelling reason for me to look forward with impatience to the beginning of training camp. At New Mexico, at Cal, at William and Mary, and in Philadelphia I had begun every season knowing that our team was outmanned. Here, with the Rams, we had talent and confidence, and I yearned to take the field with a team that had the tools and the chemistry necessary for winning. Finally, in July, we began our drills, and three weeks later we were in the Coliseum for our first preseason game against the Dolphins.

On the sideline, immediately prior to kickoff, I gathered my kickoff coverage unit about me and imparted some last-second instructions.

"Everybody stay in his lane. If you're knocked down, get up. Break down at the point of contact. Keep your head up. Nail that sumbitch on his own nine-yard line, and make him let loose of that ball. Remember now, you are playing for the Los Angeles Rams!"

None of the rookies on our coverage unit heard a word I was saying; they were all breathing too heavily.

David Ray's kick went to Miami safety Hubert Ginn on his five-yard line. My fired-up band of stalwarts raced wildly downfield sporting some of the meanest visages that ever glared out from behind a face-mask. One of our players reached out for Hubert and touched his arm at the Miami 15-yard line. That was the only contact we would subject Hubert to on that play. The only time he let loose of the ball was when he spiked it over his left shoulder in our end zone 10 seconds later. My first play for the Rams had resulted in a 95-yard touchdown return—*for the other team.* George was looking around frantically trying to find me. He'd have a tough time doing it; I was hiding behind Deacon Jones.

Fortunately, we got better quickly in our kicking team performances. By the time the regular season began we had the right players in the right positions, and our kicking teams played with distinction. We became particularly adept at returning kicks ourselves, and during the season we had several touchdown returns at crucial times.

We also had a few players on our team who had a talent for blocking kicks. On field goal and PAT defense we blocked five attempts. Most of our success there was the result of some fierce individual rushes by defensive standouts Merlin Olsen and Deacon Jones. They had the strength, height, and knack for blocking kicks. All I really wanted them to do was just tee off using a bull rush, get penetration, and then get their hands high. Nothing fancy. Such an approach, however, was not cerebral enough for Merlin, who was after me constantly to install a variety of tricks for use on our placekick blocking attempts.

Each week, during the meetings I conducted for the placekick defense unit, Merlin would recommend some maneuver. Merlin was a highly respected member of our team, and although I did not want to use his cockamamie proposals, it was necessary for me to handle the matter diplomatically. Whenever Merlin would raise his hand during a meeting, I would listen to his latest brainstorm.

"Good point, Merlin," I would say, and then I'd proceed to diagram the type of rush that I had planned to use all along.

After I had employed this evasive procedure several times, it became standard ritual for the other players in the room, following one of Merlin's suggestions, to chant in unison, "Good point, Merlin."

♦♦♦♦♦♦♦♦

Upon becoming the kicking teams coach with the Rams, I inherited some excellent kicking specialists. Pat Studstill, a 12-year veteran, was our punter. Pat and I got along wonderfully. I left him alone. Pat no longer wished to have a coach telling him what to do, and, frankly, I understood his feelings. I believe that coaches, particularly in the NFL, meddle far too much with the kicking styles and techniques of their kickers. The coaches should concentrate primarily on the kick coverage, the kick return, the kick protection, and the kick block units.

That doesn't mean that the coach should refrain from instructing his kickers on matters of obvious importance. I had always felt it vital that I convince our punters to be unselfish. That meant punting for height rather than for their statistics. Almost all touchdown returns in the punting game result when a punter is thinking only about his average distance per punt. If that is his motivation, he'll kick it long and low, well beyond the coverage capabilities of his team.

In our kicking game notebook I listed the 10 essential qualities of a great punter. Point number one read: "The best punter in the NFL will *not* lead the league in average yards per punt." For emphasis, that same declaration was included again as point number 10.

The only criticism I ever directed toward Pat was to tell him that his operation time from snap to punt was too slow. Pat countered by pointing out that he had punted more than 400 times in his NFL career without ever having had one of them blocked. Two years later, when I was coaching with the Redskins, we played the Patriots, to whom Pat had been traded in the off season. Late in the game when Pat had run his string to 499 consecutive unblocked punts, Bill Malinchak blocked one for us. We scored a safety on that play and in the process denied Pat the 500-in-a-row mark he had been seeking. Every now and then a coach experiences some bittersweet moments. That was one of them.

Our kick return specialist, Alvin Haymond, was the best all-around return man I have ever coached. I learned more from him than he did from me. He never made a mistake fielding the ball. I cannot recall that he ever fumbled. His judgments, courage, competitiveness, willingness to work hard, unselfishness, and belief in the efficacy of the kicking game all combined to make him a superior performer. Alvin was not one of those fools who refused to employ the fair catch. He knew exactly when to use it. Those who believe it is "macho" to never signal for the fair catch are afflicted with that type of misplaced bravado that causes teams to lose games and coaches to lose their jobs. Early in my coaching career, Dick Clausen had imparted to me some sage advice when he said, "Beware of the guy who will win you one and lose you two."

Alvin had only fair speed, but he could use what he had with telling effect. Balance, toughness, intelligence, and decisiveness were his tools. Too many coaches, in searching for their kick return specialist, will eliminate all candidates who do not possess blazing speed. That is a drastic mistake. They should look first for a man with the unerring ability to catch a capriciously spiraling football while 11 ill-tempered maniacs are bearing down on him. What difference does it make how fast he can run if he doesn't bring the ball along on the trip?

If Alvin had one fault it was his compulsion to recount in miniscule detail every one of his return plays. He could—to the chagrin of all coaches and teammates—take two and a half hours, during a plane trip home, to describe an eight-yard punt return.

Working for George was fun. You didn't always know it at the time, but it was. If you were interested in leisure time, however, you were on the wrong coaching staff. With George you might work until 3 a.m., and that included Christmas Eve if your team was in the playoffs. George worked hard, too. Not quite as intensely as he wanted the world to believe, but hard enough. He liked to keep his vacations secret, and there would be days when he might get into the office rather late. That imperfection inspired Ted Marchibroda to make the astute observation that once you've developed the reputation for being an early riser, you could sleep until noon.

George often left a note for a coach in order to impress upon all of us how dedicated he was when it came to working long hours. Although the message itself might vary, he made certain that the recipient was aware of exactly when he had placed that vital communication on the man's desk. For example: "Marv, Please give me the kicking reel from last year's Atlanta-Cleveland game. Signed, George Allen. ***2:09 a.m.***"

Part of the entertainment we derived from working for George stemmed from the unpredictable reactions he exhibited upon occasion to rather normal events. When we were with the Rams, it was our policy to depart on Friday mornings for our scheduled Sunday games on the East Coast. One Friday evening after we had arrived in Atlanta, Ted and I were sitting in the lobby of our hotel when George approached us, his face reflecting a mixture of anger and concern.

"We are in big trouble for this game," he sputtered. "Our players are thinking about everything else except the Falcons. Do you know what Kermit Alexander just asked me? *Do you know?*"

Neither Ted nor I could imagine what transgression Kermit must have committed, and so we waited for George to drop the bomb.

"He asked me if there is a restaurant in this hotel. Can you imagine that?" I feigned shock while hastily concealing the candy bar I had been about to unwrap.

During the off season George spent most of his time on the telephone. He had posted a sign on the wall in his office that reminded him of a self-imposed duty that really required no prompting, but George wanted all visitors to notice—and maybe even comment about—how committed he was. It read as follows: "Call at least one other team every day!" (And don't you forget that exclamation point.)

It was a rare day, however, when he called just one. This was well before the era of free agency, and George was constantly seeking to make trades for experienced players in order to strengthen our team. He had little faith in rookies. Even a first-round draft choice, he felt, was three or four years away from reaching his potential. George had no intention of losing games while some neophyte was gaining the necessary know-how. Why not trade for the players who had already served their apprenticeships, he reasoned.

There were many happy veterans on George's teams. They were players who had earned their way into the lineup on the basis of consistent top-level performance, and they combined proven ability with justifiable confidence. They were inured to the pressures of big games and able to concentrate on the tasks at hand rather than being diverted by the fear of not measuring up. The few young players whom George retained on his rosters also had some unique advantages that did not accrue to the rookies on most of the other teams. George's youngsters were not thrust into starting roles, nor was their concentration distracted by the drum beat from immediate high expectations. Instead, they would spend two or even three seasons becoming fully familiar with our system and with the nature of the NFL before being called upon to show that they were, indeed, truly pros. I cannot recall a rookie who ever started for one of George's teams.

The clamor from fans and media to get a first-round draft choice into the game is understandable. Most of those numero unos are the victims of the ballyhoo that accompanies their selection and then their signing. The teams, in their thirst to hype ticket sales, usually paint these first-rounders as the cure-alls for the club's ills. These rookies can rarely live up to such expectations. Management often believes everything their public relations and marketing departments have written about the phenom, and they think that by force of will you can make the lad into an All-Pro. Pressures from all sides to get that savior into the lineup squeeze in on the coach. If the unready player is hurried into play, he is often resented by his teammates because he not only contributes to losing, but he often makes his fellow players look bad as a byproduct of his own inadequacies. George never had that problem.

While those rookies were being patiently groomed and conditioned to play, George was sending a full contingent of salty veterans onto the field on game days, and they were ready to *win now.*

In my opinion, any team that adopts the philosophy that they are "building for the future" is always building for the future. That is the most valuable of many lessons I learned from George. He is the person who coined the phrase, "The future is now." George once told me that if you sacrifice this season in order to build for the future, what you are really doing is building for a future *coach.*

George's teams were never without the ministrations of a team chaplain. We had a chapel service the day before the game and then again prior to the pregame meal. There was a team prayer in the locker room before we would take the field, and for a game of more than routine importance, we might have another one in our team huddle along the sideline as a prelude to kickoff. I am sure that George would have called for the services of our chaplain at halftime, too, as a special supplication, if we had not been doing a good enough job of rushing the passer. A postgame prayer always punctuated our locker room celebrations.

Selection of the team chaplain was a process requiring great study, consideration, and—forgive me—soul-searching. Although George did not impress me as being any more concerned personally about spiritual matters than most other coaches, he was not going to leave anything to chance. The Dallas Cowboys were not going to outplay us, and they darn well were not going to outpray us, either.

It is a curious paradox that the players and coaches who served under George could snicker at some of his transparent gimmickry while still being able to retain their unwavering respect for him. Our players reveled in listening to the junior high school speeches George delivered in his efforts to motivate them. George believed his players and coaches would buy anything he'd say. The players, by feigning rapt acceptance of George's emotional pronouncements, succeeded in usurping his foray into con artistry. The gullible party was George, not the players, and they savored the jousting in this game of turnabout. One time, at the Coliseum, after George had spoken his final pregame wisdom to the team, we were standing in the tunnel awaiting the player introductions, and I overheard Merlin Olsen say to a teammate, "This is the fifth time this year that we are playing the most important game of our lives."

One of George's most memorable pregame orations came during my single season with the Rams. Before one game, without even knowing it at the time, he was responsible for giving birth to a term that is now an integral part of football's lexicon. The Rams' Fearsome Foursome—Deacon Jones, Merlin Olsen, Lamar Lundy, and Roger Brown—had been terrorizing opponents' quarterbacks for several years. Lundy and Brown were no longer active, however, and there was some question whether newcomers Diron Talbert and Coy Bacon could replace them adequately. The Dallas sportswriters were boasting that the Cowboys' quarterback, my former pupil Craig Morton, would leave the field with a clean jersey after the game.

Groping for some final words of inspiration as our team prepared for kickoff, George pointed across the field and blurted out, "Today we are going to take that *Morton Salt* and pour it into a sack!"

The Rams' front four spilled Craig Morton for losses eight times that day. Thus was born that enigmatic term, the *quarterback sack.*

Talbert[1] and Bacon won their spurs quickly, and the Rams' front four remained as effective with them in the lineup as they had been with Brown and Lundy.

George sought constantly to convince his players that it was "us against the world." He had a consuming penchant for security. His great dread was that some opponent might seek to spy on our practices. In order to forestall any espionage, George employed a full-time securi-

---

1. Diron Talbert was one of my favorite characters with the Rams. He was a delightful mixture of good ol' boy crude and courtly Southern gentleman. I recall a flight attendant on one of our charters asking Diron if he'd like a soft drink. "Why shit yes, ma'am," he replied in his deep Texas drawl.

ty man, one who looked the part every bit as well as he played it. Ed Boynton was a retired Los Angeles Police Department detective who always looked as if he had come directly from the set of *Dragnet.* Ed was thorough, detailed, unwaveringly conscientious, and incorruptible. The players quickly nicknamed him "Double-O."

The fence surrounding our practice field had about 50 drainage openings at ground level, spaced approximately 15 yards apart. "Double-O" had prepared 50 pieces of wood, all painted in our team colors, and every day before practice he meticulously placed one of these wooden obstacles onto the ground in front of each of the openings in the fence. At the conclusion of practice, he would gather them up to be stored for use again the following day. So much for any enemy agents who might be lying in the mud outside the enclosure trying to peer in at the mysterious maneuvers taking place on our practice field.

Upon occasion a player would hide one of those wooden squares, thereby touching off a full-scale investigation on Ed's part. His first suspect was always the chief of security for the Giants.

The players kept Ed constantly engrossed in his vigil by calling out helpful information. "Spy in the trees," or "Spy on the rooftop," were the favorite words of alarm they used in order to send "Double-O" scurrying off to check on suspicious individuals, usually 10-year-old boys. "Double-O" was the subject of numerous newspaper feature articles in both Los Angeles and Washington. On many occasions fathers would bring their young sons out to our practice facilities, where they would wait outside the fence until the day's session had ended so that they might have an opportunity to meet and to speak with "Double-O." He never disappointed them. He'd sign autographs and impart helpful hints on how to maintain law and order in a world filled with evil.

George's meetings, just like his practices, were long, but he was at least adept at finding ways to liven things up. At the first team meeting on a Monday following a victory, he would hold an Honors Assembly, during which gifts were distributed to many of the heroes from the previous day's game. These awards were not just lollipops and bubblegum, either. The outstanding player in the game would receive a set of golf clubs. Color television sets were bestowed upon the most valuable players on the offensive and defensive teams, while the standout performer from the kicking game units won a new suit of clothing. Interceptions, sacks, and big plays of any sort were all richly rewarded, as well. After we had moved to coach the Redskins, anyone on the kick coverage teams making a tackle inside the opponents' 20-yard line became the recipient of a "Garfinkel"—a $50 gift certificate from Garfinkel's department store located in downtown Washington. The NFL frowned on such awards, but our players didn't.

Following a particularly meaningful victory, George might present a handsomely inscribed game ball to every player on the team. A game ball is a prize coveted by all members of a professional football team. In our locker room after a game when a game ball was presented, George would lead the entire team as we'd all join in singing a bawdy little ditty to honor the recipient. Had Roman Gabriel been awarded a game ball, for instance, the song would go like this:

Hooray for Roman;
Hooray at last.
Hooray for Roman;
He's a horse's ass.

Even though the rhyme was strained, I've seen veteran players with tears in their eyes upon being accorded this dubious distinction.

Although George required long hours and unswerving devotion from his coaches, he treated us extremely well. Whenever any of us might convince him that we needed anything in terms of equipment, extra practice time, or additional meeting time, he would respond favorably and immediately. Most importantly, he was honest about what he could or could not do. To me, honesty from the person for whom you work is absolutely necessary if he is to gain your loyalty. He fought for his coaches, and the members of his staff were paid well.

All of the NFL teams today include automobiles for the assistant coaches as part of their contractual agreements, but in 1970 that was not standard. George, however, provided attractive ticket packages to local car dealers in exchange for their making automobiles available for every coach on his staff. The vehicles we had were jazzy Ford XL sports cars. They were pure white except for a pair of large iridescent blue Rams horns, one on each side of the car, that started at the front bumper and swept back along the fenders onto the side doors, where the painted curls in the horns culminated by wrapping themselves around the door handles. Joe Moss, my former coaching cohort in Philadelphia and still a member of the Eagles' staff, visited the West Coast one time to do some scouting of college players, and I arranged to pick him up at the airport.

When I noticed him perplexedly studying my car and told him that I'd just as soon not have that outlandish design on it, Joe offered a pertinent comment.

"If they'd give us one of those in Philadelphia," he said, "they could put a great big Eagle's ass on it, and I wouldn't complain."

♦♦♦♦♦♦♦♦

Once the regular NFL season opened we played well, but we entered the final game on our schedule with fragile playoff hopes. At that time there were three divisions (East, Central, and West) in the NFC and three divisions (East, Central, and West) in the AFC. Four teams from each of those conferences earned their way into the playoffs, which began at the conclusion of the regular season. All division-winning teams were playoff participants. One additional team from each conference—the team having the best record from among all those that had not won its division title—would enter the playoffs as well. That fourth qualifier from each conference was known as the *wildcard* team.

Our Rams were in the West Division of the NFC, but the Lions had already clinched the NFC wildcard berth by virtue of having defeated us in a squeaker the week before. Although the Lions were destined to finish behind the division-winning Packers in the NFC's Central Division, it was already determined that their final record would be better than any other non-division winner in the NFC.

For us to make the playoffs we needed to win our division title. In order for that to happen we would have to defeat the Giants at Yankee Stadium in the season's final game. It also required that the 49ers, with whom we were vying for the NFC West title, lose their game that same day to the Raiders. Our task was formidable because the Giants, if they emerged victorious against us, would wrap up first place in the Eastern Division. If they were to lose, they'd be out of the playoffs.

We played our best game of the year, and we walloped the Giants 31-3. At the airport in New York, we watched the telecast of the San Francisco versus Oakland game. One week before, the Raiders had already assured themselves of a first-place finish in their AFC West divisional race, and with little to motivate them, they turned in a desultory performance, losing to the 49ers. We had finished with a 9-5 record, but we were out of the playoffs. It was a long, quiet plane ride home. Alvin Haymond didn't even talk about his 70-yard punt return.

Christmastime in Los Angeles had never been a particularly festive occasion for George. For four consecutive years he had seen his title hopes go a-glimmering during the holiday season. Now, in 1970, right after Christmas, Dan Reeves wielded the ax. Our Rams had been eliminated from the playoffs on the final day of the season, and now George's stormy five-year relationship with Reeves would come to an end.

More than football fans are aware, losing the Rams job was an agony for George. Until the very end he had hoped some deliverance would keep him at the helm. Perhaps the team would be sold. Reeves had come close on one occasion to consummating a sale. Perhaps Reeves, now suffering through the final stages of a terminal illness, would, in a moment of magnanimity, acknowledge that George, indeed, represented the wave of the future.

George had accomplished much in his five years as head coach of the team. During the 11 seasons prior to George's arrival in Los Angeles, the Rams had been consistent losers. A procession of coaches had come and gone. Attendance, once tops in the NFL, had nosedived. George changed all of that, and he did it immediately. In his first season there the Rams broke .500. Over the next four years they compiled an impressive record, including several playoff appearances. Attendance jumped swiftly with each succeeding year.

Quickly and decisively, George resolved the long-existing handwringing over who would be the starting quarterback. He announced that Roman Gabriel would the No. 1 man. He never wavered from that decision, and Roman blossomed swiftly into one of the top signal callers in the NFL.

George put together the Rams' Fearsome Foursome, and he changed the face of defensive football in the league. By virtue of brilliantly executed trades he further strengthened the team, and he had the Rams closing in on the dominance the Green Bay Packers had maintained over all rivals during the 1960s.

Good deeds are a delight, except when they are founded on heresy. That George wanted to trade for good, experienced players was all right, but he stepped on too many toes when he determined that the trade bait he'd use would be the Rams' draft choices. Reeves had pioneered the scientific approach to personnel scouting in the NFL. As a result, the Rams had surpassed other teams for many years in their ability to evaluate and ferret out pro talent from the college ranks.

Reeves loved his system; he loved his scouts; he loved his creation. George cast it all aside like a broken chinstrap. He moved the coaching offices and practice facilities to suburban Long Beach, 30 freeway-packed miles away from the scouts and the front office people. He wanted to get away from their influence, and he wanted the players to be away from Hollywood.

George felt that the other teams had all caught up in their collegiate personnel scouting methods and were now doing as thorough a job as the Rams. He wanted an advantage, and his philosophy was simple: Rookies make mistakes. In order to win you must minimize mistakes. Let the other teams season the players and then, at this point, feed their insatiable desire for more draft choices by giving them ours in exchange for the finished products.

Because I never met or communicated with Dan Reeves, I cannot say whether he was capable of bending, but I do know how George felt about compromise. He felt that there was a definite place for it, so long as it is the other fellow who is doing the compromising. George held our personnel department in low regard, and in turn they had disdain for him. When he took the team operations to Long Beach, all the front office people viewed it as an affront, and the rift between them and George widened even more. When George was fired, they held a party back at their headquarters location in celebration of the event.

Despite the blandishments George had been receiving from other clubs and despite his abrasive relationship with the front office, he still desired intensely to remain as coach of the Rams. George wanted to build his dynasty to rival that of Vince Lombardi's Packers. He harbored no doubt that those goals to which he had devoted himself during the past five years were now within reach. Now his adversaries were raising the triumphant toast back in the downtown offices. Not having won the power struggle added even more to George's torment.

The Rams had given all of the coaches a turkey and a bottle of champagne on the day before Christmas. A few days later they gave us our pink slips. George would have to look elsewhere for the spirit of Christmas. He may not have known it then, but his best days lay ahead. Mine, too.

It was the end of another football season, and, as usual, newly created NFL head coaching job openings abounded. Several of the teams in the league were interested in signing George as their new head man, and after he had been let go by the Rams, George took several weeks evaluating his opportunities and negotiating with prospective new employers. Finally, he narrowed his thinking down to a choice between the Packers and the Redskins. Ironically, these were the two teams where Vince Lombardi had left his indelible mark.

One day, while George was still seeking to arrive at a decision, I received a telephone call from Al Davis, the managing partner of the

Oakland Raiders. Al invited me to visit Oakland so that we could discuss the possibility of my joining the Raiders' coaching staff. The Raiders were a strong team, well run, and located on the West Coast, which appealed to me, and so I was interested in the prospects of working for them. Besides, I did not know for certain, at that time, exactly what George's plans were. I telephoned George and told him that I would be going to Oakland for an interview, and he asked that I not make any commitments until I spoke with him again.

When my plane arrived in Oakland, coach John Madden met me, and we spent the remainder of the day visiting with each other. John explained to me that they expected an opening to occur on their staff within the next three weeks and that if I could afford to wait, he would like to have me fill that vacancy should it actually develop. There were now two jobs I *might* have, but none that I could count on with certainty.

Approximately one week after I had returned from my trip to Oakland, George telephoned me with the news that he had just accepted the position as head coach of the Redskins. He would like to meet with me the following day, he said, and he stressed again that I not take any other job until I could speak further with him.

The next morning Boyd Dowler and I met with George at a coffee shop in nearby Redondo Beach. George showed up for that meeting shortly after he had finished his daily jogging workout. He was wearing a baggy, stained, gray sweatsuit, and he had a soggy towel draped around his neck. He was still perspiring from his exercise, and he hadn't yet shaved that day, but he was ready to talk business.

During our discussions a matronly waitress, obviously not a knowledgeable football fan, came to our table wanting to know if any of us was a man named George Allen. George said, "Yes," and asked why she had inquired. She studied his unkempt appearance with ill-concealed disdain before responding.

"There is some joker on the phone who says he's President Nixon, and he'd like to talk with you. Ha! Ha!" she said. (George had once coached at Whittier College, President Nixon's alma mater, and they had come to know each other well.)

The call was indeed from the president, who was calling to congratulate George. Ha! Ha!

During our meeting at the coffee shop, George told both Boyd and me that he would like to have us come onto his staff with the Redskins, and although my inclination was to accept immediately, I felt that I wanted to tell Al Davis before officially accepting George's offer. George graciously allowed me that courtesy but said that he would need to know by the next morning whether I would be coming to Washington.

That evening while I was at home speaking to a friend of mine on the telephone, the operator interrupted my conversation to tell me that she had an emergency call for me. I waited with apprehension for her to put it through to me, and when I took that "emergency call," I found it was from George. He spoke to me about the many advantages that awaited us all in Washington, and he also quoted a salary figure that was more attractive than the one we had discussed earlier in the day.

I went to bed that night feeling strongly that I would be going to Washington, but the clincher in helping me to make that decision occurred as I was lying in bed about 5:15 a.m. Our windows began to shake, knick-knacks tumbled off of our shelves, chandeliers swayed, our furniture began to bounce across the floor, and our dog ran around in circles while howling piteously. A major earthquake had struck Long Beach. Someone was trying to tell me it was time to leave California.

At 8 a.m. I called Al Davis, and, after thanking him for his consideration, I told him that I would be going to Washington with George. Next, I called George with the same news.

"That's great, Marv," he said. "Can you be there in three days?"

I could. And I was.

CHAPTER 13

Mr. Allen Comes to Washington

For every working moment during the previous three weeks we, the new Redskins coaches, had painstakingly dissected every shred of information detailed in the large red- and gold-bound volumes that the scouting staff had prepared. There was a separate book for each position, and each book contained the exhaustive reports that had been compiled on all of those who were eligible for the draft in 1971.

The walls of the large room that served as our draft day headquarters were magnetized, and two of those walls were covered completely with hundreds of one-inch by three-inch cards containing the name of a player, his size, school, position, IQ score, and his scouting grade. On one of these two walls the names and the information were listed under position with the highest-ranked player's card at the top and the lowest-ranked man. The second wall displayed the exact same names and information except that all the player's cards now were shown in grade order irrespective of their positions.

These two methods of organizing for the draft allowed us to see how a player measured up against the other draft candidates at his position, as well as how highly regarded he might be as an NFL prospect without our interjecting position considerations. Some teams, for instance, might be so intent upon filling a dire need at running back that they would forego choosing a linebacker who had a higher grade. Maybe they already had a sufficient linebacking corps. Then again, maybe they'd be passing up the next Dick Butkus. There are many nuances to consider on draft day.

Walls No. 1 and No. 2 exhibited the information necessary for our draft preparations. Walls No. 3 and No. 4 were used to display draft results. Once the process began, and as each pick was announced, one of the cards for the player selected would be transferred to the third wall. That wall had 12 columns—one for each round—and so, by studying the list as it developed, you could see exactly where a player had been chosen. On the fourth wall there were 26 columns, one for each team. Upon his being selected, the player's second card (from wall No. 1 or No. 2) would be moved so that it would then be placed in the column headed by the NFL team that drafted him.

This procedure allowed us, during the course of the draft and at its conclusion, to see on wall No. 3 the round in which each player was drafted, and on wall No. 4 the team that had picked him.

It was 6:30 a.m. on draft day when George hurried off the elevator and whirled through the lobby of the Mayflower Hotel. From the bounce in his step and the gleam in his eyes you would not have guessed that he had had but two hours' sleep. Not that George had been hitting the nightspots. Heaven forbid!

At 4:00 a.m. George had completed a series of phone calls that had consumed his time since early the evening before. In fact, for most of the time the coaches spent in preparation, George had been on the telephone. Now, within the next few hours, the members of our staff were to learn that while we slumbered, George had engineered what he was to refer to later as his "Brink's job."

As George sped toward the lobby exit, the hotel doorman recognized him.

"Hey, Coach Allen," he called out. "Could I shake your hand and wish you good luck? I've been a Redskins fan all my life, and I'm really looking forward to big things from you."

George stopped so quickly that I thought he'd been clotheslined by Ray Nitschke. He grabbed the man's hand.

"By golly [strong words for George]! You are going to see a great team. And I mean this year. Do you know where I'm heading right now?" Before the doorman could even arch an eyebrow, George answered his own question. "This morning the draft begins."

"Coach, I sure hope we get some good players for a change," the doorman said. "The last good No. 1 draft choice we had here was Charley Taylor, and that was way back in 1964."

The man knew his Redskins.

"This year we're going to get a truly outstanding No. 1," George bubbled. "You watch who we pick. You just watch now! It'll be the best pick the Redskins ever made. I promise you that."

And then, like Jerry Rice on a quick post pattern, George was through the revolving door, out on the street, churning resolutely through the chill, dark January morning.

All of our coaches gathered in the office of Tim Temarario, the Redskins' director of player personnel. Tim manned the telephone that kept us in constant communication with the team representatives at the draft headquarters in New York City.

The Redskins were ready. Bring on the draft!

George did not like drafts. He preferred winds—*trade winds.* I have often read that trade winds are usually mild, but just 15 minutes before the 1971 draft was scheduled to begin, George blew into our meeting room and unleashed some high-velocity "trade winds" of his own.

"Men, a few hours ago I concluded a trade with the Los Angeles Rams," he said. And then he paused. This was going to be slow. He was going to savor once again the delight he had experienced in executing his first player deal as the new boss of the Redskins. "We have secured Diron Talbert from Los Angeles."

He stopped, but no one spoke.

"Also, Jack Pardee," he continued.

Again, a pause. Again, silence.

"And Myron Pottios—and Maxie Baughan."

You could have heard a jaw drop. George waited. He waited until he sensed that someone else was about to speak, and then, drawing his breath in sharply, he continued with his roll call.

"Besides that, we will get Jeff Jordan and Tommy Mason. And in addition to Diron, and Jack, and Myron, and Maxie, and Jeff, and Tommy, we also traded for John Wilbur."

No one dared to interrupt. No sense breaking the string now.

Finally, George asked, "Well, what do you think of the deal?"

Defensive line coach Lavern Torgeson asked the question on everyone's mind, "What do we give up in return?"

Four of the Rams' defensive starters would now be coming to Washington. The three starting linebackers—Baughan, Pardee, and Pottios—had playing experience that totaled more than 30 years. Of the Rams' Fearsome Foursome, Diron Talbert had been the youngest. He was just 26 years old, and he had five solid seasons in the league under his belt. He had speed, agility, spirit, and leadership qualities. In 1970, he had been the Rams' leader in sacking opposing quarterbacks, surpassing both Deacon Jones and Merlin Olsen in that department. John Wilbur was a starting guard, and he was destined to play a vital role as a starting lineman during several of the glory years that lay ahead for the Redskins. Tommy Mason, at one time a premier running back, may have had his best years behind him, but he could still perform well. He was an error-free type of player, who could enter a game in crucial situations. Tommy was smart, and his influence would be invaluable in helping us install the new system that the Redskins were going to have to learn quickly. Perhaps the least known player who came to us in the exchange was Jeff Jordan. George was always alert, when negotiating a trade, for players who could fulfill a specific function for us and who the other team would throw in as part of the deal in order to consummate the agreement. Jeff was listed as a running back, but his talent in that area was limited. He had been a standout member of the kick coverage teams, however, and he became a dominant performer for the Redskins' kicking game units. The Rams needed receivers and running backs. It couldn't be possible—could it?—that Charley Taylor or Larry Brown had been sacrificed.

We all waited for George's reply to Lavern's question.

"We will send them Marlin McKeever [a linebacker] *and* our first-, third-, fourth-, sixth-, and seventh-round draft choices," he said.

Our secretary sprinted out the door in order to call the paramedics, because several of our scouts were hyperventilating.

Later that day, George traded our fifth-round choice to the Packers for the playing rights to Boyd Dowler. Although Boyd was a coach, the Packers had still retained his playing rights. Boyd was a player-coach for us during the next two years, and he turned in some clutch performances when our starting receivers went down with injuries.

George still wasn't finished. Before the day was over he began to barter away future draft choices. He traded a high 1972 pick to the Rams in a deal that brought their starting strong safety, Richie Petibon, to our team. We now had half of the Rams' starting defensive unit, because their weak safety, Eddie Meador, had retired.

Most of the Rams players for whom George had traded were old, but he knew the men he was getting. All of them played with distinction for the Redskins. Jack Pardee, at age 35, had his best year in professional football with the Redskins in 1971. The three linebackers who came to us in that trade provided the knowledge and the leadership we would need in installing George's complex defensive schemes.

There would be many more trades for us before we went to training camp in July, but on this February day, when George had brought in a bunch of aging veterans, he also brought us the makings of a championship team. Most of the other teams scoffed at what George had wrought that day, and derisively, they began referring to us as "The Over the Hill Gang." It was a name we would bear proudly.

It had been a momentous two days at the draft table for the Redskins. As the final round drew to a close, George began to glow as he assessed what had been accomplished during the previous 48 hours.

"Men," he said, "we are going to have a celebration, and it's on me."

He sent out for ice cream and cookies.

On draft day alone, George had acquired nine experienced NFL players, all of whom would play well for the Redskins. He had only just begun, however. By the time we began training camp in July, George had traded away 20 draft choices—current and future—adding a total of 18 veteran players by virtue of those dealings. Our linebacker corps had been restructured completely on the first day of the draft, and on that day, also, with the acquisition of Diron Talbert, George had initiated the process of renovating the Redskins' front four. Washington's defensive line had been dismally vulnerable for many years. After reviewing films from the preceding season, our coaches had felt that only Bill Brundidge, the club's first draft choice in 1970, and Manny Sistrunk had the ability to play on a winning team. George went to work on correcting that problem.

In mid-spring we traded a future No. 1 draft pick to the Buffalo Bills in exchange for 10-year veteran defensive end Ron McDole. McDole had been an All-Pro selection two years earlier, but an injury and his being overweight had contributed to his having had a poor season in 1970. The Bills felt that at age 31, McDole would not bounce back. They accepted the draft choice gladly. George gambled on his own abilities to convince others to do what was needed to succeed. Apparently, he succeeded in convincing Ron, who reported to training camp at 265 pounds, down from a previous 295. Ron played eight more years of professional football, all of them with the Redskins. He was a mainstay among that group of defenders who, although they did not take on the catchy mantra of Fearsome Foursome, represented the second coming of those great front fours coached by George.

Today's NFL rules require that a player's status in regard to free agency be made public. In the early 1970s, however, the terms of a player's contract were kept confidential, and therefore, few people outside the Jets organization were aware that their giant defensive end, Verlon Biggs, had played out his option in 1970. George knew it, however, and he wooed Verlon vigorously, eventually signing him to a contract. The Redskins' woeful front four had been transformed during those hectic months leading up to the beginning of training camp. Talbert, McDole, and Biggs joined our two promising young players, Brundidge and Sistrunk, to give us a defensive line superior to any other in the NFL. The Redskins had allowed their opponents a total of 300 or more points during 15 of the 16 seasons prior to George's arrival in Washington. In 1971 we would give up just 190 points.

During the 1971 draft, the Saints exercised their first-round pick by choosing a highly coveted quarterback, Archie Manning, from the University of Mississippi. They felt that their incumbent quarterback, Billy Kilmer, had come to the end of his career. Billy was battered physically from having played with a weak Saints team. He lacked speed, and he threw a wobbly ball. The Saints cleared the way for Manning, and they traded Billy to us for linebacker Tom Roussel, who, following our acquisition of three starting linebackers from the Rams, no longer figured in our plans. Chalk up another addition to the "Over the Hill Gang" engineered by that loco hombre George Allen.

During staff meetings in the spring of 1971, George would constantly comment, "We've got to trade for one more good veteran player."

As soon as he'd make such a trade, he'd then want "one more." One player whose services he coveted was wide receiver Roy Jefferson of the Steelers. Jefferson was an extremely talented athlete who was considered by the Steelers' staff to be an attitude case. Shortly before training camp, George told us that the probability of our being able to bring Roy Jefferson to Washington in 1971 was about as likely as having *Thomas* Jefferson making such an appearance. Five days later he pulled off the trade, and now, with Charley Taylor and Jefferson as our starting receivers, we had the most talented duo in the NFL.

George served as head coach of the Redskins for seven years. During that time he never had a first-round draft choice. Only twice during that seven-year span were the Redskins able to pick earlier than the fifth round. In 1972, our first selection did not occur until the eighth round. Almost all of the draft choices that the Redskins lacked during the 1970s had been blown away by the unrelenting trade winds that whistled through Redskins Park in the spring of 1971.

The Redskins' kicking teams in the year prior to our arrival had been the poorest in the NFL. They had ranked last in kickoff coverage, last in punt returns, and next to last in punt coverage. After George asked me to study what we needed most to improve our kicking teams, I gave him a list of our four most important requirements:

An outstanding punt return man.
A good long snapper for punts.
We needed to change punters.[1]
Time to practice the kicking game.

George went to work. He asked me to study all of the kick return men in the league and then bring my findings to him. When I reported that Alvin Haymond of the Rams and Speedy Duncan of the Chargers were the two best, he picked up his reliable telephone. Within a few weeks we had traded for Speedy. It would take until the following year for us to get Alvin, but George eventually swung that deal, also, giving the Redskins the most prolific kick return duo to ever play the game. Speedy is the only player in pro football to have led the AFL and then the NFL in punt returns *and* kickoff returns.

There was a reserve lineman with the Rams named George Burman, who had done the long snapping for us. Burman had retired after the 1970 season, however. That didn't stop George. He sent yet another draft choice—where did he get it?—to the Rams for the rights to Burman. Within a week Burman was a Redskin, and during the next two years he was not only our long snapper but another outstanding member of a hard core kicking team.

We decided early that Mike Bragg, whose punts were not as long as Pat Richter's, would be our punter. Why? Bragg's operation time was much quicker, and he boomed skyscrapers. We were not going to get any punts blocked, and we were not going to have any returned for long gains. In 1970 the Redskins had allowed 450 yards in punt returns. In 1971 we allowed a *total* of just 45 yards. That would still stand as an NFL record today, except that our Redskins shattered that mark the next year by giving up a mere *27 yards* during the season. The longest punt return against us in all of 1972 was *eight yards*!

Finally, when it came to getting sufficient practice time allotted for our kicking teams, I harbored no concerns. George was convinced that the kicking game was truly as important as offense and defense, and so he provided equal drill time. Besides that, George relished every opportunity he had to extend the length of our practice sessions.

1. Pat Richter punted for excellent average, but his kicks were too low, inviting those long returns that had plagued the 1970 Redskins. Also, his kicking mechanics were slow, and it is difficult for a tall man such as Pat to speed it up.

If George was committed to using veteran players, the same was true in regard to the coaches he enlisted to work for him. When our Washington coaching staff was formed it included three men who had formerly been head coaches in the NFL—Charley Winner at St. Louis, Clive Rush at New England, and Charlie Waller at San Diego. Our Redskins' staff also included Lavern Torgeson, who was destined to make several Super Bowl appearances with the Redskins and the Rams. Boyd Dowler, our receivers coach, later became an offensive coordinator with the Eagles and then the Buccaneers. Ralph Hawkins, the defensive backfield coach, eventually served as a defensive coordinator for the Giants. And, of course, there was the incomparable Joe Sullivan, who became the general manager of the St. Louis Cardinals.

Joe Sullivan's finest work was accomplished during our first spring in Washington. When we first arrived there, we found that there were no adequate practice or meeting facilities.[2] The Redskins' offices were in downtown Washington, while practices were conducted five miles away at RFK Stadium.

George approached team owner Edward Bennett Williams with the idea that we build our own up-to-date practice facility on the outskirts of the city. In EBW, George would find an owner who was as far ahead of the rest of the league as George was himself. After some concern about expenses, EBW agreed that we should go full speed ahead within certain budgetary limitations. The idea had been George's, the authority for pursuing the venture had come from EBW, but the job fell to Joe Sullivan.

When our team arrived at our new practice facility at the conclusion of training camp, workmen were putting the finishing touches on the sign that would hang outside Redskins Park. A new modern building, housing offices, locker rooms, trainer's quarters, film rooms, team meeting rooms, press rooms, rooms for the scouting department, and rooms for the business office stood, gleaming and ready for the "Over the Hill Gang." Two perfectly graded practice fields—one grass and one Astroturf—lay side by side, just outside the locker room doors. An attractive tartan-surface track circled one of the fields. Around the entire complex a high red and gold fence assured privacy and secrecy. Sturdy film towers had been erected, and a wide smooth asphalt access road led from the freeway right up to the spacious paved parking lot.

---

2. When the squad broke down for their daily position meetings, they would have to find any nook or cranny or broom closet available. Practices were held on the stadium field where the grass became worn away, thereby rendering the surface undesirable for both practice and for games.

George's vision, EBW's generosity and farsightedness, and Joe's organizational genius had combined to build the NFL's first full-time practice and office complex. It had taken centuries for thousands of slaves to build Egypt's pyramids. Joe could have done that all alone over a Fourth of July weekend.

Building of this facility helped contribute to EBW's thoughts about George when he commented, "We gave George Allen an unlimited budget, and he's already exceeded it."

By June 1 each year all players notebooks are prepared, the draft is behind you, your rosters are set, and all plans for the season are ready. Once a coach reports to an NFL training camp, he will work an average of 16 hours a day, seven days a week, for the next six or seven months. Our first training camp with the Redskins was an extremely intense one. During the exhibition season George devoted all his energies and attention toward preparing those players whom he had already determined would be in our starting lineup on opening day. I remember standing on the sidelines next to 12-year veteran linebacker Jack Pardee during the final seconds of our sixth preseason contest.[3]

"Do you realize that I have played every stinking down of defense in all six of these games!" Jack said to me.

He wasn't the only one.

No one ever had any days off during one of George's training camps. It was all practices, meetings, and bed checks. Now, you might be thinking that bed check is a tame activity. Not with the "Over the Hill Gang," it wasn't. It was while conducting my first routine bed check that I became aware of man's mortality.

Normal procedure calls for the coach assigned that duty to drop by the room of every player after curfew to see that he is there. Most of the players leave their doors open, and all the coach needs to do is glance inside. When I came to Verlon Biggs's room one night, his door was closed and locked. We had keys, of course, and so I unlocked the door and began to throw it open. The biggest pair of jaws I have ever encountered came flying at me accompanied by a distinctly hostile growl. Fortunately, I was able to slam the door shut, and the creature attached to those teeth thudded heavily against the inside of the portal. Although I thought it had been the Great White Shark, I was later informed that

3. In 1971 there were six games in the preseason rather than the four-game format that prevails today.

it was Verlon's Doberman Pinscher. I had no intention of finding out for myself, and so I just took everyone's word for it.

The next time I had bed check I tapped delicately on Verlon's door and asked politely, "Verlon, are you in there?"

Although I never knew whether the answering growl came from Verlon or his Doberman, I'd go ahead and mark him "present."

♦♦♦♦♦♦♦♦

We began our initial season with the Redskins by playing the first three games on the road. On successive weekends we defeated the Cardinals, the Giants, and the Cowboys. Our No. 1 quarterback, Sonny Jurgensen, had been injured, but Billy Kilmer—that reject from the Saints—had stepped in to lead us to those victories.

We came back to RFK Stadium for our home opener against the Oilers. After the public address announcer had dutifully called off the names of the Oilers, he prefaced our players' entries onto the field by alerting the assembled throng to the momentous introductions he was about to make: "Ladies and Gentlemen—the Washington Redskins!" The din that followed drowned out completely his intonation of each individual player's name. As I stood in the baseball dugout, from which our players exited onto the field, the metal roof began to vibrate from the sound waves that were cascading down from the stands. I was stunned. It sounded to me as if I were standing under the elevated tracks in Chicago's Loop while one of those antiquated trains rumbled overhead. The roar would continue throughout the entire game.

We were well on our way to our fourth consecutive victory of the season, leading the Oilers 22-6 with just three minutes left, when the momentum switched in one stunning play. We were on their 30-yard line when a Houston defensive back picked off a flat pass and returned it 80 yards for a touchdown, narrowing our margin to 22-13. On that play, Charley Taylor, a key man on our onside kickoff defense unit, was shaken up, and he was unable to remain on the field for the certain onside kickoff that the Oilers were about to attempt.

Boyd Dowler, our player-coach who had not played a down, was Charley's backup, and he decided to have some fun with me.

"Boyd! Boyd! Get in there for Charley," I yelled.

The next play was going to be crucial. If the Oilers recovered the onside kickoff and then scored, they'd be only two points behind us. A subsequent field goal could win the game for them.

Boyd did not contribute to my sense of well-being when I heard him say, "Where's my helmet? I can't find my helmet."

The closest man to me was Verlon Biggs, and I jumped up and ripped the helmet off his head. Verlon was six foot six and weighed 285 pounds, but if he had wanted to fight, at that point I had adrenaline on my side. Again, I jumped into the air, deposited Verlon's size eight helmet on Boyd's head, and pushed him out onto the field. His lineup position was supposed to be directly in front of our bench.

The oversized headgear slid down over Boyd's eyes. He pushed it up and squinted at me.

He asked, "Where do I line up?"

George, standing next to me, was not amused by Boyd's question.

"Haven't you told him where to line up?" George screeched.

Given the situation I decided I had better answer Boyd's question first.

"Move up 10 yards, dammit," I yelled.

He moved *back* 10 yards.

"What in the hell is going on out there?" George demanded.

"What in the hell is going on out there?" I bellowed at Boyd. "Move your ass up 20 yards."

Boyd said, "Oh, *up*."

With the bottom of Verlon's helmet resting on his shoulders, Boyd groped his way to his assigned spot just as the Houston kicker bounced the ball directly at him. Boyd gobbled it up as if he were Derek Jeter handling a routine ground ball. Along with the Redskins' cheerleaders I did six aerial somersaults. Out of the corner of my eye I noticed trainers applying salve to the chinstrap burn on Verlon Biggs's throat.

We ran out the clock and won 22-13. If you think George was staring daggers at me when we left the field, you should have seen the looks I directed at Boyd Dowler.

♦♦♦♦♦♦♦♦

On the following Sunday we defeated the Cardinals for the second time that season and became the only team in the NFC to remain undefeated. We were 5-0 and heading to Kansas City, where we would be meeting one of the strongest teams in the AFC.

There always seemed to be someone who telephoned George to tell him how badly our guys were being bad-mouthed by the opponent of the week. The person with whom George spoke on the phone most often was Oakland owner Al Davis. It was at George's urging, I am sure, that on the Tuesday prior to our game against Kansas City, Al was quoted by the wire services as saying that there was no way the Redskins could expect to win against the Chiefs. It would have been very much to the advantage of Al's Raiders for us to win, of course, because they competed in the same division with the Chiefs. Al elaborated by stating that our players were not on the same talent level as Kansas City's.

George came steaming into our team meeting room on Wednesday, and anyone in the room could have written his script for him.

"Did you fellas see what those AFC people are saying about us?" he asked. "Who does that Al Davis think he is degrading you guys like that?"

On he went. It was the same speech, words altered only slightly, that we had all heard from him on many occasions.

The first time one or two of the players believed him. For a while after that they'd tolerate it. Eventually, they wound up just having some fun, play-acting as if they had been supercharged by all those heinous "insults." The prevailing philosophy was perhaps best expressed one day by Diron Talbert when he mused, "George knows that he is BS-ing us; we know that he is BS-ing us; but he doesn't know that we know that he is BS-ing us."

We went into Kansas City with our offensive unit badly banged up. Sonny Jurgensen was on injured reserve. Star running back Larry Brown was hobbled with a puffy knee and wouldn't be effective again for a few more weeks, and Jerry Smith, our starting tight end, was out with an injury.

At halftime we led the Chiefs 17-6, but on the final play of the first half, disaster hit us. Charley Taylor caught a pass for a touchdown on that play, but he also broke his ankle and was lost for the remainder of the season. The Chiefs rallied, and late in the fourth quarter their great wide receiver Otis Taylor made the most spectacular touchdown catch I had ever seen. That proved to be the margin of victory for Kansas City 27-20. We were no longer undefeated.

After the game, Edward Bennett Williams visited us in the stony silence of our locker room. He shook the hand of every player, of every coach, of the trainers, and of the equipment men. He told us it had been a great game and that he was proud of everyone in the organization. I could see that he was feeling the loss as deeply as anyone else, but he could lose like a man, and he helped to provide an atmosphere that would breed winning. We knew we had an owner who was with us when we lost as well as when we won.

After Charley Taylor had been injured in the Kansas City game, "Trader" Allen pulled off another unbelievable deal. He sent three draft choices to the Giants in exchange for Clifton McNeil, a tall, swift, and talented receiver.

We bounced back the following week against the Saints despite committing six turnovers. Our kicking teams helped us carry the day, blocking a punt to set up a touchdown and turning in two long punt returns. Also, our kick coverage units forced and recovered two fumbles. In that game Jack Pardee intercepted three passes, and he was named NFL Defensive Player of the Week for his performance.

In the fourth quarter we were nursing a 17-14 lead when Billy Kilmer gained some satisfaction against his former club by rolling out and then diving into the end zone to culminate the slowest three-yard run I'd seen since I coached the C team back at St. Louis Country Day School. We won 24-14.

Later that evening I ran into Billy at a restaurant in Washington, and we joked about his touchdown run. Billy told me it had been a carryover from his collegiate single wing days at UCLA when he was featured in their "three yards and a cloud of dust" attack. I corrected him.

"Billy," I said, "you were never three yards and a cloud of dust. You always have been, and you still are, three yards and a cloud of sparks."

Against our next opponent, we turned in one of our poorest performances of the year. In this game we turned the ball over *seven* times. With four minutes left to play, the lowly Eagles led us 7-0, and they were lining up on our 20-yard line to attempt the field goal that would have put the game on ice for them. Ron McDole got a hand on the kick, partially blocking it. Speedy Duncan scooped the ball up on our five-yard line and returned it all the way to the Eagles' 40. When I reviewed the films the next day, I counted eight key blocks by the players on our team. As the game clock wound down into its final minute, Billy Kilmer hit Clifton McNeil (that new member of our "Over the Hill Gang") in the end zone, and we escaped with a 7-7 tie.[4] In our last two games we had turned the ball over to our opponents 13 times, and we had still come away with a win and a tie.

During the locker room media conference after our game against Philadelphia, I saw George at his best. One of the writers asked George if had considered replacing Billy during the game with Sonny Jurgensen, who was now healthy and back on the active roster.

Without hesitation George told the assembled media, "I want you to write this down, and I want you to underline it. At no time did I ever consider taking Billy Kilmer out of the game. We are now 6-1-1, and it is Billy Kilmer who has gotten us here."

---

4. There was no overtime rule in effect for the NFL regular season at that time.

To the credit of George, Sonny Jurgensen, and Billy Kilmer, we never had a quarterback controversy in Washington. Both players were magnificent competitors with egos that winning quarterbacks must have, but their regard for each other, combined with George's deft touch in handling them, gave us the NFL's best combination at that position. During the next two seasons they complemented each other perfectly. Each man spent some time out of the lineup because of injuries, and when one was out, the other always rose to the occasion. I never saw a sour look on either man's face or heard a sour word emanate from either one of them.

Emotion can carry a team for only limited periods of time. After eight games our Redskins could no longer respond to exhortation. Key injuries, combined with the drained energies of our players, sent us into a midseason slump. Following the Eagles game we dropped a 16-15 heartbreaker to the Bears in Chicago. They scored the winning point on a weird PAT attempt. The center snap had sailed over the head of the Bears' holder on placekicks, Bobby Douglass. He retrieved the ball and threw a desperate, off-balance pass into the end zone, where Dick Butkus, playing wingback on the PAT protection team, gathered it in for the winning tally.

The following week we returned home to RFK, and amidst the humiliating catcalls of ever-fickle fans, we were shut out by the Cowboys 13-0. Even our kicking teams, which had played so well up to this point, performed disgustingly. We fumbled three Dallas punts. It hurt even more when George told me in the locker room after the game that he had never seen a poorer kicking game performance on a professional football field. What really made me angry was knowing that his bitter words were true.

During the five weeks we had just completed, we had won but one game. What had been a season full of promise in September was turning to ashes in the gloom of late November.

George, however, was at his best when his back was against the wall. There was no surrender in the man. When he spoke at times like those, the true toughness and tenacity of his spirit became manifest. His coaching skills would become sharpened, and his feelings of care for the people with whom he worked were laid bare. It was when George's teams were rolling along successfully that he became fearful that his charges would let up, and in those instances he would cloak the real person he was in a mantle of cute tricks. Eight games into the 1971 season our Redskins were reeling, and George pulled us back together.

Our injuries had also begun to heal. Larry Brown, the NFL's best running back at the time, was ready again for full service. So was Sonny Jurgensen, and he was inserted into the lineup in hopes that he could reenergize our sagging offensive performances of recent weeks. Jerry Smith was healthy again, as well. As a receiver he had no peer among the NFL tight ends. True, we had lost Charley Taylor, but by this time Clifton McNeil had become fully conversant with our system, and Boyd Dowler, also, had played with flashes of his old Green Bay brilliance. We were ready for the stretch run.

We squeaked past the Eagles in Philadelphia 20-13, the winning score coming when Bill Malinchak (still another of George's trade acquisitions) blocked a punt for a score. Then we trounced the Giants at RFK Stadium 23-7. Again, in this game, we blocked a punt for a touchdown. Also, special teams ace Ted Vactor blocked a field goal in that game, and we had a long punt return that set up another score. Walking off the field after the game, George actually smiled at me.

During the postgame ceremonies in our locker room immediately following our victory, I was rendered breathless when the players awarded me the game ball. Later, in the coaches' dressing quarters, George commented to me that it was a rare honor for an assistant coach to be given a game ball. He should know. After the 1963 NFL championship game, the victorious Bears' players had awarded the game ball to one of their assistant coaches. His name was George Allen.

With two games remaining, we needed one more win in order to clinch a berth in the playoffs. Next on our schedule was a Monday night game, nationally televised, in the Coliseum against the Rams. They, too, needed to win in order to keep their playoff hopes alive.

On that windy December night, George enjoyed one of his finest hours as a coach. It was a thrilling action-filled contest that had the spectators in the packed stadium on their feet during most of the game. With four minutes left to play, the score was tied 24-24. The teams had alternated scoring throughout the game, and neither team had commanded more than a four-point lead at any time. Ted Vactor and Ron McDole had each blocked field goal attempts by the Rams. They represented the fifth and sixth field goals we had blocked during that season.

As the clock ticked down to under the four-minute mark, we capped off a long drive with a touchdown plunge, and we forged ahead 31-24. Now we had to hold them. On the ensuing kickoff, Jeff Jordan, one of those former Rams players whom George had acquired by virtue of his "Brink's job" trade on draft day earlier that year, slammed into the kickoff return man on the Rams' eight-yard line, and the ball popped free. We recovered it at their four-yard line, and a few plays later we scored again to assure our 38-24 victory. The Redskins would play in the NFC championship. The last time Washington had appeared in a championship game was in 1945.

We suffered a letdown in our final game of the regular season. We had had to be emotionally high for three straight must-win games. We were coming off of a cross-continental trip after a Monday night game, and we had already clinched a spot in the playoffs. We came out flat against the Browns, and they beat us 20-13. That loss was particularly harmful to our championship hopes because it meant we would not have home field advantage for any of the upcoming playoff games.

We traveled to San Francisco for our first scheduled playoff game, arriving there the day before Christmas. On Christmas Eve, Charley Winner and I were returning to our rooms after dinner, and as we walked through the lobby, a voice called to us from out of the dark lounge.

"Charley! Marv! Can you come in here a minute?"

We recognized the voice; it was Edward Bennett Williams. He was sitting at a small table with another man. EBW did not introduce him, and because of the poor lighting I could not make out his features. His voice sounded familiar, but I was unable to place it. As my eyes became accustomed to the darkness, the man's face came slowly into focus, and I found myself sitting 24 inches across the table from Joe DiMaggio. I couldn't have been more excited if it had been Marilyn Monroe.

Joe was a friend and client of EBW. It was a thrill for me to visit with a boyhood hero of mine, but I am sure I must have bored him with all my talk about the great Yankee teams of the 1930s and early 1940s. "The Yankee Clipper" was very tolerant and responsive, despite undoubtedly having heard similar inanities many times before.

On Christmas, at the team meal, George arranged to have big Manny Sistrunk outfitted in a luxuriant Santa Claus costume. Manny distributed gifts to everyone in the room. He didn't plan to be benevolent the next day, however. On December 26 we would be at Candlestick Park to do battle with the 49ers.

Our defense stopped San Francisco on their first series, and when they attempted to punt, John Jaqua blocked it for us. A few plays later, on a scoring pass from Billy Kilmer to Jerry Smith, we took a 7-0 lead.

At halftime we led 10-3, and then Speedy Duncan opened the second half for us with a sparkling 66-yard kickoff return. We drove to the San Francisco seven-yard line but came up short when they stopped us on a fourth-down-and-inches situation.

Three plays later, John Brodie of the 49ers teamed up with Gene Washington on a 78-yard touchdown pass, tying the score, and on their next possession they scored again to take a 17-10 lead. Curt Knight added a field goal for us, but again San Francisco countered with a touchdown. Going into the fourth quarter we trailed 24-13.

Early in the quarter, Ted Vactor, who was one of our twin safeties on punt defense, returned a punt 48 yards, taking us deep into 49ers territory. We cashed in with a touchdown a few plays after that, pulling to within four points of our opponent. That's the way it ended, however. San Francisco had won 24-20. Once again, Christmas had eluded George. In his postgame press conference, George voiced a sentiment he had often expressed to our coaching staff.

"Losing," he said, "is like dying."

The hated Cowboys marched through the playoffs, climaxing their season with a 24-3 Super Bowl victory over the Dolphins. It would be a year plus five days until we would gain vengeance on Dallas.

CHAPTER 14

Hail to the Redskins

Our 1972 Redskins were much stronger than we had been in 1971. For one thing, we did not suffer nearly as many injuries. Charley Taylor remained healthy throughout the entire season, and he teamed up with Roy Jefferson and Jerry Smith, giving us an extremely diversified passing attack. Larry Brown had his most productive year as a pro, rushing for more than 1,200 yards during the 14-game season. At fullback, Charley Harraway ran well and blocked superbly in functioning as the perfect complement for Larry. Sonny Jurgensen and Billy Kilmer were the triggermen for this talented group of runners and receivers.

In addition, we had the most opportunistic defense in the NFL. We led the league in forcing opponents' turnovers *and* in sacking opposition quarterbacks. And our kicking units—that magnificent bunch of castaways who hadn't been wanted by other teams—played at a level never equaled on a gridiron before or since.

In that magical 1972 season, we led the NFL in punt returns and in punt coverage. We led in kickoff returns and in kickoff coverage. The average starting point for our opponents after our kickoffs was their *17*-yard line. Our placekicker, Curt Knight, had mastered the towering kickoff, which came back down to earth around the other team's five-yard line. No kicking off through the end zone for us so that they could start at their 20-yard line. Our ambitions were loftier than that. We wanted to nail them deeper in their territory. We wanted them to cough up the ball when our swarming horde of coverage men rattled the teeth of their return man. Our kickoff coverage units forced and recovered six fumbles during the 1972 season.

With all of these eye-popping statistics there was one record set that was more remarkable than any of the others. In 1972 the Washington Redskins blocked *15* kicks—four punts and 11 PATs or field goal attempts. Many observers feel that blocking kicks is just a matter of some fleet-footed athlete charging wildly at the kicker. If that is the way you are going to coach it, you are in trouble. Those helter-skelter kick rushers are going to run into the kicker too often, thereby allowing their opponent to keep possession. Even on those occasions when they do not rough the kicker, they will seldom succeed in blocking the kick and will probably be leaving themselves vulnerable to a fake punt.

If, as I still contend, coaches tend to overlook the importance of the overall kicking game, that neglect becomes even more pronounced when it involves the lack of attention given to blocking kicks. Teams could be blocking 20 kicks a year if they would devote the resources that they currently commit to rushing the passer or to devising pass patterns. If they'd teach the proper techniques, they could rush kicks with as little likelihood of roughing the kicker as there now is of roughing the passer on a pass rush.

Aside from the strategy involved in determining when to try to block a kick and aside from the tactical plan that is devised in attempting to block each individual kick, there are essential techniques that *must be taught* and *must be drilled.* There is no shortcut. There are techniques for lining up, techniques for getting off on the snap, techniques for getting to a specific landmark at a specific time, techniques for assuring that the assigned kick blocker makes contact with the ball, techniques for what to do after the kick has been blocked, and techniques for how to convert to setting up a punt return if the attempt to block the kick has not succeeded. Some of the best returns we had in Washington came after a failed attempt to block a kick.

There is another noteworthy advantage. Once an opponent's kicker becomes aware that he is facing a team with the intent and the ability to block kicks, that kicker is out of his comfort zone. His confidence and his mechanics suffer.

Aside from time and attention, there is one other vital ingredient required if a team is going to have an outstanding kicking game: players with big hearts who believe that their efforts are contributing as much to the outcome of their games as are the performances of the offensive and defensive players. We had men of that caliber in abundance with the Redskins. Most likely none of them will ever be inducted into the Pro Football Hall of Fame, but I think of them every time some referee blows his whistle and drops his arm to signal the opening kickoff of a football game: Mike Fanucci, Mack Alston, Speedy

Duncan, Mike Bragg, Rusty Tillman, Alvin Haymond, Jeff Severson, Paul Laaveg, Mike Hull, John Jaqua ("The Wild Angel"), Herb Mul-Key, Bob Brunet, Curt Knight, Dave Kopay, Terry Hermeling, Jeff Jordan, Jimmie Jones, Bill Malinchak, George Burman, Hal McClinton, and Ted Vactor. They were tougher than 14 miles of detour. You won't see the likes of them ever again.

One time, when our offensive line was decimated by injuries, George Allen announced at our team meeting that Paul Laaveg and Terry Hermeling would be moved into the starting lineup, Paul at guard and Terry at tackle. When the meeting broke up and I came out of the room, I found both men waiting just outside the door. They backed me into a corner, and they told me—they didn't ask me—that they were not to be taken off any of the kicking teams.

There were also some starters from our offensive and defensive teams who made meaningful contributions to some of our kicking units. These included linebacker Chris Hanburger, defensive backs Mike Bass and Brig Owens, tight end Jerry Smith, offensive guard John Wilbur, and defensive end Ron McDole. Their performances and their attitudes helped expand still more the achievements of our magnificent kicking teams in Washington.

It had amused me during the years when I was coaching to find that every member of the coaching staff fashioned himself an instant expert on kickers. We concluded every practice by having our field goal kicker attempt several field goals against an all-out rush. Because the other coaches would have finished their on-the-field duties, they would form in a semicircle and stand about five yards behind placekicker Curt Knight. The pressures Curt faced on Sundays must have been inconsequential compared to the unsolicited comments he received from this self-appointed Star Chamber.

"He looked up too soon," Mike McCormack observed.

"His plant foot was too far to the left," Torgy pointed out.

"He's hurrying too much," Boyd said.

"His trajectory is too low," Ted Marchibroda opined.

"He's got the toe of his kicking shoe tied too tightly," Charley Winner noted.

"Curt, you're not concentrating," George told him.

How the hell could he?!

Actually, the other coaches on our staff did help our kicking game prosper in many ways. There were numerous times, when we discussed personnel moves, that they agreed to keep a player at the position they were coaching whose contribution to our kicking game was the primary asset that player had to offer. Also, at my behest, Mike McCormack, our offensive line coach, was the man who installed our PAT and field goal protection techniques. We never had one blocked.

♦♦♦♦♦♦♦♦

Monday night. Metropolitan Stadium. The Redskins versus the Vikings. There was no place else on earth where I'd rather have been!

Early in the game we set the pattern for our season when Bill Malinchak blocked the Vikings' first punt and we took it in for a touchdown. It was a tight battle the rest of the way, and on the last play of the first half Ted Vactor blocked a field goal attempt by Minnesota's Fred Cox. That proved to be the margin of victory. We won 24-21. The cover of that week's *Sports Illustrated* showed a picture of Bill Malinchak—his figure blurred from the speed of his movement, the lights of the stadium reflected in sparkling bursts off of his shining helmet—at the exact moment his hands made contact with the punted ball. I've still got that one framed and displayed.

After the Vikings' game we continued to win. And win. And win. With two games still remaining in the regular season, we had clinched the Eastern Division championship. Not only that, we had assured ourselves of home field advantage for all playoff games. Our record was 11-1, and even that one loss had come as the result of a disputed call by an official. We had been trailing the Patriots 24-21, when, in the waning moments of the game, Bill Malinchak had blocked a Pat Studstill punt out around the Patriots' 25-yard line. The problem was that Bill had blocked it *too* well, because the ball flew off his hands and went bouncing swiftly along the artificial turf toward the back of the New England end zone. Bill chased it down and fell on the ball just as he and it went rolling across the back restraining line.

The referee had been unable to keep up with the lightning-like action, and he was still 15 yards away when he had to determine whether Bill had gained control early enough to rule it a touchdown. He made a quick decision and signaled that a safety had occurred. That gave us two points, and we lost 24-23. Our film review the following day showed that Bill had captured the ball before crossing the back line of the end zone, and that it should have been ruled a touchdown. Chalk up another argument for why the NFL eventually instituted the use of the instant replay camera.

Sonny Jurgensen had been our starting quarterback at the beginning of the year, and he directed us to our early successes. Seven games into our schedule, against the Giants at Yankee Stadium, Sonny limped off the field. He had torn his Achilles tendon, and he was lost for the remainder of that season. Billy Kilmer stepped in, and he continued to keep us on the winning track. George signed Sammy Wyche, a recent cut of the Bengals, to be our backup signal caller.

On week 13 we played the Cowboys in Dallas, and with our divisional title assured, we suffered our first letdown of the season. By halftime the Cowboys had taken a commanding 28-0 lead. We rallied in the second half, and by early in the fourth quarter we had narrowed their lead to 31-24. We were on the march for what could have been the tying touchdown when a dog ran out onto the field from under the Cowboys' bench. No one was able to coax the animal to the sidelines, and so Joe Sullivan, convinced that the timing of the dog's entry onto the scene was a bit of Dallas skullduggery, took matters into his own hands.

He sprinted onto the field determined to capture the mutt. For five minutes Joe and the dog cavorted around Texas Stadium, where Joe missed more tackles than our entire team had in the first half. Richie Pettibon, standing along the sidelines next to me, enjoyed the spectacle as much as the 60,000 paying customers.

"I'll give eight to five and take the dog," Richie said. I declined the offer.

Finally, the dog trotted off the field. Our drive petered out; Dallas added a field goal, and they won 34-24. After the game, Joe was the first guy on the trainer's table.

It had been an important win for the Cowboys because it assured them of the wild card playoff berth. If we both were to win our first-round games in the playoffs, we would meet again—this time for the NFC championship, winner goes to the Super Bowl.

Our final game of the year against the Bills had no bearing on the playoff picture. Reluctantly, George decided to rest our veteran players so that they would be fresh and healthy for the postseason games that were to begin one week after our matchup against the Bills. With a contingent of backup players going all the way against Buffalo, we lost 24-17. We had finished with an 11-3 record, the best mark in the NFC.

◆◆◆◆◆◆◆◆

On the day before Christmas, the Central Division champion Packers came to RFK Stadium. They had been perennial championship contenders, but this was the first appearance in the playoffs for the Redskins in almost 30 years. Less than a month earlier our two teams had met on this same field, and we had been fortunate to come away with a bitterly contested 21-16 victory. Dan Devine's Packers featured the most powerful running attack in the NFL. Running backs John Brockington and MacArthur Lane had been the key men leading the way as Green Bay finished the regular season with a 10-4 record.

George devised a special five-down linemen defensive front for that game, completely frustrating the Packers' running schemes. Brockington, who had rushed for more than 1,000 yards during the season, was held to a mere nine yards on 13 carries. They were limited to a season-low 78 yards on the ground, and their total yardage for the game (rushing and passing combined) was a scant 211 yards, the lowest single-game production in Packers history up to that time.

We played a very conservative game ourselves. Billy Kilmer threw just 14 passes, but one of them was a 32-yard touchdown strike to Roy Jefferson in the second quarter. It was the only touchdown scored in that game. Curt Knight connected on three field goals for us, and our combination of stifling defense and ball-control offense (Larry Brown rushed 25 times for 101 yards) provided us with what we needed in order to gain a 16-3 victory over the Packers.

Later that day, in San Francisco, the Cowboys defeated the 49ers 30-28. The NFC championship would be decided New Year's Eve at RFK Stadium, where the Cowboys and the Redskins would play against each other for the third time that year. We had each won one of the two previous games.

The kickoff was scheduled for late afternoon on December 31, 1972. It was a dreary, overcast day, and the darkness of the early winter evening was already beginning to settle in when the two teams came onto the field. The air may have been damp and cold, but the atmosphere inside the stadium was festive. The draped bunting, reserved for championship games, hung from the front barriers all around the lower and upper decks. Redskins fans, many of them fortified by New Year's Eve cheer, had shown up with voices set at full throttle.

To George, the Cowboys were not our opponents. They were our enemy. And now they showed up with all their best warriors. Roger Staubach, Bob Lilly, Jethro Pugh, Calvin Hill, Bob Hayes, Duane Thomas, Lee Roy Jordan, Chuck Howley, Mel Renfro, and all the other blue- and white-clad Cowboys entered the arena, accompanied by sonorous waves of boos, but ready for battle against the Redskins.

The first quarter was scoreless. Midway into the second period we edged ahead, 3-0, when Curt Knight booted an 18-yard field goal. During the course of the game, Billy Kilmer would throw just 18 passes, but late in the second quarter he delivered one of them, a 15-yard touchdown toss to Charley Taylor. Dallas surged back, and just before the halftime gun sounded, Toni Fritsch put the Cowboys back in the game with a 35-yard field goal. At the half we led 10-3.

We clung to our precarious lead, staving off several Dallas threats in the third quarter, and the fourth quarter began with the score still 10-3. It had been a brutal, carefully played game up to this point. The battle went on, and with eight minutes left to play we had the ball, third and 10, at the Cowboys' 45-yard line. On the next snap, Charley Taylor sprinted 12 yards downfield and broke toward the sideline. Billy Kilmer pumped his arm as if to throw the ball, and the Dallas cornerback jumped in front of Charley in anticipation of intercepting the pass. Charley planted his inside foot and then pivoted upfield, streaking toward the Cowboys' goal line. Billy lofted the ball perfectly, and Charley grabbed it at the Dallas 20. He raced unmolested into the end zone for his second scoring reception of the day. We led 17-3.

On the ensuing kickoff, our gallant kick coverage unit spilled the Dallas return man on his own 13-yard line. Our defense forced them to punt after three downs, and we took over at midfield. Our drive stalled, but Curt added to our margin by drilling a 39-yard field goal.

Again our kickoff coverage team stopped the Cowboys deep in their territory, this time on the 11-yard line. Again our defense forced them to punt. Again our offense moved into field goal position. And again Curt booted it through from 46 yards out. It was now 23-3 with just four minutes to play.

We weren't finished yet. On the next kickoff, our coverage team dropped the Cowboys' return man at the 14-yard line, and the entire process began again. Three plays. Punt. Short drive. Curt scores on a 45-yard field goal. It was his fourth of the game—a new playoff record.

The noise in RFK Stadium was head-splitting, but when our kick-off coverage band of marauders took the field and lined up in preparation for covering their fourth kickoff in six minutes, the sound level rose and so did every fan in the stadium. For three minutes that magnificent group of kick coverers stood out at our 35-yard line while the ovation grew steadily louder and my heart swelled with pride. Joe Sullivan came over and put his arm around my shoulder, but when we tried to speak to each other, even though we were only inches apart, we couldn't hear over the din that was rocking the old stadium.

Finally, we kicked off, and that fired-up bunch of SOBs made a swarming gang tackle at the Dallas nine-yard line. They left the field to another wild ovation. Four kickoffs! Four tackles inside the 15-yard line! Against the Cowboys! For the NFC Championship!

Our Redskins had displayed football's ideal blend of offense, defense, and kicking. Dallas had gained a trifling 169 yards against our defense. On offense we had controlled the ball for 62 plays as opposed to just 45 for the Cowboys. Billy Kilmer had completed 14 of 18 pass attempts, including two touchdowns, and no one had ever seen the equal of our kickoff coverage team. We had outscored Dallas 26-3. The "Over the Hill Gang" had won the NFC championship.

Earlier in the day, Miami had defeated Pittsburgh 21-17, thereby winning the AFC title. In two weeks we would be meeting the undefeated Dolphins in the Super Bowl at the Los Angeles Coliseum. But on this night we were going to celebrate.

George had arranged a New Year's Eve party following the game for our coaches and wives in the main dining room of the Shoreham Hotel in downtown Washington. Several of the coaches arrived before George did, and we were able to observe other New Year's Eve celebrants as they came into the room in order to join any one of the variety of parties taking place there that night. We saw many of Washington's elite—senators, network news anchors, cabinet members—filter into the dining room, with hardly a soul in the throng paying attention to them as they arrived. When George Allen made his entry, however, everyone in the room joined in the raucous welcome. George led the patrons in a "Three cheers for the Redskins!" George provided the "Hip! Hip!" three times, and the assemblage responded with the lusty "Hoorays!" George was just warming up with that one, because later in the evening he ascended the bandstand, where he led the crowd in singing "Hail to the Redskins." I counted two teetotalers who sang on tune. At midnight, George led a conga line. I wouldn't have been more surprised if I had seen Saddam Hussein doing that.

We might as well have had a good time that night. Beginning the next morning we'd be working 18 hours a day until the Super Bowl.

We spent the first week of preparations for the Super Bowl practicing at our Redskins Park facility. You have got to get the main share of your game plan installed during that first week, because once a team arrives at the Super Bowl site, the unfamiliar classroom and practice arrangements make it more difficult for the players to learn.

On the next to last day of practice in Washington, our team was surprised when a special visitor came onto the practice field just as the day's activities were drawing to a close. For the first time in our two years at Redskins Park, the gate in the fence surrounding the field was flung open while a practice was still in session. President Richard Nixon, along with a sizeable contingent of Secret Service and several photographers, came out onto the field directly toward the huddle of players and coaches clustered around George. "Double-O" began to frisk several of our offensive linemen, either as a precaution or in hopes that his vigilant actions would be noticed by the president and his party.

The president spoke to the team for a few minutes, and as he was about to conclude his remarks, he turned to George and said, "Coach, I'd like to make a suggestion. When you fellows play that game against Miami, you ought to run a reverse to the left with Roy Jefferson carrying the ball."

Our staff had already planned to install that play during the next day's practice, and of course, George had tipped off the president ahead of time so that he might appear sage when addressing the squad. It was a good play to use against the Dolphins because they tended to overpursue. We did run it in the game, with the wide field to our left. It was well conceived, and it was a good call. The only problem was that they nailed us for a 12-yard loss, but that was nothing compared to the number of votes the president lost among the Washington constituency in the next election for having made that ill-fated proposal.

When we boarded the plane for Los Angeles, where we would practice during the week prior to the Super Bowl, George was still admonishing our players about the evil he feared most in California's permissive environment. Distractions! He never specified exactly what he meant by this fearsome term, but at least twice at every team meeting he would stop whatever else he had been saying, lower his voice, and warn once again, "Be careful of those distractions." After a while I began to notice that our players, at random times, would stop short and whirl about to be sure there was no distraction creeping up on them.

During Super Week all of our players and coaches ate our evening meals each day in a special room. The coaches would all sit together around a large circular table where George would take the lead in conducting endless dissertations regarding the day's activities and the next day's practice plans. Often we'd sit there for two or three hours after the players had left. These sessions would not end until finally George decided that we (make that *he*) had talked long enough. Only when he got up and left was the ordeal over.

Toward the end of the week, after he had exhausted every subject, George would sit there pensively for 30 minutes without a word being spoken. On Friday evening, after one long period of silence, he jarred us all away from our own personal thoughts.

"You know, I'd cut off my right arm up to here to win this game. Wouldn't you?"

He illustrated by using the side of his left hand to deliver a karate chop onto his right elbow. When no one answered, he directed his left hand cleaver at a target several inches higher up on his right arm.

"Up to *here.* How about you?"

That didn't seem to win any of us over, either, and so George decided to go all out.

"In fact," he said, "I'd cut off my testicles to win this game!"

We all scrunched over and grimaced a bit, but still no one responded. George got up and stomped out of the room.

Boyd Dowler and I walked out of the room together. Boyd is the only person other than my mother who has regularly addressed me as "Marvin."

"Marvin," he said, "*maybe*—my right arm."

During my film study of Miami's kicking game, I had noticed that Howard Kindig, the player who handled their long-snap responsibilities on punts, had an unusual snapping motion. I found that, in order to generate momentum, he lifted the ball off the ground and suspended it in the air in front of himself for a fraction of a second before he sent it speeding back to the punter. Two of our players, Jimmie Jones and Hal McLinton, devised a technique for flicking at the ball just as Kindig was about to release it. Every day, for the two weeks leading up to the Super Bowl, Jimmie and Hal remained out on the field with me for 30 minutes after our regular practice session had ended in order to sharpen their ability to execute this technique. By game day they had mastered it.

We kicked off to Miami to begin the Super Bowl, and on their first possession they were forced into a punting situation at their 30-yard line. As we had anticipated, Kindig lined up as their long snapper, and as he lifted the ball and hesitated for that split second, Jimmie got a piece of it just as it was being delivered. The ball dribbled back along the Coliseum grass, and one of our players fell on it at the Dolphins' 26-yard line. The referee signaled that it was our ball, first and 10.

The head linesman, however, rushed in to inform the referee that we had interfered with the snap. We argued that our player had remained immobile and on our side of the line of scrimmage until the snapping motion had begun and that the defense is allowed by rule to cross into the neutral zone once the ball moves. The officials then huddled and held a long conference. There were 90,182 fans attending the game and a national television audience watching. If we could succeed, every time Miami punted, in doing what we had done on that particular punt, it would make a shambles of professional football's premier event. The referee instructed us, therefore, that if we interfered with any future snaps, it would cost us an unsportsmanlike conduct penalty every time. It did no good to argue that the rules allowed us to move once the ball had moved. They had made their decision. Possession of the ball was given back to Miami, and the game proceeded from there.

Late in the first quarter, Miami's quarterback, Bob Griese, connected on a 28-yard aerial to Howard Twilley for a touchdown, and the Dolphins took a 7-0 lead. Then in the second quarter, Nick Buoniconti intercepted a Billy Kilmer pass, returning it 32 yards deep into our territory. Jim Kiick then banged it in from the one-yard line, and Miami widened its lead to 14-0.

Our Redskins had been completely ineffective in the first half, but at the outset of the second we mustered a long time-consuming drive, only to have it all go for naught when Curt Knight missed on a short field goal attempt. Midway into the fourth quarter another of our drives ended in frustration when Miami safety Jake Scott intercepted a pass in his end zone and returned it all the way to our 45-yard line.

After that interception, the Dolphins' drive stalled at our 15-yard line, where they lined up for a field goal attempt. There were only three minutes left to play, and a successfully kicked field goal would have ended our last glimmering hopes for pulling the game out.

The snap, hold, and placement all went smoothly for the Dolphins. Garo Yepremian, their fine place kicker, moved forward nimbly and confidently. His foot swung, meeting the ball right on the sweet spot. As a kicking teams coach, a person eventually becomes able to recognize the sound that comes from a football that has been kicked true. This one had that sound. Almost immediately, however, I heard another sound—that unmistakable thump that always accompanies a blocked kick. Our guys had done it again!

The ball bounced onto the grass and then ricocheted directly to Yepremian, and as our 11 defenders closed in on him, Garo spotted an eligible Miami receiver, standing alone in our end zone, waving his hands frantically. Garo threw the ball to him. Well, to be more exact, he *tried* to throw the ball to him. The errant pass attempt slid out of Garo's hand and wobbled about four yards through the air. One of our defensive backs, Mike Bass, snatched it, and along with a convoy of Redskins, Mike sprinted the length of the field for a touchdown. With a little more than two minutes left to play, the score was suddenly 14-7. Now, if we could just find a way to get the ball to Garo one more time!

Miami recovered the onside kickoff that we attempted following our touchdown, but our defensive unit stopped them on three straight plays. When the Dolphins' Larry Seiple punted on fourth down, Bill Malinchak streaked in from our right side and missed blocking it by a quarter of an inch. In the few seconds that remained, Miami was able to keep us bottled up in our territory, and in so doing, they capped their undefeated season with a Super Bowl victory. The feat had never been accomplished before, and it hasn't been equaled since.

Statistically, it had been a very even game. We had a total offensive production of just 228 yards, while Miami registered a modest 253. We had notched 16 first downs to their 12, and we had controlled the ball for 64 plays to their 48. But the score was Miami 14, Washington 7, and they would wear the Super Bowl rings.

When I reflect back even today on Super Bowl VII, I find it ironic that the thing most people recall about that game is Garo Yepremian's ill-fated forward pass. During his career with the Dolphins, Garo became Miami's all-time leading scorer. He kicked 165 field goals—a team record—out of 242 attempts, a 70-percent rate of success. He added 335 successful PAT tries. Yet Garo Yepremian is remembered more for that one freak play in Super Bowl VII than for any of his accomplishments. It's a funny game.

Some people find it easy to ridicule the Garo Yepremians for a misplay. They are the fools, however. There is only one way for a person to assure that he will never make a mistake on the football field—or in any other endeavor, for that matter. How? Don't enter the arena. And that, of course, would be the biggest mistake of them all.

Perhaps the lesson about how perspective on a sport is often warped was best driven home to me on the first day I came to work for the Chiefs in December 1977. As I sat at the emptied desk where my predecessor, Paul Wiggin, had worked for three years, I found just one scrap of paper jammed into the back portion of a lower drawer. It was a cartoon that Paul apparently had clipped from a newspaper at some earlier time. In the cartoon, two bedraggled, weary players of college age were walking crestfallen off the football field after what had obviously been a losing effort. All about them angry alumni were gathered shouting invectives and shaking fists at the two forlorn gridders. The words under the drawing were from one player as he spoke to the other. "Wouldn't it be great if football was just a game?" he asked.

♦♦♦♦♦♦♦♦

On the day after the Super Bowl, George informed me that a few weeks earlier he had received a call from J.I. Albrecht, the general manager of the Montreal Alouettes of the Canadian Football League. J.I. had requested permission to speak with me regarding the head coaching position with the Alouettes. George had told him that it would be all right, but then he had stipulated that J.I. should wait until after our season had been completed. Now, George advised me that if I were interested in the Montreal job, I had his permission to telephone J.I., and I decided that I should at least investigate the situation.

When I reached J.I., a longtime friend of mine, he told me that his call to George had been six weeks earlier, and that the Alouettes, feeling that they had needed to proceed, had progressed to where they were about to offer the position to another candidate. I forgot the matter, but a few days later, J.I. called me back, inviting me to Montreal so that I could meet with him and with team owner Sam Berger.

When I left Los Angeles on a mid-January morning it was 80 degrees. In Montreal, when I arrived, there were two feet of snow on the ground. Because the Celsius scale thermometer didn't mean much to me, I cannot tell you what the temperature was, but—take my word for it—*it was cold!* I spent the day with J.I. and Mr. Berger, and late that evening they offered me the head coaching job.

It had been four years since I had served as a head coach, and I had missed the stimulation of putting all of the pieces together. I missed making the decisions that only a head coach had the authority to make. The experience I had gained in working for and in observing George had been invaluable, and I felt a desire to convert my newly acquired knowledge into action. Also, J.I. was an acknowledged whiz at talent scouting. He knew where to find good players, and he knew how to sign them. I took a deep breath of frigid arctic air, and I accepted the position. Besides, there was something about Sam Berger I thought I was going to like. I never called a shot any better than that one.

My hectic three years working for George were drawing to a close. At times it had been sheer hell, but there had been other times when the ecstasy of victory had made it all worthwhile. I hadn't slept more than five hours a night during those three years. When you work for George, you don't live longer; it just seems longer.

There were many times when our coaches and our players bitched about George and about the needless hours he sometimes wasted so that we rarely saw our families. There were times when we all laughed at him and at some of his transparent utterances. We scoffed upon occasion at the imperial lifestyle George lived—chauffeured limousines and formal White House dinners during the season—while he lectured us on the merits of the Spartan life and the constant vigil we must hold against diversions.

George took great pride in his collection of inspirational signs and quotations. His favorite item in this array was a list of his "Ten Commandments for Success," which he himself had authored. Even Moses would have batted about .300—.400 tops—in complying with those 10 stringent directives. One of the commandments specified all of a person's leisure time should be confined to the four or five hours a night when he slept. One of our coaches composed a three-point summary of those "Ten Commandments for Success," which he maintained embodied the essential features of George's credo:

1. Never have a good time.
2. Never drink anything except milk or eat anything except ice cream.
3. If you spend any time with your family, you *and your family* are not dedicated.

If my observations indicate that George had some quirks, I am sure that some other person can point out many of mine, as well. George's attributes and his human qualities far outweighed his idiosyncrasies. He cared about the individuals who worked for him and who played for him. George was instrumental in helping many of his former assistants get head coaching positions. That includes me. He involved himself in helping players with their personal or health problems.

Everyone who has striven toward a common goal with George had learned the value of hard work, and they learned it first from the examples he set. An association with George taught a person how to win and how to derive great joy from the preparation for winning. George usually won. When he didn't, he started—right then—preparing to win next time.

Another of George's admirable qualities was that he let you know exactly where you stood. He didn't go off half-cocked, but if he believed you had done something nonproductive, he'd tell you straight out, no dancing around the subject. By the same token, George would be lavish in his praise for a job well done. He'd listen to you with an open mind, and when he responded, you wouldn't have to read between the lines. When George said he was going to do something, he did it.

Someone once said to me that George was a genius. He wasn't. He just worked hard and had an indomitable spirit. How come all of the geniuses in this world seem to be football coaches? Every time I read the newspaper or turn on my television, a new coaching genius is being discovered. Perhaps the best definition of a genius that I ever heard was offered by former Buccaneers coach John McKay, "A genius in football coaching is the guy who won last Sunday."

As the years have passed, I have had opportunities, on occasion, to visit with the other assistant coaches who shared with me those glorious years in Washington. When we talk, we forget the discomforts, the lack of sleep, the boredom of endless meetings, and the inane projects that we had been assigned. Instead, we remember the game balls, and "Hail to the Redskins." We remember the "Hip! Hip! Hoorays!" We remember "Hooray for Pat Fischer . . . and Lenny Hauss . . . and Rusty Tillman . . . and all those other 'horses asses.'" Most of all, we recall with fondness, good old George Allen. We remember him—"The Ice Cream Man"—with his pinched face, clapping his hands, wetting his thumb on the tip of his tongue, tugging at the peak of his cap. And to tell you the truth, we'd even enjoy hearing him say once again, "This is the most important game of our lives."

♦♦♦♦♦♦♦♦

After accepting the position in Montreal, I returned to Washington, where I had agreed to spend one week with Paul Lanham, the man who would be taking over as the Redskins' new kicking teams coach. We met for six full days reviewing the Redskins' schemes, their practice structure, and the individual players who made up the various kicking units. When we had finished scrutinizing every item and had wished each other success in our new jobs, I headed for the door of the office in which I had lived for the past two years. Just before I exited the door for the last time, I stopped and turned to Paul.

"Paul," I said, looking at his full head of black hair, and recalling when mine had been the same, "if you are going to work for George Allen, you'd better go buy yourself an ample supply of Grecian Formula."

SECTION V

NORTH OF THE BORDER

CHAPTER 15

Take This Job and Love It

I love Mexican food and I also love Mexican music. Mariachi bands, castanets, and Dolores del Rio and Leo Carillo movies all gave me a thrill. When Bing Crosby sang "South of the Border," I always felt compelled to sing along with him. Once, in 1942, I put the last five nickels I owned into a jukebox so that I could listen to good ol' Bing croon that number five straight times. "Ay, ay, ay, ay—ay, ay, ay, ay." I had never thought that "South of the Border" would mean International Falls, Minnesota. At least not until I moved to Canada.

When I interviewed with J.I. Albrecht, he told me that we would be able to have 12 men on the field for every play. That sounded like a darn good deal to me. Imagine my surprise after I arrived in Montreal and found out the other teams were also allowed to use 12 men. Most American coaches, when they come to the CFL for the first time, can't figure out what to do with that additional player. "Greasy" Neal, once a head coach for the Eagles, came up with a rather innovative solution when he took over as coach of the Saskatchewan Roughriders in the CFL. Here it is, in his words: "I'll just flanker one man out all the way to the sideline, and they'll have to put one of their players out there to cover him. I'll leave our guy out there with their man, and then we'll go ahead and play football."

When "Greasy" had come to Canada, he was heralded as a defensive (here's that word again) genius. In his first game his team was beaten 62-0, but "Greasy," never at a loss for words, had a pertinent comment ready for his postgame press conference. "Think how bad it might have been if I wasn't a defensive genius," he said.

In one respect Montreal was similar to all of the other head coaching jobs I had taken. The Alouettes, too, had been heavy losers. During the season prior to my arrival there, they had posted a 2-14 record, finishing deep in the cellar of the CFL's Eastern Division. There was one big difference this time, because the Alouettes had better-than-average talent, and we would quickly be adding several more outstanding players to our roster. Less than one month after I came to work in Montreal, J.I. and Sam Berger collaborated in executing the CFL's greatest personnel coup ever—they signed that year's Heisman Trophy winner, Johnny Rodgers from the University of Nebraska.

Johnny Rodgers had many attributes. Modesty was not one of them. After he arrived in Montreal, Johnny sought to have his name changed to "J.R. Superstar." Although he never did follow through with the necessary legal steps to make it official, he always continued to cherish the idea.

Not long after we had signed Johnny, my old friend, Bob Devaney, then the head coach at Nebraska, telephoned. After telling me all about Johnny's unique talents, Bob left me with a disquieting prediction.

"Marv, he said, "you are going to have to spend 80 percent of your time dealing with Johnny Rodgers."

This proved to be one of those rare instances where Bob Devaney was wrong. In fact, I told him so three years later when I called him and asked if he could remember having made that statement.

"I sure do," he acknowledged.

"Well, Bob, it didn't work out that way," I said. "He's taking up *95 percent* of my time."

The roster of a CFL team was limited to just 32 men when I was coaching in the league. Seventeen of those players were required by rule to be Canadian, and, if it was to be a Canadian game, that rule certainly was an understandable one. By sheer weight of population and by virtue of the high-powered U.S. athletic programs, a preponderance of players who possessed outstanding ability came from that group of 15 Americans each team was allowed to have. When it came to toughness, however, the Canadians were able to stand right in there with the most ornery of the players who had traveled north. Noteworthy speed, also, was a quality provided primarily by former collegians from the states although occasionally there were exceptions. One of the fastest players who played for me when I coached in the CFL was a Canadian flash named Brock Aynsley. Also, we had a Canadian tight end named Peter Dalla Riva, who had the ability to have played in the NFL if he had so desired. He chose to play his full career with his hometown Alouettes, and, after completing his playing career, Peter was inducted into the CFL Hall of Fame.

Since the CFL's inception, the teams had chosen to use almost all of the 15 American players whom they were allowed to include on their rosters by playing them on their offensive units. Our staff played 10 of our Americans on *defense*. During the five years I coached in Canada we ran the ball—every year—more than any other team in the league. Foolhardy! Oh, yeah! That's what they said when we did it. During those five years, using this seemingly unorthodox approach, we were in the playoffs all five years. We played in three Grey Cups, and we won two of them. During that five-year period, we won more games that any other team.

My first season in Montreal got off to a slow start, but by midseason we began to click. Johnny Rodgers proved to be all that we had hoped for. As a runner, a receiver, and a kick returner he was the most feared player in the league, capable of breaking any game wide open on any play. At the end of the year he became the recipient of the Schenley Trophy, awarded annually to the CFL's Rookie of the Year. At the same time, attendance in Montreal began to perk up, again because of the excitement that our team was providing. After several years of losing, interest in the team had fallen to low ebb. It didn't help that the team played its games in a dank, morbid old stadium.

The Autostade, as its name indicated, had been built originally as a venue for automobile shows. The stands were low and far removed from the playing field. Traffic around the stadium, where several freeways met and tangled, was heavy and chaotic. The parking lots were ill lighted, unmarked, and filled with deep, jagged potholes. An insufficient number of toilets, even for the sparse crowds, helped to sour further the dispositions of the fans. The walkways were damp and slippery. Aside from all of those "amenities," the Autostade sat in a soot-covered field, devoid of landscaping or vegetation, with no structures on any side to deflect the icy, knifing winds that attacked during Quebec's early arriving winters. Try selling tickets to that show!

Two years earlier, the Montreal franchise had been about to fold. If the nation's most populous and cosmopolitan city could not field a team, then the CFL would go under. That is when Sam Berger stepped in.

Sam Berger was almost 80 when he bought the Alouettes. He knew he was buying a white elephant. He knew, also, that he was likely the only person in Canada who could breathe life back into this critically ill team and who could, in doing so, save and revitalize the CFL. He was too refined a gentleman to have stated such a sentiment in blunt terms, but in his heart he knew that was true.

Sam had served his country well. During World War II he had been in England serving as a general in charge of coordinating the logistics involved in supplying the Canadian forces stationed in the British Isles. He had also been a member of the Canadian Parliament, and, like Edward Bennett Williams, he had been one of his nation's most renowned trial lawyers. As he had done so many times before, Sam stepped into the breach once again. He attacked all of the team's problems with the vigor of a man 50 years younger. He knew he would be losing money at the outset of his seemingly hopeless endeavor to save professional football in Montreal, but he didn't intend to be the caretaker of a dying enterprise, either. Although he was alone in his belief that he would succeed, Sam was confident that he would.

A team doesn't win just because they have good players. They don't win just because they have good coaching. It isn't just good marketing, good scouting, good business procedures, or a good public relations operation that makes a team successful. *Total program* is needed in order to win. Sam didn't know what an audible was. He couldn't tell you the difference between a long-yardage and a short-yardage situation. The nickel defense was an insolvable mystery to him. But he knew his people, and he cared about them. Also, he was a master at coordinating *total program*. That's why Sam was a winner.

Sam was at his leaky office in the Autostade every day. He was on top of all that was happening. He was a totally involved owner, and he was a totally honest one, as well. I never heard him speak a false word. He was concerned about the integrity of the team and of the league. He devoted every effort possible toward seeing that the fans who came to the Alouettes' football games got their money's worth. He signed good players, and he invested heavily in improving conditions at the stadium. He projected a cheerfulness and a sense of optimism that became contagious. Sam had a sharp wit, and he called upon it at all the right times. He used it with grace and kind intent and left those in his company feeling better for having been in his presence.

One more thing—he let his coaches do the coaching. That is what he had hired them to do, wasn't it?

Every time we'd win a game, he come up to me and say, "Well, I guess you're the coach for another week."

Then he'd always slide a cigar into my breast pocket. He'd have a quip when we lost, too, and it was never mean. They don't make many men like Sam Berger.

With a strong finish in 1973, my first one in Montreal, we squeaked our way into the playoffs. Our first game was against the Toronto Argonauts, a team that had defeated us all three times we had met during the regular season. The game was to be played on their home field. In a swirling snowstorm—the condition that prevailed for 90 percent of all games played during November in the CFL—we tied them late in the game, sending the match into overtime. In Canada, the overtime rule was utilized only during playoff games, and overtimes were a full 20 minutes in length. No sudden death. We outscored Toronto 22-0 in that overtime period, winning the game 32-10.

The following week we were to meet the Ottawa RoughRiders for the Eastern Division Championship.[1] The winner would advance to the CFL's Grey Cup. Ottawa was the class of the league that year, and they showed it by defeating us and then going on to win the Grey Cup.

For reasons that I wished had not existed, Sam and J.I. became engaged in an escalating clash of personalities. In the area of football operations J.I. was remarkably capable, but Sam was not happy with the increasing fiscal morass into which the team was sinking. Also, J.I. had a rather short fuse. His emotions were always close to the surface, and they erupted frequently into displays of temper. The two men just did not get along. Every time they'd meet to discuss an issue, they'd part with feelings between them further strained. If I may borrow from the wisdom of Richie Pettibon, any time the team owner and someone who works for him are contesting, I'll give eight to five odds and take the owner. One month after the conclusion of my first season in Montreal, Sam fired J.I.

I was sorry to see him go. We had worked well together, and I had great faith in J.I.'s ability to find good talent. He had a sensitive touch in dealing with the players, as well. That is a trait that all good general managers possess. It is a difficult quality to refine, and there are many general managers—well qualified on every other count—who do not succeed because they come to be viewed by the players as being antagonistic. Those general managers who treat the players fairly, who tell them the truth, and who feel and display a personal interest in sincerely getting to know them individually are the GMs who succeed.

1. In the CFL there were the Saskatchewan Roughriders *and* the Ottawa RoughRiders. The only difference was that the second "R" in Ottawa's version of RoughRiders was capitalized. Please don't ask me why. At that time I was still trying to figure out what to do with that doggone 12th man.

When Sam told me that he had fired J.I., he also asked me to serve as the team's general manager in addition to my responsibilities as head coach. Any coach who thinks he can handle all duties required by both of those positions is a fool. How do I know that? Because when I agreed to take on that additional role, I became one of those fools. During the months leading up to the beginning of our second training camp in Montreal, I found that I was devoting 75 percent of my time to the general manager's responsibilities. We made healthy progress in instituting sound fiscal policies. We eliminated a multitude of needless expenditures, and there was a sharp increase in our season ticket sales, although we were still far short of filling the Autostade. Our improved performance on the playing field during the preceding season, of course, helped contribute to the more brisk action at the ticket window. That and the exciting presence of Johnny Rodgers. Many players are touted as being "box office attractions." Few really are. Johnny Rodgers was one of those few. He was colorful *and he could play!*

J.I., in addition to his general manager's duties, had functioned, also, as the team's director of player personnel. He was good at this latter responsibility, but many other areas, which required his attention, suffered from neglect because of his having to dedicate so much time to his consuming search for new talent. There were no other scouts—it was just J.I.—and he was determined to visit all American and Canadian colleges each year in his quest to find good prospects. A program of that scope was expensive and extremely time-consuming, and it spread him very thin.

There was one other problem involved in directing attention so heavily toward the American colleges. At graduation time, the competition to sign that year's crop of seniors was intense. In order to convince a player to forego a crack at the NFL, the Canadian teams had to negotiate contracts that were far more attractive. If you could score big by landing a Johnny Rodgers, that was one thing, but having to double the NFL bonus and contract offers in order to sign some fourth-rounder was foolish. If we had gone head to head in trying to sign NFL first-round picks, we would have been forced out of business faster than you can say "World Football League." Big money! For a guy with "potential." That is too heavy a gamble to take.

"Potential" is an imposter. Potential has gotten more coaches fired than injuries have. Potential has served to erode the credibility of many general managers. Unrealized potential has turned off more fans than predictions of thunderstorms. Team owners have forfeited more money because of potential than they have from IRS audits.

Sam and I both knew that I could not simultaneously handle my in-season coaching duties and still be able to scout college player prospects. I proposed, therefore, that we should employ a full-time director of player personnel, and Sam readily agreed. I recommended a former college coach who was then working as an NFL scout. His name was Bob Windish, a marine corps veteran who had seen action at the Battle of Guadalcanal during World War II. We hired Bob, and he would play a key role in the successes we enjoyed during the next four years.

Together, Bob and I recommended an unprecedented restructuring of our approach to scouting. It dealt primarily with those prospects who had played their collegiate football in the United States. The Canadian colleges were scouted by a CFL combine, and so our information on the Canadian lads was as good as that of any of the other teams in the league. Besides, there was seldom competition for Canadian college players from the NFL. The startling proposal that Bob and I presented to Sam was that we should not scout the American colleges at all. He had to like that, because such an approach would result in huge financial savings, *but*—where would new players from the states come from?

The answer: Let the players go to NFL teams. Then scout them carefully and thoroughly during the NFL training camps and preseason schedule. Commit all the resources we had to zeroing in on scouting just those 28 NFL teams. Other CFL teams also scouted the NFL, of course, but they did it in combination with their scouting of the U.S. colleges. Using this method, their scouts could afford just cursory glances when they were in the NFL camps. They were more concerned with airlines schedules to Baton Rouge, Louisiana, to Ames, Iowa, to Athens, Georgia, and to other college towns. Our scout stayed at training camp, looking closely at the NFL players, while we prepared to make our move at those players who failed to make final NFL rosters.

But these players are rejects, you might be saying. Not really. Almost all NFL teams part with players late in training camp for whom they have high regard. Only the restrictions posed by roster limits dictate that they be released. Even among that group, we were selective, and whenever we had determined that one of those prospects was a desirable fit for our team, they usually came in and upgraded us immediately. We had seen a player work for eight weeks against professional competition. We knew how tough he was; how good a learner he was; what his work habits were like. Often a player would have talents particularly suited for the Canadian game, talents that had not been beneficial to him in vying for a spot with an NFL team.

Sam saw to it that our veteran players, when they deserved it, were well compensated. Our active players were the best paid in the CFL, but our overall player payroll was far from the highest in the league, because we used the funds we had to pay those players who had produced. There were no big rookie signing bonuses for us other than the one given to Johnny Rodgers. We were now able to operate with a sharply diminished scouting budget and a more effective and efficient scouting system. We committed far fewer mistakes in selecting player personnel. We rewarded those players who deserved it most, and that led to excellent player morale. We kindled fan interest because of the continuity on our roster. We won more as we spent less.

The plan sounds like a simple one, but we were the only team to operate that way. The others were too ready to sign press-release heroes straight out of college and to get those immediate "saviors" right into the lineup. Remember: *What it takes to win is simple—but it isn't easy!*

Bob Windish spent all of the training camp period at NFL practices and preseason games. In addition, Bob had enlisted the part-time services of three other men, former coaches who were then in other lines of work but who had remained football personnel hobbyists. For minimal stipends, these men, too, visited NFL preseason games, sending reports back to Bob. They continued to attend regular-season games, and, throughout the whole NFL season, they fed us information about players and teams in the NFL. It was an opportunity for them to become associated with professional football and to attend NFL games as press box spectators. They loved it, and they helped us become a better team. As guests of our official party, they were on hand to share the thrills of the three Grey Cups in which we would play over the next four-year period, and Sam always saw to it that they were rewarded even beyond the amounts for which our agreements had called.

Before I had met personally with any of these part-time scouts, I did have numerous opportunities to review the written reports they had been sending in. One of those men had been an assistant coach at Fordham and the Coast Guard Academy. He kept submitting some of the most superlative scouting reports I have ever seen.

One day I asked Bob, "Hey, who is this guy, and what does he do now?"

"He sells advertising for some trade magazine," Bob responded. "His name is Bill Polian."

"If he ever gets up here, Bob, please be sure to introduce us to each other," I said. "I'd like to get to know him."

Did I ever get to know him!

When we entered training camp at the outset of my second season in Montreal, I found that I continued to be overwhelmed by my general manager's responsibilities. I wanted to prepare practice plans and to review films of our practices and of our early-season opponents. I wanted to be immersed in the refining of topics I would discuss at our team meetings. I wanted to be able to take time to know our players, to find the key to each man's psyche so that I could help him realize his full capabilities. When it came time to release a player, I wanted to be able to explain to him, patiently, why we were doing so.

Instead, I was devoting my time to meetings with our ticket manager, with the people we had contracted to repave the parking lot, with the concessionaires. I was spending hours in meetings with Sam on matters of vital financial importance to him and to the franchise. I was doing everything except being a good football coach. In fairness to Sam, to our players and coaches, and to myself I realized that I'd better be either the coach *or* the general manager. That decision was easy. I wanted to coach. Convincing Sam was another matter, I thought.

When I approached him and asked to discuss the situation, he listened carefully and made some sensible suggestions, and we worked out a solution to concerns that we both had. I was to remain as the football coach with full responsibility and authority for football operations. This was to include my having jurisdiction over all coaching staff and player personnel decisions except for the negotiation of player contracts. The person in the front office who handles contract negotiations is thrust into an adversarial relationship with the players, and I felt that a coach should not be involved in any way in those discussions.

Sam determined that his two young sons, David and Robert, both recent law school graduates, would be in charge of most of the business operations for the team. Bob Windish was already aboard as director of player personnel. There was one other man, Bob Geary, who would be promoted and who would have responsibility for most player contract negotiations and for a broad variety of time-consuming tasks that fell within the scope of the general manager's duties.

I have never seen Bob Geary's family tree, but I would not have been surprised if he's is a descendent of Diamond Jim Brady. Bob loved opulence. He drove an Austin-Healy automobile, flashed solid gold cuff links and jeweled rings, dined at the most expensive restaurants, and wore custom-made suits tailored at the finest men's shop. That was the outer man. The real Bob Geary had rougher edges.

Bob was a native of Montreal, having been born and having grown up in the toughest part of the English-speaking section of the city. In the earlier days of the CFL, when they played without facemasks, Bob had been a lineman with the Alouettes. Players' salaries were meager in those days, and Bob had supported himself primarily through his employment as a bouncer at several of the city's less elegant bars and nightclubs. Bob's face—fashioned over the years by his many encounters on and off the field—looked like a relief map of the Rocky Mountains. I do not know whether he had always talked out of the side of his mouth, but that is how he spoke when I came to know him.

Bob was a gregarious man with a heart of gold and with fists of iron. He had outgrown his barroom brawler days, but his reputation lingered. He still talked a good fight. His vocabulary, fairly limited to begin with, was printable only about 40 percent of the time, but that never kept him from getting his point across.

Although Bob lacked polish and formal education, he was no dummy. He understood instinctively what other people felt and what was important to them. He was at ease with anyone, be it the prime minister or some unfortunate wino on skid row. Better still, people always seemed to be at ease in Bob's presence. Also, Bob had an admirable knack for getting things done. He never procrastinated. If he said he'd get back to you by the next afternoon, you'd hear from him the next morning.

At my urging, Sam agreed that Bob should be given the title of general manager, and the announcement of this appointment was met with hearty approval by all of the media and football fans in Montreal. He moved in; the sparks began to fly, and they ignited all of the right pieces of kindling. Players got signed, and tickets got sold. Bob's press conferences were great theater, but there sure were a lot of "bleeps" edited into his tape-recorded pronouncements.

Bob went along with my recommendations, and he signed the players I wanted even though he might disagree vehemently with some of my judgments. Speed, size, skill, intelligence, and experience were all meaningless to Bob. They served only to confuse the issue so far as he was concerned. According to Bob there was a simple method for classifying players. They fell, he believed, in just one of two sharply defined categories, and in his Player Evaluation Notebook he kept but two pages. A prospective player's name would be listed on only one of those two sheets. One sheet was titled: "He'll Knock Your Jock Off," while the caption on the other page bore the words: "He's a Pussy."

There was one habit Bob developed that I could tell was beginning to irritate Sam. Whenever Bob referred to any aspect of the organization, there was a decided proprietary cast to his words. At a typical pregame press conference, Bob might conclude his remarks by saying,

"*My* coaches and *my* players are going to see that *my* team wins this game right here in *my* stadium. That's what I spent all *my* money for."

One time, when the Alouettes had to pay a $25,000 compensation fee in order to convince one of the other teams in the league to switch home game dates, Bob had commented, "It cost *me* 25 grand to get those [bleeps] to change that schedule."

That was one "me" or "my" too many for Sam. After thanking Bob for his generosity, Sam asked him if he'd prefer to have the $25,000 deducted from his salary in five or in 10 installments.

In the CFL's Eastern Division, our main competition came every year from the Ottawa RoughRiders. In 1973, my first season north of the border, they had won the Grey Cup. A year later it was 1974, and, as we entered our final game of the regular season, Ottawa and Montreal were tied for first place in the division. The one remaining date on our schedule pitted us against the RoughRiders on their home field, and the team that won that contest would also capture the Eastern Division title. Going into the game, both teams had already qualified for the playoffs, but there is an overwhelming advantage enjoyed by the division champions. They had a first week bye during the postseason and needed to win just one game to get to the Grey Cup, as opposed to the two wins required from the wild-card contender, and that one game was played at the division champion's home stadium. Over the previous 30-year period, teams that had not won their division title had advanced to the Grey Cup just three times, and they had won it but once.

Our defense had done an outstanding job all season long, and again at Ottawa, on the season's final Sunday, we turned in a superior defensive performance. Tommy Clements, the former Notre Dame All-American, was Ottawa's quarterback, and he was the best in the league at his position. Tommy was a brilliant tactician, with a celebrated ability to execute the sprint out pass. On the CFL's spacious playing field it was almost impossible to contain him.[2] On this particular afternoon, however, we had held him well in check, so that by late in the fourth quarter Ottawa had been able to score just 10 points, their season low.

2. The Canadian football field is 110 yards long, and the end zones were then 25 yards deep (in recent years they have been reduced to 20 yards). Also, the field is considerably wider. There are more than twice the number of square yards on a Canadian gridiron than there are on the standard American field.

Unfortunately, that is all we had been able to put on the board, too, and so the count was knotted at 10-10 late in the game as the RoughRiders punted the ball to us from the midfield stripe.

Johnny Rodgers gathered in the punt on our 15-yard line, and then he exploded 95 yards for a touchdown. It was Johnny's fourth kick return for a touchdown that season, and this one won the Eastern Division Championship for our Alouettes, the first time a Montreal team had accomplished that in many years.

Two weeks later, after Ottawa had advanced to the final round of the Eastern playoffs, we met again. The winner would be representing the East in the Grey Cup. For the first time in its history, the Autostade was filled to capacity for a football game, and our players responded by cruising to an easy victory. In just one week from that day we would be playing the Western Division champion Edmonton Eskimos in the Grey Cup at Empire Stadium in Vancouver.

The Grey Cup was Canada's premier sporting event. It is different from professional hockey and baseball because every team is based in a Canadian city. On a national level, the Grey Cup is as publicized and as attention-consuming in Canada as the Super Bowl is in the United States.

Grey Cup Week brings to the game's host city large contingents of visitors from all over Canada. The hotels, the restaurants, and streets are filled with Grey Cup Week revelers. There is no need for Canada's prime minister to make a telephone call to the victor's locker room because he is always in attendance, presenting the Grey Cup to the winning team's owner. The game is usually played in bitter weather conditions, but that merely adds to the enthusiasm exhibited by Canada's hardy fans.

Edmonton was favored to win the 1974 Grey Cup. They had been the most productive offensive team the league had seen in many years, averaging close to 40 points a game.

Both teams spent the full Grey Cup Week at the game site, conducting their practices there and holding daily meetings with the large media corps that had gathered for the week's activities. During our daily media sessions, the interest of the writers and broadcasters was consumed, understandably, with Edmonton's offensive capabilities. By week's end they had convinced themselves and the fans that the Eskimos were an unstoppable scoring machine.

At the final press conference, attended by the head coaches of both teams, I was asked how we hoped to win the game. It often amazes me how a journalist hopes that a coach will reveal, before the game, what his specific game plan is. Usually the coach must dredge up some evasive answer, and that is how I responded.

"We'll just have to find a way to stop them," I said.

Brilliant!

"Do you think *that* will be enough to win?" they all scoffed.

When the media are able to light a short fuse, they usually succeed in triggering the kind of reaction that delights them. They sure did it this time.

"Edmonton has the best offense in the league," I snapped. "We've got the best defense. When an outstanding offensive team meets an outstanding defensive team, the defense will win every time."

Oh! Oh! Now I'd done it! Although the basic premise was one that I believed devoutly, I have to admit it was a dumb overstatement. I sure would look foolish if they went out and beat us 38-13 or something like that. There was no way I could call back my foolish words. We had better play one helluva defensive game.

♦♦♦♦♦♦♦♦

If you have ever looked carefully at the weather map published in your daily newspaper, you will see that from November through April there is a football shaped design that includes Vancouver, British Columbia, and Seattle, Washington. The diagonal dashes within that illustration will tell you that rain is falling in that section of the continent, just as it did yesterday and was expected to do again throughout today and tomorrow. It rained heavily on our practice sessions every day during our week of preparation for the Grey Cup. On game day, the weather pattern changed slightly—it rained even more intensely. With the temperature at 36 degrees, it was a *cold* rain. At least it wasn't snowing.

The first task a coaching staff must tackle when they begin planning to play an opponent is determining what it is that their rival does best. What is it that must be stopped, and what must be done in order to stop that main threat? The defensive plans employed by our Alouettes and by the Eskimos in the 1974 Grey Cup were strikingly similar. We each had to shut down our opponent's outstanding pass receiver. Larry Highbaugh of the Edmonton Eskimos was a 9.4 100-yard dash man. He had great moves; he could get open; and he could catch the ball. Whatever else we might have to sacrifice, we were going to have two—and sometimes three—men on every down responsible for coverage on Highbaugh. In describing Highbaugh, I have also described Johnny Rodgers. Edmonton assigned three defenders in their efforts to contain Johnny. They succeeded. We were unable to get our most formidable weapon into the battle.

So we tried something different. We ran the ball. Wait a minute! You don't run the ball in the CFL! Not with just three downs, you don't.[3] We did. We ran. And ran. And ran. We controlled the clock. Johnny was in motion more than a break dancer, and three or more Edmonton players chased him toward the sidelines while our two running backs, Larry Sherrer and Steve Ferrughelli, powered away at their thinned-out defensive alignments.

All of that offensive strategy would have meant little, however, if it hadn't been for our dominating defense. One of the reasons I believe so strongly in defense is that there is more consistency of performance. Offenses have off days. Freakish plays occur in the kicking game. But defenses tend to play at the same level, game in and game out. If they are bad, they stay bad. If they are good, they stay good. Ours stayed good.

We won the Grey Cup 20-7. Larry Sherrer was selected as the game's MVP. That night, at our hotel in Vancouver, Sam hosted a victory dinner for all of the coaches and their wives. We all had a turn at sampling a toast from the Grey Cup itself. Sam enjoyed that almost as much as the five-dollar cigar I gave him.

The front page headline in *The Montreal Gazette* the next morning blared forth the news: "Levy Was Right—Defense Wins It." You know something? Those writers aren't such bad guys, after all.

---

3. In Canadian football, the offense is allowed just three downs. That rule helps to assure that the passing game will almost always predominate.

CHAPTER 16

'Twas Not the Season to Be Jolly

A happy landing does not always mean that you had a good flight. We had had to overcome a festering problem within our team. Johnny Rodgers had begun to exhibit some attitude problems, which, despite his enormous talents, served to antagonize not only our coaching staff, but his teammates, as well. Frequently, when it had come time to run our opponent's plays to help prepare our defense during practice, an assignment in which all members of our offensive unit participated, Johnny would be beset by any number of difficulties. His tape was too tight, requiring him to return to the locker room for an adjustment; his asthma would act up; he would have cramps; his shoulder pads were slipping; he had spots in front of his eyes; he had a toothache. I admired his imagination, but I didn't appreciate the type of contribution he was making to help us prepare for the next game. Neither did his teammates who had to carry his load.

During his rookie season, Johnny had been on top of all his assignments. In his second year, he began to show up for practice at the last instant. Frequently, he was several minutes late, and his concentration in our team meetings was minimal. He took to wearing sunglasses at the meetings, behind which he would catch a periodic nap. When he was told to take them off, Johnny complained that the lights hurt his eyes. Maybe so, but how about when the lights were turned off so that we could show films? On many occasions he called in sick. His brand new Rolls Royce broke down more often on the way to practice than any of our defensive linemen's 1958 Chevys did.

Naturally, I fined him for his transgressions, but our fine schedules were structured in accordance with the modest contracts held by the rest of the players on the team, not with Johnny's. He could miss practice completely, do an endorsement instead, and come out way ahead. One time, he merely called in to find out what it would cost him to miss practice. I told him. He didn't show up for practice. When, as I had warned him, I benched him for that week's game, it had little impact. Johnny had a guaranteed contract, and he was paid for the game, whether he played or not.

Once a team's fine schedule was submitted to the league office before each season began, the team was obligated to stick to the maximum amounts detailed in that schedule. Toward the end of the 1974 season, I informed our players that the fine structure for the following year would be the same, except that there would be steep, escalating amounts assessed for repeat offenders. Few of them were fined at all during an entire season. They knew it was a "Johnny Rodgers clause."

Johnny found a way, he thought, to thwart my attempts at disciplining him. In 1975 he would be entering the option year of his contract. The World Football League was functioning then, and they had expressed interest in him. Johnny had been drafted by the Chargers of the NFL, and they, too, would have liked to sign him. With this leverage, Johnny and his agent, Mike Trope, entered contract renewal negotiations with Sam Berger. Johnny's talents were ideally suited for the CFL. Playing on the Canadian-sized field and with the use of CFL rules, he could have prevailed for many years as the league's star attraction and its most outstanding player. In the American professional game, he would have been just another good player. I knew that, and I made certain that Sam knew it. Johnny and Mike knew it, too. In the mid-1970s Johnny could command a much better contract in Montreal than he could in the WFL or NFL.

When Johnny and Mike met with Sam, they asked not only for a whopping raise but for a clause in the contract that would make Johnny not subject to any team fines. My advice to Sam was to release Johnny. Let him go sign with a team in another league. Despite his talents, I felt we would be a better team overall without the problems he was causing us. Sam said that he could not do that without alienating our fans. Johnny was *the* gate attraction on our team, and he was capable, when properly focused, of turning in some scintillating on-the-field performances. I understood Sam's position on that point, but I told him that it would be impossible for me to continue as the coach if the "no fine" clause was included in the contract.

Several hours later Sam telephoned me. He told me that he had worked out a new and lucrative contract for Johnny. But he also informed me that he had refused to include the "no fine" stipulation. When he had told them to take it or leave it, they took it. Sam Berger—what a man!

♦♦♦♦♦♦♦♦

Johnny had walked out of Sam's office with a blockbuster of a contract, by far the best ever written in the CFL. He showed his appreciation by leveling some public blasts at Sam following their sometimes contentious negotiations. Sam was too much of a gentleman to respond in kind. A reporter, who covered our team regularly, told me of the only time Sam had given in to an even mild retort. One day he spotted Sam riding to the stadium on Montreal's subway. Sam usually came to work in a limousine, but on this day he stood, grasping a strap, as the subway cars careened along the tracks.

"Sam Berger, what are you doing riding the subway?" the astonished reporter asked him.

"Anyone who gives the kind of contract that I gave to Johnny Rodgers deserves to ride the subway," Sam answered.

We began the 1975 season as the defending Grey Cup Champions, and we did justice to that role. Once again we engaged in a season-long struggle with Ottawa to see who would be the Eastern Division representative in the Grey Cup, and once again we prevailed.

During the previous two seasons, Johnny had carried our offense. In 1975, however, although he still played well—brilliantly at times—he was much more inconsistent. For most of 1973 and 1974 J.R. had been all football. Now he became engaged in a multitude of outside activities—a partnership in a plush new Montreal nightclub, for instance. His energies were low, and his concentration was often elsewhere. He tired easily and seemed never to be able to practice because of a variety of injuries—real, imagined, and invented—which disappeared on game days. He dropped more passes and began to fumble and miss assignments more frequently. His fines mounted as he continued to show up late for meetings and practices.

There was one occurrence during that season that is humorous to me now. At the time, however, it didn't amuse me at all. Johnny had stayed out of a midweek practice complaining of a tender leg. The next morning I read in the Montreal newspapers that he had won a dance contest at one of the downtown discos the night before. I congratulated him on this accomplishment and then hit him with a fine big enough to put a dent in even his hefty paycheck. That weekend we played a key game against Ottawa, and, on the morning of the game, J.R. told me that he had an upset stomach and wouldn't be able to play.

We beat the RoughRiders soundly without Johnny in the lineup. At the postgame press briefing, one of the reporters asked if I would be taking disciplinary action against J.R.

"What for? He told me he had an upset stomach, and so I held him out of the game," I explained.

"Didn't you see him sitting at the end of the bench eating hot dogs and smoking cigars?"

"Of course I didn't see him doing that," I said. "It's hard for me to believe that he would."

"Believe it!" several of the gathered writers chanted.

Johnny was very good at making excuses. But he was not very good at making convincing excuses. When I confronted him about the incident, J.R. told me that the hot dogs help settle his queasy stomach (huh?) and that he was smoking cigars in order to keep the mosquitoes away. They have some damn tough mosquitoes in Canada, but the thermometer had hovered around 20 degrees Fahrenheit that day. I sure didn't have any bites. That is one paycheck Johnny didn't get to pick up.

Throughout that 1975 campaign many other players on our offensive team played superbly, giving us a more diversified attack than we had had in previous seasons. Our defense continued to excel, and our kicking game was by far the best in the league. Don Sweet, our place kicker, had succeeded on 21 consecutive field goal attempts that season, a new professional football record at the time. His feat was all the more remarkable because of the harsh weather conditions that prevail during a CFL season. There were no indoor stadiums, and most of the fields in the league had grass surfaces.

Our Grey Cup opponent in 1975 once again was the Edmonton Eskimos. There would be no heavy rain again this time, however. We played it in Calgary, located in the Canadian Rockies, on the last Sunday in November, and, although the official start of winter was still almost a month away, the temperature was -7. Snow was falling at game time with 30-mph winds whistling through the stadium. Yet the stands were filled to capacity. I still cannot believe those fans.

The weather, combined with our staunch defense, kept Edmonton from scoring any touchdowns in that 1975 Grey Cup. They did put up three field goals, however. Late in the third quarter we managed a touchdown, and as the final quarter began Edmonton led 9-7.

Midway into the fourth quarter we stymied the Eskimos deep in their territory, and they were forced to punt. We began our drive at midfield and advanced to their three-yard line where, with six minutes still to play, we had a first down. On the next play from scrimmage Johnny fumbled, and the Eskimos recovered. They were able to move the ball enough to use up four minutes. When they punted to us this time, we had to begin our last drive from deep in our own territory with just two minutes remaining on the clock. Our quarterback, Sonny Wade, directed a heart-stopping drive for us, and with 10 seconds left in the game we lined up at the Edmonton 11-yard line for a field goal attempt, which would have given us a 10-9 Grey Cup victory.

The snap was good, but in the icy cold weather, our holder was not able to place the ball accurately. As the ball slid onto its side, Don Sweet swung his foot at it desperately. The kick missed the uprights by a wide margin and skittered out the back of the end zone.[1] We had lost the Grey Cup Championship 9-8.

On the plane trip home, Dan Sekanovich, one of our assistant coaches, commented that it was going to be a long, cold winter. The fall had been cold enough for me.

In three seasons the Alouettes had come a long way. We had become a fixture in the playoffs. Twice we had played in the Grey Cup, winning it once and then coming within a point of repeating as champions. Our meager attendance had picked up each year, although the improvement had not been as much as we had hoped. Average attendance, which had been only 12,000 a game the year before my coming to Montreal, had crept up each year, and in 1975 we had averaged 25,000 a game. The fans were proud of their team, but too few of them were willing to cope with the discomforts of the Autostade.

We all believed that 1976 was a year that held special promise. Our team was solid. It was still a young team, and it was getting better all the time. We were the heavy preseason favorite to win the Grey Cup. And a magnificent, new 75,000-capacity stadium, completed for the 1976 Olympics, would be available to us early in October.

Our team, unfortunately, did not fare well. By a freak of schedule planning, we played five games during the first 22 days of that 1976 season. We won our opener and then tied our next one. In the third game, Andy Hopkins, our star running back, suffered a severe knee

1. In the CFL, any time the ball is kicked into or through the end zone, the kicking team scores one point.

injury, and he was out for the rest of the year. We lost our next three games, and we continued to flounder right up to the midseason point. The new contract that Johnny had wrangled had done little to change his attitude, and he became more recalcitrant than ever about complying with team rules. His outside interests multiplied, and as they did, his performance diminished.

In one game at Toronto, after he had dropped several passes in the first half, he asked, at halftime, if he could address the squad. We were being soundly whipped by the underdog Argonauts, and I thought Johnny was going to own up to his poor performance. Perhaps he had come to his senses and was about to apologize and let his teammates know that he was turning over a new leaf. It would be an ideal time for such a catharsis, I felt, and so I encouraged him to speak as he wished. His words stunned me, and they further alienated his teammates.

"There is not one of you guys in this room who gives a damn if we win or not," he scolded.

Some of our coaches had to restrain a few of our players or we would have had a fight during that halftime break. We lost the game.

Sam had wisely arranged to have our first game in Olympic Stadium scheduled against the best drawing card in our division, the Ottawa RoughRiders. Activity was brisk all during the week leading up to that game, and, on Friday, Sam told me that he was optimistic. He expected a crowd of more than 40,000, he said. He was right. We did have more than 40,000—more than *76,000* to be exact. It was, and it remains, the largest attendance ever at a CFL game. When we came onto the field prior to the opening kickoff, there wasn't an empty seat in the place. People were standing along the broad walkways behind the last row of seats. Another large throng was down on the field, restrained only by ropes hastily thrown up to keep them off the playing areas.

Ottawa's heavily favored RoughRiders were greeted by thunderous boos as they came onto the field. The noisy electricity of the crowd was at a level I hadn't heard since leaving Washington. I do not know whether it was because we were inspired by this show of support or whether it was because Ottawa was intimidated by it—probably both—but we shellacked them 21-3 that day.

In the VIP Stadium Club, immediately following that victorious inaugural game, Bob Geary was at his most expansive.

"Did *my* team do it today?" he kept asking.

As the postgame party gained momentum, Bob's spirits continued to soar. Later, when I was driving away from the stadium, Bob's car zipped by mine. He waved cheerfully as his Austin-Healey gained speed, disappearing quickly from view. I continued driving, but after five minutes I ran into a traffic tie up. Apparently, there had been an accident ahead. The long lanes of cars inched forward, and finally I drew abreast of the accident scene. Bob had plowed his car into the rear end of the Ottawa team bus. Fortunately, he was uninjured, but his car and the Ottawa bus were badly damaged. I got out of my car to see if I could be of help. Bob was unfazed because he continued to gloat over our team's victory. His only comment about the accident was vintage Bob Geary.

"Wait till *my* law firm gets those [bleeps] in court," he said.

We played the remainder of our home schedule games before crowds in excess of 60,000, and, by virtue of a late-season rally, we managed to salvage something from what until then had been a disastrous year. We made it into the playoffs, but we'd have to be on the road for all postseason games. The first one would be at Hamilton. If we could win that matchup, we would then move on and play the first-place RoughRiders in Ottawa.

There was little satisfaction in Montreal with the way our season had gone. We certainly had not lived up to preseason expectations. We had been bludgeoned by injuries, especially at running back and at wide receiver. We traveled to Hamilton with just two healthy receivers. After Andy Hopkins had been injured earlier in the season, our once sturdy running attack had become more enfeebled with each passing week. Our record was responsible for our forfeiting more than just a home-field competitive advantage, because we also suffered the loss of sizable revenues we would have realized from playing those games in the Olympic Stadium.

The media were acutely aware of the internal problems festering on our team stemming from the squad's ongoing conflict with Johnny. This issue, including what they perceived as my ineffectual dealing with J.R., dominated the sports pages. Many of the media, noting that I was on the final year of my contract, were predicting that, unless we could accomplish the unlikely and win the Grey Cup, I would be fired at season's end.

At the team meeting the night before the playoff game against the Hamilton Tigercats, Johnny did not show up. Later that night, when I confronted him in his hotel room, he told me that he had been out to dinner with an old friend and that he had lost track of the time. What to do? If we had had another healthy receiver to put on the field in his place, I would have held J.R. out of the game. We did not have any, however, and we had to play the game. I gritted my teeth, cussed under my breath, and started Johnny.

We didn't have to worry about traveling to Ottawa the following weekend because we were out of the Hamilton game from the outset. Early in the game they punted the ball 23 yards deep into our end zone. Standard procedure in such an unfavorable situation is to concede the single point to your opponent. By doing so a team, despite giving up that one tally, is able, according to CFL rules, to retain possession of the ball and put it in play on the next down at its own 35-yard line. Instead, Johnny tried to run the punt out of the end zone. He fumbled, and the Tigercats recovered. As the result of that play, we trailed 7-0 early in the game, and the tempo for the remainder of the contest had been established. Hamilton went on to win 22-0, the first time the Alouettes had been shut out in my four years as coach. Also, it was the earliest we had been eliminated from the playoffs during that four-year period.

Little was said in the subdued gloom of our locker room after the game. Sam did tell me, however, that he would like to talk with me the first thing the following morning. I went to bed that night feeling that it was probably my last as head coach of the Alouettes.

When I came into Sam's office early the next day, he did not look up immediately from the papers he was reviewing.

After a brief pause (it didn't *seem* brief to me), he said, "I want to talk with you about your contract."

I waited silently while he continued to shuffle through the clutter on his desk. Finally, he found what he had been searching for, looked up, and passed the sheets of paper across to me.

"How does that look to you?" he asked. It was a new three-year contract, one that included a generous raise. "You are a great football coach, and I want you to stay with us. Take it home and read it."

There are some people in this world you can trust completely. Sam Berger was one of those people. I didn't take the contract home. I didn't even read it through. I signed it that morning in his office.

"There is something else I'd like to talk about with you," he said after I had returned my newly signed contract to him. "Do you still feel we should release Johnny Rodgers?"

I told Sam that I believed doing so would be in the best interests of the team.

"Okay," he said, "but I want to tell him."

Johnny had been trying to renegotiate his own contract with the Alouettes, and when Sam had refused to do so, J.R. had unleashed a public diatribe against Sam. I was present in Sam's office when he met with Johnny. Sam got right to the point.

"Johnny, you're fired!" he said (and I'll bet Donald Trump thinks he is the one who invented that phrase).

For a moment J.R. was stunned, but he soon recovered, telling Sam that they had a contract.

"You're fired *with cause,*" Sam responded.

I am not sure about the legalese, but, after Johnny had discussed the situation with his agent, they decided not to contest Sam's action.

From 1914 until 1941, the University of Illinois had just one head football coach, Bob Zuppke, and during my playing days and early coaching years, Coach Zuppke had already achieved legendary status. The first book I ever read about coaching was written by Zuppke, and although most of the technical information he presented has long become obsolete, the old mentor also included numerous coaching aphorisms, as fresh and applicable today as they were the day he first wrote them. There is one that has stayed with me: "A tragedy in sports occurs when the man of outstanding ability does not achieve his full potential."

Next to Don Perkins, Johnny Rodgers had more raw football ability than any other player I had coached up to that point in my career. When he first came to Montreal, his teammates and everyone in the city welcomed him enthusiastically. At first, he displayed many qualities that made him easy to like. Johnny was a personable young man, and he had a sharp mind. He was full of energy and could do many exciting things on a football field that I have seen no other player do. But then he began to let it all slip away. For almost two years, as a professional, the flame from his talents burned brightly, and then, just as quickly, it flickered and went out.

I have always felt a personal sense of failure in not having been able to help Johnny direct his efforts and concentration so that he might have continued to realize the benefits from his unusual talents. I tried to help him on many occasions. But I did not get through to him.

For several years after he was no longer playing football, Johnny[2] went through some difficult times, but, thank heaven, this is not a story

2. Johnny Rodgers joined the Chargers in 1977. He didn't start many games for them. A year later he was out of football.

with an unhappy ending. In recent years I have been delighted to hear that he has redirected his life in positive directions. Someone reported to me that Johnny works in the athletic department at his alma mater, the University of Nebraska, and that his counseling of the young athletes there has been a healthy and effective addition to their program.

There is one unfortunate irony in this recounting of my years in Montreal. Although I have written primarily about Johnny Rodgers, I have scarcely mentioned the names of the other players or of the assistant coaches who contributed so much to the successes we enjoyed. Fellows such as Peter Dalla Riva, Chuck Zapiec, Dickie Harris, Larry Smith, Glen Weir, Gordon Judges, and Carl Crennel all were named to the All-CFL teams. Like their stalwart teammates—too numerous for me to mention in this account—they were at practice every day. They worked to the limits of their abilities. They were the ones responsible for the winning of our championships. Because these players made no waves, little has been written about them. As I said before, the world isn't always fair.

CHAPTER 17

My Grey Cup Runneth Over

Late in the summer of 1977 I began my fifth season as coach of the Montreal Alouettes. With the Johnny Rodgers saga behind us, harmony prevailed. We packed big crowds into the Olympic Stadium, averaging more than 60,000 spectators a game. We started the season winning, and we kept on winning, until midseason, that is, when we were hit, once again, with injuries at the running back position.

While we were straining to get back on track, I received a timely telephone call from former Redskins player Richie Pettibon. Richie's playing days were over, and he was now serving as an assistant coach with the Oilers. The Oilers were about to release a little-known rookie running back named Horace Belton, and Richie was calling to alert me that Horace had been impressive in their training camp.

Because we were hurting badly at running back, we signed Horace, flew him to Montreal, and exposed him to a crash course, hoping that he could learn our offense quickly. In his first game, Horace was still feeling his way, and we absorbed one of the few losses we experienced that season. By the following week, however, he was ready. He rushed for 177 yards, and we cruised to victory.

Horace had helped us win the game that day, and he also won the hearts of the Montreal fans and of his teammates. Horace was built like a bowling ball—five foot seven, 210 pounds—and once he got rolling he kept on rolling—all the rest of that season. We rolled with him, right on into the Grey Cup, where once again we would be playing the Edmonton Eskimos for the CFL Championship.

♦♦♦♦♦♦♦♦

The 1977 Grey Cup was played before a capacity house in Montreal's Olympic Stadium. A heavy snowstorm and 10-degree temperatures couldn't discourage those Grey Cup fans. All 75,000 seats were filled, most of them with Montreal partisans. Their beloved Alouettes did not disappoint them. We were the best team in Canada, and we proved it convincingly. No desperate last-second field goal heroics would be needed this time. We kept the assemblage roaring throughout the contest as we brought the Grey Cup back to Montreal. The final score was 41-6.

With about a minute left to play in the game, we scored our final points when one of our defensive backs, Vernon Perry, returned an intercepted pass 70 yards for a touchdown. He was the toast of Montreal.

After Vernon's long touchdown run, Brock Aynsley, our star wide receiver, clasped me in a bear hug and cried out, "We've done it, Coach! We've won the Grey Cup!"

Ever the coach, always conforming to the philosophy that the game isn't over until the last tick is off the clock, I played the role to the hilt.

"We haven't won anything until that clock runs out," I admonished him. "We aren't going to do any celebrating until this game is *all* over."

Brock was the most gentlemanly player on our team. He was polite to a fault. On rare occasion he might call me "Coach," but most of the time it was "Mr. Levy" or "Sir." After my mild rebuke to him, however, he stepped back, studied me briefly, and then said, "Aw, bullshit, Marv, we've won the damn game."

Then he hugged me again. This time, I hugged him, too.

The locker-room festivities following the game had run their course, and most of our squad had departed when Sam Berger stopped by the coaches' dressing room. When I presented him with a victory cigar, he lighted it and savored the first puff. Then, a benign smile spread across his face.

"Well, Marv," he chuckled, "I guess you're our coach for another week."

Neither of us knew then that his words had been prophetic.

Two days after the Grey Cup I received a telephone call from Edward Bennett Williams. He asked if I could meet him later that week at Logan Airport in Boston. I had barely set the phone down after that call when it rang again, and this time it was Jack Steadman, president of the Chiefs. He invited me to visit Kansas City. I arranged to fly to Boston on Thursday, where I would confer with Mr. Williams. On

Friday and Saturday I stopped in Chicago in order to see my mother who had been hospitalized with a heart condition. On Sunday I proceeded to Kansas City for my session with the Chiefs' braintrust of Jack Steadman, Lamar Hunt, and Jim Schaaf.

I was taken by surprise when EBW told me that he was not expecting George Allen to return as coach of the Redskins for the next season. Only two weeks remained, and, for the second time in the past three years, the Redskins were out of the playoffs. The advanced age of their former star players was swiftly taking its toll on the team. Many of the original "Over the Hill Gang" had retired, and those who still remained were now far past their prime. Besides that, all of the Redskins' top draft choices for the past, and next, several years had been traded away.[1]

There appeared to be several lean years ahead for the once proud Redskins, EBW forewarned me. That honesty on his part, combined with the knowledge that he had thought of me first as his new coach in the event that George did leave, served to further augment the esteem in which I held him. There was, however, an uneasiness that had come over me during our discussion. George was still the coach of the Redskins, and I had no intention of seeking a position he held until his departure, if it were to occur, had become a reality. EBW and I agreed that when the season had ended and when George's status with the Redskins had been determined, we would talk further.

As matters eventually developed, George did part company with the Washington Redskins following the 1977 season. He returned to the West Coast for another crack at the Rams head coaching job.[2] George's move to L.A., however, would not occur until several weeks after I had met with EBW in Boston. In the meantime, events had moved swiftly for me, also.

The Chiefs were in the final stages of finishing a dismal season when I met with Lamar Hunt, Jack Steadman, and Jim Schaaf at the Marriott Hotel near the Kansas City airport. At midseason, head coach Paul Wiggin, serving his third season with the Chiefs, had been fired. One of his assistants, Tom Bettis, had taken over as the interim coach, but the club had managed to win just one game since Tom had been given the job. It was no fault of his, because the team was a weak and

---

1. In the 1970s, free agency did not exist, and so there was no access to "get well quick" star players from other teams in the NFL except via trades.

2. Ironically, he came back to the team to which he had traded all those high-round draft choices a few years earlier. The players the Rams had acquired from those drafts had by this time developed into outstanding experienced pros, and the Rams' personnel was now right up there with the best in the NFL.

demoralized one. They had liked and respected Paul, and they had been dismayed over Paul's dismissal.

My interview with the Chiefs' top executives went well, and I left my meeting with them feeling that I would be offered the job soon. Naturally, they wanted the time to review and digest the substance of our interview, and I, too, welcomed a chance to be off on my own so that I could speak with Sam and so that I might mull over my future decisions. I returned to Montreal with the understanding that the Chiefs and I would talk again as soon as their season had ended.

What to do? The Chiefs had a definite vacancy. Washington was a "maybe." Neither team was going to be strong for a few years, but the Chiefs brass had told me that they understood the depths to which the Chiefs personnel situation had sunk. They would be patient, they had told me, especially because they were determined to build through the draft. Granted it was the slow way to do it, but it was, they felt, the surest way to get to the top and to stay there. Wasn't that how Dallas had done it? And Pittsburgh? Those were the points that club president Jack Steadman put forth so strenuously during our visit.

In Washington, people were not used to being patient. They had just experienced seven consecutive winning seasons, and the fans expected their Redskins to continue as a strong team. Never mind that old "building for the future" conundrum.

There were some other appealing advantages I saw in the Kansas City situation. They would be a young team on the rise, not the remnants of the squad George had left behind. George had won numerous battles, but he would be leaving a shattered army, lying spent on its broken shields. To me, the most compelling lure in Kansas City would be the nature of the responsibilities I was promised during my negotiations with the Chiefs. I would have sole authority over all matters relating to selection of the coaching staff and player personnel. Without interference, I was to determine which players we played in the games, which players we would release, and which players we would retain on our roster. Decisions on trades were to be mine, subject to sanction and counsel by general manager Jim Schaaf, because contract and financial implications had to be considered.

We agreed that we would take a consensus approach in formulating plans for the annual draft of college players. When it comes to drafting, I have always felt it is wise for a coach to adhere to the judgments made by the men in the scouting department. They are the people most knowledgeable regarding the relative abilities of graduating college players. I would still shape our draft philosophy and retain final approval on all draft choices the club would be making, however, but it would be a rare instance indeed for me to go contrary to the recommendations made by our director of player personnel.

It would be my responsibility, of course, to determine our style of play, our strategy, and our game-day tactics. That was exactly the way it had been for me while I was coaching in Montreal, and these were the promises that Chiefs president Jack Steadman made during our meetings. It sure sounded good to me.

♦♦♦♦♦♦♦♦

After that round of interviews, I returned to Montreal where I informed Sam and Bob Geary that I had had discussions with the two NFL teams. I also told them that in neither situation had I been made a specific job offer. We all agreed that there was no need to address the matter further unless a concrete proposal was made by an NFL team. One week later, Jack Steadman telephoned me again with the message I had been hoping to hear. He told me that the Chiefs wanted me to be their new head coach, and he asked me to meet him in Chicago as soon as possible so that we could discuss the details of a contract.

In the time that had elapsed since my first meeting with EBW and with the Chiefs officials, I had had ample opportunity to weigh the pros and cons. Despite the high regard I had for EBW, and despite the wonderful memories I retained of those thrilling Sundays at RFK Stadium, I felt that the path to winning soon enough to survive in Washington was strewn with land mines. If the Kansas City job were offered, I determined, I would accept it. I had not at that point discussed salary with either Washington or Kansas City, but that was not going to be the deciding factor for me, anyway.

Now I had the distasteful task of telling both Sam and EBW about my plans. EBW understood that I had made a difficult decision, and he wished me well. Sam was not happy about my intended departure. He reminded me that there were two years remaining on an attractive contract he had given me a year earlier at a time when so many fans and the media had been speculating that I was about to be fired. His words hurt, but, as always, what he said was the truth. I explained to him how seldom someone who enters coaching as an assistant high school coach and who fantasizes about someday becoming a head coach in the NFL ever sees that dream realized. I explained to him further that such an opportunity very likely would never come for me again. My words did not have the impact on him I had hoped they would have, however, and I could understand the agitation he felt.

He had taken over a dying franchise in a dying league. He had plowed large amounts of his own resourced into the enterprise at a time when only he had faith that he could cause the CFL to survive. He had stuck by me in dark times, and now, he felt, I was abandoning him.

"If you are determined to go, then do so," he said, "but it is not with my blessing."

I had hoped that it would be. What Sam thought of me was important.

"Sam," I said to him, "I don't know if you recall this, but last year when I signed my contract with you, I said that if an NFL head coaching job were offered to me I would ask that you allow me to take it. You said that you would."

"That is not written into our contract," he noted.

"I don't need Sam Berger's word written into a contract," I told the elderly lawyer.

There was silence as he looked across his desk directly into my eyes.

"Of course you don't," he told me.

There weren't adequate words I could find to thank Sam for all he had meant to me during the five years I had been in Canada, but I tried. As I was leaving his office for the last time, he came out from behind his desk and grabbed my arm.

"Marv, you *do* have my blessing," he said.

He knew those words would mean a lot to me. And they did.

Two days later, I met with Jack Steadman in Chicago. We agreed on the terms of a contract and established plans for me to come to Kansas City where a formal press conference announcing my appointment would be held. It should have been a happy occasion, but later that day my mother's physical condition took a sharp turn downward.

I contacted Jack in order to arrange for a delay in the press conference he was going to schedule, and then I rushed to the hospital in order to be with my mother. Through her suffering she still managed a smile and a joyful sigh when I told her that I would be returning to the United States and that I would be coaching in Kansas City. My mother knew little about football, but she knew much about people's heart desires. She drifted into peaceful slumber, and in the early hours of the next morning, the sweet lady died in her sleep.

SECTION VI

THE BATTLE OF KANSAS CITY

CHAPTER 18

Can We Go to the Super Bowl with This Quarterback?

At the press conference where I was presented for the first time to the Kansas City media, I learned a valuable lesson. Toward the end of the session, I was asked by one of the journalists to describe the style of play our fans could look forward to seeing in Arrowhead Stadium.

My answer was, "Offense sells tickets. Kicking wins games. Defense wins championships."

Nothing earth shaking about that. It's true. But hardly anyone likes to hear it. Never mind that the team that has led the NFL in passing yardage for the season has won the championship just one time in NFL history, while the best defensive team has won it so often that I've lost count. People want to hear about offense—"Big O" as Jack Steadman would call it.

So here is my advice to all coaches: Talk about offense. Talk about your aerial circus. Give it a signature name. Call it "The Coast-to-Coast Offense," or announce, as an alternative, that it will be known—if your last name is Kappelmeier—by the appellation "Air Kappelmeier." Talk about how innovative you are. Tell them you invented the spiral. Tell them that you like to roll the dice, that punting is for sissies, and that defense is for criminal lawyers. Use words like "razzle dazzle" and every synonymous term you can dredge up. Don't talk about reverses; talk about *triple* reverses and *fake* reverses. Tell the world how you are going to go for it on fourth down, probably with a play-action pass. Say something catchy, such as, "Our offense will take no prisoners" or "Wait until you see *our* weapons of mass destruction." And then—*do what it takes to win.*

As we began preparations in the spring of 1978 for my first draft with Kansas City, I saw immediately why the Chiefs had sunk to such a lowly spot in the NFL standings. Over the preceding three years the team had given up a staggering average of 30 points a game, more than any other team. They were woefully weak on defense, and it was easy for me to see why. Going all the way back to 1970, the Chiefs had used their first pick in the draft for a defensive player just one time. Even here they had fared poorly. Of the seven offensive players they had chosen with those first selections, only one still remained on the roster. He was a reserve lineman whom we did not retain after my first season as coach of the team.

As our predraft meetings intensified I became increasingly aware of how often Jack Steadman would pop in. His interest I could understand, but then I began to notice how vigorously he would express opinions about so many of the areas which I believed fell into the category—as it had been described to me during my interview—of football operations. Jack knew business, and he knew it well. He knew a lot about a lot of things, but he didn't know much about football. Trouble is, he *thought* he knew more than anyone else about it.

As the team's president, Jack had every right to be kept abreast of my thinking and my reasons for taking actions that affected the club. Furthermore, I expected that there would be differences of opinion from time to time. A rational give-and-take discussion can often lead to both parties being better informed and can conclude in an atmosphere that allows them to work together more closely.

I had that type of relationship with the team's general manager, Jim Schaaf. Jim was a former Notre Dame lineman. He knew football. He was forceful and straightforward. We could have heated discussions with each other—even disagreements—and still keep each other's trust. If I ever felt that Jim crossed the line where he was meddling with responsibilities we had all agreed were mine, I told him so. If he concurred, he'd back off. If he didn't agree, he'd tell me why.

Unfortunately for the Chiefs, Jim was not allowed to function as a general manager should. Jack also interfered in the areas where Jim was responsible. Jim never told me that, but it was obvious, just as it was apparent to all observers that Jack sought to influence so many decisions that were in the domain of the head coach.

Jim had been serving as the Chiefs' director of media relations, but when Hank Stram was released following the 1974 season, Jim had been named as the team's new general manager. Jack made certain, however, that Jim's activities were confined to matters of contract negotiations and to many of the functions usually assigned to an assistant general manager. Jack retained for himself all authority for the policy matters that were normally handled by the GM. Unfortunately, for Jim and for me, Lamar Hunt, a truly well-intentioned gentleman, lived in Dallas, and almost all communication with him about such issues was channeled through Jack.

Jim stayed current with what was happening on our team. He knew the players well, and he communicated with them. He watched our films; he attended many practices, and he was open-minded in his dealings with us all. Jim won the confidence of our players and coaches alike. Jack would show up for practice for 15 minutes two or three times a year. He rarely spoke with our players. That was fine with them.

Now, in 1978, without having examined the personnel department reports, Jack was campaigning for us to use our first-round draft choice to select a quarterback. He opened our discussions by asking me a question that I soon learned would be his constant query.

"Do you think we can make it to the Super Bowl with Mike Livingston [the Chiefs' veteran signal caller] as our quarterback?"

I didn't have to ponder long in order to come up with an answer.

"Until we cure our problems on defense, Jack, neither Mike Livingston nor any other quarterback can lead this team to the Super Bowl," I responded.

I didn't bother to add that in 1970, when the Chiefs had won the Super Bowl, Mike Livingston had played quarterback during a large part of that season, because starter Lenny Dawson had been injured.

In the 1978 draft, we had the second pick in the first round. Our scouting department had designated running back Earl Campbell as the top player among that year's prospects. Ranked number two was a six-foot, seven-inch, 260-pound defensive end from the University of Kentucky named Art Still. Everyone knew that the Oilers would name Campbell as their first choice. There was no question in my mind that we should follow by selecting Art. During the weeks leading up to the draft, Jack continued to lobby for us to take a quarterback.

On draft day, Jack was still pushing for a quarterback. I persisted, however, and we chose Art. In the second round we picked up another defensive lineman, Sylvester Hicks, and in the third round we selected a linebacker, Gary Spani. Art was an All-Pro player for the Chiefs on several occasions. Several years later, when I was coaching in Buffalo, we acquired him in a trade, and he help propel the Bills to their first division title in many years. Sylvester was also a valuable addition to our defense. Gary won a starting position as a rookie, and he continued to be an outstanding leader and the Chiefs' best linebacker for many years.

♦♦♦♦♦♦♦♦

As we prepared for the 1978 season, our coaching staff, knowing that we were going in with a weak defense, believed it was essential that we find a way to keep our defenders off the field as much as possible. I decided that we should utilize a run-oriented offense, one that could help us maintain ball control and use up big chunks of the clock. If we could combine those qualities with an outstanding kicking game, I felt, we could stay close in every game and be in position to pull off some upsets. Even on those days when we might not win, we would have fought a tough battle, and our players could leave the field with their morale intact and their self-respect growing. With these thoughts in mind, we installed my old-time Wing T formation, a power-based, time-consuming ball-control offense.

It was my intention to use the Wing T for one year, perhaps two at the most. We wanted to give our defense time to gain experience. We wanted to develop toughness and discipline. We wanted our players to be in every game. We wanted them to develop spirit and confidence. Given the makeup of our squad, the Wing T formation was the ideal vehicle for helping us accomplish those objectives.

♦♦♦♦♦♦♦♦

We opened the 1978 season on the road against the Bengals. The year before, Cincinnati had drubbed the Chiefs 27-7, and that game had been played at Arrowhead Stadium. We figured to have our hands full on the first Sunday of my NFL head coaching career.

We brought our Wing T to Riverfront Stadium, and we ran the ball. We ran it, in fact, more times than any Chiefs team had—or has since—run the ball in a single game. We had *69 running plays* that day, and we controlled the ball for 41 minutes compared to 19 for the Bengals. We took an early lead, but Cincinnati rallied in the fourth quarter. With just over six minutes remaining, the Bengals scored a touchdown, cutting our lead to one point. They never got the ball back again. We stayed on the ground, grinding out first downs, retaining possession until the clock ran out. We had won our opener 24-23.

The following week we took a 17-6 halftime lead against the Oilers, but then they did even better at what we had hoped to do to them. With their sensational rookie, Earl Campbell, chewing up yardage, they maintained ball control throughout most of the second half. With less than two minutes to play, Campbell went into the end zone for the touchdown that won the game 20-17. During the five years I was to coach in Kansas City, we never again lost a game after taking as large a lead as we had that day against the Oilers.

We continued to play close games. Against Denver, the defending AFC champions, we lost in overtime. After each narrow loss our team played harder, but we didn't get our second win until the eighth game of the season, when we defeated the Browns 17-3 at Arrowhead. The following week we lost a 27-24 heartbreaker to the powerful Steelers in Pittsburgh. We then lost in overtime again, this time to the Chargers, and a week after that we dropped a 13-10 squeaker to the Seahawks. We headed into the final four games of our season with lots of fight but without many victories to show for it. Toward the end of the previous season, the Chiefs had collapsed, being routed in the final six games of the year. This year's team wasn't ready to surrender.

Our team, and especially our defense, came of age after the Seattle loss. We came back to Arrowhead Stadium and shut down the explosive Chargers offense, beating them soundly 23-0. We followed that victory with a 14-10 win over the Bills. For the first time since early in the 1976 season, the Chiefs had won two straight games. The Broncos snapped our streak the following week, and we finished the season one week after that with a 23-19 loss against Seattle.

We had won only four games during the 1978 season. Still, that was twice as many as the Chiefs had won the previous year, and although we were a long way from where we intended to be, there were some encouraging signs. There had been a sharp improvement in our defense, and the young players had gained in experience and confidence. Our kicking game had already become the equal of any in the NFL, and by the following year we would have no peer in that department. Most important, our players believed they could win.

Mike Livingston had done an excellent job of implementing our Wing T attack. He had been an unselfish player, and he had won the respect of his teammates. Although Mike was past his prime, he could still play well, and his grasp of the game, combined with his calm personal manner, helped the young players at a time when they most needed the type of leadership Mike provided.

It was now time to draft a young quarterback. We needed to give him time to learn for two or three years, while Mike continued to function as our starter. Meetings, film sessions, game planning involvement, studying opponents' offenses and defenses, drilling and refining his fundamental position skills, playing the role of the opposing team's quarterback at practice, seeing some mop up action in a few games, playing in preseason games—these were the kinds of activities that would pay off handsomely for a newly drafted quarterback and for our team.

When that young signal caller had gained maturity and familiarity with professional football, he could then take over a solid team, one that had been strengthened by three years of solid drafts and by experience. That is the way to bring along a promising quarterback. Provide him the advantage of learning without undue pressure, and you will greatly increase his chances to succeed and to grow in confidence.

Jack, of course, was all for the draft-a-quarterback premise. There was a problem, however. Once again, in 1979, we had the second pick in the draft. Once again, the second-rated player in that draft was a defensive end, Mike Bell from Colorado State University. When the scouts around the league categorize the draft-eligible players each year, very few of those players are designated as surefire first-year starters in the NFL. There are usually two or three draftees each year who are worthy of being so considered. In 1979, Mike was one of them.

The top-rated quarterback in that year's draft class was Jack Thompson of Washington State University, but his scouting grade rating was nowhere close to Mike Bell's. Also, Jack had a history of injuries, and our team doctors, upon examining him, advised that his previously injured knees would serve to shorten Jack's career considerably. There was no question in my mind that we should select Mike with our first choice. With him in the lineup, we would have two outstanding young defensive ends. The cornerstones for our defense would have been laid. We had the second pick in the second round, also, and we could get the premier defensive end available that year *plus* a good quarterback prospect.

Jack Steadman was having none of that.

"We need *the* top quarterback available now," he insisted. "Let me ask you, do you think we can go to the Super Bowl with Mike Livingston? Won't we be a better team with Jack Thompson at quarterback?"

"I do not know." I countered, "but I do know that we *will* be a better team with Mike Bell in the lineup. I also know that we can get a good quarterback prospect with our second choice."

That conversation took place in February. I wasn't to hear the last of Jack's quarterback harangue until the exact moment we finally drafted Mike Bell in May.

The night before the draft, Jack; Jim Schaaf; Les Miller, our director of player personnel; and I met for several hours finalizing our strategy for the next day. At this meeting Jack turned up the heat in his efforts to get me to back off from my position on Mike. When he realized that I remained resolute, he spoke some words to me, which I was to hear often from him whenever I made a personnel decision that was not in accordance with what he had been advocating.

"Okay, but you will be held responsible for how this decision works out."

Hell! I knew that. I went to bed late that night feeling that at last a great load had been lifted from my shoulders. We were going to pick Mike Bell with our first choice.

One hour before the draft was scheduled to begin, Jack called us all together again.

"I cannot believe that we are not going to select a quarterback first," he proclaimed.

After the hour had passed, we were still talking about it, and even as we walked to the drafting room the conversation continued. Jack didn't like it, but we picked Mike Bell. It was the right choice.

Mike broke into our starting lineup immediately, and he led the squad in sacking opponents' quarterbacks several times in the years that followed. Teaming with Art Still, Mike gave the Chiefs a defensive line on a par with any in the league.

♦♦♦♦♦♦♦♦

Because we all knew that Jack Thompson would be selected by some other team before we'd get a shot at him in the top of the second round, we began to maneuver and plot our strategy so that we could pick one of the other quarterbacks we had rated highly. We—and everyone else in the NFL, too—knew that the San Francisco 49ers would be going after a top-notch quarterback in that year's draft. San Francisco did not get to pick until the bottom of the first round, and as the draft moved along, approaching the time when the 49ers could make their choice, we speculated that they would be going after Clemson's Steve Fuller, the highest rated quarterback still on the board.

We liked Steve, too, and if it worked out that he would be available at the top of the second round, we planned to choose him. He had been a rollout quarterback for a run-oriented college team, but he was big, strong, bright, and athletic, and he would have been a good selection if we were willing to be patient as he developed his pro-style talents.

If the 49ers did take Steve at the bottom of the first, I had my eyes on another quarterback whose grades in that year's draft really didn't merit his being selected early in the second round, but there was something about that man that told me he was worth the gamble.

All during the spring of 1979 as we prepared for the draft, we had sent our assistant coaches out to the colleges where they would meet with the highest rated player prospects at the positions they coached. Kay Dalton, the coach on our staff responsible for the passing game, was assigned to work out quarterbacks. When he returned from his trip, his initial reports were about those who were potential first-round selections, but he, too, felt that none of them merited being taken with the second overall pick in the draft. Kay spoke highly of Steve Fuller, but he went on to comment that there was one fellow, a non-first-rounder, Kay said, whom he liked best—*better than any of the top two or three!*

I was intrigued, and so I watched some films of Kay's favorite guy. His arm was okay, but it wasn't the kind of gun that made you gasp. He was, however, very quick, and he displayed a flair and a competitiveness that was eye-catching. The more I watched him the more I came to understand Kay's enthusiasm. I called the lad's college coach, and, in terms of coach-speak, it had to be the most gushing endorsement I've ever heard this side of an Academy Awards presentation.

If San Francisco did go ahead and pluck Steve Fuller off the board with their low first-round pick, I would have been quite content to use our top of the second choice on the quarterback that Kay had recommended so highly. When I told that to the other men sitting in our draft headquarters room, their response was understandably lukewarm. Jack made a good case for why we should seek to trade away our second-round pick plus several other draft choices in order to move up and get a first-round slot just ahead of the 49ers.

"How long are we going to continue to bypass *the* best quarterback available?" he demanded to know. "The man you are willing to settle for does not have a scouting grade anywhere near high enough for us to use our early second-round pick on him. Besides, Marv, he really isn't very big—just average height for a quarterback and real slim, too. You already have acknowledged that his arm is nothing that will blow you away. C'mon, it's time for us to get that best QB right now!"

Everything Jack had said made sense, and, realizing now how many times I had persisted in having it my way, I listened and then agreed with the logic that Jack had put forth. We went to work on the phones and managed to swing such a trade just moments before San Francisco would have had their opportunity to exercise their first-round pick. We picked Steve Fuller. We had our quarterback.

Just seconds after our selection of Steve Fuller was announced, the telephone in our draft room buzzed. The call was for me, and, on the other end of the line I heard the voice of my old friend, Bill Walsh, who was now the head coach of the 49ers.

"Marv, you no-good so and so!" he shouted. "We were going to pick Steve Fuller, and you guys knew it, didn't you?"

He said it with no rancor in his voice, because he knew the chess games that were always played out on draft day. In fact, Bill was a master of such shenanigans himself.

The disappointed 49ers did not select a quarterback when their turn to pick came. They didn't take one in the second round either. They waited until late in the third round, and it was there that they chose the young prospect that Kay had called to my attention. I haven't mentioned that player's name up until now because he was some guy you football fans have never heard of. His name was Joe Montana.

We began my second season at Kansas City on a high note, shutting out the Colts 14-0 at Arrowhead Stadium. Our defense and our kicking teams played superbly in that game. Led by Art Still and Mike Bell, our defensive line completely throttled Bert Jones and the potent Baltimore attack.

We had brought a free agent rookie punter named Bob Grupp to training camp, and, by the end of the preseason, it was obvious that he had won the competition for the position. Against Baltimore, in his first NFL game, Bob punted 11 times, a Chiefs' single-game record that still stands. Time after time, from deep in our own territory, Bob sent towering punts booming into the late summer sky, forcing the Colts to start their drives a long way from our goal line. Bob Grupp averaged better than 45 yards per punt that day, and when the weekly statistics were published the following Tuesday, he was leading the NFL. Bob continued to lead the league all season, and he was selected as the AFC's punter in that year's Pro Bowl.[1]

Although we had combined Bob Grupp's sterling punting performance and the tenacious play of our defense to win the Baltimore game,

1. The following summer Bob injured a groin muscle while working as an instructor at a punting clinic. He was never again able to punt as well as he had during his rookie season, and eventually we had to replace him. Without that injury, he was destined to have become one of the greatest punters ever. He told me that he had punted more than 80 times one day during that ill-fated clinic. We believed that 20 times a day should have been the maximum.

we had failed to move the ball on offense with any authority. The following week our offense started even more poorly, and at halftime we left the field trailing the Browns 20-0. I decided at halftime to give Steve Fuller some game experience. He had quite a debut.

Steve, relying mostly on his hair-raising scrambling ability against Cleveland's loosened defenses, rallied our team. In the fourth quarter we took a 24-20 lead, only to see it slip away when Cleveland quarterback Brian Sipe connected on a 35-yard touchdown pass to Reggie Rucker in the closing moments. Cleveland won the game 27-24.

The real blow, however, was not the loss of a single game. Mike Bell had torn a bicep muscle free from its attachment. The injury required surgical repair, and Mike would have to miss the remainder of the season. We had lost Mike, but sometimes the effect on a team's morale, when a key player is sidelined with an injury, is even more devastating than the loss of his services. We reflected that the following week when Houston pushed us around at the Astrodome, inflicting a 20-6 defeat upon us.

On the basis of his excellent second-half showing in Cleveland, I started Steve Fuller against Houston, and he played the entire game. They threw a blitzing, stunting pass rush at Steve, sacking him six times during the contest. I did not want to put him back on the bench after just one poor game, however, and so I decided that he would get the starting call again the following week when we would be meeting the Raiders.

At one time the Chiefs versus Raiders rivalry had been the most hotly contested matchup in the AFC. The Raiders had won the previous seven games between the two teams, however, and the Chiefs had become twice-a-year patsies as the Raiders laughed their way through their long winning streak. It was time for us to regroup. The loss of one player did not diminish the talents of the other players on our team, I told our squad. We could put our tails between our legs, curl up, and die, or we could show that we were made of sterner stuff. Our team responded with a 35-7 thrashing of the Raiders. It was the most satisfying day the Chiefs and their fans had known in many years.

After Oakland, we beat the Seahawks 24-6. The Seahawks had come into the AFC West as an expansion franchise a few years earlier, but our triumph on this day marked the first time that the Chiefs had ever defeated Seattle. Next, we scored our third consecutive victory by nipping the Bengals 10-7. Not since early in the 1975 season had the Chiefs won three straight games.

Our streak ended there, however. The Broncos beat us 24-10. Then, against the Giants, we played poorly in the first half, falling behind 14-0. That was the third week in a row that our offense had been ineffective. Steve had been at quarterback ever since we had inserted him into the lineup for the second half of our second game of the year in Cleveland. Now, against the Giants, he was once again struggling badly, and, feeling that a change of tempo was needed at that key position, I sent Mike Livingston out to play at the start of the second half. It was Mike's turn to spark an exciting comeback, and he did.

We moved the ball smoothly throughout the entire second half, and, with five minutes left to play, Mike completed a long touchdown pass to wideout Henry Marshall, putting us in front for the first time in the game. We led 17-14. New York could not move the ball, and they had to punt to us. With just a minute and a half remaining in the game, one of our rookie running backs fumbled. A Giants' defender scooped the ball off of the turf and ran it into our end zone for the touchdown that broke our hearts and won the game for New York 21-17.

In the second half of that game against the Giants, we had moved the ball, for the first time that season (now at the halfway point), with the type of rhythm that coaches envision when they devise their game plans. Our offense had shown cohesion, understanding, and the promise of continuing to get better. True, Steve had shown some encouraging qualities. It was obvious that he was a keen competitor. We had won three games in which he had been the starter, and we had also lost three with him in that role. Many of the big plays that had occurred while he was on the field had been the result of helter-skelter improvisation on his part. He had talent: no doubt about that. In my opinion, he now needed to come out of the lineup for a while. He needed to digest what had been force-fed to him during the past several hectic weeks. He needed to see some games from the close proximity of the sidelines while profiting from the new and expanded perspective now open to him.

Besides that, we still had a mathematical chance to make the playoffs. Considering the strength of our team, it was a long shot, but, if we were to overcome the odds, we needed to have a veteran signal caller to lead the way. I felt that Steve, if we were to play him, would win a few and lose a few at this early stage of his career. The likelihood of our making the playoffs with a rookie, subjected to intense pressure and trying to run the show, was exceedingly slim.

There were no guarantees that Mike could pull it off, either, but I decided that our best hopes at that time lay in going with Mike. On Monday, I told the two players of my plan. Steve understood, and he accepted my decision. At my weekly Tuesday media meeting the next day, I announced that Mike would be our starting quarterback that coming Sunday when we were scheduled to meet the division-leading Broncos.

Early Wednesday—the busiest preparation day of the week during the season in professional football—Jack came to my office saying there was something he wished to discuss with me. I didn't need three guesses. Since the first day of training camp, Jack had exerted every influence he could contrive in his efforts to get across to me his conviction that Steve should be our starting quarterback. After our first training camp scrimmage, held specifically for rookies, in which Steve had completed about 50 percent of his passes, Jack asked me what I had thought of Steve's performance.

"He looked pretty good to me," I said. "I'm pleased with how well he did for a first scrimmage."

"Pretty good!" Jack exclaimed. "He was *awesome*."

One of Jack's favorite buzzwords was "awesome." In my five years with the Chiefs there was one constant upon which I could always rely. After our first rookie scrimmage in training camp each year, Jack would inform me that the offensive player we had selected first in that year's draft had looked "absolutely awesome." After this particular scrimmage, however, Jack advanced a further opinion regarding Steve.

"If he continues to progress like this, he'll be our starter. Don't you think?"

"Jack, he's not ready for that, yet," I said.

In my own mind I tried to rationalize that Jack wanted merely to be informed about my thinking and that he wasn't seeking to interfere in personnel matters. Deep down I knew better.

That exchange had taken place back in July, but it was now halfway through the season when Jack came into my office on the Wednesday before our Denver game in order to discuss once again what he so often referred to as "the quarterback situation." I have often wondered why no football team ever has a "left guard situation."

"I heard on the news last night and saw in the newspaper this morning that you're planning to start Mike Livingston this week," he said.

"That's right."

"But you didn't tell me; you didn't even talk it over with me."

I guess I was supposed to feel guilty. Wearily, I pushed aside the practice and game planning materials on which I had been concentrating and told him why I had made the decision to start Mike. I could see the agitation growing in Jack's face.

"You didn't have the guts to tell me," he exploded.

That was the exact moment I became aware that the working relationship that existed between Jack and me was in serious jeopardy, and, for the first time since I had come to Kansas City, I raised my voice in talking with him.

"What you mean is that I *did* have the guts to make a decision, which I am supposed to make without interference from you," I snapped back. "I plan to keep making personnel decisions that are in the best interests of the team, and, so long as they do not involve financial matters, I am not going to seek your permission in instances where it has already been agreed that I have responsibility and authority. I've got one life to live, and I am going to walk through it, standing straight, on my own two feet; not crawling along on my belly."

Now, at least, we understood each other. I understood, also, that unless our team showed unwavering improvement, Jack would work to have me replaced as coach of the Chiefs. For the most part we remained civil in our dealings with each other. Not once during my five years with the team did I ever allow the fallout from a disagreement between Jack and me to spill outside of our discussions with each other. Never—to the media, to the members of our coaching staff, to Jim Schaaf or anyone else in the Chiefs organization, to owner Lamar Hunt, to any fans, or to any friends—did I say or hint at anything disparaging regarding Jack. While I worked for the Chiefs, I owed him that. However, I no longer work for the Chiefs.

I wish I could write now that our performance against the Broncos at the end of that tumultuous week would have vindicated the decision I had made. It didn't. The Broncos, with the best-ranked defense in the NFL, won easily 20-3. Nevertheless, I started Mike again the following week against San Diego. He played well, and our offense did succeed in moving the ball against the Chargers. Not quite well enough, however, because San Diego came away with a 20-14 victory. With six games remaining in the season our record was 4-6, and next on our schedule were the powerful Steelers.

The Steelers were the defending Super Bowl champions from the year before, and they were destined to win it again during this 1979 season. Early in the preparation week for that game, I received a long, carefully crafted letter from team owner Lamar Hunt.

One of the items that Lamar addressed in his letter concerned our quarterbacks. The main point he made was that, although he understood the reasons for reinserting Mike as our starter, he felt that the situation had changed drastically from what it had been two weeks earlier. Realistically, he noted, we were no longer a viable contender for a playoff spot. The time had come for us to think creatively.

"The future of the Kansas City Chiefs," he wrote, "*and your future with the Chiefs* [the italics are mine] depend upon how quickly Steve Fuller develops into a strong NFL starting quarterback."

He suggested that I take advantage of the remaining games by allowing Steve to play and to gain valuable game experience.

So far as Steve's development was concerned, my thinking had evolved in this direction, also. For two reasons, however, I would have preferred going one more week with Mike. First, if we could win all of our remaining six games, we still had a mathematical—granted, highly unlikely—shot at the playoffs. Second, I would have preferred that Steve's reintroduction to combat be against a team less formidable than the Steelers. But there are issues worth fighting for, regardless of the consequences. Waiting one more game until we would insert Steve into our lineup was not one of them. We started Steve that Sunday against the Steelers.

As I had studied my letter from Lamar, I sensed that his words about my future with the Chiefs bore an ominous tone. Perhaps he did not mean them to resonate that way. I would have welcomed a face-to-face, one-on-one discussion with Lamar about our quarterbacks and about a variety of other topics relating to the football operations of the team. I truly liked Lamar, and I felt—and still feel today—that he is a straight shooter. We were not structured that way, however. Once Jack had succeeded, following the 1974 season, in railroading longtime Chiefs head coach, Hank Stram, out of his job, Jack had supplanted Hank as the person responsible to Lamar for the team's football operations. After that, easy-flowing, direct communication between Lamar and the head coach became more cumbersome.

As I look back now, I wish I would have had the good sense to have initiated more direct one-on-one discussions with Lamar, but, at that time, I felt doing so might have been interpreted as a power-play on my part to bypass Jack's authority. I did not want to be the cause of any such internal in-fighting. Upon occasion, I did have telephone conversations with Lamar, but these did not serve sufficiently to cover the detail needed in the coordinating of a successful program. Whenever Lamar was in Kansas City or with us on trips, our discussions about football operations were always held with Jack present.

On the Sunday after that week of "Who should be quarterback?" Pittsburgh inflicted upon us our season's worst defeat 30-3. It wasn't Steve's fault; we had been overwhelmed by a far superior team.

Our players refused to quit in the late stages of the season, and we came back the following week in Oakland where we defeated the Raiders 24-21. On the last play of that game, with the ball on our one-yard line, their place kicker missed a field goal attempt, and we danced off the field with our astounding victory. We deserved a break like that, I felt, after what had happened to us in the waning minutes of our game against the Giants earlier that season. In beating the Raiders, we had swept the season's series from them. The win was the first for the Chiefs on the Raiders' home field since 1966.

We won two of our next three games, and with one game remaining, our won-lost mark stood at 7-8. We would have finished with a break-even year if we could have won the season's finale in Tampa against the playoff-bound Tampa Bay Buccaneers. The game was played in a deluge of rain. Neither team could move the ball, but, late in the fourth quarter, despite the adverse weather conditions, Neil O'Donoghue, the Bucs' place kicker, booted a field goal for the only score of the game. Tampa Bay had won it 3-0.

We had narrowly missed becoming a .500 team, but, once again, we had improved over the previous season's record. Our defense had allowed 60 fewer points than we had the year before. We had gained more experience at all positions, and, although we still lacked adequate depth, we had some excellent starters, especially on defense.

On the field we were becoming more like contenders. In my meetings with Jack about matters of player personnel, however, we were becoming more *contentious*. That is not a good formula for teamwork, for harmony—or for *winning*.

CHAPTER 19

Stick to Your Guns

As we prepared for opening day in 1980, we made two bold personnel moves. One of them was at quarterback. During Steve Fuller's rookie season in 1979, he had started 12 games. Steve had been plunged into action more quickly than I would have liked. He had played as well as could be expected, but he had operated on instinct, and he still had a lot to learn. Steve would have benefited from more observing and from less exposure to pressure during his rookie year.

In San Francisco, by contrast, Joe Montana had spent most of his rookie year watching veteran Steve DeBerg play quarterback. The 49ers had resisted the urge to rush Joe onto the field even though they had labored through a 2-14 season. Joe threw just 23 passes during the year, and his first start did not come until the 14th game of the season. Again, in 1980, the 49ers held Joe back. After the first four games, he had thrown only six times. Then he began to see a little more action, and in their seventh game he was given the starting assignment.

The 49ers brought Joe along exactly as a young quarterback should have been. They had minimized the pressure on Joe, while allowing him to learn, to gain confidence, to master the tools he possessed. San Francisco's head coach, Bill Walsh, was also the man in charge of football operations for their team, and he had no Jack Steadman hovering about to divert him from good coaching procedures.

It would have been my preference to bring Steve along in much the same way, but the off-season discussions between Jack and me began with his expressions of concern about the "quarterback situation." On many aspects of the topic we were in agreement. We both felt that our quarterback of the future was Steve, and we both agreed that he should be our starter as soon as it was wise for us to install him in that role.

Jack (and Lamar Hunt) wanted the path to be cleared for this step by eliminating Mike Livingston from the equation. I would have preferred that Mike be our starter at the beginning of the season, but I came to realize that his presence would result in more problems—so far as my dealings with the front office were concerned—than benefits.

In 1979, when we drafted Steve, we also had brought to camp another quarterback whom we had signed as a free agent. His name was Bill Kenney, and on the strength of a strong training camp performance, we kept Bill over several other candidates who were vying for the No. 3 quarterback slot on our roster. Bill did not see any regular-season game action throughout his rookie year, but he did serve as the scout-team quarterback as he helped our defensive unit prepare for each week's opponent. We liked what we observed in him. He had a strong arm; he was a quick learner; he was intelligent, and he had an excellent understanding of the passing game. At six feet, four inches and 215 pounds, he also had ideal size for the position.

With Bill on our team, untried as he was, I felt better about our strength at quarterback. Between Steve and Bill, however, we would still have too little experience there if we traded away Mike. Then something happened that made such a trade more feasible. The best CFL quarterback over the previous several years had been Tom Clements. Tom was undersized, but he was an outstanding athlete and field general. He had just played out his option with the Hamilton Tigercats, and so we signed Tom to a Chiefs contract. The way had been cleared for us to part with Mike.

Late in the spring, we traded Mike to the Vikings for a lower-round draft choice. Upon doing this, we all concurred that Steve would be our No. 1 quarterback going into the 1980 season.

The other personnel decision that I made prior to the beginning of the regular season in 1980 had greater traumatic effect on our team than any of the repercussions that emanated from our ongoing quarterback carousel. For more than a decade, Jan Stenerud had handled all place-kicking responsibilities. Jan was more than just another player; he was a favorite of the fans in Kansas City, the last player remaining on the roster from the Chiefs' 1969 Super Bowl Championship team.

Although Jan still had a couple of productive years remaining before he would retire, his level of performance had tailed off a bit from what it had been during the prime of his career. In the late 1960s and the early and mid-1970s his booming kickoffs had sailed repeatedly through opponents' end zones. That was no longer happening. Also his percentage of misses on field goal attempts, particularly those from more than 40 yards, had increased in the last couple of years. Jan was a dogged competitor, however, and for several years, including my first two as coach of the Chiefs, he had staved off the challenges of the young hopefuls we had brought to training camp each year.

During the off season, following the 1979 campaign, we had signed a little-known free agent out of Dartmouth named Nick Lowery. Nick had been cut by five other NFL teams, and so we brought him to training camp with little thought that he would still be with us once the season began. From the outset, however, Nick established himself as a serious contender. Day after day, Nick excelled. His kickoffs were averaging 15 yards more than Jan's, and they were hanging in the air much longer. His accuracy on field goals was astounding, and he kept displaying a machine-like consistency, never having a bad day.

It is one thing to kick well in practice and quite another to do well in games. When the preseason games began, however, Nick's performances in those contests continued to be of the highest caliber.

Only three weeks remained until our final cutdown, and it had become apparent that Jan was up against the most serious challenge he had faced since joining the team in 1967. Almost all of our players were pulling for Jan. He was personable, mature, and team oriented. No one could imagine the Chiefs starting a season without Jan teeing up for that first kickoff just as he had done for every one of the previous 13 years.

From the standpoint of his relationship with teammates, Nick was not helping his own cause. In training camp, veteran players usually inflict some verbal harassment upon the rookies. Most of those neophytes endure it, keep quiet, and maintain as low a profile as possible. Not Nick. He tended to return their jibes, trying to upstage them with the cleverness of his remarks. Because of Nick's proclivity to respond in this manner, I began to see the attitude of our players toward him turn from one of light-hearted ribbing into displays of resentment.

It was bad enough for a rookie to answer back, but if he happened to be a kicker, his sins were compounded in the eyes of the established players. Not only that, this smart ass from the Ivy League was trying to unseat one of the most popular and respected players that had ever worn a Chiefs uniform. Nick became an outcast. I saw the makings of a serious morale problem beginning to take shape. It was time for me to have a talk with him.

"You are going to make this team with your foot, not with your mouth," I told him.

We talked at length, and after that Nick went quietly back to work, biting his tongue at times, I am sure. One day in practice, he kicked two 65-yard field goals, and his abilities continued to win the grudging respect of the other players.

We were late into our training camp when I made the decision that Nick would be our kicker and that we would have to release Jan. I felt it best that we make such a move before our final preseason game. In that way we would not go into the preparation week for our opener grappling with the immediate reactions to our having cut Jan.

When I informed Jan that we were going to waive him, he was understandably bitter about it. I could fully appreciate the wound he was feeling. He accused me of conspiring with our front office to have him replaced because he had an attractive contract. That was not the situation. The decision was mine and mine alone. It was based purely on my belief that Nick, at the time, was a better kicker.

In one sense, being waived two weeks before the regular season worked to Jan's benefit. It afforded other teams the opportunity to assess their own place kicking needs, and they had time to sign Jan so that he could work with them in preparation for their season's opener. I admit that was not the primary reason I made the move when I did, but it was a fortunate byproduct. The Packers signed Jan, and he played two years for them before moving on to the Vikings with whom he finished his illustrious career.

Jan was hurt deeply when he was released by the Chiefs, and I feel badly that my action caused a fine man so much pain. For many years afterward Jan continued to harbor resentment toward me, and that further magnified my sorrow, because I have always held Jan in the highest esteem. Cutting players, especially longtime veterans, is the most distasteful part of being a professional coach. I was never more aware of that than I was the day I broke the news to Jan.[1]

How about Nick Lowery? In our 1980 season opener against Oakland, Nick had no opportunities to try a field goal. The following week, however, when we played Seattle at Arrowhead Stadium, he kicked a 57-yarder on his first attempt. It was the third longest field goal in NFL history, and it established a Chiefs record that still stands. Later in the

1. One day, seven years later, while I was attending the NFL off-season meetings in Palm Springs, California, I was having breakfast with Seattle Seahawks coach Chuck Knox. As Chuck and I talked, I sensed someone standing next to my chair. I glanced up, and there stood a smiling Jan Stenerud. "I'm not mad anymore," he announced, as he reached out to shake my hand. Jan joined us for breakfast, and, since that happy peacemaking moment, I have shared some laughs and some pleasant conversation with Jan at numerous NFL-sponsored events.

game, Nick was successful on a 52-yard effort. Before the game was over he booted another one through the uprights. During his rookie season, Nick made 20 of 26 attempts, including four from more than 50 yards.

Nick went on to become the best place kicker in the NFL, and he, like Jan, enjoyed many years of stardom. He also won the respect and affection of his teammates who, after a few years had passed, elected him as their NFL Players Association team representative. Not too long ago, his name was added to the nominee list for the Pro Football Hall of Fame. He would be a most deserving inductee, and when that happens, Jan and Nick will once again become teammates.

The biggest distraction during the preseason resulted from a different contract matter, one that involved our two starting running backs, Ted McKnight and Tony Reed. They didn't report to training camp, and their angry and ongoing negotiations dominated the attention of the media and fans in Kansas City for several weeks. In addition to our other problems in the early going, Mike Bell was injured once again. This time it was his knee, and it would cause him to miss a large portion of the 1980 season. We worried that Mike might be injury-prone, but, in the seasons that followed, he proved to be hardier.

Reeling from these preseason upheavals, we began the 1980 regular schedule by losing to the Raiders 27-14. It was the Raiders' first victory on their way to winning that year's Super Bowl. Next, Seattle downed us 17-16, and then Cleveland defeated us 20-13. What a start! We were 0-3.

During the 1979 season, we had begun to gravitate away from the offensively conservative Wing T that I had employed in 1978. We had installed it as a stop-gap measure until such time when our defense would be able to perform more respectably. Now, in 1980, we were ready to be bolder. Our defense had become much stronger, and I felt the time had come for us to move to a more wide-open style of play. By 1980 we had evolved completely to the pro style of attack.

Once a coach had been branded as a conservative, however, there is no shaking the label. Whenever his team might lose a game, the Monday morning quarterbacks know the reason. It was because he was "too conservative." If they ever needed an alternate term in order to show that they—the critics—could change up, then the coach was "too predictable."

Because of our once having operated a Wing T offense, I became known as conservative. There are, I guess, worse things that a person can be called.

Following our three consecutive losses at the beginning of the 1980 season, Jack, once again, entered the picture. He sent me a memo, dripping with coaching advice, in which he presented his thoughts and observations. "Thoughts and Observations" was Jack's favorite title to use whenever he really wanted to present his "Do this, you jerk!" manifest to me. In this particular memo, Jack included the following "thoughts and observations":

> "We have lost faith in what we are doing." (What did he mean "we?" I hadn't.)
>
> "I am concerned that we are too conservative in our offensive philosophy, and, as a result, too predictable." (At least he was reading the newspapers.)
>
> "We must open our offense up more to attack our opponents' weaknesses like they are attacking our defensive weaknesses." (Whatever the other teams were doing was always what we should do, according to Jack.)
>
> "If we cannot attack those weaknesses because of Steve Fuller's inexperience, we must consider a change at quarterback." (The old panacea: change quarterbacks.)
>
> "Let the players know that we are doing everything possible in order to win. That is the mental part of the game." (More wisdom from Chairman Jack.)
>
> "If you sit back and analyze the difference between ourselves and the teams we have played the past three weeks, it probably boils down to the level of experience at the quarterback position more than anything else. Because of their experience, their quarterbacks have been able to come up with the big play when they needed it, while Steve, because of his inexperience, has not." (Jack, I hate to say, "I told you so," but—.)
>
> "Either design our offense to more effectively use Steve's ability to move or go to Tom Clements, who is our most experienced quarterback." (This meant junking almost everything we had worked on since the beginning of training camp when we had all agreed that Steve would be our No. 1 quarterback. In our efforts to bring Steve along he had been allotted all the work at quarterback during our practices. At that time, we had determined that Bill Kenney would be our No. 2 man. There is only so much practice and preparation time available.)
>
> "It would seem logical that we go with Tom. We are not going to sit back and do nothing different while we are getting

> our tails whipped week after week." (Someone once spoke similar words to General Ulysses S. Grant. He didn't listen either.)
>
> "If we are not successful with this plan of attack, then most assuredly we would need to go back to Steve and continue his development for the future." (Two years later, when I did make some changes at quarterback, Jack cited my actions as examples of indecisiveness on my part.)
>
> "No reply necessary." (Thank goodness.)

I started Steve again the following week when we played the Chargers. Going into the game, their record was 3-0, and after they defeated us 24-7, it became 4-0. We were 0-4, and our next game was in Oakland against the Raiders. I started Steve in that one as well.

We stunned the Raiders with a 31-17 upset victory. And then we defeated Houston 21-10. We won again the following week by downing the potent Broncos 23-17, the first Chiefs' triumph over the Broncos since 1975, and then we made it four straight when we nipped the Lions 20-17. The Chiefs hadn't won four straight games since 1971, the year they were the defending Super Bowl Champions. Despite Jack's ominous memo of four weeks earlier, I had stayed with Steve, and he had been our quarterback in all four of the games we had won. We entered the second half of the season with a shot at qualifying for the playoffs.

We weren't really a strong enough team to pull that off, however. Over the next four-week period we won two games and we lost two. We entered the final four weeks of the season with a 6-6 record. In our next game against Cincinnati, we played poorly, and the Bengals beat us 20-6. When the game was over, we learned that Steve had suffered torn cartilage in his knee and that the injury required surgery. Steve was out for the last three games of the season.

I was now faced with the decision of whether to play Bill Kenney or Tom Clements. Jack was insisting that we should play Tom now that Steve had been sidelined. There were some difficult issues that clouded the situation, however. Bill's development in practice had exceeded all expectations we had for him when we first signed him. Tom had had no practice time since the beginning of the regular season. The little that hadn't gone to Steve had been assigned to Bill. Steve had by this time established himself as our No. 1 quarterback, and he would be reinstalled as our starter the following year when he had recovered from his injury. Tom, understandably, would be very reluctant to remain on our team as a non-starter. We had to find out if Bill had what it took to merit the backup role, and so I did what I was hired to do—make coaching decisions that I believed were in the best interests of the team. I announced that Bill would start against Denver.

Jack was dismayed by my decision, and he asked me to reconsider. I told him my mind was made up. All week long, he asked me if I had changed my mind.

In retrospect, it had been unfair for us to bring Tom to Kansas City. During the preseason games, Tom had performed extremely well, and he had joined us with the intention of winning the top spot. We—and that included Jack and Lamar Hunt as well as myself—were committed to Steve being our starting quarterback, however, even before the beginning of training camp.

Jack was correct in believing that Tom was a talented player, and in this instance my long-term future with the Chiefs might have been aided had I gone along with Jack's urgings following the four losses we incurred to open our season. Had we gone into training camp more open minded about allowing there to be a true competition for the starting quarterback position, there is a strong possibility that Tom would have emerged as our starter, but we all knew now, nine games into our schedule, that Steve would be reassigned that role when he was healthy.

Bill Kenney had a sensational debut as a professional quarterback. He executed our offense with perfection. We had our best showing on that side of the ball in the three years I had been there. Bill threw two touchdown passes in the game, and we trounced the Broncos 31-14. We had swept the season series from them, the first time the Chiefs had succeeded in doing that since 1972.

Bill played well again the following week in Pittsburgh, but Chuck Noll's still strong Steelers won a hard-fought battle 21-16. Just as in the season before, we now had to take our 7-8 record on the road in our efforts to avert another one of those losing seasons that had plagued the Chiefs for six straight years. This time we would be facing the Colts, who had defeated us in our home stadium earlier in the year. We had a difficult task confronting us.

We could do nothing wrong in the first quarter of that game, and we jumped out to a 21-0 lead. In the second quarter, however, we did nothing *right!* Baltimore's quarterback, Bert Jones, carved out large, repeated gains. The Colts scored four times, and by halftime we had fallen behind 28-21.

For the first time in the three years since I had become coach of the Chiefs, I was disappointed with our players' effort and concentration. They had gone into the tank after the first quarter. I rarely castigate players during a game. Usually, when a coach displays anger toward his team while the game is underway, it backfires. When you do that, they don't think you are in control; they think you are *out of control.* In this instance, however, they deserved to be told how lousy they had played, and they knew it. There were no blackboard Xs and Os at halftime that day in Baltimore. I fired both verbal barrels at them, and it wasn't for show, either. I meant every abusive word I spewed out.

Late in the third quarter, we tied the game at 28-28. Then, midway through the fourth quarter, Nick booted a long field goal, and we inched ahead 31-28. With three minutes remaining to play, we had the ball, third down and 17 yards to go, on our 25-yard line. We called a timeout in order to discuss our next crucial play selection.

I told Bill that I felt it would be best if we ran a draw play, thereby taking no chances against the seven secondary defenders the Colts used in such obvious passing situations. It was a low-risk play, and we'd probably have to punt to them after we ran it, I said, but then we'd rely on our defense to hold Bert Jones at bay, just as it had been doing throughout the second half.

Bill talked me out of it. There was one pass play on our ready sheet that Bill believed he could make work. As he trotted back out to our huddle, I remember thinking that, at least, they'd no longer be calling me "conservative." I just hoped they wouldn't be calling me "stupid."

Bill threw a beauty to Henry Marshall. Henry took it in full stride, and no one caught him. He zipped 75 yards for a touchdown. We won the game 38-28.

For the third consecutive year, we had improved our record. The Chiefs had registered their first non-losing season since 1973. It had been the toughest, most disruption-filled season since I had come to Kansas City, but our promise for the future was bright. We had two solid, young quarterbacks. Our defense and our kicking game were both vastly improved from what they had been when we first arrived. Our patience and our persistence were beginning to pay off. I had stuck to my guns in the face of Jack's mounting interference, and I hoped that now, at last, he might get off our backs.

The plane ride back to Kansas City was a happy one, far different from the season-ender the year before in Tampa Bay. Once we were airborne, I pulled a *Time* magazine from the seat pocket in front of me. While reading it, I came across a full-page advertisement for a large insurance company. The caption on their ad read: "As Safe as a Twenty-one Point First Quarter." When I arrived home, I checked my insurance policies. I wanted to be certain that we weren't carrying any coverage from that company.

CHAPTER 20

Turning a Corner?

We were doing it the old-fashioned way—building slowly, primarily through the draft, but we were continuing to make progress as we entered the 1981 season, my fourth with the Chiefs. Our recent first-round selections of Art Still and Mike Bell, combined with the fine play of a seventh-round 1979 draft choice, Ken Kremer, gave us a very solid starting defensive line. In Steve Fuller and Bill Kenney we had two promising young quarterbacks, both of whom now had NFL playing experience. Nick Lowery had emerged as the best place kicker in the league, and, until Bob Grupp was injured, we had a top-quality punter, as well. J.T. Smith, whom we picked up as a free agent halfway through the 1978 season, had become the leading punt returner in the AFC. We still needed to improve our kickoff returns, however.

Our defensive backfield was shaping up as one of the best in the NFL. When I had come to Kansas City, Gary Green and Gary Barbaro were already excellent players. Green was a cornerback, and Barbaro was our free safety. The other two secondary spots had been weak, and we needed to improve at both positions if we were going to be able to cope with opponents' passing attacks.

In 1977, the Chiefs had drafted a player named Eric Harris, a first-team All-America cornerback from Memphis State University. Eric had signed a lucrative contract with the Toronto Argonauts, however, and he became an All-CFL selection all three years that he played in Canada. Prior to the 1980 season, Eric's contract with Toronto expired, and he was then free to negotiate with NFL teams.

NFL rules at that time specified that if a player did not sign with the team that had drafted him within one year's time, then the player was free to negotiate with any of the other teams in the league. If the team that originally drafted him, however, matched the best offer the player received, then they would retain his playing rights. The Saints offered Eric Harris an attractive contract, and he informed us that he wanted to play for the Saints. Jack Steadman, Jim Schaaf, and I conferred in order to discuss whether we could afford to match the figures New Orleans had put on the table.

Jack rightly pointed out that, in giving a large contract to Eric, we would breed discontent among some of our current defensive backs. I countered that here was a player whom *we* had drafted and who was an outstanding talent at a position where we were badly in need of help. Yes, we would create some other problems, but we had to decide whether we were ready to deal with those issues or continue to be mediocre. Jim supported my position, and Jack agreed. We informed Eric, the NFL office, and the Saints of our decision.

When we came better acquainted with Eric, we found him to be a quiet, gentlemanly person, but in his early days with the Chiefs he was full of anger and resentment. When he reported to training camp, he informed me immediately that he did not want to play for the Chiefs; he wanted to play for New Orleans. He could not understand why I insisted on keeping a player who wished to be elsewhere. Then, he carried his fight to the media, and, in doing so, he incurred the displeasure of the other players.

One day, Eric and I had a showdown meeting in my office. I informed him that I would not consider trading him to the Saints or to any other team. He was a fine player with a reputation for high character, and I told him that I felt he was diminishing his abilities by focusing on the wrong target. He should be thinking about getting ready to play to the highest level of his capabilities, I said.

"You don't give a damn about Eric Harris," he responded.

I tried to explain to him why we wanted him as a member of our team, and I told him, also, that if we let him go, every player who ever had a gripe would be in our offices seeking to be sent elsewhere. Given his state of mind at the time, all of my reasoning meant nothing to him. He felt he was being used, and his frustration over being denied what he wanted pervaded all of his thinking.

We met for over an hour, and finally I, too, became angry.

"Eric, in all the time we have been talking, all I've heard you say is 'I,' 'I,' 'I.' Not once have you said 'win' or 'compete' or 'team,'" I exploded.

He left my office still smoldering.

The day following our meeting, Eric sustained a mild knee injury during our drills, and he had to leave the practice field. Most of his teammates and many of the media covering us suspected him of malingering. I did not agree with that assessment.

"Eric Harris has told me he is injured, and I believe him," I announced. "Right now he might be an angry person, but he is a truthful person, as well."

After our team doctors examined him, they confirmed that Eric did, indeed, have an injury that would require us to keep him out for a couple of weeks. Just a few days later, while I was standing along the sideline at practice, Eric told me how much he had appreciated my public words of support at a time when everyone else was doubting him.

Slowly, Eric adjusted to the idea that he would be playing in Kansas City. He said little, and he worked hard. After a while he won the respect and then the friendship of his teammates. When he recovered from his injury, he competed vigorously to make up for the time he had lost. By the third game of the year, we moved him into the starting lineup. During his NFL rookie season, Eric intercepted seven passes, and the following year he was second in the league in pass thefts when he intercepted seven more. Toward the end of his first season, we were walking side by side off the field after having beaten the Raiders.

In the glow of victory, Eric turned to me and said, "You know, Coach, I really love wearing this uniform."

I didn't know whether to smile or to cry.

With the addition of Eric, we now had three-fourths of our secondary. One more good man and we'd be equal to any defensive backfield in the league. In 1981, we were able to add that player. In fact, we added two good defensive backs. In the third round we drafted Lloyd Burress from the University of Maryland, and in his rookie season, Lloyd became our starting strong safety. A free agent signee out of Rutgers, Deron Cherry, also came in and performed well enough to win a spot as our fifth defensive back. After the Chiefs lost Gary Barbaro to the fledgling United States Football League a few years later, Deron moved in and became the AFC's All-Conference free safety.

At wide receiver, we had the respectable trio of Henry Marshall, J.T. Smith, and undersized, but highly productive, Carlos Carson.

Three years earlier, the Chiefs had been in a state of disarray. We now had a first-rate defensive line, defensive backfield, and kicking game, while our quarterback and wide receiver situations also looked encouraging, but there were still areas of play where we needed to improve. When I had arrived in Kansas City, the offensive line was undersized and aging. In 1980 we selected offensive guard Brad Budde in the first round of the draft, but it takes longer to develop an offensive lineman than it does a player at any other position. Thus, I still felt that overall the offensive line was not yet near where it needed to be.

There were other position needs to be addressed, also. Gary Spani was our only big-league linebacker. Tight end, too, needed strengthening. Most of all, I worried about our running backs. Both Tony Reed and Ted McKnight could no longer perform as they had a few years earlier. Before the 1981 season began, we traded Tony to Denver for a draft choice, and we used it to get our new starting strong safety, Lloyd Burress. We were fortunate to solve our running back problems during that 1981 draft. In the second round, we chose Joe Delaney, a little speedster out of Northwestern Louisiana, and, in the seventh round, we drafted fullback Billy Jackson from the University of Alabama. Both of them moved immediately into our starting lineup.

Joe played brilliantly. He was voted the AFC Rookie of the Year. During that season, Joe rushed for 1,121 yards. In one game he racked up 193 of those yards. Five times he ran for more than 100 yards in a game. All three of those marks established new Chiefs records. Billy scored 11 touchdowns during his rookie year. Joe and Billy, along with our third running back, James Hadnot, led us to the second greatest total team rushing yardage mark for a season in Chiefs history, surpassed only by our 1978 Wing T practitioners.

In 1981, we would once again feature our running game. We had the backs to do it, and we lacked an offensive line capable enough to protect our young quarterbacks if we had sought to rely primarily on the forward pass. Again, I was to hear accusations, led by Jack, that I was being—this was getting really serious—*"ultraconservative,"* but we would not have won as many games as we did during that season had I relied on a more pass-oriented attack.

When we reported to training camp in 1981, Steve had already started 25 games at quarterback for us, and Bill had started but three. Steve had been a first-round draft choice two years earlier, and, seeking to hurry his development, we had invested a heavy amount of playing time in him. The last thing I wanted was a continuation of what had been a major distraction, and so I announced from the outset that Steve would be our No. 1 guy at the position. That would put to rest all this "quarterback controversy" idiocy. That's what I thought!

Tom Clements had returned to the CFL, and Bill was firmly entrenched as our backup quarterback. Our new No. 3 man was Bob Gagliano, that year's 12th-round draft selection out of Utah State. Bob had good talent, but he would need several years of seasoning.

Late in the opening quarter of our first preseason game, against the Redskins, Steve injured his other knee. Arthroscopic surgery was required, and, again, Steve would be out of action, this time for six weeks. Nice situation we were in at quarterback. Bill, with three games of NFL experience, and a rookie 12th-round draft choice would be carrying our hopes. Talk about fun!

We opened the 1981 regular season in Pittsburgh. The last time the Chiefs had won a game against the Steelers had been in 1971. It was a thrilling seesaw battle, and Bill picked up right where he had left off. He connected on touchdown passes of 48 yards to Henry Marshall and 53 yards to Carlos Carson.

Pittsburgh quarterback Terry Bradshaw and his contingent of great receivers, led by Lynn Swann and John Stallworth, were hot also, and with less than two minutes remaining, we trailed 33-30. Pittsburgh had control. It was their ball on our 35-yard line, and it appeared that they would run out the clock while preserving their narrow lead.

As the Steelers lined up for their next play, our kicking teams coach, Frank Gansz, grabbed me by the shirtsleeve and screamed, "Coach, we are going to win this damn game!"

I made a mental note to have the poor fellow examined by a battery of psychiatrists as soon as we returned home.

Our defensive coordinator, Rod Rust, called for a three linebacker blitz, and one of our inside linebackers, Frank Manumaleuga, slammed into Pittsburgh running back Sid Thornton, just as Bradshaw was handing Thornton the ball. Thornton could not hold on to it, and as soon as the pigskin bounced to the ground, our outside linebacker, Thomas Howard, scooped it up and ran 65 unmolested yards for the touchdown that won the game for us. We had beaten the best, and we had done it in their ballpark.

On the plane trip home, I took the seat next to Frank Gansz and asked him if he had any good stock market tips for me.

Next we defeated Tampa Bay 19-10, before dropping a scoreboard-exhausting 42-31 decision to Don Coryell's explosive Chargers. In the

Tampa Bay game we lost Carlos Carson for the season when he suffered a broken leg. We bounced back with a 20-14 victory over Seattle, but we followed that by losing to the Patriots in Foxboro.

By this time Steve had recovered from his injury and was ready for action, but Bill had been playing extremely well, and so I continued starting Bill at quarterback. He responded by leading us to a resounding 27-0 trouncing of the Raiders. The week after that, Bill directed us to a 28-14 win over Denver.

We were 5-2, and just two weeks after we had defeated the Raiders, we were scheduled to play them again, this time in Oakland. They jumped all over us in the first half, taking a 17-0 lead. When you fall behind by a sizeable margin early, your game plan goes out the window. We were going to have to go to an almost exclusively pass-oriented, catch up-style approach on offense to get back into this game. We knew that, and so did the Raiders. They mounted a murderous pass rush, and they continued to shut down our offense in the third quarter.

Steve was a more swift-footed and mobile player than Bill, and so late in the third quarter, I sent him in to replace Bill, hoping that by doing so we could alter the tempo of the game. Steve led us on three consecutive long touchdown drives, and with five minutes left to play we forged ahead 21-17.

Now it was the Raiders' turn to mount a drive. With less than a minute remaining, they reached our three-yard line. There quarterback Mark Wilson rolled out to pass. Again Rod Rust called for a three linebacker blitz, and again, one of our blitzers, Charles Jackson, jarred the ball loose. Gary Spani picked it up this time, and he rumbled 95 yards for the score that clinched our 28-17 victory. For the third year in a row, we had beaten the hated Raiders right in their own backyard.

Despite Steve's heroics and on the basis of one poor outing, Bill did not deserve to lose his starting position, and so he was back in the lineup the following week in San Diego. Bill played well, but with just 13 seconds remaining, their place kicker, Rolf Benirschke, connected on a field goal, giving the Chargers a 22-20 win.

The Bears were next. Again, our offense was sputtering, and in the second half, trailing 13-3, I replaced Bill with Steve. We rallied, and on the last play of the game, Steve hit Henry Marshall on a touchdown pass, and the score was tied at 13-13. The game went into overtime, where unfortunately for us, the Bears kicked a field goal, and they escaped with a 16-13 victory. Our season's record now stood at 6-4, but we had lost our last two games.

Still, I stayed with Bill as our starting quarterback. Despite all Bill had accomplished during the season, for several weeks, Jack had been sending me memos "suggesting" that we ought to make the change to Steve. I stuck with Bill as our starter, and we defeated Houston 23-10. Then we demolished Seattle 40-13.

I still recall an incident during our pregame warmup in Seattle that always amuses me whenever I reflect back upon it. The longest two hours of the week for a football coach are those that come immediately prior to the opening kickoff. Once his team has arrived at the stadium, there is really nothing more a coach can do to prepare for the game. For the most part, the players need to be left alone. Each player has his own pregame ritual. Some review their game plan notes; some seek quiet so that they can concentrate on the strenuous physical and mental challenges they are about to face. It is no time for a coach to introduce new ideas; they tend only to cause overload and breed insecurity.

Usually the coaching staffs from both teams stroll out onto the playing field, pretending they are examining the condition of the turf. Perhaps they'll study the scoreboard, or they will test the wind direction and velocity for the umpteenth time. When the teams come onto the field, the players go through a prescribed warmup procedure, one that has become second nature to them. The coaches still have little to do, and often members of one staff will exchange informal pleasantries with the other team's coaches. The talk is guarded and respectful. Whatever you do, don't get the other guy fired up.

I was surprised, therefore, when, after I said hello to Seattle's offensive coordinator, Jerry Rhome, he responded with a belligerent, "Your punter is standing in our territory; tell him to get his butt out of there."

I like Jerry, and I admire him as a coach. It was obvious that his adrenaline was running high and that he was in his full game-day mood, but it's hard not to snap back when your own emotions are near the surface, and so, after I had our punter relocate, it was my turn.

"Don't worry about it, Jerry," I said. "We're going to be in your territory all day." Fortunately for us, we were.

After Seattle, we were 8-4, with four games left in our season, but three of those four were to be played on the road. On Thanksgiving we played a nationally televised game in the Silverdome against the Lions. We should have stayed home and eaten turkey. Instead, we played like turkeys. Detroit took a 20-3 halftime lead, and for the third time in six weeks I called on Steve. He played well, but not sensationally, and the Lions coasted to a 27-10 victory.

On all of the occasions when I had made the change at quarterback, I felt my reasons were sound, but I also knew that the process was having an unsettling effect on our team. The distracting uncertainty that resulted from these moves was exactly what I had hoped, going into the season, we had put behind us. Unfortunately, the preseason injury to Steve had served to reopen that Pandora's box. Now, Bill, after a barnburner of a start, had become somewhat inconsistent. Steve had played well in all three of his appearances. I felt the time was ripe to rest Bill, to let him regroup, and to have Steve carry the load.

The following week in Denver, we were locked in a tough defensive struggle. Late in the game we trailed 16-13, but Steve had moved us to a third-and-three situation on the Broncos' 22-yard line. At that point, Denver linebacker Bob Swenson picked off one of Steve's passes, and we lost the game by those three points. It was no time to backtrack, however. When I had made the decision to start Steve against Denver, I determined that, barring injury, I would stay with him through our final three games of the regular season.

Miami was next. Midway through the fourth quarter, the Dolphins were clinging to a 10-7 lead. We marched to their 30-yard line, where our drive stalled, and so we lined up to attempt the field goal that could tie the game. Our regular field goal snapper, Todd Thomas, had dislocated his shoulder earlier in the game, and we had to call on our starting center to handle that chore. He had never snapped for kicks in a game, and this one went high. How high was it? Too high for our holder to handle. It went over our holder's upstretched arms, *and* it went over the head of our kicker, Nick Lowery, who was six feet, three inches tall. That's how high it was!

The errant snap rolled, and it rolled, and it rolled. A Miami player fell on it after it came to rest on our side of the 50-yard line. From there the Dolphins consumed much of the remaining time on a march that culminated with their scoring a touchdown less than a minute before the final gun. We lost the game 17-7, our third consecutive defeat.

With one game remaining, we were out of the playoffs. We still had a lot to play for, however. If we could beat the Vikings up at Metropolitan Stadium, we would register the first winning season for a Chiefs team since 1972.

That game and its aftermath proved to be a magical experience.

It was one of those old-time "blood in the mud" games, played so often on the cold, soggy turf at time-scarred Metropolitan Stadium.

This one, however, was special. Only a down or two remained to be played in the 1981 season, and then the old arena would hear no more cheers. They were going to tear it down, and some new modern buildings were to be raised on the site where Fran Tarkenton had scrambled and passed his was into the Pro Football Hall of Fame and where the Purple People Eaters had devoured quarterbacks, while spearheading the Vikings to four Super Bowl appearances. The memories might remain for a long time, but the stadium would be gone the next time they teed up for the kickoff in Minneapolis.

For a few more ticks of the clock, however, this was still "football," played as it should be played—outdoors, on the weekend, in the afternoon, on the grass, in the elements. None of that Thursday night in the cozy warmth of the Dotcomdome crap. This was a sentimental day for all Vikings fans, and, under different circumstances I am sure that, standing there in the darkening chill of that late December afternoon, I could have savored these last few nostalgic moments with them.

No touchy-feely sentiments were gripping me at the time, however. The outcome of the game, the success or failure of our season, and probably my job, too, all depended on what was going to happen on the next snap from center. For more than three hours my Chiefs had struggled valiantly against the favored Vikings, and with just 15 seconds left, we were clinging to a narrow 10-6 lead. That was the good news.

The bad news? The Vikings had the ball on our two-yard line, with fourth down and goal to go. For the past six excruciating minutes, Vikings quarterback Tommy Kramer had been engineering a long drive, the only one the Vikings had been able to muster all through that dreary afternoon. A few plays earlier, I thought we had them stopped as they faced a fourth-and-long situation on our 40-yard line, but their resourceful veteran quarterback had connected on a short pass to running back Tony Galbreath. Before we finally spilled Tony with a heart-stopping, shoestring tackle, he had turned it into a 35-yard gain, and we were now being listed in critical condition.

Three downs and three yards later it came down to one decisive play. If we could hang on, it meant a 9-7 season for us. A loss, of course, would leave us at 8-8, the same record we had posted the year before. I was aware that any season without improvement would be treated by our front office as an embarrassment. For three consecutive years we had improved on the previous season's record, but this was the NFL.

The ball was snapped. Kramer rolled to his right. Tony Galbreath slipped into the flat, and—*he was open!* As I peaked through spread fingers, laced in front of my eyes, Kramer drilled the ball unerringly at

Tony's chest. Our outside linebacker, Whitney Paul, who had dropped more coverages than a strip-tease dancer, streaked from out of the pack, and then I heard that sweet thunk as his beautiful left hand swatted the ball to the ground. It was the prettiest sound to reach my ears since Glenn Miller's "In the Mood."

One play later, Steve ran my favorite play. He took the snap, and he knelt down. The clock ran out, and the game was over. We had won.

Only then did I recall the words spoken to me before the game by Vikings coach, Bud Grant.

"Marv, when this game is over, get off the field in a hurry or your ass is going to be a souvenir. These fans are going to grab everything in the place as a remembrance."

As I glanced up, I saw the horde of Vikings faithful beginning to come over the walls. They looked like my old Redskins kickoff coverage team thundering straight at me. Behind them I could vaguely see and hear the bleacher seats being ripped from their moorings. I did the only sensible thing. I ran, beating our fastest wide receiver to the locker room door by four steps. I'd hug Whitney later.

CHAPTER 21

Strike Three! You're Out!

For four consecutive years, beginning with my first as coach of the Chiefs, we had improved the team's won-lost record over what it had been the previous season. No other team in the NFL had matched that.

Not once however, do I recall Jack Steadman saying to me or to the media that our coaching staff had done a good job. There had been numerous expressions on his part of dissatisfaction after some of the losses or on occasions when we used players he didn't believe we should have used, but never was there an unqualified "good job."

There was one coaching decision I made, however, about which Jack was pleased. We had started Steve Fuller in the final three games of the 1981 season, but it was not because Jack had decreed we should. I had started Steve because *I* believed we should. On the day after our victory over the Vikings, Jack sent me the following note:

> "Observation—I thought Steve was a better-looking QB on Sunday than Kramer [Minnesota's quarterback]. Threw better, more effectively, and handled pressure better. Both good QBs, but Fuller better at this stage. I'm sure in reflecting on it, you'll agree."

That was all he wrote. No congratulations on our winning season. In actuality, there had been little difference in how effectively the two signal callers had played, but Jack was seizing the opportunity to kick off on the spate of advice he would be offering regarding who should play quarterback for us the following year.

It was important to Jack that our drafting decisions appear to be infallible, because after he had unseated Hank Stram, one of his pet projects had been the restructuring of the Chiefs' scouting procedures. In many respects, he had done excellent work here. He had hired well-qualified men for our department of player personnel, but Jack kept such pressures on them and looked over their shoulders so intently that they became inhibited. If scouts are to make bold judgments, they must also be allowed to make occasional mistakes. They had no such leeway while working for Jack.

During the off season, I spent many hours in the offices of our scouting department. For the most part, I was seeking to learn as much as I could about that year's crop of draft eligible players. There were about 75 thick volumes of reports that lined the walls of their meeting room, and the only way to learn what was in those books was to review, over and over, the boringly repetitive contents.

Once in a while, however, I visited for reasons other than edification. I came to be entertained. The scouts in the NFL fill out thousands of dull report forms every year. In the process, they adopt a certain writing style. The most notable feature of the "NFL Scouting School of Writing" is that no sentences begin with a subject because the player's name will appear on his folder. Some of the writers, while still managing to adhere to the basic style, also developed a flair for the picturesque. Many coaches and personnel men are familiar with the literary creations of our most imaginative scouts. Here are a few of the most noteworthy:

> Blazing speed. Can run the minute in 58 seconds.
> Quicker than a hiccup.
> Could throw a ball through a car wash and have it come out dry on the other side.
> So dumb that when he was a POW he gave only his name and rank. Couldn't remember his serial number.
> Dow Jones-type player—up and down.
> Looks like Tarzan; plays like Jane.[1]

♦♦♦♦♦♦♦♦

We entered the 1982 season with the threat of a players' strike looming. The Chiefs' players were among the most militant in the NFL, believing that a strike was the only way in which they were going to

---

1. There have been variations—"Looks like King Kong; plays like Fay Wray," for example—but the original still ranks as the finest in scouting literature.

achieve the National Football League Players Association's goals. One of our starting offensive linemen, Tom Condon, who, following his playing career, gained a law degree and went on to become a renowned players' agent, was at this time the players' representative for our team, and Tom was a strong and eloquent public advocate for the players' demands. In the process he incurred the wrath of Jack.

All of that was none of my business. Other people were dealing with the management-NFLPA negotiations. I had a team to get ready, and I had to start by determining what we were going to do in regard to naming our starting quarterback for opening day.

Steve and Bill had both been with us for three years, and yet neither one had clearly established that he had clearly beaten out the other. Steve had started 26 games, and we had an 11-15 record in those contests. Bill Kenney had been the starter 17 times with an 11-6 record to show for those starts. Many more factors than just who had started at quarterback affected the outcomes of our games. I recognized, for instance, that we had won several games when Steve had come off the bench to salvage come-from-behind victories.

Had Steve not been injured during the past two years, he probably would have had a lock on the position by the time our 1982 season began. His injuries, however, had allowed Bill to play, and Bill had responded by playing his way into contention. I told both players that I would name our opening-day quarterback on the basis of what happened during our training camp and preseason.

I realized that such a process would continue that old coach's nemesis—"the quarterback controversy," but this was the only way I felt that I could be fair to both men and to our team's aspirations. Even then I was aware that coaches have been fired more often than a Civil War cannon when they get entangled with this issue. Less than a year later I was to learn how right I was—about the getting fired part, that is.

As training camp drew toward its close, our coaching staff, which had been paying close attention to the competition between the two men, felt that Bill had inched ahead, and I was in agreement with them. Ten days before the opening game of the season, I informed them both that Bill would be our starter.

Jack questioned me extensively about why I had reached such a decision. This was an important step we were taking, and I could understand fully his reasons for wanting to know what had brought us to this point. After a while, however, I realized that he was questioning the validity of my decision.

"I cannot understand how we have failed to make a No. 1 draft choice capable enough to be a starting quarterback after three years in our program," he stated.

"I am not ready to give up on Steve Fuller," I told him, "but right now I feel our offense is running more smoothly with Bill Kenney at quarterback. Therefore, I have decided that he will be the starter. Our players need to know that the issue has been settled; they need to concentrate on getting ready for the regular-season's games."

"Well, that's your decision," Jack said. "You still have 10 days until our opening game. Let me know if you change your mind."

Several times during the next week, Jack asked me if I had reconsidered.

Steve never showed any outward reactions whenever I informed him about our plans at quarterback. He was a keen competitor, and I knew that he was not about to give up. He wasn't one who ran around saying, "You know how much I hate to lose." From the intensity with which he played and from the tenacious way in which he bounced back from disappointment, I knew he didn't like to lose.

"You know how I hate to lose," was one of Jack's frequent pronouncements. Whenever I hear any player or coach dredge up that hackneyed old statement, I detect an arrogance that implies that the *other people around here* do not really dislike losing. Who the hell doesn't hate to lose?

I never heard Art Still, or Gary Spani, or Tom Condon, or Gary Green, or Jack Rudnay, or Fuzzy Kremer, or any of the guys who put on that Chiefs helmet speak those words. Yet, I was constantly aware that they were the type of men who were willing to do what was required in order to keep from losing. They reminded me of another of my old college coach Dick Clausen's favorite slogans: "What you do speaks so loudly no one can hear what you are saying."

I particularly recall one play in a game we lost to the Chargers in 1980. On the last play, San Diego scored a touchdown, thereby taking a 20-7 lead. The try for the extra point, of course, which was attempted after the final gun, was meaningless. Gary Green, nevertheless, exerting great individual effort, succeeded in blocking the Chargers' place kick. So what? It showed me and his teammates how much pride Gary possessed, and it provided the springboard from which we bounced back to win the following week in St. Louis.

♦♦♦♦♦♦♦♦

Even though talk of the impending strike had dominated the media and fan attention throughout training camp, we opened the

1982 season with high hopes. We had been doing it the patient way, and we had been getting steadily better. The time had arrived, I felt, for our breakthrough season. On opening day, playing in Buffalo, we were trailing 7-6 late in the first half. The Bills had moved the ball to our eight-yard line where their quarterback, Joe Ferguson, drilled a pass into our end zone. Gary Spani intercepted it, and, with a convoy of Chiefs blockers clearing the way, Gary returned the ball deep into Buffalo territory before finally being dragged down. There was enough time remaining in the period for us to score.

To my dismay, however, I saw an official pick the ball up and start a long trek back toward our goal line. We had been guilty of pass interference, and the Bills were awarded possession and a first down on our one-yard line. On the next play *they* scored a touchdown. Instead of leading at the half, we were behind 14-6. The penalty had cost us not only a potential touchdown; it had resulted in Buffalo scoring one. It had been a 14-point (or at least a 10-point) turnaround. That was the difference in the game, because, although we held the Bills scoreless in the second half, we were able to add only a field goal. Buffalo won 14-9.

In our home opener one week later, we faced the Chargers. Against the teams in our AFC Western Division, we had experienced the most difficulty when our opponent was San Diego. We had learned to take the measure of the other three teams in the division. While I was coaching in Kansas City, we won five of the last seven games we played against the Raiders; we won five of the last six meetings with Seattle and four of the last five against the Broncos. No such luck against the Chargers. In my first four years in Kansas City, we had beaten San Diego just one time, and that happened on a day when their brilliant quarterback, Dan Fouts, had been unable to play because of an injury. Now, in 1982, he was healthy, and the Chargers were flying high.

We stopped them on their first possession and forced them to punt from midfield. Gary Green (him again!) blocked the kick, and when the ball scooted all the way back into their end zone, we recovered it for a touchdown and an early 7-0 lead. We never relinquished that lead.

Although we struggled on offense for the second week in a row, our defense and kicking teams turned in superior performances, limiting the potent Chargers' offense, Fouts included, to one touchdown all afternoon. We won 19-12.

Everything was looking bright. And then the players went on strike.

Most interested parties thought that it would be a short-lived hiatus, but the strike dragged on acrimoniously for eight weeks. Some of the players on teams such as the Dolphins stayed together and practiced so that they would be more ready to perform at high level whenever the walkout might end. The Dolphins, in fact, were so ready once the strike ended that they went on to become the AFC's representative in that year's Super Bowl.

Our team, more than most, needed repetition. We had a simple approach, and it depended heavily on the type of execution that is derived from daily practice. Our players, however, were strongly supportive of the strike, and they dispersed. Once the season resumed, it took us several weeks to regain adequate playing form and attitude.

When an agreement was finally reached, it was determined that every team in the league would play only the final seven games of their regular schedules. Because we had all already played two games before the strike had occurred, it meant that the full 1982 season would be comprised of nine games for each team rather than the original 16 that would have taken place under normal circumstances.

Of our seven remaining games, four were on the road. That difficulty was compounded further because our first three were all away games. We could find ourselves out of it before we ever lined up to play at Arrowhead Stadium. Wouldn't that be nice for our attendance figures?

After a hectic week of practice, we traveled to New Orleans, and we turned in the worst performance I can recall during my time with the Chiefs. The Saints whipped us 27-17, but we were beaten more soundly than the score might indicate. Again, we sputtered on offense, making a number of errors that led to New Orleans scores. We were now three games into the abbreviated 1982 season, laboring with a 1-2 won-lost record.

I contemplated making a change at quarterback (here we go again), and although most of our offensive coaches felt we should go one more week with Bill Kenney, I decided that we had to take immediate action. Accordingly, I designated Steve Fuller as the starting quarterback for our upcoming game in Los Angeles. This was the single most difficult quarterback decision I had to make during all my years as a professional football coach. Although I realized that we required stability at the position, I had felt more strongly that our team needed to be shaken out of the doldrums.

The Rams scored a fourth-quarter touchdown to beat us 20-14, but we stayed with Steve again the following week when we traveled to Pittsburgh. It was no contest. The Steelers overwhelmed us 35-14. Since returning from the strike, we had now lost three straight games.

Usually after our games, Jack visited our locker room, but following the Pittsburgh loss he did not. The media made quite an issue over his absence, and several of the writers and commentators speculated that it was an early indication that the Chiefs would be making a coaching change, if not immediately, at least at the conclusion of the season.

Every Tuesday at noon, during the football season, I met with the members of the media in the Press Club at Arrowhead Stadium. At the session following our loss to Pittsburgh, I was surprised when Jack entered the room and asked to make a statement. It was the first time I could recall that he had ever attended that function. He told the assembled group that the Chiefs would be retaining me as their coach for the remainder of the year and for the following year, as well.

The next day, as I was leaving our offices for the half-mile walk to our practice field, Jack met me in the parking lot and asked me to ride to the field with him in his car. He told me during the short trip that he wanted me to know, person to person, that what he had said the day before was 100 percent valid—I would be the coach of the Chiefs in 1983. I thanked him for having been so emphatic in the support he had demonstrated.

That weekend we finally returned home to Arrowhead Stadium for a game against the Raiders. In the first half, we continued to flounder, and the Raiders took a 14-6 halftime lead. We had managed a couple of field goals, but overall our play, once again, had been feeble on offense. There had been previous times when I had brought Steve off of the bench in an effort to change the tempo, but on this occasion I called on Bill to replace Steve, hoping that Bill might help provide the spark to get us back into the fray.

Bill succeeded in leading us on two second-half drives, one of which culminated in a touchdown and another that produced a field goal. We took a 16-14 lead, and it appeared that we were going to break our losing streak. If we could hang on, it would mark the fourth time in a row that we had defeated the Raiders.

With just 20 seconds remaining, the Raiders had the ball on our 35-yard line, where they faced a third-and-13 situation. We anticipated a short pass play from them, thinking they would seek to get better position for a fourth-down field goal attempt. Instead, their quarterback, Jim Plunkett, defied the percentages by lofting a long pass into our end zone, where Calvin Muhammad, a reserve receiver, made a difficult diving catch. As he tumbled to the ground with his victory catch, we tumbled to our fourth straight defeat. The Raiders won 21-16.

Despite our having lost the game, I could see some signs of improvement that encouraged me. We had played with spirit during the second half, and, for the first time since the strike ended, I saw our team execute well. We had gone through some tough weeks, but at last we were looking competitive once again. Also, finally the previously muddled quarterback picture had become clear in my mind. I felt that Bill was the man who should be installed and left in the starting role, and I told Jim Schaaf of my feelings during the following week. In looking back, I regret that I had benched Bill earlier in the season, but at the time I made that move it had seemed appropriate. Every decision does not always turn out to be the right one, but choices must be made. If a person is to take bold steps, all that can be asked is that he considers all the facts and that he applies his best judgment.

♦♦♦♦♦♦♦♦

We were back on the road again—for the fourth time in five weeks. This time we would have to play in Denver, but I felt confident that our team was now hitting its stride. We dominated the Broncos, defeating them for the second time in our last three meetings at Mile High Stadium. We came away with a 37-16 victory. Our last two games of the season would be at home.

The first of those two was against the 49ers. Like us, they had not done well since returning to action after the strike. Late in the game we trailed 19-13, but Bill had directed a long drive that brought us deep into 49ers territory with a minute left to play. A converted touchdown would have given us a 20-19 win. The next play cost us the game. It probably cost me my job, too. Defensive back Ronnie Lott stepped in front of a flat pass on his own eight-yard line, and he returned it 92 yards for a San Francisco touchdown. We lost 26-13.

In many respects, the last week of the season was the most pleasant and exhilarating of any I had spent in Kansas City. The tough Jets would be coming to Arrowhead Stadium riding the crest of a six-game winning streak. The Jets had already clinched a playoff berth, but this was to be a vitally important game for them. By winning it, they could assure themselves home-field advantage in the postseason.

What made the week so delightful, however, was that not once did Jack visit or call me. No questions. No memos. No observations. No suggestions. No distractions to keep us from preparing, as we should have been able to prepare all along. Finally, after five years, we had a week without any interruption. We all knew that Jack's failure to have any contact with our coaches had ominous portent, but there was no way that our staff was going to approach this one with a whimper, and we knew that our players would not go in with a losing attitude.

They didn't. We drubbed the Jets 37-13.

Perhaps our resounding win against New York would make a difference, I allowed myself to hope. It was obvious to me that through five patient years we had finally become a solid team. We had improved our personnel considerably, and the quarterback competition had been settled. We were no longer reeling from the strike, and we had regained our sense of direction. Now was the time to persist—to forge forward. It wasn't the time for disruption.

True, for the first time in five years, we had faltered, but the crazy quilt of events emanating from one little old strike would undoubtedly be taken into consideration, wouldn't it? After all, the Bears and the 49ers had finished with 3-6 records, just as we had, and we were on a par with them at this stage. If we would remain resolute and stay on course, we would have as good a chance as either of them to be a Super Bowl Champion within the next two or three years. Anyone could have seen that.

I should have known better.

On the day after our game against the Jets, I arrived at the stadium early so that I could prepare for our final team meeting, scheduled for 9 a.m. When I drove into the parking lot at 7 a.m., I noticed that Jack's car was parked in the space reserved for it. Jack rarely showed up for work before 10 a.m., and so it didn't require three guesses for me to figure out why he was there early on this day. As soon as I entered my office, the phone rang. Surprise! Jack asked me to come to his office in order to meet with him and Jim Schaaf.

"Um, uh, well, uh, yes," he began. I remained silent. "We are going to change coaches." I said nothing. "Would you prefer to resign?"

"Why should I do that?" I responded.

There was still a year remaining on my contract. I speculated that Jack would have loved to avoid having to meet that obligation.

"I just thought you might prefer to do it that way," he answered.

"You should know from the outset," I told him, "that I am not going to resign. There is no reason for me to resign. I've done a good job. And I shouldn't be fired, either. For you to fire me now is a conscienceless act."

"How do you figure that?" he wanted to know.

"You told me personally that I would be the coach in 1983. You also announced it publicly. Since that time we have trounced two good teams, and we came very close to beating two other good teams. We are back on the track, and now you are about to do something that will screw up everything valuable we have accomplished over the past five years." As I talked, I felt the pent-up anger and frustration rising within me, and I cared nothing about trying to be diplomatic. The words spilled out. "If you do this, Jack, the fortunes of this team will take a plunge. How the hell can you justify firing me?"

"We have hit a plateau," Jack said, "and the fans want a change."

"For four straight years this team has improved, and our attendance during that time has risen swiftly," I countered. "Only this year did it fall off, and you know damn well what a terrible effect this year's strike had on those figures. There are always some fans who want to see coaching changes take place, but, mark my words, if you fire me, the Chiefs' fans will perceive the move for what it really is—a transparent act on your part to try to divert their attention from what is really wrong with this team."

"Oh, yeah, what's that?" Jack challenged.

"Your constant, ill-advised interference in coaching matters."

"Me interfere? That's ridiculous," Jack fumed.

The time for our scheduled team meeting was approaching, and I suggested to Jack and Jim that I conduct that session and then return afterward to Jack's office. They agreed. In meeting with the squad, I said nothing to them, of course, about what had transpired between Jack and me earlier that morning. Routinely, I dealt with plans for the off season. I complimented them for the way they had played during the final weeks of the season, and I told them that I believed they would be rewarded with championships in the years ahead. Purposely, I kept the tenor unemotional, even though I knew that I was most likely saying goodbye to them for the last time.

When I returned to Jack's office after the team meeting, I was mildly surprised to find that in addition to Jack and Jim, Lamar Hunt was present, also. Jack asked me to repeat to Lamar the statements I had made to Jack earlier that morning. I knew that Jack wished to show that it would be impossible for him and me to work together effectively. He was right about that, and so, for the second time that day, I expressed myself forcefully.

Lamar listened carefully, but I was aware that he had already given Jack the backing Jack had desired. When I finished talking, Lamar asked me it I would be willing to take a break until the next day, so that they might have time to reflect fully on all that we had discussed. Unless I was willing to walk away from the job at that moment, that delay was the only other open option. I told Lamar that I would wait, and then I left them so that they could review their plans among themselves.

Lamar was a likable man, and he had always dealt with me fairly. On the few occasions when he had expressed some displeasure to me, he had done it gracefully, and I knew that he listened with an open mind to my opinions. I felt badly for him now that he had placed his trust in a man whose counsel did not serve him well in matters that involved the team's player personnel and football operations.

I should have known how it would all turn out, however, because Jack had served Lamar well in handling many of the team's other functions, especially those relating to business operations. I was aware also that Jack would not now have progressed this far in seeking to have me replaced before having received prior sanction from the team owner. Nevertheless, it was difficult for me to leave the Chiefs without fighting to the end for what I believed was right. I had spent 30 years as a coach, working toward the time when I might be a head coach in the NFL. Since arriving in Kansas City, our coaching staff had endured some rough times so that we could bring our team to this stage. Now, at last, we had a good chance to win, to savor the joys of victories that result from having paid a price.

When I arrived at Jack's office the morning after we had taken that recess in our talks, Jack was the only other person in the room.

"We are going to go ahead with our plans to make a change."

There was nothing more to be discussed as far as I was concerned, and so I nodded my understanding and departed.

That afternoon, the Chiefs held a press conference at which Jack announced that I had been fired. As I had anticipated, the members of the media bombarded him with repeated questions about his earlier, in-season pronouncements wherein he had maintained that no coaching change would be made. The best Jack could muster in response was his "plateau theory." Several of the newspaper columnists wrote blistering articles decrying these contradictions, and one of the major television stations in Kansas City conducted a viewers' call-in poll asking respondents whether they supported the Chiefs' action in dismissing me.

When I learned that this poll was to be initiated, I cautioned Dorothy that it was likely, given the results of the season just completed, that those fans who were opposed to retaining me as coach would probably be the ones most active in calling in. I underestimated our fans. Sixty percent registered disapproval of the Chiefs' decision. Many of them elaborated, saying that Jack should be the one to go.

After I had been fired, I waited two days before I met with the writers and the broadcast media. I had wanted time to gather my thoughts, and I wanted to be rational when I did speak with them. I felt no bitterness, only disappointment, I told them.

Asked what it was that disappointed me the most, I responded, "For five years our coaching staff has been fighting a battle in the trenches against heavy odds. Now, when we are on the brink of capturing what we have fought for so long and so hard, we have been told that our uniforms are too dirty for us to march in the victory parade."

Perhaps my words were overly dramatic. At least what I said at my press conference was the truth.

Among my greatest regrets in leaving Kansas City was having to witness the break up of my outstanding coaching staff. I was saddened to see loyal, competent people, who had worked together so effectively and so congenially, have to disperse. The lot of assistant coaches in football is a difficult one. They have even less security than the head man. Their fate is tied closely to that of the head coach. Players have their union; head coaches usually have multiple-year contracts; assistants have neither. Their families are frequently uprooted, their children pulled away from friends and school ties, and their wives must often give up good jobs and seek to start anew in strange locations.

About one week after our dismissal following the 1982 season, Don Lawrence, one of our coaches, and his wife, Barbara, hosted a party at their home. All of our coaches, their wives, and our two secretaries, Ann Roach and Betty Swanson, attended. As Dorothy and I approached the Lawrences' home, a large banner displayed above the entrance greeted us. It proclaimed: "Welcome to the Plateau Party."

We had a wonderful time that evening. The coaches gave me an attractive stained walnut cigar humidor. Fastened to the top cover was an engraved brass plate that bore the following inscription:

TO COACH MARV LEVY
from
1982 KANSAS CITY CHIEFS FOOTBALL STAFF
In War: Resolution   In Defeat: Defiance
In Victory: Magnanimity In Peace: Good Will

Those were the words that had appeared at the beginning of Winston Churchill's six-volume history of World War II. It is a gift I treasure, and whenever I gaze upon that humidor, I recall fondly all those good souls who have enriched my life.

Within two weeks, all members of my coaching staff had been snapped up by other teams. Their talents had not gone unnoticed by others around the NFL. Walt Corey and J.D. Helm remained with the Chiefs. The others went elsewhere.

I did engage in one more farewell meeting with the media in Kansas City. They had requested it, and I was happy to have that opportunity to thank them for the professional relationship we had enjoyed. The Kansas City media were fair-minded. Upon occasion I had been subject to their criticisms, but I never felt that they had been dishonest. Also, I had, and I retain, a respect for their intelligence and impartiality.

At this session I was asked to make some prognostications about the Chiefs' immediate future. For the most part I demurred, but I did venture one not very daring opinion that, if Jack had his way, Kansas City's first choice in the 1983 draft would be a quarterback. I might as well have predicted that the sun would rise in the east. The Chiefs selected quarterback Todd Blackledge with their No. 1 pick in 1983.

One year later, they traded Steve, thereby squandering the five years of development that they had invested in a far better than average player. Although Steve did not become the regular starter with his new team, the Bears, he did lead them to a number of crucial victories during playoff and Super Bowl seasons. In bringing in a new first-round quarterback and in parting with Steve, the Chiefs may have resolved the long-lived Steve Fuller/Bill Kenney quarterback controversy. They also reopened the path for Jack to begin once again his badgering about who should be playing the position. Welcome to the new era—to the *Todd Blackledge/Bill Kenney* quarterback controversy.

In enlisting the services of a new head coach for the Chiefs, there were two main items that dominated Jack's agenda. First of all, he wanted to see instituted a glittering passing attack. None of that conservative, predictable stuff; let's "air it out." If we do that, we'll be able to achieve our second goal, which involved getting off of that darned "plateau." He achieved both objectives. In the next year or two, the Chiefs set a lot of new passing statistics records. Indeed, they invested so much time in their new passing attack that they became the poorest *rushing* team in the NFL, and their kicking game became a comedy of errors. They got off that plateau, too. In 1983 their record was 6-10.

A year or two after I left, the Chiefs also parted company with my friend Jim Schaaf, and they continued to struggle for a while. Although I am not privy to all the innerworkings that transpired there after I no longer coached in Kansas City, there came a time when Lamar made a monumentally important decision when he removed responsibility for the team's football operations from Jack's control. When he brought in Carl Peterson as his new general manager, Lamar turned over those duties to Carl. Carl is an outstanding football executive. He knows the game, and he knows how to work cooperatively and productively with the outstanding coaches he has brought to work there. Marty Schottenheimer and then Dick Vermeil have helped to finally propel the Chiefs to the level where they are legitimate contenders, although they have still not been able to make that Super Bowl appearance they so earnestly covet.

Jack has continued to work for the Chiefs, and it is obvious that, in the more limited roles he now handles, he continues to be a magnificent contributor to the franchise's successes. The Chiefs' marketing programs and their facilities serve as examples that all other teams in the NFL seek to emulate. The contentious relationship that I had with Jack is something that I have acknowledged, now that I recount my days in Kansas City, but I bear no lingering animosity toward him. I see signs that his feelings toward me have mellowed, also. Whenever our paths cross at league functions, we have a cordial exchange of conversation, and we endeavor to recall the more pleasant events when we worked together in Kansas City.

A few weeks later, when Dorothy and I departed from Kansas City for our home in California, we did not leave in sadness. We carried with us memories of the many exciting moments and of the many fine people we had known. We would always fondly recall the coaches and their families; the players, who had given to the limits of their abilities; my secretaries, Ann and Betty; the fans, who sometimes had booed us but who usually had cheered us lustily; Lamar and Norma Hunt; Jim and Julie Schaaf; our friends in the media; and many of the other friends we had in that delightful middle-American city.

This had been my fifth head football coaching assignment, and I had the satisfaction of knowing that, in every one of those jobs, our teams had recorded a better record in the very first year upon my taking over than they had in the season prior to our staff's arrival. In

Kansas City I felt I had done the best work of my coaching career to date, and I was leaving now with my self-respect intact.

Best of all, I experienced no sense of defeat. I looked forward to the days ahead, to more coaching, to more kickoffs, to the thrills and the quickening heartbeat that comes whenever 11 men line up, ready to do their best against 11 others in America's finest game.

SECTION VII

THE STATE BETWEEN THE WARS

CHAPTER 22

Have I Got a Deal for You

My intentions, and my desires, were to continue coaching, preferably as a head coach in the NFL, and, within a few weeks after my firing by Kansas City, I received two telephone calls from NFL owners.

I visited first the Nordstrom family in Seattle, at that time the Seahawks' majority owners, and my former Redskins coaching colleague, Mike McCormack, who had taken over as general manager. Although I received strong consideration, they eventually offered the job to Chuck Knox, who was leaving his position as head coach of the Bills. Seattle made an excellent choice when they hired Chuck, a man whom I felt was one of the best two or three coaches in football.

Another NFL team owner asked me to come visit with him, because he, too, had a head coaching vacancy. I did not get that job, either. A few days after I returned home from our meeting, he telephoned to tell me that he had decided to promote an assistant who had been on the staff the year before. In losing out on this opportunity, I was disappointed, but I understood his thinking, because I, too, in hiring members for my own staffs, had experienced similar difficulties in choosing between two qualified candidates.

During the course of our interviewing process, I came to know and to like the owner of this team. I speculated about how enjoyable an experience working under him would have been. Oh, well. What wasn't meant to be, wasn't meant to be. That owner's name, by the way, was Ralph Wilson Jr. The team was the Buffalo Bills.

♦♦♦♦♦♦♦♦

In that spring of 1983, the newly organized United States Football League was scheduled to begin, and I was offered the position of general manager with the USFL's Los Angeles Express. At that time, however, I felt strongly that if I returned to active work with a team, I wanted to do so as a coach rather than in an administrative capacity.

Just before the USFL season got underway, I received another telephone call. This one was from Shelby Whitfield, the director of sports programming for the ABC Radio Network, and soon afterward I was working as an analyst on ABC's broadcasts of USFL games. That activity kept me close to the game, and I enjoyed the work tremendously. I soon found that I was much smarter in the broadcast booth than when I was on the sidelines coaching. My meals after the games were more relaxing and enjoyable, as well.

By this time, several coaching opportunities had developed. The USFL had granted six new franchises for 1984, and two of the expansion teams had asked me to become their coach. Then I received a call from a man named Ron Potocnik. Ron was serving as the point man for a physician in Milwaukee who was in the process of purchasing the USFL's Chicago Blitz franchise. The current Blitz ownership, Ron explained, was about to conclude a deal whereby they were buying the league's Arizona Wranglers, and they had agreed that my old friend, George Allen, who had been at the helm of the Blitz during the past season, would become the new coach with the Wranglers. George's departure from Chicago meant that the Blitz had a head coaching vacancy to fill.

Ron arranged to have me meet with him in Chicago, and, at the conclusion of our discussions, he offered me the job. The Blitz had a strong team. They had come close to winning the USFL championship the season before. Besides, I loved Chicago. It was my hometown. My father, my sister, and many relatives lived there. I had countless friends in the city. I accepted the job Ron offered me.

♦♦♦♦♦♦♦♦

From that day almost two years earlier when I had walked out of Arrowhead Stadium for the last time, I had missed coaching. I yearned to organize a staff, to work with young men, to teach fundamentals, to plan strategy, to pore over films and scouting reports, and to compete every week against worthy opponents. I had heard and read about coaches having experienced "burnout," but I knew I wasn't afflicted with that malady. I have noticed, also, that no one ever seemed to suffer from burnout unless he was in a very strong financial condition. I wasn't tired, and I wasn't clipping coupons, either.

Now, for the first time in my coaching career, I would be taking over a strong team, one that was ready to challenge for the championship right from the outset. On the day I arrived back in the old hometown, I learned that the complicated Chicago/Arizona deal had included an exchange between those two teams of their complete rosters of players. I was Chicago's new coach, all right, but Arizona's 4-14 last-place team from the year before would be the *new* Chicago Blitz.

After learning about the trade that sent the strong Blitz roster to Arizona in exchange for a much less talented group, I spent several days in intensive care. Then I was ready to go to work on what would prove to be the most bittersweet football season I have ever known.

Ron, who was now the general manager of the new-look Blitz, and I were able to immediately establish a good working relationship. Ron was aggressive and optimistic as he attacked the difficult job that lay ahead for both of us. He moved swiftly in his efforts to sign new talent, directing his attention, at first, toward adding players who had formerly been standout performers with the Bears. Most of these men—Dan Jiggetts, Vince Evans, Doug Plank, Revie Sorey, Kris Haines, Jerry Doerger, Perry Hartnett, Oliver Williams—were no longer in the Bears' plans, but they brought solid NFL experience to our team. Also, they were players whose names were recognized by the football fans in Chicago. With a couple of exceptions, however, they were too far past their primes to help us, but at least, we were making efforts to strengthen a woefully weak team.

At my suggestion, Ron was able to lure Bill Polian away from the Winnipeg Blue Bombers of the CFL, where he had been serving as their director of player personnel. Bill joined us and took over that same responsibility with our team, and he was to help us immeasurably in our efforts to stay competitive throughout a year that was punctuated by a succession of problems that eventually assumed comic proportions.

Bill's scouting staff with the Blitz included just one other man. That was John Butler, who was a holdover from George Allen's regime. When George had taken the job with the Wranglers, he had wanted John to move out there with him, too, but John was a native Chicagoan, and it was his desire to continue working in his home city. When he asked George to recommend him to Bill and me, George obliged him by providing us with a glowing endorsement of John's abilities and qualities. Little did I know that the two most astute player personnel men the game of football during the next 20 years had just come to work for the rather obscure Chicago Blitz.

As preparations began for our opening season in Chicago, Bill and John put together for us a draft that was the envy of every fantasy football fan who has ever overindulged on carbohydrates. In the first round, we drafted the top player in the nation, wide receiver Irving Fryar of Nebraska. We also selected Albert Bentley, the star running back from the University of Miami's NCAA National Championship team. Then we picked Greg Bell, a breakaway speedster from Notre Dame. Off the board we plucked Terry Taylor from Southern Illinois, that year's highest rated defensive cornerback.

Round after round we came up with excellent choices. There was just one problem. We didn't have the money that was needed to bring aboard *any* good players. When the ink had dried on that year's contract signings, we had succeeded in adding just one of our draft choices to our roster. He was an unheralded eighth-round defensive safety.

Irving Fryar was the first pick in the entire NFL draft that year, and he signed with the Patriots. Lacking the funds to sign Albert Bentley, we traded his rights to another USFL team. He joined the Michigan Panthers and helped lead them to the USFL championship. Greg Bell was a first-round draft choice of the Bills. He signed with them and rushed for more than 1,000 yards in his rookie season. The Seahawks made Terry Taylor a first-round selection also, and he became an immediate first-year starter for them. Except for that eighth-rounder we had signed, all of our other draft choices wound up playing for other teams.

We went to training camp in February 1984 with Arizona's last-place roster from the year before augmented by a group of castoffs who had big hearts and diminishing abilities.

As training camp progressed, Ron, Bill, John, and I continued our efforts to improve our personnel. Bill's abilities I had known before, but it was refreshing to see how effectively Ron was helping us. Ron's only previous experience had been as general manager of a semi-pro team in Chicago known as the Chicago Fire, and he had handled those duties while working a full-time job at the First National Bank. Now in his first year serving exclusively as a football executive, he was exhibiting the type of acumen that had eluded many who had worked in similar capacities for many years. Yes, experience is an asset, but there are exceptions to every foregone conclusion.

The quest for talent continued. Ron signed free agent Vagas Ferguson, who became a starting halfback for us. Vagas had been Notre Dame's all-time leading rusher, and he had played well in the NFL before injuries had slowed him down a bit. Still, he was a heady player; he was experienced; and he provided outstanding leadership qualities.

Even though he was a starter on offense, Vagas was consistently our best coverage man on our kicking teams, as well. He was always thoroughly prepared and he always put forth maximum effort.

Bill and I succeeded in completing a trade with the Denver Gold for fullback Larry Canada, another NFL veteran, and he rushed for more than 900 yards during the year with us. Then, Bill and Ron collaborated in signing punter Jeff Gossett, who had most recently been with the Browns. Jeff proceeded to lead the USFL in punting during the season.

Bill and John continually combed the waiver wires, and during training camp they claimed several players, who, even though they were rejects from other USFL clubs, helped to make us more competitive than we might otherwise have been.

In February, during our training camp, held at Scottsdale, Arizona, I began to hear disturbing reports coming out of Chicago. Dr. James Hoffman, the team owner, had plunged large amounts of money into an elaborate marketing program, but the response from potential ticket buyers in Chicago had been dismal. The fans and media had been irate when the exchange of rosters between the Arizona and Chicago teams had taken place, and they had no intention of supporting a team whose ownership, in their minds, had betrayed them.

Dr. Hoffman blamed Ron for the mounting financial problems our team was having, and two weeks before our regular season opener, he fired Ron. Three days later, Dr. Hoffman quit. That's right! He quit! He didn't sell the team. He didn't even put it up for sale. He merely told the league office that he was bowing out, that he was not going to pour any more resources into the hopelessly plagued enterprise.

Up until that time, I had heard of coaches quitting, or of players, or even equipment men. Lots of guys working at a gas station have told the boss to take this job and shove it. But when Dr. Hoffman called it quits, it was the first time I had ever heard of an owner bolting. They say that everyone likes to be in on things when history is made, but this time I would just as soon have declined the honor.

The USFL could not afford to operate without a representative team in the Chicago market, and so they decided that they would take over running the operation while searching for a new owner. Enter Carl Marasco, sent out from the league office to oversee the team's business affairs. Just one year earlier, USFL commissioner Chet Simmons had hired Carl and put him in charge of coordinating the league's player personnel matters. Now, he arrived in Chicago with instructions to serve as the team's temporary general manager until such time as new ownership was found. Carl's one overriding instruction was to see that a stringently frugal approach be taken regarding expenditures for the team. The other club owners in the USFL were being charged with underwriting the Blitz during this interim period, and I could fully understand that we could spend only for necessities.

I felt they were carrying matters a bit too far later that spring, however, when we could not get an authorization to buy toilet paper for the locker room and office washrooms. I became known as "The Scot Tissue Hero" the day I purchased, at my personal expense, several cases of this vital commodity. I had each roll gift wrapped separately, attached appropriate nametags, and conducted a ruffles and flourishes ceremony as I distributed these care packages to everyone. Modestly, I accepted the serenade of "For He's a Jolly Good Fellow" directed my way by those grateful members of the Blitz family.

We also dealt with persistent rumors that the club would not be able to meet the biweekly payrolls, but, so long as Chet Simmons was commissioner, the Blitz met those financial commitments. It was after Harry Usher took over that responsibility that the USFL began to renege on its contractual obligations to us.

Carl Marasco came into a difficult situation, and I knew that he would have to make many tight-fisted decisions relating to the club's finances. I instructed everyone in the Blitz organization to be aware of the constraints within which Carl would be required to function, and I urged them all to be cooperative and understanding.

Prior to his having joined the USFL headquarters staff, Carl had been one of those player personnel hobbyists with no working connection to any professional team. Men such as Carl, his brother Peter, Mel Kiper, and Joel Buschbaum had been enamored by the player personnel articles in the Street and Smith sports magazines and other publications such as *Pro Football Weekly*. Over the years, they had devoured all the information they could lay their hands—and eyes—on regarding football players. They had structured mock drafts, and eventually, as some of their conclusions and handiwork began appearing in print, their reputations as player personnel authorities grew. Carl became a master of lists and categorizations. He was the ideal man for the record-keeping job the USFL had hired him to do, but he had scant understanding of the chemistry needed to put together a functioning team.

Shortly after Carl came to Chicago, it became apparent to me that he was far more concerned with rosters and our personnel usage than with the financial affairs he had ostensibly been sent to monitor. He became much more aggressive in advising me about prospective trades and the waiver wire claims he thought we should be making.

My response was to tell him that Bill was our director of player personnel, and that I wished Bill to take the lead in these areas. Talking with Carl during the early stages of the season was not very productive. He did not see himself as a fiscal overseer. He visualized himself as a classic general manager. All of a sudden he was Branch Rickey, Bill Veeck, Al Davis, Red Auerbach, and George Young. Whenever I came to his office, I would find him at his desk poring over our roster, making theoretical position switches, or talking with other general managers around the league about possible player trades.

All of this he did independently of what we were seeking to accomplish with our team. We had a confrontation one day when I learned that Carl had instructed Bill's secretary to not send any of Bill's routine communications to the league office without first clearing them through Carl. Had he talked with Bill and me about such a procedure, I would have understood his wish to be informed, but for him to undermine Bill in the eyes of his own secretary was something I felt needed to be addressed. Address it we did.

Carl, Bill, and I had an amicable meeting at which Bill and I accepted Carl's contention that he needed to be kept fully abreast of all steps we were taking that affected player personnel matters because of monetary repercussions. We did not desire to—nor would we have wanted to—complete any transaction without Carl's final okay. This all seemed to make good sense, but I soon learned, however, as Carl frequently interjected his opinions about the performing abilities of every player we discussed, that his professed reason for wanting to be in on the mechanics of every transaction was a mere smokescreen to cover up his ardent desire to be the true dealmaker.

Our season opened in Detroit, where we lost on the final play of the game to the defending USFL champion Michigan Panthers. They kicked a field goal as time expired, and they beat us 22-20. Unbelievably, we lost the next four games, too—*all of them on the last play of the game!* Our team was struggling badly during the early part of the season, but it was only because we had a weak defense. On offense we were moving the ball as well as any team in the league. We just could not hold on to a lead.

In our sixth outing we faced the Washington Federals at RFK Stadium. With two minutes remaining, we forged ahead 21-20. The Federals took over for their last possession and moved the ball all the way to our 10-yard line with just five seconds left on the game clock. There they lined up for a field goal attempt. If they made it, we would skid to our *sixth straight defeat,* once again on the last play of the game.

Their snap was off the mark, and they never got the kick away. Finally, we had won one. There would be more victories for us, but in the indelicate words of one of my assistant coaches, we were no longer pushing that 200-pound ball of manure up a steep hill.

One of the few good players who had come to Chicago from Arizona was a gifted wide receiver named Jackie Flowers. Jackie was a sure-handed young man out of Florida State University, and he had been one of the top performers in the USFL the year before. We were delighted to have him. Through no fault of his, however, Jackie was responsible in a way for my almost getting sacked once again. It all happened one Monday early in the season, and it had nothing to do with having lost a game. What I had lost was my temper.

When I reported for work on that memorable Monday, Carl was waiting to greet me.

"I've traded Jackie Flowers to the Pittsburgh Maulers," he informed me.

I am sure that I set a new high-jump record for athletes more than 50 years of age upon hearing that news. Nine and a half swear words had spewed forth from my mouth before my feet returned to the floor, according to reports from witnesses. During the next 10 minutes, while several secretaries ran for cover, Carl and I engaged in a most unbecoming shouting match.

Carl told me that he damn well was the general manager and that he was going to make bold personnel moves. He didn't have to clear it with some Neanderthal coach. I, in turn, had a few valuable suggestions for Carl.

Upon learning the details of the trade, I became even more agitated. From Pittsburgh, we had received a 16th-round draft choice and an amount of cash that would have barely reimbursed me for my earlier toilet paper extravagance. It was at this point that I told Carl that his idiotic trade would be remembered forever as "The Marasco Fiasco."

Then, I jerked the phone up from the desk, and, with Carl present, I called Chet Simmons in the commissioner's office.

"Mr. Commissioner," I stated, "I cannot work with Carl Marasco under the present conditions. He is making decisions that have nothing to do with finances and that are destructive to our team's performance and morale."

I realized that my blunt words had placed me on the brink of being bid farewell.

Fortunately, the commissioner did what he could to diffuse the matter. Later that day, I received a call from another high-level USFL official urging that I seek to patch up the personal animosity from our verbal exchanges. The league officer explained to me that, although Carl would continue to supervise the team's fiscal policies, he would not be involved in any personnel matters that were unaffected by finances.

Some of the vitriolic words that I had directed at Carl during our classic argument had been personal in nature, and, with true contrition, I apologized to Carl for having spoken them. He, too, proffered his apologies for intemperate statements he had uttered. Before the afternoon was over, we were on friendly terms again, and, on a number of occasions, we were able to scare up a laugh or two by recalling the comic scene. It's a good thing we could, because there was not much else to laugh about during that "season without a reason" as one of the Chicago sportswriters had so aptly dubbed it.

With good relations reestablished, Bill and I took extra care in seeing that Carl was informed about all we were doing in relation to player personnel moves. Carl, by the same token, did not seek to interfere with our decisions so long as we operated within the established financial guidelines.

Three weeks before the end of the season, Carl asked to be relieved of his duties in Chicago. The league's controller, Joe Cussick, replaced him. Joe was happy to confine himself entirely to financial matters. With the team we had, I could understand why he didn't want to be associated with what was happening on the field.

We played our home games in historic old Soldier Field, located on Chicago's downtown lakefront. Most of the time we played our games in front of 70,000—*empty seats*, that is. We averaged just a trifle more than 5,000 fans per game. They were a tolerant bunch of die-hards, however, and I really came to love them. Even on our bad days, we heard no boos. After a few games, our coaches and players came to know many of our regular supporters on a first-name basis.

Actually, after our string of last-second losses early in the season, we played well during the middle part of our schedule. Bill and John had continued to scrutinize the waiver wire, and based on their recommendations, we added several players who made us better. By midseason, our linebacker corps, for instance, comprised players who had been cut by other USFL teams. Yet they constituted a far better group than those with whom we had begun the year.

During the middle part of the season we won five games, including a 49-29 rout of the Los Angeles Express. The Express quarterback, Steve Young, later of 49ers' fame, passed for more than 300 yards and rushed for more than 100 yards against us on that day, but we still managed to win the most important statistic of them all—*points scored*. We also defeated the Denver Gold 29-17 in Denver. Denver had won seven games in a row prior to our knocking them off.

As the season moved into its later stages, however, our problems multiplied. Injuries had dwindled our numbers, and by that time we did not have the funds that would allow us to replace incapacitated players with new additions to the roster. It wasn't just a matter of our not being able to give a new man a paycheck; we didn't even have the money to provide a plane ticket so that a replacement could be brought to Chicago. We made do by patching up, by shifting player positions, and by holding our breath.

Our final four games were against strong teams, and we weren't able to beat any of them. We played some of those contests with no backup players available at several positions. Following our last game of the year, played at Soldier Field, we couldn't even provide towels for our players when they showered after it was over. It sure would have been more fun leaving the stadium soaking wet if we had won the darn game.

Our players took it all with good nature. Instead of griping, they laughed and they persevered. They continued to prepare and to play as hard has they could right up to the final gun of the final game. I admired them then, and I am still proud today to have had that association with a group of underdogs who may have lost games but who never lost their sense of humor or their dignity.

Despite the many problems with which we dealt throughout that year, our team still bettered their record of the previous season when they had been known as the Wranglers. That, too, was a source of satisfaction to me.

When that "season without a reason" (or was it?) came to a close, the Blitz ceased operations, and the players were dispersed among the other clubs in the USFL. It has been more that 20 years now since the team went out of existence, but I still wear my Blitz coaching cap whenever I go for my daily run along the lakefront paths that border Chicago's beautiful Lincoln Park.

CHAPTER 23

When a Coach Is No Longer a Coach

After more than 30 years of coaching football, I finally was presented with the opportunity to engage in more leisurely activities. There were no more pressure-packed games for which I needed to prepare; no player problems; no recruits on campus or drafts to be readied; no staff to coordinate; no alumni or team owners to be appeased; and no more criticisms from the media.

At last, there would be regular meals, full nights of sleep, and a time to play golf or go hunting and fishing. Some other former coaches may have enjoyed, or even reveled, in such a change in lifestyle. Not me. I have nothing against golf or golfers, and I know that the sport provides a happy diversion for millions of people. It is a wholesome game, played outdoors in inviting surroundings—usually with good companions—and so I can understand why so many people enjoy the game. For me, however, golf is just a good excuse to keep from exercising.

How about hunting and fishing? I'll answer that question with another question. Killing living creatures is *sport?* Somehow, to me, it seems like an ultimate act of cruelty. I've heard and read all that malarkey about "harvesting the herd," and I don't believe a word of it. That phrase ranks high on my list of heinous euphemisms. It has always mystified me that someone can snuff out the only life one of God's creatures will ever have and then blithely call himself a "sportsman" for having done so.

I have many friends who do hunt and fish, and I love them dearly. I probably won't succeed in changing their minds, and I am certain that they, too, have strong opinions on the subject. I do not deny them the opportunity to express their views, but I am entitled to present mine, as well. Go ahead and get mad at me if you wish. I've heard worse condemnation after some of the games we lost.

No golf, hunting, or fishing? That didn't leave a great deal for me to do with my newfound leisure. Now that I was no longer a football coach, what did I do with my time? For the most part, I worked at trying to become a football coach again. Other than that, I sought opportunities to stay as closely associated with the game as possible, and, again, working as an analyst on football broadcasts and telecasts helped me to stay in touch with the events and with the coaches and players.

ESPN hired me in the spring of 1985 to work alongside play-by-play announcer Fred Manfra on their telecasts of USFL games, and, for the third consecutive year, I teamed up with my friend, Rick Azar, of WBKW-TV in Buffalo, on the telecasts of the Bills preseason games. Then, in the fall of 1985, I returned to Cal, this time as part of the radio broadcasting team for the Golden Bears' football games.

What could I, as a former coach, do to honestly inform viewers and listeners and to enhance their enjoyment of the game? I could contribute best, I felt, by lending insights into the thought processes that grip coaches and players during the course of the action.

Too often producers and executives measure an analyst's merit by his proclivity for being acidly critical. If there was ever an on-the-field decision or action with which I firmly disapproved, I felt an obligation to state my feelings, but, too often, there are people who go looking—indeed, searching—for something to criticize. That is hitting below the belt, and it really does not offer any intelligent insight into the game. Actually, the most vigorous and constant faultfinders aren't nearly so bold and tough as they'd like you to believe they are. They lash out knowing that their position affords them immunity from being criticized themselves. They are the "pitchers" not the "catchers."

When a man no longer has to work 18 hours a day, seven days a week, matters that he once found to be routine begin to assume a place of major importance in his life. Nothing consumed me more, for instance, once I had returned to Southern California, than my quest to find the right barber. Society had advanced swiftly during the last half of the 20th century, and for the most part, I felt good about how I had been able to change with the times. The appearance on the scene, however, of the men's hair salon sorely tested my confidence in my ability to adjust. Unfortunately for me, California was in the forefront of the movement away from the good old striped barber pole.

I began my search at the small shopping center just six blocks from my home, and there, nestling right next to the Safeway, was Suzette's Creations Pour Mademoiselle et Monsieur. Not without trepidation, I entered and walked up to a person whom I took to be Suzette.

"Are you Suzette?" I inquired.

"Funny man, I'm David," he said, before stamping his foot and walking off in a huff.

I felt better knowing that there were some men working in the shop because I had never had my hair cut by a woman. Just having walked through the doorway had provided adventure enough for me on that day, and so I scanned the room seeking to find men who might be on duty. The nameplates on the first four chairs told me that Raoul, Yves, Emile, and Gilles were at my service. Figuring that I might have a language problem with those fellows, I strolled toward the back of the shop hoping to find a name I could pronounce.

Conrad had a customer, and Chuckie was busy arranging a dozen long stemmed roses he had just received from his boyfriend for Valentine's Day. That left just one chair available. It belonged to a spiky-haired, platinum blond lad who was wearing a baggy-sleeved white blouse that had countless ruffles down the front.

"Hey, Mac, may I sit here?" I asked.

"The name is Mister Lionel," he informed me. "Do take a seat."

It took Mister Lionel almost 10 minutes to ready all of his equipment and lotions. Finally, poised for action, he asked me, "Do you prefer the Deauville, the Charlemagne, or the Meuse-Argonne?"

"I just want a haircut, not an automobile," I told him.

After some additional discussion, I copped out and told Mister Lionel to give me the haircut he thought would be best. That ranked as the biggest mistake I ever made up until the time my daughter talked me into ordering sushi at a Japanese restaurant.

"Mais oui!" he said. As he entered final preparations before cutting my hair, however, Mister Lionel laid down his scissors, closed his eyes, and shook his head disdainfully. "Monsieur, your nails are a scandal."

With that said, he snapped his fingers and beckoned to a young woman, one of the manicurists at the establishment.

"Natasha," he lamented when she arrived, "would you look at this gentleman's fingernails!"

"Sacre Bleu!" she exclaimed. "Look at your nails."

Upon heeding her instructions, I could not suppress a spontaneous "Mon Dieu!"

Natasha and Mister Lionel then double-teamed me. He went after my hair while she began an assault on my virgin fingernails. Forty-five minutes later the "new me" emerged—part Liberace, part early-day Phyllis Diller, part Boy George, and part NBA basketball player.

The bill came to $293, but that included the headscarf and the sunglasses with the inset rhinestones that I bought at their novelties counter so that I might disguise myself during the dash to my car. I bolted through the parking lot, knocking over several abandoned Safeway shopping carts. For the next 10 days I remained in the house, shades drawn, watching *The Phil Donahue Show*, *People's Court*, some *Barney Miller* reruns, and an assortment of soap operas and game shows.

The next time I needed a haircut, I was much more selective, driving around for hours until I spotted a window sign that appealed to me. It was Gus's Barber Shop. I entered only to find that Gus was taking the day off. He was at home trying to repair his outboard motor, I learned. There were two other men working that day, however—Leo and Burt—both of whom had customers when I arrived. I decided to wait.

Leo was the first to finish, and so I placed my fate in his hands. Leo's full name was Leo Gibson, but ever since he had been a boy back in Ada, Oklahoma, everyone called him "Hoot" he informed me. "Hoot" still had a bicycle clip around the right ankle of his dark brown gabardine trousers. He was wearing a white polo shirt that had a bright red collar, and the flap on the shirt's pocket bore the proud words, "Go Sooners" scripted in the same striking crimson hue that adorned the collar.

The toothpick jutting from the corner of his mouth did not distract me from noticing that his thin (and obviously artificially colored) brown hair had been left long on the top so that it could be swept from one side to the other in an inadequate attempt to cover a bald expanse across the crown. His pork-chop sideburns were gray and full with the front inside tips reaching almost to the corners of his mouth.

"Hoot" fancied himself an entertainer as well as a barber, and he proved it by regaling me with a couple of jokes that I hadn't heard in the last 20 years. Not wishing to hurt his feelings, I manufactured a guffaw and asked "Hoot" to write that last one down for me, promising that if I ever wrote a book I'd be sure to make reference to his sense of humor. With one hand he scribbled it onto a piece of paper while continuing to cut my hair with the other.

It required just seven minutes for "Hoot" to complete cutting my hair, and I left the shop with a small piece of toilet paper on my ear, placed there in an effort to stanch the bleeding where he had nicked me. Everything considered, it was still better than the spit curls that had adorned my forehead the day that I exited Suzette's Creations Pour Mademoiselle et Monsieur.

♦♦♦♦♦♦♦♦

So there I was, sitting in California's golden sunshine, continuing to reflect on the uncertainty of the days that lay ahead. Two objectives consumed me. One was to get that chance to coach football once again, and the other involved my finding a worthy barber. The tireless search for each went on.

Even today, as I glance into the mirror from time to time, I cannot be convinced that the master hair cutter I have sought so fervently has yet been identified. Also, when my 60th birthday passed in 1985, I was gripped by the crushing realization that I might never be given the opportunity to once again lead a group of ardent young men back out onto those fields where my heart was yearning to go. Little did I know how close I was to beginning a coaching odyssey that I never could have imagined on that first day I had left the looker room on my way to practice, as a high school assistant football coach, 35 years earlier.

Those years in the mid-1980s that I spent in my constant search to reenter the NFL as a head coach were traumatic ones for me for reasons that extended well beyond my thwarted desires to gain such employment. Not only were the bills beginning to pile up, but I was grappling with the twin devastations of seeing my father's health deteriorate as cancer ravaged his body and of becoming aware that my marriage to Dorothy was heading toward a breakup.

During part of the time when my father was ill, I was coaching the Blitz and residing in Chicago. Living there allowed me to closely monitor his treatment and his heroic battle against the disease. Through it all, he remained remarkably self-sufficient. His bed was made; his shoes were shined; his clothes were washed, cleaned, and pressed; his apartment was in order; and he still, at age 84, would have been able to pass inspection if his old drill instructor from the Parris Island Marine Corps Base would have come marching in.

In 1985, when his condition worsened noticeably, I was living in California, and I made several trips back to Chicago as my concentration became more consumed with the reality that the end was drawing near for this man I so loved and admired. On St. Patrick's Day of that year, he passed away and joined my mother, who had preceded him in dying seven years earlier. Sam and Ida have been gone for many years now as I write this account, but there have been countless times since their passing that I have been struck by an awareness of their presence.

Trying to explain how or why a marriage of many years could possibly reach a conclusion is an undertaking that is beyond my ability or desire to tackle. Perhaps the unsettled nature of our lives that set in during the four years following my firing by the Chiefs contributed. We were living in California. No! It's Chicago. Wait a minute; I *think* it might be California again. Or is it?

We had been drifting apart, and, although I believe that neither of us can give any deeply insightful analysis as to why, that process continued. Soon we were separated, and, eventually, we both agreed that formal termination of our marriage should occur. Personal matters such as this one are difficult and they are painful to explain, and so, other than acknowledging that we are no longer married, I will eschew giving any play-by-play account. Even in parting, I will always know that Dorothy is a fine lady, and I retain warm memories of our years together. Today, neither one of us bears any animosity toward the other, and, as the years have passed, we have stayed in touch, visiting, upon occasion, for a social breakfast outing in Chicago where she, too, now lives.

In September 1986, I received a call from Norm Kimball, at that time the president of the CFL's Montreal Alouettes, inviting me to come back up there to serve as their director of football operations. It wasn't coaching, and it wasn't the NFL, but it was intriguing enough for me recognize that offer as an opportunity to get back close to the game I loved, in a city where I had enjoyed living and competing for those Grey Cups a decade earlier. I jumped at the overture Norm had presented. I put away my sunscreen, took my scarves, mittens, and earmuffs out of storage, and headed north.

SECTION VIII

REBORN

CHAPTER 24

Nothing Is as Beautiful as Niagara Falls

Norm Kimball had been a highly successful general manager for many years with the Edmonton Eskimos before he was lured to Montreal where the new owners (my old friend, Sam Berger, had sold the team) hoped he could help them resurrect their struggling franchise. On the field and at the gate, things had turned sour for that sturdy team I had coached to its last Grey Cup Championship nine years earlier. Norm had found that he was so consumed with solving the team's marketing and administrative woes that he was unable to afford sufficient time to overseeing the activities of the coaching staff and the personnel department. I had always had high regard for Norm when we had competed against his outstanding Eskimos teams, and apparently he admired my abilities because I was the person he wanted as his director of football operations as he sought to revive the once-proud Alouettes.

The 1986 season was already almost halfway over when Norm enlisted my services, and, at that point in the campaign, the team had lost several more games than they had won. Once again, I arrived on the scene and went to work for a losing football team. So what else is new?

What they required most, we all agreed, was an infusion of some new playing talent at positions that were obviously in need of being upgraded, and so it was to that task that I turned my primary attention. Historically, the CFL was well into its season when the final training camp cuts from the NFL occurred. Of course, the teams in the CFL were waiting eagerly to enlist the services of those newly available high-grade performers, and so every September the competition to sign them was keen.

To operate effectively in this environment, not only did a team have to be aware of whether each one of those former NFL prospects had the talent that would help them improve, but also they needed to have marshaled their strategy so that they could compete with all other CFL teams that were vying in this spur-of-the-moment bidding contest. There also is a delicate balance that must be achieved whereby in the excitement of seeking to bring in new blood, you do not create such turmoil and turnover in personnel that all the teaching invested since the beginning of training camp is forfeited in this headlong rush toward creating something that is "new and improved." It was upon this endeavor that I focused my main concentration and energies.

My stay in Montreal was short lived—you will soon learn why—and so I will not contend, despite a flurry of activity during my few weeks there, that my actions had any long-term impact on the Alouette's fortunes. Only one episode from Montreal remains still vivid for me today. Among the few player prospects we brought up there in an effort to strengthen our team was a young linebacker named Ray Bentley who had competed in the now defunct USFL. Ray had impressed me when our Blitz teams had tangled with his, and his dominant talents continued to grab my attention during those seasons when I served as a radio and television analyst for USFL games.

We contacted Ray at his home in Michigan, and I told him that we would like to have him as a member of our Alouettes. He seemed excited about the prospect also, and we arranged to have him travel to Montreal the next day in order to have him sign the contract we had agreed upon with his agent. Upon arriving at the airport, Ray came directly to our offices, and he had just finished signing his contract when my secretary, Celeste, came into the room. She told me that a man was on the telephone saying that it was imperative that he speak to Ray immediately. That man was Ray's agent, and he informed Ray that an NFL team had just contacted him. They, too, had made an attractive offer, and they guaranteed that Ray would be added at once to their active roster.

Uncomfortable and apologetic, Ray told me of the dreams he always had that he would someday play in the NFL. Never before, or since, have I ever seen such a plaintive look on the face of a pro football linebacker. I understood why, and I told Ray that, indeed, I did understand. With that I tore up his contract, presented him with the shredded remnants, smiled, and shook his hand. After Celeste had dried her eyes and returned to her desk, Ray and I chatted for a few minutes, and then, when he got up to leave, I said, "Goodbye, Ray, and good luck."

I didn't know it then, but that would not be the last time I'd talk with Ray Bentley.

In late October 1986, just one week after my aborted effort to add Ray to our Montreal roster, I received a telephone call from the general manager of the Bills. He informed me that the team's owner, Ralph Wilson, would like me to come visit with him at his home in Detroit. Four years earlier, I had interviewed with Ralph for the head coaching vacancy that had existed with the Bills at that time, and even though I didn't get the job then, I had liked the gentleman, and I had sensed that a healthy rapport existed between us.

Going into the 1983 season, the Bills had decided to hire Kay Stephenson, a respected assistant from the staff of departing coach, Chuck Knox. After a breakeven record during his first year at the helm in 1983, the Bills slipped to 2-14 in 1984, and they were struggling badly again in 1985 when Ralph made a midseason switch. He fired Kay and replaced him with Hank Bullough, who had been serving as an assistant on Kay's staff. Once again, however, the Bills muddled through and repeated their 2-14 finish from the year before. It was now 1986, and Hank was feeling the heat. Halfway through the season, they were wallowing with a 2-6 record.

That sixth defeat of the season had been a 27-3 home game embarrassment administered in front of a crowd of more than 77,000 Bills fans by the division rival Patriots. It was the day after that debacle when the call came to me in Montreal from the Bills' general manager. *His* name, by the way, was—Bill Polian. Yes, it was *that* Bill Polian, the one who had left the Blitz two years earlier in order to become a personnel scout with Buffalo.

As the Bills had floundered during the mid-1980s, Ralph made some bold moves in an effort to reenergize his team. Besides changing coaches, he had also released his general manager and instituted a shakeup in the department of player personnel, as well. More than 10 years earlier, when I was coaching the Alouettes, I had been fortunate enough to discover that there was a man filling a rather obscure role in our organization, one who possessed unique talent and leadership qualities. Now, in 1986, Ralph had come to the same realization, and when he did decide to replace his general manager, he had the courage and the foresight to elevate this same man—Bill Polian—from his job as an out-on-the-road scout to his new role as general manager. With that move, Ralph succeeded in halting the Bills' downward spiral, and he set in motion the synergy that would propel his team to heights to which they had never ascended before.

When Ralph conferred with Bill about coaching prospects, Bill's first recommendation to him was that he consider interviewing me. Ralph liked that idea. And so did I! I was on my way to Detroit to meet for the second time in four years with the owner of the Bills.

It was midweek when I met with Ralph in Detroit, and during that session he told me that there was a strong possibility, following the Bills' game Sunday in Tampa Bay, that he would relieve Hank from his responsibilities as head coach. He did not want, however, to elevate any of the current staff members to the head coaching slot, and, after we had talked for several hours, he asked me if I was interested in taking over at this midseason juncture. I assured him that I would welcome the opportunity, and he told me that he would be back in touch with me immediately after the game that weekend.

I had enjoyed our meeting immensely, and I left it feeling that Ralph sincerely wanted me to be his next head coach. Nevertheless, I returned to Montreal without the certainty of knowing whether that "strong possibility" Ralph had mentioned would ever become a *reality.* He had not stated that he absolutely would take such action, and I could understand that the timing for making such a irrevocable future commitment was awkward when the team was just a few days away from playing a game.

Sunday arrived, and I sat in my hotel room in Montreal watching the telecast of the Bills at Tampa Bay. The favored Bucs dominated from the outset, and, as the final two-minute warning was sounded, they had an apparently comfortable 34-21 lead. It seemed obvious that the Bills were heading toward their seventh loss of the season. Then "the obvious" disintegrated. The Bills' up-until-then porous defense finally succeeded in forcing Tampa Bay to punt. The punt was an excellent one. The punt *coverage* wasn't. Buffalo's safety, Ron Pitts, brought it back more than 70 yards for a touchdown, and now the score stood at 34-28.

If somehow, in the waning moments of the game, the Bills could eke out one more touchdown and the extra point, they would come home with an always-to-be-remembered one-point victory. Would a thrilling comeback win, on the road, against a favored opponent cause Ralph to refrain from making a coaching change? Would I once again come "that close" (but not close enough) to becoming the head coach of the Bills? I've got to admit, I was worried.

I relaxed, however, when the Bills' ensuing onside kickoff attempt was recovered by Tampa Bay. Two plays later, they fumbled, the Bills recovered, and I spilled my popcorn and soft drink all over the carpet.

The Bills had a first-year quarterback who, despite the team's woes that season, had shown some definite promise. He went to work, executing a magnificently directed last-ditch drive toward the Tampa Bay goal line. With seconds remaining in the game, the Bills had a fourth down on the Buccaneers' four-yard line, and, on a called pass play, ace running back, Robb Riddick, hooked up wide open in the end zone. The quarterback drilled the ball right at Robb's chest. There was only one problem. Robb, who had played courageously with his arm in a cast after having fractured it the week before, was unable to catch the ball, and it slipped to the ground. For the fifth time in six weeks the Bills went down to defeat. Ten minutes later my telephone rang.

The caller was Bill Polian.

"Get your *** down here right now!" he shouted jubilantly. "We are having a press conference tomorrow morning to announce—and to present—our new head coach, and you are that man."

Early Monday morning, I informed Norm, packed my bags, turned in my hotel key, made plane reservations, and got my *** out to the airport in less time than it has taken me to type this sentence.

Late Sunday night the Bills had announced the dismissal of Hank Bullough. Because they preferred presenting their new head coach for the first time at a press conference scheduled late Monday morning, they did not want me to fly into the Buffalo airport where they knew that the members of the media would be hanging out in heavy numbers. It was arranged, therefore, that I would arrive at the airport in Toronto—a 90-minute drive from Buffalo—where I would be met by the Bills' director of security, Ed Stillwell.

Ed did meet me there early in the morning, and we proceeded toward the Canadian-American border. During the trip, as we got to know each other, I recall musing to myself that if everyone in the Bills' organization was as friendly and as entertaining as this man, I was really going to enjoy working there. How right I was!

As we approached the customs booth just before crossing into the United States, for the first time in my life, I saw the inspiring beauty of Niagara Falls. It is a moment and an experience I will always remember.

Thirty minutes later, our car pulled up in the parking lot at Rich Stadium, and Ed led me up the tunnel, past the team dressing room, toward the elevator that would take us up to the media headquarters several floors higher. Just before entering the elevator, I peered down the long darkened passageway that led out to the playing field. At the end of it I saw sunlight, and I could see the goalposts and the empty grandstands beyond that opening. For the next 12 years, I would be walking up that tunnel. The seats would always be filled, and, on many occasions instead of sunshine there would be swirling snow and icy winds. But the gridiron was always there and so was the rush of adrenaline and those feelings of gratitude that always washed over me every time I strode out into that most special arena.

CHAPTER 25

The Pendulum Begins to Swing Our Way

The excitement of the introductory press conference was over, and then it was time for me to move on to an even more important gathering. The Bills players were assembled in the team meeting room for their regularly scheduled day-after-the-game session, but they all knew that this would not be one of those "business as usual" get-togethers. It was time for me to address the players, and it was time for them to meet yet another new head coach.

They may have been apprehensive, but I was exhilarated. This was a team that had been losing, but sitting in that room when I walked in were some budding young players who were destined for stardom in the years that lay ahead. Looking at me from those seats I saw faces of men whom I could not at that time identify. On that Monday morning, fellows such as Bruce Smith, Andre Reed, Darryl Talley, Kent Hull, Jim Ritcher, Pete Metzelaars, Mark Pike, Jerry Butler, Fred Smerlas, Frank Reich, Dwight Drane, Mark Kelso, and all of the rest of the men gathered there were merely names that had appeared on a roster handed to me by media relations director Denny Lynch just a few moments earlier.

Somewhere in that audience, also, sat that first-year quarterback whose performance had impressed me so favorably just two days earlier when I had watched the Bills versus Bucs game. As I stood there at the front of the room, I was not, at that moment, able to point him out, but I did, at least, know his name. It was Jim Kelly.[1]

When I entered the team meeting room on that first day, Bill Polian introduced me to the squad. I kept my remarks to them simple and direct. I told them there were just three questions we all had to answer and that I was there to help *them* provide those answers: Where are we now? Where do we want to go? How do we get there?

I pointed out my basic belief that what it takes to succeed is simple—but it isn't easy, and then I emphasized that we were going to do the ordinary things in an extraordinary way.

"If we can dedicate ourselves so that we are able to run, throw, block, tackle, catch, kick better than our opponents, we will be winners," I told them. "That's really simple, isn't it? But it isn't easy. Let's go to work."

There was not time, nor was it appropriate, for me to do any more speech-making than that. It was right in the middle of the season, and on that Sunday we were scheduled to play the powerful Steelers. I needed to turn my attention to meeting with the coaching staff, to game planning, and to preparation—not to any more talking. Before dismissing the players from the meeting room, however, I did speak one final sentence. I directed it at one of the Bills' players sitting in the front row.

Pointing to that man, I said, "Ray, since you wouldn't come join me in Montreal, I decided to come join you here in Buffalo."

That's right! It was Ray Bentley, the linebacker who, five days earlier, had asked me to release him from the contract he had just signed with the Alouettes so that he could come play for some NFL team. That team was the Bills, and for the next six years Ray was our starting inside linebacker. His play and leadership helped contribute to many of the victories our team would enjoy during his time there.

As you, dear reader, are undoubtedly aware at this stage in my story, there were numerous career-impacting telephone calls that I received during my lifetime (and I didn't even have a cell phone). On Tuesday morning, the day after I had arrived in Buffalo, there was another one. This time it was from Ralph Wilson's wife, Jane, whom I had met when I visited Detroit for one of the interviews I had with Ralph. One evening Ralph and Jane had invited me to join them for dinner, and she had been a friendly, pleasant lady. The three of us talked about a variety of topics, but whenever the conversation turned to football, she withdrew from the discussion until we might turn our attention back to other subjects that seemed to me to be of more interest to her.

---

1. Fifteen years later, I found myself standing before a different crowd. It was in Canton, Ohio, and I was there in order to introduce Jim on the day of his induction into the Pro Football Hall of Fame. Among the words included in my presentation at that ceremony I was able to say with clear recollection, "From the very first day that I took over as coach of the Buffalo Bills, I became aware of what a special player, and what a special person, Jim Kelly was."

That assumption on my part was accurate, I learned, because when she called me that Tuesday morning she began the conversation by stating she knew very little about the game. On the heels of that admission she went on to say that she was calling, nevertheless, to offer some advice which she believed would be vital in enhancing my chances for success as the coach of the Bills. I remember her exact words.

"Marv, *talk* to Ralph."

I was perplexed. Of course I intended to talk with him, and I asked Jane why she might think that I needed to be prompted to talk to the man who had just hired me. Her explanation was priceless.

"So many of the coaches who have preceded you here never seemed to have the time to listen to some of Ralph's opinions," she told me. "They'd become defensive whenever he might directly question some of their decisions or their reasons for using certain players rather than some of the others. They always acted as if he was butting in. They'd cut conversations short, and only rarely did they ever initiate a phone call to him. Whenever Ralph would call them, they'd always convey the impression that they were too busy right now for some 'small talk.'"

Jane did not need to elaborate. I got the message, and, other than the admonition I had received as a young boy to "always zip up after you go to the washroom," hers was the best advice I have ever received.

During the next 12 years I did speak with Ralph often, in season and out. Every Tuesday morning, after our coaches had completed our thorough Monday review of the game tapes from the previous day's game, after we had conducted our staff meeting at which we discussed our conclusions, and after we had received a full medical report from our team doctors, I would telephone Ralph and spend an hour filling him in. Often he would ask some probing questions. Upon occasion he might offer a criticism about a player, about one of our coaches, or about a decision that I had made with which he did not agree. I always responded by addressing his concerns, and I found out something extremely valuable. He'd listen! Most of the time he was satisfied with the answer he got from me. On a few occasions I recall him finally bringing a topic of discussion to a close by saying, with no rancor in his tone, "Well, I still don't agree with you, but you're the coach."

There were also times when his comments and suggestions merited consideration, and when we implemented some of those ideas that he had advanced, they helped us to perform at an improved level. Over the years our feelings of mutual trust and regard for each other grew, and our conversations were enjoyable adventures. I came to know a man whose sense of humor I savored and whose friendship I valued. He was a person who said what was on his mind, but he never rammed it down your throat. He was willing to listen, to weigh, and to respond to the other person's point of view, even when it might be one that was contrary to his.

One of the qualities I admired most about Ralph was his straightforwardness. If he made a promise, it was kept. In all the time I worked for the Bills I never had an agent. Maybe I was foolish, but I am content with the nature of the negotiations (and the attendant *lack* of complications) that took place at renewal time while I coached in Buffalo. I recall one instance in the mid-1990s when I was about to enter the final year of my contract. I was standing in the hallway outside of my office chatting informally with Ralph, and when I mentioned that situation to him, he suggested that we step into my office in order to discuss the matter.

Once we were seated, Ralph asked me what I had in mind in terms of a contract extension. I took a deep breath, and then I blurted out some figures, some time-frame considerations, and a list of perks that I would wish to present for his consideration. As I was reaching into my desk drawer in order to pull out a 45-page, handsomely bound treatise that detailed all the compelling reasons why this proposal of mine should be carefully studied, Ralph said, "Okay," and then he got up and walked out of the room. Three days later a new contract, containing the exact terms I had presented, arrived for me in the mail.

Several years have passed since I retired as the coach of the Bills, but from time to time I still talk on the telephone with Ralph. As always, we sometimes don't agree, but we sure do have fun.

All of the assistant coaches who had served on Hank Bullough's staff were still under contract on that day I arrived in Buffalo. Some of them I had known personally, and a few of the others were men about whom I had heard favorable reviews. Although I could not offer assurances regarding their job status beyond that current season, to their great credit, and despite the uncertainty, which undoubtedly plagued them, they all worked as earnestly as any coaches with whom I have ever been associated. To them I owe a considerable debt for helping me to come in and to deal effectively with what might have been an even more unsettling transition situation. When the season was over and I turned my attention toward putting together my permanent (as if anything in coaching is "permanent") staff, I retained four of them—offensive line coach Jim Ringo, defensive line coach Ted Cottrell, strength and conditioning coach Rusty Jones, and running backs coach Elijah Pitts.

When a coach takes over at midseason, the stupidest thing he can do is change the team's offensive and defensive schemes. There is already enough confusion, and by implementing "adjustments," he succeeds only in elevating the level of befuddlement that prevails into the realm of the chaotic. I let the coaches know that they should continue to employ the terminology and the playbook, which had been used since the beginning of training camp. My only admonition to them was to simplify the game plan material and to then teach it so that it could be executed with confidence and enthusiasm. We weren't going to win with bells and whistles. We (once again) intended to win with fundamentals—run, throw, block, tackle, catch, and kick better than our opponent did.

At the end of my initial week on the job, defensive end Bruce Smith, the first pick in the first round of the draft the year before and eventually the man who would set the NFL's all-time record for sacking quarterbacks, approached me with a question.

"Hey, Coach, could you tell me, please," he asked, "who put the *fun* in 'fundamentals?'"

I responded that the fun came when, because of "fundamentals," you won the game. On Sunday—my first game as coach of the Bills—we had *fun!* We upset the Steelers 16-12, in front of 72,000 *fun-loving* fans.

By virtue of that memorable triumph in early November 1986, I became the only undefeated football coach in the history of the Bills. By the time the sun set late on the following Sunday afternoon, that distinction no longer applied. The Dolphins, for the fifth year in a row, came into Rich Stadium and went home with a victory. We had led during a large portion of the game, but, behind some fellow named Dan Marino, they rallied. The final score was 34-24. On that somber afternoon we lost more than a football game. The team's most accomplished wide receiver and inspirational leader, Jerry Butler, while catching a touchdown pass on the last play of the first half, suffered a broken leg. It was a severe and complex injury. Jerry never played again.

Throughout a long coaching career there are incidents that, despite the passage of time, a person can recall vividly. Some of those scenes are joyful, and some are devastating. I will always remember the ecstatic celebration we enjoyed in our locker room immediately after our win on my first Sunday in Buffalo. And then, I can never forget the feelings of sadness that I experienced one week later when that injury to such a fine young man ended his NFL playing days.

Jerry did remain with the Bills, however. Ralph hired him to work in the front office, and it was during those years that I really came to know what a bright, competent, honest, high character, family-oriented person Jerry was. Although he was able to play in just two games during my 12 years as coach of the Bills, to this day I am still proud to boast, "I coached Jerry Butler."

There was one part of the coaching staff structure I inherited in Buffalo that stunned me. They did not have a full-time kicking teams coach. Each of the position coaches was assigned to handle one of the special teams segments. What type of a message regarding the importance of the kicking game are you sending to your players when that department of play is treated in such an afterthought manner? I had determined that I would not, in midseason, come in and "shake things up" so far as the coaching staff structure and duties were concerned, but there is an exception to every rule. As the great statesman and orator, Winston Churchill, once said, "I'd rather be right than consistent." Therefore, I made a huge and immediate change in how the kicking game would be approached and appointed myself as the full-time coach of those units for the remainder of the season. Now I was really going to have fun.

On Monday evening following my second game as coach of the Bills (the 34-24 loss to Miami), Joe Faragalli, a member of our coaching staff, approached me. He had a copy of that day's waiver wire. During the previous season Joe had served as member of the Oilers' coaching staff, and Joe had noticed a name placed on the list by the Oilers that he thought he should mention to me.

In 1986, an NFL rule then in effect provided that anytime a team had placed a player on injured reserve, they could not add him back to their active roster without first exposing him to waivers. During the next 24-hour period, every other team in the league was eligible to log a claim for the player. If more than one team took such action, the one with the poorest won-lost record would have priority. If no one exercised a claim, only then could the player be reactivated by his original team. In most instances, however, when a player was placed on waivers, it was because his team was merely releasing him. There were those few instances, however, when a club took a chance and tried to sneak through the process a player they had, at an earlier time that season, put on the injured reserve list.

Joe told me that he was almost certain the Oilers were seeking to activate this young man.

"With Jerry Butler injured, Coach, you'll find this guy to be a very reliable receiver," he told me. "Not only that, he is extremely bright, and he'd pick up our terminology and system very quickly."

"How big is he?" I inquired.

"He's about five-nine, and he must weigh at least 175."

"Uh, huh. How about his speed?" I wanted to know.

"Pretty good. And he's real quick, too," Joe added.

"*Pretty good?*" I winced. I could see poor Joe beginning to perspire. "How high a draft choice was he?"

Joe wasn't quite sure whether the young man had been a low-round selection or a free agent out of college.

"Joe, what is it about this fellow that makes you think he can be of help to us?" I asked. "He lacks size. He's doesn't have blazing speed. He's been injured. He wasn't a falling-down-gotta-have-him draft choice coming out of college, and I've never heard his name before today."

Finally, I had given Joe reason to be bold.

"I know how strongly you believe in the kicking game," Joe said, his voice now dripping confidence, "and you are never going to find anybody who will match this guy's special teams talents and enthusiasm."

"Why in the hell didn't you say so in the first place," I chided him. "Come on, Joe, you and I are going to go see Bill Polian and ask that we put in a claim on this man. I hope you are right about him, but it really sounds like it's worth taking the chance. And by the way, it's not the *special teams;* it's the *kicking teams.*"

Later that evening the Bills made a roster move. After placing Jerry on injured reserve, we informed the league office that we were claiming off of waivers, from the Oilers, a player named Steve Tasker.

It would be 12 years later (all of them spent with the Bills) before Steve would finally retire as an active player in the NFL. By all who follow the game of football it is acknowledged that Steve was the greatest hard-core kicking teams player to ever take the field. Not only that, he was a darned good wide receiver, as well. Thank you, Joe.

Following our loss to Miami, there were five games left in that 1986 season, and four of them were on the road. The first one would take us into Foxboro, Massachusetts, were we would face the Patriots, the team that had humbled the Bills 27-3 and whose victory led to my being hired, just four weeks prior. Already it seemed like a lot longer than that.

By the time we began to implement and practice our game plan on Wednesday of that week, Steve had joined our ranks. After practice that day I kept Steve out on the practice field, and I began to drill him on a technique for blocking punts. Most coaches and players make the mistake of thinking that you need to get your hands high as you approach the punter in order to succeed in blocking the kick. Wrong!

What you should do is thrust your hands forward at waist height toward the spot six inches *in front* of where our scouting report tells you the punter's foot will meet the ball. Stretch! Push your extended hands forward as you lay out, being certain to not allow your body to enter the space the punter will enter. You must contact the ball, *not the punter.* Use your eyes to help you push your hands as far forward as possible. Stare through your outstretched fingers at the spot where you know the ball must be contacted. Visualize—and then feel—that sweet contact of your hands on the ball just as it explodes a few inches off of the foot of the kicker. It's really very simple—but it isn't easy! Learning to do it takes countless practice repetitions along with the determination and the understanding of *how* to do it right.

Steve and I, along with our punter, John Kidd, who had been a college teammate of Steve's at Northwestern, stayed out on the practice field for 45 minutes after all the others had left late that Wednesday afternoon in order to work on that skill. We did it again during a chilling drizzle after practice on Thursday, and once more in the darkening loneliness following our Friday drills. I was aware, almost eerily so, of how swiftly Steve was mastering the techniques involved. He was getting good at it, but remember, this was only practice. We'd have to wait until Sunday in order to really find out just how good.

It was Sunday, and we were in Foxboro. This time we were not the patsies that the Patriots had demolished a few weeks earlier. It was a close and hard-fought contest, and we trailed 14-12 in the third quarter, when the Patriots lined up to punt. From the outside, No. 89 Steve Tasker, in his newly issued Bills uniform, streaked around the corner, and for the first time in his NFL career (it wouldn't be the last), he blocked an opponent's punt, setting us up to score a go-ahead touchdown. We took a 19-14 lead.

There was not to be a happy ending that day, however, because New England was able to rally, and they eked out a 22-19 win. Although we hadn't won the game, we had shown great improvement over the Bills' previous performance against the Patriots. Besides that, we had taken the first step toward establishing the dominating kicking game that would become the trademark of the Bills' teams during the years that lay ahead.

With that heartbreaking three-point loss in Foxboro, the Bills established an all-time NFL record for futility away from home. The team had now suffered 22 consecutive road game defeats. The news was even worse than that because our next game also had us packing our bags for a trip out of town. We would be traveling to Kansas City for a matchup against the team that had fired me four years earlier.

I never have been much of a believer in locker-room pep talks just before the team is about to take the field for the opening kickoff. Throughout the entire week leading up to a contest, the players have been immersed in the arduous study and mastery of the game plan essentials. They have exerted themselves physically in practice. They come to understand their opponents, especially those against whom they know they will be facing one on one. Their adrenaline will be flowing as game time draws near, and some ranting by some guy who isn't going to have to lay his body on the line the way they are going to is unsettling. For the most part they want to concentrate on the task at hand, and so they usually scoff at and tune out any babbling orator as the time for keen competition is about to arrive.

I utilized a different method of conveying any pertinent pregame thoughts—ones that I wanted to be meaningful and not just routine. On every Saturday night prior to our Sunday games, whether we were playing on the road or at home, our team would stay at a hotel. Once there we would hold our final team meeting of the week. The agenda included showing a videotape of the opponent's kicking game to our full squad, accompanied by commentary from the kicking teams coach and from the head coach in order to reaffirm what we had preparing to do in that area of play all week long.

After that I would speak to the entire team and coaching staff about any topics that I felt had specific application to the next day's game. I gave considerable thought to what I wanted to say at these sessions, but at the same time I sought to limit it to no more than 10 minutes. When I finished my remarks, the players would break off into separate meetings with their coordinators and position coaches to reestablish their understanding of the game plan. The entire meeting process usually lasted about an hour and a half, after which a late-evening snack was served and the players would retire to their rooms. At 11 p.m. one of the assigned assistant coaches took bed check. And those players better be in their rooms!

At the meeting the night before our game in Kansas City, I decided to confine my comments to just one issue. I didn't talk about offense, defense, or the kicking game. I began my remarks by saying to the players that I wanted to tell them a story, and with that I launched into a tale that, in its initial stages, had them all glancing sideways at each other with a "has this man lost his sanity" look on their faces.

I asked first if any of them had heard of Adolf Hitler, and a few of them actually raised their hands, albeit somewhat hesitantly. I went on to tell them that in 1939 Hitler had commanded the biggest, the best trained, the best equipped military machine in the world, and, with that armed might, he had overrun almost all of Western Europe and Poland. I told them how he then invaded Russia and advanced farther into foreign soil. And then I said that as winter hit and as he found his supply lines stretched, his armies began to falter. In the west, when he tried to invade England, he also failed, and eventually, despite all of his initial advantages, he was crushed and inflicted with ignominious defeat.

I was aware that all the players (not to mention the members of the coaching staff, as well) were squirming uncomfortably in their seats while wondering what in the world did this soliloquy have to do with helping us stop the Chiefs' running attack. It was then that I asked the question toward which only I knew I had been proceeding.

"Do you know why Hitler lost the war?" I challenged.

Silence greeted my inquiry. I raised my voice still more as I supplied the answer.

"Because he couldn't win on the road," I bellowed.

Our players must have somehow understood my message, because on the next day at Arrowhead Stadium we defeated the Chiefs 17-14. For the first time since midseason 1983, the Bills would be coming home celebrating a victory.

It is logical to ask whether winning that first confrontation against the team that had fired me a few years earlier had any additional gratification attached to it. I could be nice, and then again, I could be honest. I've decided to be honest. Yes, it did!

We were getting better and gaining confidence, but the roadwork that would allow us to travel more smoothly toward becoming consistent winners was still in its early and difficult stages. At home the following week against the Browns we lost a tough one 21-17, and then we were back on the road for our final two games of that 1986 season. We were competitive, but we suffered losses by narrow margins to the Colts and Oilers.

The season was over, and although we had won only two of the seven games since my taking over as head coach, those victories meant that our team had totaled twice as many wins in 1986 as they had in each of the previous two years. I was excited about the prospects for our immediate future, and I looked forward to the coming off season when I could work in conjunction with Bill and Ralph as we built the structure for championship-level performance.

Now I would have time to put together the proper mix of qualified men for my coaching staff. The philosophical approach to kicking, defense, and offense would be ours as would the playbook materials and the practice procedures. We would have time now for the thorough study needed as we got ready for the draft. Our choices would be tailored to our needs. We would have the time we required, as soon as the 1987 schedule was announced, for the minute off-season study of the opponents we would be facing. And you call that work? No way! It's fun!

I was greatly encouraged by our personnel situation. Because of a string of disastrous seasons, the Bills for several years in a row had high draft selections, and they had chosen wisely. Those players were now young veterans. They had weathered the learning period, and they were on the brink of blossoming into star-caliber performers.

After a difficult two-year adjustment period, defensive end Bruce Smith was about to change from being a somewhat overconfident and self-indulgent individual into a dedicated athlete whose combination of conditioning and ability would lead to an 18-year career during which he would, in my opinion, establish himself as the greatest defensive end to ever play the game.

Bill's signing, at the beginning of the 1986 season, of that free agent quarterback from the USFL named Jim Kelly had energized the team. Immediately, that vital position was filled by a man whose combination of talent, leadership, toughness, and ability to inspire confidence has rarely been matched. In the third round of the 1985 draft, the Bills had quietly selected another quarterback out of the University of Maryland named Frank Reich. One of Frank's noteworthy achievements as an undergraduate had occurred in a game when he led his team to the greatest come-from-behind victory in the history of collegiate football. Try duplicating that! With Jim and Frank as our quarterbacks we were ready to thrive.

Bill's USFL coup was not confined to the heralded signing of Jim. He also added to the roster another man whose only pro experience had come from playing in that league. This fellow was the ultimate unknown. He was an offensive center (who ever heard of those guys?) who had gone to the USFL straight out of college as a free agent, undrafted by any NFL team. His name was Kent Hull, and he was to become the driving force in our front line for the next 11 years, winning recognition as the premier center in the NFL as evidenced by his being selected numerous times for the Pro Bowl and All-Pro teams. The responsibility for seeing that our difficult to run, but vaunted, no-huddle offense would rest just as heavily upon the physical and mental abilities of Kent as it would upon those of our quarterbacks.

By virtue of some sharp dealings with other clubs, Bill had been able to acquire, during the 1985 and 1986 drafts, a total of four first-round picks. In addition to selecting Bruce with the No. 1 choice in the entire 1985 draft, the Bills used the other three top-round choices available to them by choosing running back Ronnie Harmon, cornerback Derrick Burroughs, and offensive tackle Will Wolford, all of whom were on the brink of developing into high level performers.

But it wasn't just in the landing of recognized top-notch talent that Bill's expertise was manifest. Some of his lower-round picks and the way in which he was capable of ferreting out so many "Who's he?" free agents gave credence to how brilliant Ralph and I had been when we each had decided to enlist the services of this former advertising salesman from *The Farm Journal.*

In 1985, for example, after the excitement involving the picking of Bruce had begun to subside, the draft proceeded. By the time the fourth round rolled around, all of the high-profile names had disappeared from the board, and so, I am certain that even the most ardent of Bills fans must have yawned when the announcement was made that their team had just used that available choice by picking a player they undoubtedly had never heard of, from a school they *probably* had never heard of.

"From Kutztown State," the commissioner had droned, "the Buffalo Bills select wide receiver Andre Reed."

On that day, no one in Buffalo knew who Andre was. Fourteen years later, when Andre's NFL playing days were finishing, there wasn't anyone in Buffalo who did not know who he was. He was the Bills' all-time leading pass receiver and the third most prolific in the history of the league at the time of his retirement.

A seventh-round pick in 1986 was a defensive lineman out of Georgia Tech named Mark Pike. Mark played with the Bills for the next 12 years, but he never started one game as a defensive lineman. But his contributions were every bit as important as Steve Tasker's were in making our kicking teams the most devastating in the NFL. Former NFL assistant coach Mike Giddings, who for the past 20 years has provided the most respected pro player personnel evaluation program existent, wrote in his description of Mark's talents, "Best big man special teams player in the NFL—EVER!"

Although there were countless more occasions when Bill's acumen helped the Bills to enlist the services of players with talent and *high character,* there is one last example to which I will point because it so firmly affirms that contention. Floating around out there as a free agent was a defensive back of little renown who had been cut by the Eagles. Bill (don't ask me how) was able to pick out this particular Eagles reject and bring him onto the Bills' practice roster at the beginning of the 1986 season. He was not a real big lad, sort of slender in build, with a rather polite and scholarly demeanor. His speed was okay, but nothing that would make your eyes widen. What in the world was it that Bill could have seen in this player that would motivate him to use one the five practice roster spots that each team in the NFL was allowed to fill during the regular season? I soon found out.

By 1987 that young man—his name was Mark Kelso—had moved onto our active roster, and in 1988 he became our starting free safety, a position at which he would excel for the next six seasons. Considering the somewhat limited size, speed, and strength upon which Mark was able to rely, his level of play was astounding. His contributions went far beyond the physical. From the moment he stepped onto the field, our overall secondary came as close to flawless execution as it is reasonable to conceive. He always made the right calls. He always recognized the tipoffs we had tried so hard to coach our players to be aware of. He always conveyed the necessary information to his teammates in a manner that made it possible for them to translate our plan into action once the ball was snapped. He was brilliant, and he made that brilliance contagious so that all the players in our secondary could more effectively profit from the spontaneous wisdom he was dispensing.

That wasn't all, however. We found out that the man could really play, too. In 1988 he led our team with six interceptions. In week four he was named the AFC Player of the Week. In 1989 he led the team again by intercepting seven passes, and he came back with a team-high six more in 1990. Mark's three-year total of 19 interceptions during that three-year period was the highest number for any player in the NFL during that span. He played at that consistently superior level for the next four years until a series of concussions finally caught up with him and served to bring his playing days to a close.[2]

There is one piece of the puzzle, however, that does help me to understand why this young man might have been able to achieve such prodigious accomplishments. You may recall in an earlier chapter I commented that the most astounding group of overachievers I ever coached were those lads back at the College of William and Mary in the mid-1960s. Although Mark graduated from college in 1985, I note with interest that it *was* from the College of William and Mary.

As we began off-season preparation, I had still more reason to be encouraged because I knew that we were about to add several top-notch player prospects. True, our 4-12 finish had been bad news, but the good news was that, because of that dismal mark, we would be positioned among the first to choose in every round of the upcoming draft. That, of course, included the first round, and among those initial eight or 10 eligible draftees, there were some real difference-makers.

The pieces were falling swiftly into place. Bring on the draft! Bring on that 1987 football season!

---

2. Today Mark Kelso remains as an outstanding citizen living in the Buffalo area, where he is employed as a school principal. There is no other player I have ever coached who was any smarter, and there is no other player I have ever coached who was able to reach a level of performance so far beyond what anyone believed he might be capable of reaching than Mark Kelso.

CHAPTER 26

Strike Four!

What a joy it was working with general manager Bill Polian, with director of player personnel Norm Pollom and with everyone else in the Bills' organization as we zeroed in on becoming familiar with that year's crop of draftees. We had determined early that it was on defense where our needs were most acute. We felt fortunate that the top echelon of those so-called "can't-miss" prospects comprised almost exclusively linebackers and defensive linemen because those were the two positions to which we had assigned our highest priority. There is no lawyer in the land who studied any harder for his bar exam than I did while scrutinizing the talents and qualities of those few college seniors.

The most coveted defensive player in that year's draft was linebacker Cornelius Bennett from the University of Alabama. We knew that the Colts, who occupied an even higher spot on the draft order list, would name Cornelius as their first choice.

Okay. Where did that leave us? A number of good linebackers would still be available, and one of them was a guy who had impressed me more and more favorably as I proceeded through the evaluation process. Norm, while acknowledging the lad's considerable ability, pointed out that there was a defensive lineman on the board who had a scouting grade higher than the one posted for the linebacker upon whom I had focused. Norm reminded me—although I really didn't need reminding—that our defensive line concerns were at least equal to those that we had at linebacker. In discussing the superior scouting grade given to the player he was recommending, Norm advised me that his man's assigned score would have been even more lofty had it not been for serious questions that had arisen regarding his character and attitude.

"He is a truly unique talent, and, if you can find a way to get to this guy, you are going to have the best player to come out of college in the past 10 years," Norm asserted.

"Norm, you've made your point about how much ability this fellow has, but you've also cited all the reasons why I *don't* want to draft him," I responded.

In the weeks and the days leading up to the draft Norm urged me to reconsider. But in this instance I was not swayed. Bill and I had both agreed that high character and good attitude needed to be essential ingredients in the makeup of any players brought onto the roster.

To Norm's credit, he was tenacious without being confrontational. Just before we sent the notification of our selection up to the rostrum at draft headquarters in New York City, Norm tried one last time.

"Marv, if you take my guy, I guarantee you he'll go to the Pro Bowl."

"Norm," I countered, "I want to pick someone who is going to help us go to the *Super Bowl!"*

With that the Bills selected in the first round of the 1987 draft linebacker Shane Conlan from Penn State University. Shane became an immediate starting inside linebacker for us, and he went to four Super Bowls. About a year or so after the 1987 draft, the defensive lineman Norm touted went to jail.

In the first four rounds of the 1987 draft, Bill, through some of his magic dealings, had manipulated it so that we had a stockpile of six choices. We used five of those picks on defensive players—two linebackers, two defensive cornerbacks, and a defensive end. One of the cornerbacks, Nate Odomes, who we selected early in the second round, quickly became a standout defender, while fourth-round defensive lineman Leon Seals moved into our much improved up-front rotation.

The one offensive player in that initial group of six was a fullback out of tiny Benedictine College in Missouri named Jamie Mueller. Add one more kamikaze to our hard-core kicking team ranks. Believe me, the man could block, and he could cover kicks just the way you draw it up on the blackboard. We didn't pick another offensive player until we chose a *basketball player* from another small school (Jacksonville State in Alabama) in the ninth round (there were 12 rounds in the draft in those days). His name was Keith McKeller, and it was after Keith, a tight end, that we would name the quick-striking "K-Gun" attack that we featured during the Super Bowl years that lay ahead.

Way down there in the 11th round we ventured again to the offensive side of the ball. Our scouts had journeyed onto another small college campus, Alabama A&M, and there they discovered an offensive tackle. The school may have been small, but, take my word for it, this guy was mammoth. Don't ask me how much Howard Ballard weighed. Our scales did not register that high, but it might give you some indication of his size when I tell you that no one called him Howard. He was known by all—family, friends, foes, and associates—as "House."

Both "K-Gun" and "House" played key roles in contributing to the ascent our team was about to enjoy. The heroics of "House" resulted in his being named as a Pro Bowler more that just once.

♦♦♦♦♦♦♦♦

Going into the 1987 season I knew we would be a better team than any the Bills had sent out onto the field for several years. I believed, being as young as we were, that we might not show it early, but I was convinced that we would improve swiftly as we progressed through our schedule. In front of a crowd of more than 76,000 enthusiastic Bills fans we played well on opening day against the Jets. Not well enough, however. We dropped a heart-stopping 31-28 thriller to our division rival. Our offense, led by Jim Kelly, performed effectively and smoothly, but it was obvious that our defense was still a work in progress.

The Oilers, with their high-powered run-and-shoot attack spearheaded by their superb quarterback, Warren Moon, came to town the following weekend, and although we, like everybody else in the NFL, had trouble slowing them down, we put on an even more explosive display of offense ourselves. At the final gun we danced off the field celebrating our 34-30 victory over the Oilers.

We were rolling now. Our offense was already in high gear. Our kicking teams, tutored by recently hired coach Bruce DeHaven, were beginning to assert themselves already, and I felt that our young defenders were starting to understand and gain confidence in the newly installed 3-4 scheme that defensive coordinator Walt Corey had brought with him from Kansas City. Besides all that, four of our next six games were at home, and the first team that would be visiting us was the weakest one in our division, the Colts. As an oft-quoted U.S. President once said, "Bring 'em on!"

And then it happened! Again! The NFL players went on strike!

Five years earlier, as an offshoot of the 1982 players' strike, I had wound up getting fired as head coach of the Chiefs. If remembering that episode caused me some uneasiness, think about how I must have felt after we played our first game with the hastily assembled off-the-street, nonunion "bodies" (I hate that word when it is used to refer to stopgap players) that we, like all the other teams in the league scrambled to sign so that the flow of the season would not be interrupted. The NFL owners had determined that if the threatened strike became a reality, they would somehow assemble, from any available source, enough players to continue to play the scheduled games.

I hardly knew the names of the players we rushed out onto the field for our game against the Colts. Neither did our fans. Only 9,860 of them showed up. (I counted them myself.) Indianapolis, a team we would have been favored to beat if we had both sent our regular players out to play, won the game—*47-6!*

It got a little bit better the following week when our pickup squad journeyed to New England. We fumbled and stumbled our way to 14-7 loss at the hands of the Patriots. They at least had a whopping throng of more than 11,000 fans on hand to witness that epic struggle.

It was time for me to take a closer look at where we stood. We were now 1-3. All three of the losses had been against division opponents, thereby burying us uncomfortably in the AFC East cellar. More than half of our remaining games were on the road. There was no end of the strike in sight, and we had probably the most nondescript group of fill-ins of any team in the league. Our attendance was setting records, also—for the *smallest* number of people in stadium. My won-lost record since having taken over the team in midseason the year before now stood at 3-8. If the strike were to end soon, two of the games still left to play were against the Dolphins, the toughest team in our division. Also, I hadn't received a telephone call from Ralph in five days. Frankly, I didn't like my chances.

The heck with all that. We had a game to get ready for. The Giants were coming to town. As we entered the third week of competition since the beginning of the strike, our coaches had begun to know the members of our team better, and those players, in turn, were also beginning to grasp how to prepare. We saw improvement, and that at least was encouraging. As time passed, my frustration diminished, and I began to develop a liking and respect for these young men who were living a dream they had never imagined would become a reality. They were playing in the NFL! How about that!

On Sunday, the Giants came to Orchard Park, and our Bills met them in what I will always insist was the worst played game in NFL annals. There were more dropped passes, missed signals, stupid penalties, botched center/quarterback exchanges, blown assignments, shanked punts, bobbled handoffs, sloppy tackles, miscommunications, bad measurements, and flubbed field goal attempts in that one game than I ever recall happening in an entire season. Only the coaching, of course, was superlative.

The Giants had one huge advantage on which they were able to call. In a few instances around the league there were players who had decided not to go on strike. One of them was the Giants' Hall of Fame-bound linebacker Lawrence Taylor, and if you think he was a dominator prior to and after the strike, you should have seen the devastation he wrought upon those unfortunate replacement players who had to line up opposite him. Against us, the Giants' game plan called for L.T. to position himself directly across from our center with the instruction to blitz on every down. He spent more time in our backfield that day than our starting two running backs did.

In the locker room at halftime I remember approaching the man who was playing at center for us in that game. His name was Will Grant, and he had been a good player for the Bills a number of years earlier. When the strike had occurred, Will was intrigued by the thought that he might be able to put on the uniform again and relive some of his exciting days of yore. So what if he was too old and so what if he wasn't in condition, he reasoned. Neither were the other guys. No one had told him that he would have to line up and play 60 excruciating minutes opposite Taylor.

When I spoke with Will during halftime, I was all "Coach."

"Will," I remonstrated, "what in the world is going on out there? You have been called for holding *six times* in just one half!"

"Hey, Coach," he explained, "that's really good because I've been holding him on every down."

He had a point there, and even though we hadn't been able to move the ball at all, neither had they. Maybe we'd get lucky.

As the game ground down to its final seconds, neither team had scored a touchdown. From the many field goal attempts (all coming after the other team had fumbled deep in their territory) that had been tried in the game, each team had been able to convert one of them. The score was 3-3 with 30 seconds left to play when the Giants lined up on our 15-yard line to try for a game-winning field goal. They missed it, and we took over. I instructed our quarterback to kneel down so that the clock would run out. We'd take our chances in overtime.

As he moved back out onto the field toward our huddle, I shouted, "And don't fumble!"

He fumbled. The Giants recovered it. They missed yet another field-goal try. Time ran out, and the game did go into overtime.

With the passage of time, I can't remember exactly how we got down there, but somehow we got close enough to kick the game-winner. The six fans in the stands who were not yet dozing, awakened the other four, and they all headed out to join the merriment at the Anchor Bar. Those 10 people will always be able to tell their grandchildren that they were there that night back in a previous millennium when the Bills defeated the Giants in overtime 6-3.

Winning is always good news. And then we got some even better news. The strike was over. Yahoo! Our regular guys, much improved over previous seasons, came flowing back into the locker room, eager and hungry to put on the pads once again. And then I looked at the schedule, and there was some bad news. Our first game back would pit us against our longtime nemesis, the strong and experienced Dolphins. Even *worse* news was that we would being going on the road after a short and hectic week of preparation. We would be traveling down to South Florida in order to play the Dolphins in their stadium.

It was, I reasoned, our turn to get some *good* news, and, man, oh man, did we ever get it. It didn't come until the exact moment when the final gun sounded down in Miami on that first Sunday back in action for the NFL players. That really good news was displayed right up there on the scoreboard. Our Bills, in overtime, had defeated the Dolphins 34-31. One of Scott Norwood's two field goals that day had tied the game for us. The other one won it. Do you think we celebrated?

Maybe we became a bit too giddy following that landmark triumph, because we came home the next weekend and disappointed a crowd of more than 71,000 Bills fans when we bowed to the Redskins 27-7. Despite the sobering disappointment we experienced as a result of that loss, there was a redeeming lesson for us, and that lesson was: Whether you have won or lost, be ready to put the result behind you after a short period of joy *or* of distress. That is the best method for assuring that you will perform to your fullest capabilities in an even more important game—the next one.

We must have been maturing because, despite our so-so defensive production up to that point of the season, I could sense that our players were gaining a level-headedness that helped provide that essential self-direction required of them in their efforts to continue getting better. Also, our defense was about to get an infusion of talent that served to propel us from the ranks of the "I think they are getting better" into the more exclusive group known as the "Look out for these guys" bunch. Credit Bill Polian.

After our practices every day, I would drop by Bill's office where we would examine the waiver wire and where we would discuss any routine items. On Monday, following our defeat by the Redskins, when I made my usual stop to see Bill, he greeted me with a question.

"How would you like to have Cornelius Bennett come play for the Buffalo Bills?" he asked.

The Colts had secured the rights to the top-rated defensive player in the draft earlier that spring when they selected Cornelius with their early first-round pick. Their contract negotiations with Cornelius's agent had gone nowhere, however, and seven games into the season the ongoing talks appeared to be hopelessly stalled.

When I arrived for our meeting on that Monday afternoon, it was probably apparent that I was feeling a bit low after the previous day's loss, and so I didn't take his inquiry seriously. As Bill continued to stay on the subject, I found myself on the brink of being exasperated. Is the man losing it, I wondered?

"How in the hell are we going to be able to get Cornelius Bennett come play for us?" I asked dismissively.

"Trade," he said. All of a sudden the loquacious Bill had become a dealer in one-word answers.

Now I became frightened. We had some outstanding ready-to-emerge young talent on our team. Flashing across my mind flew the names of Darryl Talley, Shane Conlan, Nate Odomes, Ronnie Harmon, Will Wolford, Jim Ritcher, Pete Metaelaars, Andre Reed, and even those of—oh, my gosh!—Bruce Smith and Jim Kelly. Was this newly drunk-with-power general manager going to offer up a combination of players such as these in order trade for Cornelius? And even if we somehow swung such a trade, how were we going to be able to get him under contract? I caught my breath long enough to utter four desperate words.

"Who? How? What? When?" I gasped.

And then Bill explained. Indianapolis was in dire need of an outstanding running back. They had their eyes on Eric Dickerson of the Rams who, at that time was the premier player in the NFL at his position. Things had turned a bit sour between Eric and the Rams' brass, and, although the Rams were willing to consider trading him, they wanted heavy compensation in draft choices. The Colts, by now stymied in their attempts to come to an agreement with Cornelius, figured that by sending him elsewhere (at a steep price) they could stockpile some of the draft choices they needed to provide for the Rams to order to consummate the deal for Eric.

When Bill had heard about the nature of the discussions taking place between Indy and L.A., he sensed an opportunity for us to step in. He advised me of his plan. It sounded good to me, and so Bill picked up his telephone and went to work while I returned to join our coaching staff as we began our game planning for the Broncos.

At midnight, Bill came to my office and told me that he was very close to working out a complex three-way exchange in which we were involved along with the Colts and the Rams. He explained that we would gain the rights to Cornelius and that Eric would be traded to the Colts. In exchange for Cornelius, we would be required to send our first draft choice in 1988 and our first and second draft choices in 1989 to Indy. Indy would then use those newly acquired choices as payment to the Rams for the rights to Eric.

There was an even more stringent bounty required from us, Bill continued. The Rams would not complete the deal without getting a capable running back to fill the void that would result from Eric's departure. Indy did not have anyone of sufficient talent to satisfy the Rams, and so that meant that Greg Bell, who had been Buffalo's first-round pick in 1984, would have to be included as part of the package going to the Rams.

"Bill, we have to give up far too much," I told him. "Two firsts, a second, *and* a starting running back for a guy who has never played a down in the NFL, who hasn't been to training camp, who is coming in to take up a roster spot even though he's not ready to play, and who isn't even signed to a contract. I don't think we should do it."

"Marv, he's worth it; believe me," a weary Bill said.

He pointed out that despite having to include Greg in the deal, we'd be okay at running back where we still had veteran Robb Riddick and our first-round pick from the 1986 draft, Ronnie Harmon.

"No way," I stated flatly.

Bill didn't give up easily. We continued to talk, and talk, and talk. By 3:00 a.m., as I was beginning to have hallucinations, he finally convinced me. Man, am I glad he did. By 4:30 a.m. it was done.

As I went back to getting ready for Denver, I heard Bill sigh and then say, "Now, all I have to do is get Mr. Wilson to agree to their contract proposals."

He did that, too. By midafternoon the following day, Cornelius, the most recently signed member of the Bills, was in our equipment room, checking out his red, white, and blue No. 55 uniform.

We didn't know it at the time, of course, but, when we were humbled in that game by the Redskins, we had been beaten by the best team in the NFL. They went on to prove it with a resounding 42-10 victory in the Super Bowl at the conclusion of the season. The team they faced in that championship game was the Broncos, our next opponent. In successive weeks we had to meet *both* of the participants in that year's Super Bowl. Don't we ever get a break? Oh, well, at least we'd be playing at home.

We were far more competitive against Denver than we had been the week before. It was a closely fought battle all the way, but I believe the key moment in the game came midway through the second quarter when we sent into the game a young fellow who had been exposed to just four days of practice with us. Cornelius needed to get his feet wet, and we had determined before the game that we would spot him in for a play or two on a few occasions throughout the game.

The ball was snapped, and a blur, wearing No. 55, exploded from off our left outside and proceeded to greet Denver quarterback, John Elway, eight yards into the Broncos' backfield. On his very first play, Cornelius had sacked the quarterback, and it wasn't just *any old* quarterback, either. We left No. 55 in the game for the next play, too, and for the one after that, as well. And then—what the heck!—we kept him in on defense for the rest of the game. From that point on we shut down Denver's offense. We began to move the ball as our defense succeeded in giving us opportunities to do so. When it was all over, we had upset the Broncos 21-14.

In our festive locker room after the game, Cornelius, to the accompaniment of his teammates' discordant rendition of "Hooray for Cornelius; he's a horse's ass," received the first game ball of his NFL career. It wouldn't be his last. When the excitement finally quieted down, I spotted Bill standing on the other side of the room.

I strode over to him and said, my voice dripping with authority, "Damn it, Bill, aren't you glad now that you listened to me?"

It's never easy in the NFL, and 1987 was proving to be a worthy example of that reality. Our next two games had us going back on the road once (make that twice) again. The first of those upcoming opponents was the Browns, again one of the stronger teams in the AFC. In Cleveland we continued to move the ball well on offense, but we still were unable to play effectively enough on the other side of the ball. Cleveland beat us 27-21 in a skirmish that went right down to the wire.

Now it was on to the Meadowlands to play the Jets, a team that had beaten us in our own backyard 11 weeks earlier. Had we improved enough to reverse the outcome and to do it right there in that hostile environment? And the answer *was*—yes! It wasn't easy, but we scraped out a 17-14 victory. We *were* heading home, and the following week at Rich Stadium we would be playing—guess who? You're right! It was those dad-gummed (to borrow a term from my old mentor, George Allen) Dolphins, once again.

It was Saturday night at our team hotel in Buffalo, and I was conducting the usual night-before-the-game meeting in accordance with our standard pregame procedures. We had just completed an intense week of practice. Since coming to Buffalo, I had never observed such a complete commitment on the part of our players toward preparing for an opponent as I had noted during this particular week. Even as I spoke to them on this night, I sensed emanating from them a magic mix of eagerness to play combined with a confidence in themselves, in their teammates, and in the plan they were expected to execute the next day.

Frequently, but not always, when I was about to finish my portion of the meeting, after which the players would move on to their positional breakdown sessions, I might present a non-technical thought that had special application to the opponent they would be facing. On this night, when I closed the game plan book and then hesitated, they knew that this was one of those occasions. Although it smacks of pompousness for me to say it, I do believe that they had begun to enjoy listening to these little sidebar presentations as much as I enjoyed delivering them.

I began by directing a question at one of the players.

"Cornelius," I said to the newest team member, "how old are you?"

It was obvious that the poor young man was uncomfortable being the sole object of this interrogation, but he did manage to respond.

"I'm 21," he said.

"Oh, I see," I commented, feigning surprise. "Does anyone here in this room know how long it has been since the Bills won both of the games they played during a single season against the Dolphins?"

It was apparent that there were no scholarly football historians in attendance. Swiveling heads and silence greeted my query.

I reached onto the hidden lower shelf in the speaker's stand and pulled out a heavy volume titled *NFL Record Book*. Then I licked my thumb and began to hum as I leafed through the pages.

"Ah, here it is. It has been *22 years*—one year before Cornelius Bennett was born—since the Buffalo Bills have won two games in one season from the Miami Dolphins. Can you imagine that?"

I could tell that they couldn't. But I'd have to wait until the next day to find out what they were going to do about it.

There is nothing like an autumn day outdoors in a packed football stadium in upstate New York, and the Bills and their fans would be able to savor this late November Sunday afternoon in 1987 like none they had known before. When it was all over, we had defeated the Dolphins. We had moved the ball. We had covered kicks in a manner never before witnessed at Rich Stadium. *And*—we had done the near impossible—by keeping a Marino-led team from putting one point on the scoreboard. The final count was Buffalo 27, Miami 0! You can look it up.

Now came the really tough part. Two of our previous three games had been away from home, but if you think that had presented a difficulty, it was inconsequential compared with the final four games on our schedule. Three of them were on the road, and the first one had us journeying all the way out to the West Coast for a contest against the

Raiders. The roller-coaster nature of that disruptive, strike-beleaguered season prevailed, and we fell to the Raiders 34-21.

We came home, changed our underwear, and got back on the plane for our next trip. This one was to Indianapolis where we were scheduled to play the Colts. On the first weekend when teams in the league had to take the field with replacement players because of the strike earlier that season, the Colts had come to Buffalo and demolished us. Now, with our regular rosters and even though we were playing at their place, we took full command and came away with a rather comfortable 27-3 victory. Too bad that we couldn't have played both games against them using our regular players, but that sentiment ranks as 281st on a coach's list of top 1,000 "What Ifs."

Apparently, we still were not good enough to win with consistency. New England came to Orchard Park the next weekend and squeezed by us 13-7, and then we ended the year with another loss, this one played against the Eagles in the *unfriendly* confines of Veterans Stadium.

What a hectic season it had been. (Come to think of it, I can't recall any NFL seasons that have qualified as "serene.") There was, nevertheless, much for which I had reason to be thankful. In our non-strike games we had gone 6-6, not overwhelming, but certainly an improvement over the depressing results from a succession of preceding years. I was truly excited about the young players (who would be young *veteran* players when they reported for training camp in 1988) on our roster. We even had some superstar talent at several key positions. The agreement between the team owners and the NFLPA assured that, for the future, there would be no more of the player walkouts that had resulted in screwing up my chances (and those of a lot of other coaches, too) of developing the kind of team I envisioned.

Beyond that, I was working with the best general manager in football and for the best team owner in the NFL. That resulted in my functioning as part of an organization that was by far the most cohesive of any I had observed or worked for during my years in the league.

Not least among my reasons to be grateful was that this time, despite the ominous similarities to the events that had impacted me by the players' strike back in 1982, I was not sacked. This time it was not "Strike Out!"

Through the turmoil, my relationship with Ralph had grown into an enjoyable and productive one (for both of us, I hope). I no longer needed to be reminded to "talk to Ralph." I wanted to. He and I both looked forward to that new and exciting era that was on the horizon for the Bills and our fans.

I could hardly wait.

CHAPTER 27

The Day They Tore the Goalposts Down

Once a team's training camp is over and the regular season begins, all other objectives, so far as the coaching staff is concerned, take a backseat to game planning and the all-consuming striving for victory on Sunday.

As soon as the season ends there occurs an immediate switch of focus. For the next seven months there will be no games. It is time to direct all energies toward *getting better* so that when the stadiums are once again packed with faithful fans, we will have forged a marked improvement in our chances for more often achieving victory.

For two compelling reasons, matters involving team finances, contract negotiations, marketing, and ticket sales should be left completely in the hands of other people. First, those people are far better qualified than the coach is to deal with such necessary issues. And—I will resort to a question in order to emphasize the second reason—why in the world would any coach ever want to distract himself by becoming mired down in what keeps him from directing all his energies toward working on specifically what it takes in order to constantly improve the team's performance? Is it just ego? (I know, that's *two* questions.)

Between seasons, there are several areas toward which a coach must turn his attention because they contribute to nurturing that desired on-the-field improvement process. A team's off-season conditioning program is of vital importance, and in that department we had an advantage. We had a man named Rusty Jones, our strength and conditioning coach, who not only was eons ahead of others in his field but who was also a masterful teacher and persuader.

Beyond that, Rusty was an expert nutritionist, and he succeeded by inculcating in our players an understanding of, and even a joy in applying, good eating habits. The days of Big Macs, fries, and cola drinks were over for the Bills. Our players became leaner, stronger, and healthier. Bruce Smith, for example, went from being a 315-pound, rotund, self-indulgent rookie to a lean 265-pound, rock-hard energy machine three years later. It turned out that everyone in the organization profited from Rusty's ministrations, because the training table breakfasts and lunches were also made available, by Ralph Wilson's authorization, to everyone working at our facility.

By the time training camp began in 1988, I felt for the first time since having come to Buffalo that we were fully girded for the challenges we would be facing. This wouldn't be a "take over a sinking ship" year like 1986, nor would it be an "Oh, no, not another strike" year like 1987. We had been able to fine-tune what I now believed was a superbly coordinated coaching staff. Our playbook had been adjusted to fit our personnel, and, to some extent, our personnel had been tailored to fit our playbook. We had had ample time to give close study to the teams in our division and to the other rivals whom we would be meeting in the fall. Via my newsletters, our off-season conditioning programs, our minicamps, and other indoctrination activities, we had conveyed to our players our philosophy and our convictions.

Those were some of the responsibilities that commanded my attention during the off season, but the time I directed toward augmenting player personnel was preponderant. Bill Polian and I, along with our director of scouting, ruled out no possibilities. Trades, free agents, players from the CFL, the USFL, or "any FL," along with the upcoming crop of draftees, were all possible sources for helping us to get better.

Our organization also had experienced a major change following the completion of the 1987 draft, and it didn't involve even a single player. Norm Pollom resigned his post as director of scouting, and so, in addition to all the other tasks we were handling, Bill and I were commissioned by Ralph to find the right man to fill that vacancy. We interviewed a number of highly qualified candidates, many with glittering credentials and reputations. We agreed to speak, as a personal courtesy, with a man who was in his second year on the scouting staff with the Chargers. It was John Butler, the man who had been our only scout when Bill and I had been with the Blitz four years earlier.

When John walked out of Bill's office after his presentation outlining how he envisioned conducting the scouting department and how he foresaw his role and working relationship within the organization, Bill and I looked at each other incredulously. Silently, wide-eyed, and with a questioning look on his face, Bill raised his eyebrows. I responded with one short, quick bob of my head, whereupon Bill picked up his telephone and dialed. A few seconds later I heard Bill speak to the person on the other end of the line.

"Mr. Wilson," he said. "we've found our man."

Did we ever.

With John installed as our new director of player personnel, we all went to work on preparations for the 1988 draft. We were always desirous of increasing our depth and improving our talent along our defensive line, and shortly before draft day we made a trade that addressed that concern in a way that far exceeded any expectations I could have had.

The Chiefs' coaching staff and their outstanding defensive end, Art Still, were clashing. I knew Art. He was the first player we had picked in the 1978 draft when I had taken over as coach of the Chiefs. He was different and he was eccentric, but I never found him to have traits that would place him in that category labeled "bad attitude." Although by this time he had been in the league for 10 years, our study showed that he was still on the top of his game. He had always been an individual who conditioned himself well, and that dedication to good work habits was reflected in what we saw on the game tapes that we reviewed. We jumped on the opportunity to add him to our roster. The trade was consummated.

With that need addressed, we now turned our attention toward filling the second highest priority that we originally had listed while preparing for draft day. We were uneasy about our depth at running back. Robb Riddick was drawing swiftly toward the end of his career. Age and injuries were taking their toll on Robb. That left only Ronnie Harmon, and Ronnie's main abilities were as a pass receiving back rather than as an every-down ball carrier. We needed one of the latter.

Our chances for landing one of the top-rated running backs in that year's draft, however, were limited. We had traded away our first-round pick. We wouldn't have a shot at the top one or two, but our scouts had placed the names of six of them on a list of the elite. Surely, there would be at least a couple of them still on the board when we made our second-round selection.

In 1988 the world must have been hungering for running backs because, when it came time for us to pick, all six of the players we had in our sights had been claimed. Bad luck was haunting us, I fretted. When were we ever going to get a stroke of *good* luck? Stay tuned.

Our offensive backfield coach, Elijah Pitts, a former outstanding running back himself with the fabled Packers teams in the 1960s, came rushing into our draft room with an unusual combination of glee and urgency showing on his face. Elijah had been sent out during the weeks preceding the draft in order to screen about 20 running backs who were draft eligible.

"Coach, Bill, John, Mr. Wilson," he called out, "the very best running back I worked out on my trip is still on the board."

Elijah hastened over to the display on the wall and pointed out the name of the player about whom he was talking. I knew, from our exhaustive study during our pre-draft meetings who the lad was, and I knew, also, that he had racked up some impressive statistics as a collegian. Nevertheless, he wasn't real big. He was five foot 10 and about 195 pounds. At that size would he be able to withstand the heavy pounding that an NFL running back is exposed to, *and* would he be able to pick up those frenzied blitzes by 245-pound linebackers? Also, although his rushing yardage totals bordered on the sensational, he had no pass receptions, and our style of offense required that our running backs be involved as an integral part of our passing attack.

There was an even more compelling reason why our scouts had listed this young prospect far down the board. In his junior year he had sustained a severe knee injury. He had not had it surgically repaired, and every day, in practice and during games, he wore a bulky brace.

We didn't have much time available to us now for a leisurely discussion. Once it is a team's turn to pick on draft day, they must announce their choice within 15 minutes or else the next team in the draft order gains the right to make their selection. When Elijah offered his opinion, there were only 10 minutes left.

All the scouts, along with Bill, John, and I agreed that the young man under discussion would have merited a far higher grade had it not been for the concerns about his knee.

"When I worked him out two weeks ago," Elijah interjected, "there was no problem with that knee. He made moves I haven't seen since my wife, Ruth, made me go to the ballet with her a couple of years ago. Not only that, we threw a ton of passes at him, and he is as good as any back I've ever seen when it comes to running routes and catching the ball."

There were now six minutes left until our time ran out.

I grabbed the telephone and placed a call to the player's college coach, and during our conversation he told me that the young man hadn't missed a single practice or game since returning from that injury. I thanked the coach, hung up the phone, and then I turned and faced the other people in the draft room. We now had one minute before our time would expire.

"He sounds good to me," I said simply.

"I'm all for it," Bill added.

"What the hell; let's take a chance," John chimed in.

"Go for it," Ralph said.

As the clock ticked down to 20 seconds, we informed our representative at draft headquarters to send up to the rostrum the name of the man we were selecting in the second round. Ten seconds later the commissioner announced it.

"The Buffalo Bills, with the 40th pick in the draft, select Oklahoma State University running back Thurman Thomas," he said.

Think about it. If we had had a first-round draft choice available to us in the 1988 draft, we wouldn't have used it to pick Thurman. If any of the six other running backs (I can't remember the name of any one of them) had still been there in the second round, we wouldn't have picked Thurman. If we hadn't just recently acquired the services of Art Still, we wouldn't have picked Thurman; we would have picked a defensive lineman instead. If we hadn't made that trade six months earlier for Cornelius Bennett—the one I had been reluctant to make until convinced by Bill—we wouldn't have picked Thurman. *(And we wouldn't have had Cornelius, either!)* If OSU coach Pat Jones hadn't been sitting next to his telephone at the exact moment I called him, we wouldn't have picked Thurman. If Thurman had not sustained the injury that scared so many other teams away, we wouldn't have been able to pick Thurman. So what? We *did* pick Thurman!

In selecting Thurman, it turned out that Ralph, Bill, John, Elijah, and I sure did look smart. Or was it just lucky? Whatever.

Thurman became a starting running back for the Bills in his first year with the team. He didn't rush for that magic 1,000 or more yards as a rookie, but he came close by gaining 881 yards on the ground. That was more than O.J. Simpson, the Bills' all-time leading rusher up till that time, had registered in his rookie season. Before his playing days with the Bills came to an end, Thurman went on to shatter almost every record that O.J. had established as a member of the team. For the next eight consecutive years Thurman rushed for more than 1,000 yards compared to O.J.'s mark of five straight seasons. On 46 occasions Thurman ran for more than 100 yards in a game. O.J. accomplished that feat 41 times. By the time both of those men no longer wore a Bills uniform, Thurman had more carries (2,874 to 2,188), had gained more yards on the ground

(11,938 to 10,183), and had scored more touchdowns rushing (65 to 57) than O.J. had. And those figures pertain only to the running game.

Despite his not having been a pass receiving back in his college days, Thurman, by the time his playing days were concluded, had gone on to become the second all-time leading receiver in Bills history. Only teammate Andre Reed, a wide receiver, exceeded Thurman's total. No other running back is listed in the team's top 10. As a pass receiver, Thurman added 22 more touchdowns to those he had scored on the ground, and beyond that he could pick up a blitz as well as any fullback I've ever seen (well, *almost* any).

The "little guy" from OSU, extrovert that he was, was still one of the most unselfish players I have ever known. He, like so many of the other star performers on the Bills teams that I coached, never once mentioned statistics, and their accomplishments are made more noteworthy because we never resorted to tactics designed with the purpose in mind of padding any player's numbers.

When we luckily drafted Thurman in 1988, we had added an irreplaceable part of an offense that would help us stampede our way, a few years later, to four consecutive AFC championships. O.J. is in the Pro Football Hall of Fame. The greatest running back in Bills history, Thurman Thomas, belongs there, too.

Okay, we had made our move at running back. Now it was back to defense. Those often overlooked late-round draft choices provide a source of talent that helps prove my contention that the scouting of personnel is not an unerring scientific procedure. We had two eighth-round picks available to us now in 1988, and with them we selected strong safety John Hagy and defensive nose tackle Jeff Wright. In the ninth round we picked linebacker Carlton Bailey from the University of North Carolina. All three of those "who are theys" won starting positions with us early in their careers.

No more distractions. It was all football, and we were ready for it. Sure, we had a stable of outstanding players, but the quality that impressed me the most about this group of warriors was the poise they exhibited at times of greatest stress. How do you measure poise? The best indicator of that in an athletic contest, I believe, is found in how a team fares in its most keenly contested games. Are they able to prevail

in the close ones? We squeezed by with a 13-10 victory in the opening game of the season against the Vikings. We followed that with a 9-6 win at home against Miami in front of almost 80,000 revved-up Bills fans. Then we were on the road to meet another division rival, the Patriots. We won that one, too, 16-14. How's that for winning the close ones?

Our defense had come of age, and we were rolling now. Next, the Steelers came to town, and it was our offense that came alive that Sunday afternoon as we trounced the Steelers 36-28. We were 4-0. True, three of those victories had come at home, but what difference did that make? We found out the following weekend in Soldier Field where the Bears brought us back to earth, inflicting a 24-3 shellacking.

What a wake-up call that was for us. We went back to work, and we began another winning streak. We won the next five straight, and then we traveled down to Miami where we made it six in a row by demolishing the Dolphins 31-6 right there in their own backyard. There were still five games remaining in the regular season, but if we could win the next one, at home, against the Jets, we would clinch the AFC East Division crown. If you think the adrenaline was running high in our locker room shortly before the kickoff of that game, you should have sampled those tailgate parties out in the parking lot.

We gave all 78,389 fans in attendance that day reason to stay excited every second of the way. The Jets were ready for this one, too, and they played as sterling a game on defense as our guys did. They kept us, in fact, from scoring any touchdowns during that long, chilly afternoon. Scott Norwood's two field goals allowed us to put a miniscule six points up on the Jumbotron, and we clung tenaciously to that tenuous lead throughout most of the second half. The Jets were not going to give in easily, and late in the game they scored a touchdown. The score was 6-6, and they lined up to kick the game-winning extra point.

Remember how often I have emphasized how important the kicking game is? We deemed it to be so important that we had included a starting *offensive* tackle on the kicking unit designated as our "point-after-touchdown defense" team. It was "House" Ballard, and the big fellow bulled his way through the front of the Jets' place kick protection unit, threw his massive paw into the air, and deflected the attempt. The game went into overtime.

The Jets won the toss, and they elected to receive. They then moved the ball deep enough into our territory so that they were in easy range for a game-winning field goal. This time it was veteran defensive nose tackle Fred Smerlas who provided the heroics as he came barging through to block their field goal effort. (By the way, have I ever mentioned how important to a team's success I believe the kicking game is?)

We took over, and now it was the Bills who moved the ball into field goal range. Scott nailed his third successful kick of the day between the uprights. We had won the game 9-6, and with it we won also the AFC East Division championship.

Ecstatic Bills fans poured out onto the field, and I still have a treasured picture, taken in the dusk on that late November afternoon by our team photographer. It shows a group of our jubilant supporters bringing down the goalposts. Other celebrants surround them, and glee prevails. A few days later, the members of the grounds crew came to my office with a piece of that yellow-colored metal mounted handsomely on a polished walnut backing. With it they delivered an enlarged color photo taken at the exact moment those descending goalposts were at a jaunty 45-degree angle. I proudly displayed both of those items on my office wall during my Bills coaching tenure.

We had now won seven games in a row, the longest winning streak the Bills had ever enjoyed since entering the NFL. We had clinched the division title, but there were still important games left to play. Our next two games were away from home, and, nursing a multitude of injuries, we lost them both. First we fell to the Bengals 35-21, and as we would learn later, that loss would have far-reaching repercussions. We were duds the following week in Tampa Bay also where the Buccaneers took a 10-5 decision.

Yes, we were division champs, and we were in the playoffs, but we wanted to capture home-field advantage, which is so important in helping a team to advance all the way to the Super Bowl. We had two games remaining, and we rallied from those two road losses by coming home the next weekend where we defeated the Raiders 37-21.

It was to no avail, however, because the Bengals, at the conclusion of that weekend's games, had won one more game than we had. Even if they lost their final game of the season and we won ours, we would have finished with identical records, and because they had beaten us in our head-to-head encounter three weeks earlier, they owned the tiebreaker. If we had won that earlier contest, we would have been the ones in that most enviable position. What a meaningful loss that turned out to be, because it meant that Cincinnati, and not Buffalo, had first call on home field throughout the playoffs.

Because our last regularly scheduled game was a meaningless one when it came to our playoff positioning, I made the decision to rest many of our starters so that they could be fresh, and in some cases healed from injuries, when the playoffs began. Our reserves played well, and they gained valuable experience by taking the field for us in Indianapolis, but the Colts' regulars came away with a 17-14 win. Our regular season was over. We had finished with a 12-4 record. Only once before had the Bills matched that 12-victory mark, and that had been back in 1964 when they competed in the AFL prior to its merger with the NFL.

As division winners, we had a bye in the first round—known as the AFC Wild Card Playoff. Besides that, we were assured of a home game the following weekend in our AFC Divisional Playoff. If we were to win that one, it was even conceivable that the week after that we could play the AFC Championship in Orchard Park, as well. That would require, however, that Cincinnati lose their Divisional Playoff. If this all sounds confusing, I have a simple solution designed to help you understand all these complexities, and that is, in the words of the venerable Al Davis, owner of the Raiders, *"Just win, baby!"*

The Oilers came to Rich Stadium on New Year's Day, and so did 79,532 clamoring red, white, and blue-clad fans. We followed Al Davis's advice. We won.

It wasn't easy, but it was vintage Bills. In the second quarter our strong safety, Leonard Smith, blocked a punt, and a few moments later, Robb Riddick rammed it in from the one-yard line. The Oilers countered with a field goal, and the score at halftime was 7-3, in our favor. In the third quarter, Thurman climaxed a 60-yard drive by bolting the final 11 yards to paydirt. Early in the final period Mark Kelso picked off a Warren Moon pass and brought it back 30 yards to the Oilers' 18-yard line. Our drive sputtered, but when Scott added a field goal, things were looking rather rosy for us as we took a 17-3 fourth-quarter lead. Not so quick, mister!

Don't ever count Warren Moon out. He led a Houston drive, and, with about five minutes to be played, an Oilers' touchdown narrowed our lead to 17-10. After they kicked off, we tried to milk the clock, but they succeeded in stymieing our efforts, and with just under two minutes left in the game we were forced to punt. Moon and the Oilers would get one more opportunity to score and to send what had appeared a few minutes earlier to be a victory for us, into that uncertain land called "overtime." Again—not so quick, mister!

John Kidd boomed the punt, and, just after the Houston safety gathered it in on their 20-yard line, a streak, wearing No. 89 (oh, yeah, it was that doggone Steve Tasker, once again) stripped him of the ball. Our Ray Bentley pounced on it. We ran out the clock, and then, we ran off the field with the victory. We had advanced to the AFC Championship game.

The Bengals won their Divisional Championship game on that same weekend, also, and so that meant that the AFC title game would be played at Cincinnati's Riverfront Stadium where we had lost to the

Bengals 35-21 just a few weeks earlier. We didn't do any better this time. Cincinnati won the game—*and* the trip to the Super Bowl. The final score was 21-10, but they had dominated by more than that modest figure might indicate. All of a sudden, our season was over.

What a shock it is when your expectations are so high, and then, all of a sudden you are eliminated. All coaches know that, as hard as we all strive to make the playoffs, only 12 of the 32 teams will advance. We know, also, that of those 12 teams there will be *11 of them* who end their season with a loss, and that the emotions we will experience after those losses are even more intense than after regular-season defeats. Why then would any sane person expose himself to such likelihood of impending misery?

First, let me ask you, who ever said football coaches were sane?

That established, let me seek still to provide a rational answer to why we allow such uncertainties to invade our daily life. We love it! We love the competition. We love the people with whom we strive, and, yes, we even love the people against whom we strive. Don't ask why we love it, please. Most people will acknowledge unqualifiedly that they love their spouse, and yet, when asked to detail why, they'll most often say, "Because I just love her/him, that's why." I know, coaches aren't "married" to football (an assertion many coaches' wives might refute), but I hope you get the drift.

How you deal with those grinding disappointments shows best whether you will merely continue to lie there and whimper or whether you will show the resolve that leads to rekindling the love and enthusiasm you have for the pursuit of victory and the art of coaching. If a crushing defeat on the football field winds up defeating you, then you have, indeed, become a loser. But if you rise above it, if *you* overcome defeat, then you are a winner.

We had accomplished much during that 1988 season. Just two years before, the Bills had finished in the AFC East Division cellar (for the third straight time) with a 4-12 record. Now we were East Division champs sporting a 12-4 mark. Our player personnel situation was extremely encouraging. We had inherited some budding young prospects who were now maturing into the type of star performers that exceeded all initial expectations. We had added others whose talents fit perfectly with those already on the roster. There had been a few disappointments and numerous startlingly uplifting surprises. Late-round picks and unknown free agents had added to that latter group.

It wasn't just the talent these players possessed that was so noteworthy. These were men of unique character. These were team-oriented guys who were a joy to coach. These were fellows who responded to teaching and who you knew were going to improve. And, with men such as Bill Polian and John Butler on board, you knew that the process—and the on-field product—would become increasingly better.

Our defense had gone in four years from being the Bills' all-time worst to becoming close to its all-time best. In 1984 the team had allowed 454 points, the most ever given up by a Bills team. Now, in 1988, by holding opponents to 237 points for the year, we had come within eight points of bettering the team's best NFL season, when they had given up 230 points back in 1973. At this time our defense was a bit farther along than our offense although there was also noticeable improvement on that side of the ball. The 329 points we had put on the scoreboard was the best in that department since 1975 when the Bills had led the NFL in scoring.

We were solid at quarterback with Jim Kelly and Frank Reich providing what I felt was the best one/two combination in the league. Our offensive line, with players such as Will Wolford, Jim Ritcher, Kent Hull, Joe Devlin, and Howard Ballard was really beginning to shape up. Tight ends Pete Metzelaars, Keith McKeller, and Butch Rolle combined to give us superb depth at that underrated but important position. True, there were still questions at running back (it would take until the following year before Thurman would emerge as an almost unstoppable talent).

It was at wide receiver where we believed we would need to focus our main attention, however. Andre Reed, that 1985 fourth-round draft choice out of Kutztown State, was beginning to show some real promise, but other than that we felt we needed to improve at that position if we wanted to capitalize fully on Jim's quarterbacking abilities.

We were excited. And so were our fans. How excited were they? In 1988 we set a Bills all-time attendance record. It was a figure our team would exceed two years later, and then the year following that we shattered that newly established mark. During the six-year period from 1988 through 1993 the Bills—in that "small market" city—led the NFL in home game attendance every one of those six seasons. That's how excited they were.

We had momentum. We had great young—and some experienced—players. We had the best owner, the best front office, and the best personnel department in the NFL. I had a super coaching staff working with me. We had the best fan support in the league. Everything was smooth and harmonious as we looked forward to the 1989 season. We were really ready to hum now.

Let's hear it one more time—*not so quick, mister!*

CHAPTER 28

The Bickering Bills

We approached that 1989 season with great expectancies. Almost every player on our team demanded the best from himself and from his teammates as we dedicated ourselves to resuming the steep climb that had been momentarily delayed by that setback we had sustained in Cincinnati the previous January. The same anticipation that permeated our players and coaches was shared and expressed, also, by our fans, by the media, and by Ralph Wilson.

The demanded level of play that our players exacted from themselves and from their teammates was commendable, and they reflected that high degree of motivation that is so essential for achieving success. Sometimes, however, the passion that wells up inside a man becomes so intense that it results in his making a critical remark about another player, in the hope that such goading will get—what he perceives to be—that errant teammate back on track. The critic's intentions are benign, but the sparks that fly off as a result of his comments often land on material that is also highly flammable.

As the strain from the season's heated competition increased, a few minor conflagrations of this nature were ignited, and the media—I don't blame them—were quick to fan the flames. I had to be the guy who knew how and when to use the fire extinguisher.

Initially, there were no signs of discord within our ranks, and it was the unfolding of events that led, well into the season, to our becoming anointed with that unwanted and, I truly feel, unwarranted (but catchy phrased) "Bickering Bills" moniker.

In 1989, similarly to how we had operated during all other off seasons, we turned our attention first toward filling personnel needs. At the forefront of these efforts, as usual, was preparation for the draft. But this year we could sit around in our meeting room on draft day watching ESPN and eating pretzels until late in the third round because we didn't have a first-round *or* a second-round pick available to us because we had traded them away in 1987 to get Cornelius Bennett. Our initial choice in the 1989 draft wouldn't come until 81 other players had already been taken. Maybe John Butler would come up with some sleeper wide receiver from some small college somewhere out there on the prairies.

When our time finally came to make a decision, John nudged me awake and told me that he recommended a lad named Don Beebe.

"Never heard of him," I said.

"He's from Chadron State," John elucidated. "It's located halfway between Harrison, Nebraska, and Pine Ridge, South Dakota."

"Never heard of it," I droned. "And never heard of either town."

"He's a wide receiver," John persisted, as he injected a tone of enticement into his pronouncement.

"Now that I *have* heard of," I acknowledged.

John proceeded to tell me that the player he was recommending was the fastest man in that year's draft, running the 40-yard dash in under 4.3 seconds. (If you don't think that is swift, dear reader, try doing it yourself.) He told us about the intelligence, the character, the work habits, and the competitive attitude that all combined to make this fellow the right fit at the right time for the Bills.

Our needs at the position were dire, and all the glamour receivers from Florida State, Southern Cal, Michigan, Oklahoma, and Notre Dame had already, earlier that day, been picked. Because we all believed that John knew his business (and apparently his geography, too), we went along with his bold recommendation.

Our corps of receivers now included one fourth-round afterthought selection out of Kutztown State (Andre Reed) plus our newly acquired third-round "reach" from Chadron State. Ask of the other teams in the NFL, back there in April 1989, how much fear this daring duo struck in the hearts of their defensive coordinators, and I'd wager that your inquiry would elicit a yawn in response. Ask them the same question three years later, and then be prepared for one of those, "What are you, a wise guy?" retorts. What no one in professional football knew at that time, and that included us, was that there was still a missing piece in a machine that would become the most feared and respected pass receiving trio in the NFL. I guess that third part was still on order, and it was delivered in the middle of the season when we lucked into adding to our roster one of the brightest and most talented receivers to ever play the game.

It wasn't mid-season yet, however. It was, instead, time to begin the season, and what a start we had. The Bills had begun to build a reputation for being unbeatable when another team had to come to upstate New York to play in January's bitter cold. The icy winds and swirling snow served to make us even more invulnerable. But what about when the situation was reversed? What about when we had to invade South Florida and grapple with the merciless, squint-inducing sunshine and the attendant stifling summer heat and humidity?

To cope with those challenges we adopted the attitude that we were not playing against the weather; we were playing against a worthy opponent. In our season's opener we made that demanding late-summer trip to Miami where we met the Dolphins. We came away with a hotly contested (no pun intended) 27-24 victory. In the last three and a half minutes of that game we rallied from an 11-point deficit, capping off those heroics when Jim Kelly scrambled into the end zone for the winning touchdown on the final play of the game.

We were rolling now, and we continued to roll right up until—our next game. It was our home opener, and we got handled by the Broncos. More than 78,000 disappointed fans watched us limp to a 28-14 loss right there in the venue where we had won all nine games we had played there one year earlier. Those first two contests of the new season provided a preview of the vicissitudes that would afflict us during that tumultuous 1989 season. Against Denver we had been bums, but the following week down in Houston we were heroes once again thanks to a 60-yard touchdown pass from Jim Kelly to Andre Reed in overtime that put away a head-swiveling 47-41 victory for us.

That's the way it seemed to go all year long, and there must have been similar experiences haunting the other teams in our division also, because although we found ourselves late in December sporting an unimpressive 8-7 record, we still had a chance, by winning that final game on our schedule, to capture the division crown once again. There had been some stirring moments along the way.

As 1989's finale drew near, I struggled to recall back in late October when, for the first time in the history of the franchise, more than 80,000 fans overflowed into the stadium where they watched us defeat the Dolphins 31-17. And then, one month after that, a raucous throng of Bills fans, again topping 80,000, had seen us play the Bengals, the team that had kept us from going to the Super Bowl the year before. Our players and our partisans exacted sweet retribution as we coasted to a 24-7 victory over the humbled Bengals.

But there were some darker recollections in that memory bin, also. Early in the year we had gone into Indianapolis as solid favorites and had gotten wiped out 37-14. We bounced back and won *three* straight right after that before striding confidently into Atlanta where the underdog Falcons deflated us on the last play by kicking a 50-yard field goal that gave them a 30-28 upset win. Matters became worse than that as we began to show disturbing signs of a late-season collapse.

After "Revenge Sunday" against Cincinnati, bad things really began to happen. For starters, we lost the next three games in a row. The scene we had all envisioned back in midseason depicting us wrapping up another division title was on the brink of fading away. The worst of our problems, however, were taking place off of the playing field.

The sporadic flow of successes and failures during the season was beginning to frustrate us all—players, coaches, fans, ownership, and even the media. No one wants to look bad or, worse yet, foolish. Not only were we appearing to be overconfident and too self-satisfied after our good outings, but we were confounding the writers and announcers by bouncing back with resounding victories immediately following their assertions that we had tanked. To justify these contentions some members of the media sought to highlight examples attesting to the existence of dissension in our ranks. We accommodated them.

Postgame press conferences can be dangerous, especially after a loss. It is difficult to be responsive and courteous when anger and humiliation are still fresh on one's mind, when one is tired and bruised from several hours of extreme exertion, and when a question directed at the interviewee implies that perhaps he must explain his personal responsibility in having contributed to the team's failure.

Remarks such as, "I wish our defense had not stayed on the field so long that we cooled off while waiting to get back in there," by a member of the offensive unit, or a "We've got to stop turning the ball over so damn deep in our own territory, if they want us to keep those guys from scoring," by one of his defensive counterparts were honest expressions of how a player might be feeling. What you feel and how (and when) you express those feelings have considerably different consequences. Normally such statements are dismissed as innocent venting of postgame angst. Not, however, when other indications of unrest become manifest.

After one game, in which Jim had been the victim of five quarterback sacks, he responded to a reporter's question after the game regarding what needed to be done in order to rectify the situation, by pointing out that "House" Ballard, who was in his first year as a starting right tackle, had struggled with some of the line calls made by our center, Kent Hull. Jim expressed confidence that "House" would benefit from some of the mistakes he had committed and felt that his remarks had been honest and innocent.

That same writer moved on to Thurman's locker, and the manner in which he conveyed Jim's comments to Thurman left our star running back with the impression that Jim's words were more like, "It was all Howard Ballard's fault." Thurman, never one to watch his own words carefully anyway, leapt to the defense of his offensive line teammate by shooting back with a "Maybe Jim ought to get rid of the ball more quickly himself."

By the time Jim and Thurman left the locker room that day, they had talked with each other, had come to a full understanding of what each of them had intended by his remarks, and were once again the closest of teammates and friends. They remained close friends throughout their long careers with the Bills and even beyond. Immediately, on that day, they had put the issue behind them, but by the next morning the newspapers, wire services, and broadcast media were serving up juicy tidbits regarding the newly anointed "Bickering Bills."

From that point on, every utterance from every player, was examined by the media and by the public to see if there might be any innuendo indicating internal strife. Of course there was; players carp at each other all the time, and then they go out and have dinner together. My telephone conversations with Ralph began to be punctuated by his asking, "What's going on there?" I'd tried to explain patiently, but to be honest, I was losing patience with this distracting situation.

There were a couple of other incidents also that served only to sharpen the unsettling image we had created. In the event you don't know it already, I am compelled to point out that coaches, too, experience emotions, sometimes so volatile that they erupt. One day during the staff conference we held every day prior to our team meeting, I stepped out of the room briefly for a call of nature. As I was returning down the hallway, our kicking teams coach, Bruce DeHaven, called out breathlessly, "Coach, you better get back in here right away."

When I had left the room a few minutes earlier, our offensive line coach, Tom Bresnahan, and our wide receivers coach, Nick Nicolau, had been in heated debate about some aspect of the planned practice schedule for that afternoon. When I hurried back into the meeting area, I found that Tom and Nick were no longer exchanging words. They were tussling—not verbally, but physically. Headlocks, kicks, a few swings of the fists, and some attempts at tackling that would have embarrassed our linebacker corps greeted my eyes as I reentered the room. Along with a couple of the other coaches, I succeeded in breaking it up. We declared the match a draw.

After Tom and Nick simmered down, they looked at each other, laughed through swollen lips, and then, sheepishly, apologized and shook hands. It was time for our team meeting to begin, but the two gladiators needed a little time for repair. I sent them down to the training room to see Richard Weiss, our team physician, while, along with the rest of the staff, I headed for the team meeting room.

The team meeting had been underway for about 20 minutes when Tom and Nick tried to slip in through the back door. They knocked over a chair, and, as all heads turned to see what the commotion was all about, there were Tom and Nick with ice packs on their cheekbones, band aids on their foreheads, salve on their lips, and scrapes on their elbows seeking to appear nonchalant. Word had already filtered down to the players, courtesy of some still unidentified "Deep Throat,"[1] that an altercation had taken place, and, now as our players had verification of those early reports, they were delighted. Some spontaneous applause, accompanied by a few enthusiastic cries of "Yo-yo!" greeted the two warriors returned from combat. They were welcomed with open arms into the hallowed ranks of "The Bickering Bills."

Later that day, the ever-vigilant media, after thorough investigation of the rumors that circulated through our practice facility, substantiated that, indeed, members of our coaching staff had joined the players in the activities of this scandalous society of troublemakers. That's all I needed. That night I received another telephone call from Ralph. Guess what it was about?

It wasn't the so-called bickering that was the cause of all our problems, however; it was the losing. From being a 12-4 team just one year before, we now brought an 8-7 record into the final Sunday of the regular season. Lose this one and we'd be out of the playoffs completely. We had lost three in a row entering that game, and now we had to travel to the hostile Meadowlands to face the Jets. What to do? We came up with a brilliant solution. We went out there and mangled the Jets 37-0. We had our winning season. We had our second straight AFC East Division title. We had a bye in the first round of the playoffs. We had pulled together at the most crucial time of that otherwise dispiriting season. We had begun to show the fiber that would hold together that unique group of Bills players as they marched forth into the next decade where they would be confronted with new and exhilarating challenges.

---

1. For those few of you who might possibly be younger than I am and who are not familiar with the details of the Watergate scandal that captivated the nation's attention in the 1970s, it should be noted that "Deep Throat" was the code name assigned to the anonymous person within the Nixon administration who leaked information to *Washington Post* journalists, Bob Woodward and Carl Bernstein, so that they could break the story.

We were truly the hardest to predict team of the year in 1989. Our offense was coming alive as Jim moved into high gear, as our offensive line gained experience and rhythm to go along with a solid trio of tight ends, as Thurman registered the first of his eight consecutive 1,000-plus yard seasons, and as Andre Reed established himself as the premier receiver in the AFC by setting an all-time team mark of 1,312 yards receiving. We remained one dimensional at the wide receiver position, however, because rookie Don Beebe was still a couple of years away from emerging as an accomplished NFL receiver.

Even as the season was in progress, we felt the need to find help outside so that teams wouldn't gang up on Andre. Week after week, we brought in prospects for tryouts, and then one day, we were surprised to see on the waiver wire the name of a former star player. We needed immediate help, and because it was the middle of the season, we preferred someone who was both smart, experienced, and able to step right in and contribute. We placed the waiver claim, and 24 hours later, James Lofton became a member of the Bills.

James broke into the starting lineup on his first weekend with our team, and he continued to start in every game for the next three and a half years. During that time he helped us make three successive trips to the Super Bowl. One overcast Sunday afternoon in Rich Stadium in 1992, James caught a pass for a four-yard gain. Why am I telling you about that dinky little reception? Because when he pulled that ball into his chest, James broke the all-time career record for pass receiving yardage by an NFL player. He caught some more after that one, too.[2]

While our offense was going through "The Great Awakening" (we scored 409 points, only the second time in team history that the Bills had surpassed the 400 mark), our defense was not as effective as it had been the year before. It was obvious that some ongoing restructuring in that area would be necessary if we were going to become legitimate championship contenders. Any doubts we might have had that that assessment wasn't accurate were dispelled, to our chagrin, when we traveled to Ohio early in January for our 1989 season divisional playoff against the Browns.

The weather may have cold, but our offense was really hot that day. We racked up 453 total yards. Jim connected on a 72-yard touchdown

---

2. In August 2003, I was in Canton, Ohio, to join his family and his former teammates and coaches in celebrating his induction into the Pro Football Hall of Fame. Most of his playing days had been with the Packers, but a magnificent chapter in his career had been written in Buffalo, also. Today, Bart Starr, his coach in Green Bay, and I are both able say with pride, "I coached James Lofton."

pass to Andre and on a 33-yarder to James. He hit Thurman for two more, giving him a Bills playoff record of four touchdown passes in one game. In that game, Thurman had 13 catches for 150 yards, and Andre added six more for 115 yards. And yet, we trailed for most of the game. How could that possibly be?

It happened because we were lousy on defense and because—this really galled me—our kicking game stunk! Late in the third quarter, we scored a touchdown to narrow Cleveland's lead to 24-21, and then, on our ensuing kickoff, we allowed their safety, Terry Metcalf, to bring it back all the way—90 yards. In a matter of less than 10 seconds, the Browns had regained their 10-point lead. Early in the fourth quarter a Scott Norwood field goal moved us to within seven points, but the Browns' offense ate up time on the clock. Their drive finally petered out, and with 8:10 remaining to be played, Cleveland place kicker Matt Bahr booted a three pointer. Once again, they led by 10, 34-24. That's when I made a decision.

I sent our offense out onto the field with instructions to go—right now!—to our two-minute drill. We needed to score twice, and I wasn't going to wait patiently until the last gasp moments of the game to see if we could pull it out. "Gunslinger" Jim went to work, throwing 23 consecutive forward passes. It really wasn't my style, but at least they'd never called me "too conservative" again.

We marched, and with less than four minutes left to play, it was Jim to Thurman on a three-yard, play-action touchdown pass.

The horrors of our kicking game performance that day continued. We botched the snap/hold process on the PAT, and instead of being in position to tie the game with a field goal, we were faced with a 34-30 deficit. Oh, well, all we had to do then in order to win the game was score another touchdown. First, however, we had to get the ball back.

Our kicking teams could have redeemed themselves at this juncture if they recovered the onside kickoff that followed. They didn't. It was now on the shoulders of our up-until-then vulnerable defense to find the means of securing for us one last fleeting opportunity to become the feature story on that evening's sports' telecasts, and, whaddaya know, they did force the Browns to punt. When we finally regained possession of the ball, however, it was deep in our territory, and there was only a little more than one minute left to play. But don't forget, we had Jim and Company assigned to the task.

Again, operating from our hurry-up, no-huddle, two-minute drill offense, we gobbled up sizeable chunks of yardage. We reached the Cleveland 12-yard line and had a first down. There were only 15 seconds left on the scoreboard clock. It was here that Jim lofted a perfectly thrown pass into the corner of the end zone to Ronnie Harmon, one of the most dependable and sure-handed receivers on our team. Ronnie had executed his route just the way you draw it on the blackboard, and he was open. As the ball began to settle into his hands, Ronnie glanced down quickly in order to be certain that both of his feet would come down inside of the end zone's back stripe. That fraction of a second of divided concentration was responsible for causing the pass to slither through his hands and onto the ground. It was incomplete.

On the next play, Jim tried to drill the ball over the middle, but it was tipped and deflected just enough so that Cleveland linebacker Clay Matthews intercepted it on the one-yard line. The Browns ran the last few seconds off the clock, and, all of a sudden, our season was over.

We had lost, and, as I reflect back now on that somber occasion, I am reminded of something that a coach from Michigan State University named Duffy Daugherty once said in jest while he was lecturing at a coaching clinic I had attended back in the 1950s. Duffy had quipped, "If you don't learn something from losing, there's no sense losing."

For me and for two outstanding coaches on my staff, offensive coordinator Ted Marchibroda and offensive line coach Tom Bresnahan, there was an important lesson that we did learn as a result of that loss and of that hectic fourth quarter on the scarred grass of grimy old Cleveland Stadium. As we walked off the field immediately after the game, however, we were all too distraught to reflect upon any educational benefits that could be derived from that unhappy ending. Many months later it would hit us, and when it did take hold, it would be a revelation that helped inspire a decision that would lead to energizing the Buffalo sports scene as never before.

For the time being, however, all we knew was that we had just lost the damn game.

CHAPTER 29

It Wasn't All Football

Many football coaches love to create the impression that they are workaholics. My old mentor, George Allen, was at the forefront of this movement. One of his favorite lectures to those of us who were assistants on his staff involved letting us know that he, despite all tales to the contrary, was a magnanimous soul who was concerned that we all be provided with some recreational activity in order to recharge and thereby be able to meet the demands he would be putting on us.

"Leisure time," George said, "should be between 2 a.m. and 5:30 a.m. when you are sleeping. That way you can combine, into one time frame, two healthy methods to rejuvenate."

Now there was a man who was ahead of his time.

I believe that I worked hard and that I put in long hours, but (and please don't tell this to any other coaches) there were rare occasions, during the off season, when I might take a day off or even (is anyone listening?) a week's vacation. One summer, between seasons, I visited Chicago. I came to see friends and family and to see if there was something I could do to help the Cubbies win the National League pennant. I didn't ring the bell on all of those objectives, but you've got to admit, two out of three isn't bad.

During my stay in the Windy City, I put in a call to our former equipment manager with the Chicago Blitz, my old friend "Malaprop Bob" Colonna. He was delighted to hear from me, and after reminding me how much he disliked having to eat meals alone, he invited me to come have Sunday morning breakfast with him at a coffee shop that we both used to frequent. He explained that his wife, Alma, had left for the weekend because of an obligation she had back East.

"She went to Jersey so she could help her young niece, Gwendolyn, get her *torso* ready for her upcoming wedding," Bob informed me.

Unfortunately, I had other obligations, I told him, that would keep me from joining him. At the last moment, however, it ended up that I could make it. I knew he'd be there, and so I decided to just pop in at the restaurant and surprise him. As I wended my way through the aisles and past numerous tables and alcoves, there was Bob, in the back, sitting all alone in his favorite booth scattering cigar ashes all over his eggs Benedict.

I sat down across from him, and as we chatted, I happened to notice a strikingly attractive woman enter the coffee shop. As Bob said something or other, I continued staring as she stood there and gazed about perplexedly until she apparently spotted some person in the recesses of the room for whom she had been searching, and then she proceeded, her posture regal, in the direction of her intended companion. Bob continued to talk. And I continued to look.

As she advanced in our general direction, I noticed that several heads swiveled to admire her. When she was within a few yards of our table, her face lighted up, and I spun my glance quickly toward the cubicle behind me to see who was the lucky recipient of her radiant smile. That booth was empty, and when I turned back, she was standing beside our table. She looked at me and spoke a magic word, "Hi."

When you got it, you got it, I thought. And then Bob broke the spell.

"Hey, Coach, you know Fran, don't cha?" he said.

I didn't, but I sure wanted to.

"May I join you?" she asked. I was out of my seat before the question mark was added to punctuate her inquiry, and after she sat down next to me, Bob explained. He told me that after I had said that I'd be unable to join him for breakfast, he had invited Fran, who lived in the neighborhood and was the ex-wife of the man who had handled the transportation for the Chicago Blitz.

During our conversation, I learned that Mary Frances Kozlowski (her full name) had remained on friendly terms with her former husband, Bill, and through him she had gotten to know Bob. She was now a single mother, working as a secretary while raising a rambunctious teenage daughter.

While I toyed with my multigrain pancakes, I became more charmed (and I hope *charming,* as well) as I got to know the beautiful lady. I was amused as I learned that she had no idea, even after being told, what kind of a job I had. Other than rookie quarterbacks, I have never met anyone who knew less about the NFL than she did. That added to my intrigue. Bob sought to clarify the matter by telling her that I was an instructor of men who engaged in a rigorous physical activity, and when Fran heard that, she inquired eagerly about whether I might be able to design an exercise program for her. There it was—my invitation to ask for her number so that I could call her as soon as I had prepared the information she had requested.

I was on vacation, but that afternoon, instead of making my intended trip to Wrigley Field, I stayed in my hotel room where I plotted a workout that embraced the same attention to detail that I would have devoted to a plan for a playoff game against the Broncos. By midnight I had finished it, but I decided, discreetly, to wait until the following morning to telephone Fran with the breaking news that it was ready.

When I did call early the next day, she had already left for work. That evening I tried again, but she was at a PTA meeting. I was too late again the next morning, and that evening she was at the dentist where she had taken her daughter, Kimberly, who needed to have her braces refitted. On Wednesday, it was more of the same: work in the morning and a student art fair with Kimberly in the evening. Finally, when I couldn't connect once again on Thursday, I left a voicemail for Fran.

"If you don't get going on this exercise program," I admonished in a voice that would have frightened a blitzing linebacker, "you are going to get fat and dumpy. You will see your gorgeous figure, your creamy complexion, your magnificent facial features, your elegant posture, your glistening smile, your kind disposition, and your alert, facile mind all disintegrate before your previously dazzling eyes. Call me immediately at my hotel number or you can visit at my web site, www.blockthatkick.com. This offer is good for a limited time only, so please avail yourself of this once-in-a-lifetime opportunity. Call before sunset and you will also receive a complimentary 10-day free supply of nonfat blueberry yogurt. If I do not hear from you by then, I will be compelled to consign this carefully crafted program to the paper shredder."

A few hours later my phone rang, and when I picked it up, I heard Fran's sweet voice, tinged with a bit of panic, pleading for me to not destroy the information that contained her passport to everlasting health and beauty. We arranged to meet the next day in the hospitality room of the apartment complex where she lived. There I reviewed with her every detail of the program. It was thorough, but I have to admit that if she had adhered to it in the exact form that I had outlined, she would have been ready to cover kickoffs by the time the football season opened. She thanked me, and with a wan smile, she set it aside while telling me that she would begin the routine "soon." I'm still waiting.

Thinking as quickly as I had two football seasons before, when I had intuitively called for a fake punt against the Lions, I saw an opportunity, and I seized it.

"Exercise is only part of the equation. Proper diet is every bit as important," I emphasized. Expanding on that pearl of imparted wisdom, I made my move. "With that in mind," I continued, "I would be pleased to invite you out to dinner tomorrow evening so that I can communicate with you about proper dietary guidelines in an atmosphere that is conducive to such a conversation."

It was an offer she didn't refuse.

We dined at Le Fountainebleu, and there, after two martinis (olives are good for you, I pointed out) and some appetizers dripping in a *magnifique* cholesterol-laden beure et creme sauce, prepared only on Saturday evenings and holidays by Chef Gabrielle, I began to enlighten Fran regarding the proper approach to wholesome nourishment. I must admit that I interspersed other topics that were of considerably more interest to me, but those must remain confidential. By the time we had discussed proper consumption of fiber, of fresh fruits and steamed vegetables, and of lean protein, Fran and I were already eating our dessert of triple chocolate cake with ice cream, candied nuts, whipped cream, and strawberry compote topping.

The session was drawing to a close, but I told her there was so much more that she still needed to know. We arranged to meet again for dinner the next evening as well, so that I could continue with the educational process. Even after that, there were still loose ends, and so for several more nights we got together at some newly discovered restaurant where I supplied Fran with the information she needed to help her implement her determined pursuit of knowledge. By the time my stay in Chicago was drawing to a close, she could have written a master's thesis on the subject. She probably needed to know that much about it, too, because we both must have gained at least five pounds during our Bacchanalian eating orgies.

That wasn't the only result of my trip to the old hometown. Something else I never could have anticipated happened the moment that Mary Frances Kozlowski sat down with Bob Colonna and me in our booth at the Omega Coffee Shop on that Sunday morning. I fell in love. And during the rest of that week in Chicago I had fallen more in love, and it wasn't with the food.

After I returned to Buffalo, Fran and I remained in touch with each other. Whenever I could, I came back to Chicago so that we could be together. On several occasions she visited Buffalo, and our romance blossomed. I learned that this lovely lady was a lot more than just beautiful. She was warm, sweet, smart, sociable, and wholesome, as well, and what an exemplary mother she was. Not only that, when we were alone, she never wanted to "talk football." How refreshing that was!

When Kimberly left for college, Fran moved to the Buffalo area, and in February 1990, we ran off one weekend and got married. We had a fantastic one-day honeymoon at Niagara Falls (who ever heard of

having a honeymoon there?), and then it was back to the job. And so we live happily ever after, while I continue to fall more in love every day.

In marrying my dear Frannie (as I now call her), I also brought into my life my darling daughter, Kimberly. I had never, until now, had a child, and so if I continue to spoil her a bit, it's understandable. Not only that, she deserves it. She is now a young adult, having finished her undergraduate studies and then going on to get her law degree. No man ever could have asked for a more bright, energetic, honest, loving (and pretty like her momma, to boot) young daughter. Thank you, Frannie, my love. And thank you, too, "Cutie Beauty" (my name for Kimberly).

So there, you see, there is something in a coach's life besides just double reverses and onside kickoffs. That said, it's time to get back to work.

SECTION IX

THE BUFFALO BILLS RIDE HERD

CHAPTER 30

1990 Was a Super Year

We had ended the 1989 season with those last two chaotic no-huddle drives in Cleveland. How appropriate. After all, turmoil had been the prevalent characteristic associated with our team most of the season anyway. Why change for the playoffs? Although I can't supply an answer for that one, I knew full well that I had better come up with a solution for curbing all that unrest and that I'd better do it quickly.

Even before our equipment men had thrown the last jock strap into the washing machine after our loss to the Browns, my phone was ringing. It was Ralph Wilson summoning me to come visit him in Detroit. I ventured a guess that he wanted to address head-on all this clamor about the Bickering Bills that had been so distracting for us all. Or I wondered if perhaps he was so miffed that he might speak those words so many of us in my line of work hear with such demoralizing frequency at that time of the year, "Coach, you're fired."

He darn well did want to know, "What the hell is happening?" I had come to Detroit determined to be forthright and to acknowledge the validity of accusations that confrontations and disagreements had marred our season. The night before this trip to Detroit, I prepared what I felt to be a comprehensive presentation of the steps I planned to take in order to put out the fire that was in danger of destroying our team. My off-season communications with the players, at a time when a more stress-free atmosphere prevailed, would provide a starting point for such a program. I showed to Ralph, in outline form, exactly what I would be conveying to the players and what the time schedule for such indoctrination would be. It was a specific, detailed plan. Included would be a brief segment at the beginning of our team meeting each evening once our players had reported for training camp that coming

July. At those sessions I would expand upon the attitudes and actions that I believed were required from a group of dedicated athletes who are seeking to achieve a true sense of teamwork.

This approach, I told Ralph, did not involve my implementing draconian disciplinary measures. There weren't any "troublemakers" on our team. If there were, they'd be gone by morning. This was as fine a group of men any coach could have ever hoped to lead. During my discussions with Ralph I was able to give voice spontaneously to what role I felt a leader must play in order to merit such designation. Leadership, I told him, is the ability to get *other* people to get the very best out of themselves. And it is manifested, I continued, not by getting them to follow you, but by getting them to join you. You don't get the best out of people by bulldozing them; you do it by educating (or convincing) them.

In accordance with that line of thinking, I told Ralph that I would like to have, at two of our training camp meetings, a professional media consultant conduct a seminar for all players and coaches to help us understand and develop healthy media and fan relations. As it turned out, all of these program proposals were implemented with positive effect on team morale, team cohesiveness, and on-the-field results.

I didn't do all the talking at that meeting in Detroit, however. Ralph had plenty to get off his chest, as well, and he did. That's one of the things I always liked about him. Our failure to make the improvement we had expected going into the season coupled with a few unwarranted gripes (from sources even to this day unidentified) about members of our coaching staff led Ralph to suggest that some changes needed to be made. I had come to Detroit anticipating that this would be a likely topic of discussion, and so, even before arriving in the Motor City, I had done a thorough job of assessing the work of every member of my staff. They were outstanding teachers; they were loyal; they were hard workers; they were men of solid character. I determined, therefore, that I would not make any of them sacrificial, even if it cost me my own job.

Once again, Ralph listened. Although at the time he continued to harbor doubts, he accepted my explanations without hitting me with, "Okay, but you better be right or else." I am gratified to report that just a year or two later, a couple of the coaches about whom Ralph had expressed reservations were among his favorites.

I left Detroit feeling regenerated and looking forward already to the 1990 season. I left it with an increasing regard for this man for whom I was working. But I left, also, knowing that my obstinacy, my decisions, and my actions had better lead to a bright new year for the Bills.

When I returned to Buffalo the next day and called for a staff meeting in order address some of the many items that needed attention as soon as a season was finished, I detected an uneasy sense of quiet apprehension accompanying the assistant coaches as they filed into the room. They knew I had been called to Detroit, and they had speculated about the reasons why. Some expected that we were all going to be fired. Some thought that I might be forced to let one or two of them go in order to save my scalp. There were a variety of other possibilities that invaded their thinking also, and none was pleasant.

I told them that Ralph had wanted to be filled in on all of the furor surrounding the Bickering Bills. I didn't talk about the discussions we had had relative to the coaching staff, but I was able to read in the eyes of almost every one of them that they knew that had been a prime item on the agenda. I could sense also that they had been aware that I might have been pressured to dump some of them and that I had remained steadfast in sticking by these men who deserved such loyalty from me. And, strangely, I felt an aura of increased allegiance as they realized we had all somehow survived. They still hadn't actually heard those words from me, however, and so I put them all at ease when I brought the meeting to an early close by saying, "Okay, fellas, take the next 24 hours off, and then get your butts back in here. We've *all* got to start getting ready for our season opener next fall."

And so came to an end the era of the Bickering Bills.

Fine-tuning the personnel makeup of a team is always an ongoing process. There are careers cut short because of injuries. There are players who choose to retire. There are other star players who, although they are reluctant to acknowledge it, have seen their talents decline. The toll from the passing years has slowly rendered them incapable of performing up to the required demands of the game. There are changes in styles of offense and defense, which dictate the need for a different type of player than the staple position player who has been on the team for many years. There are some desirable free agents floating around out there (if you can identify them), and, of course, there is always this year's over-hyped crop of draftees.

The coordination of all matters relating to improving and developing our player personnel with the Bills was the best I have ever experienced or observed. I can't explain all the intricacies that come together to make the solar system work, but it keeps functioning anyway. Neither can I present a formulaic answer as to why the player personnel operation fashioned by Bill Polian, John Butler, Ralph, and me, plus our director of pro player personnel, Bob Ferguson, ran so smoothly and harmoniously, but it sure did. It was an integral feature in the equation explaining why we kept getting better.

It was time to get specific regarding how we were going to continue to strengthen our team. Our defense had not performed nearly as well in 1989 as it had the year before, and I had determined that, for starters, we needed to make some adjustments in how we utilized our defensive line personnel. The game had changed, and the tempo up front had intensified so that I felt a defensive lineman could no longer play the whole game and still be able to sustain top effort on every snap. It was akin to a track coach asking a great miler to run his event while maintaining the pace used by a 100-meter sprint champion.

If we wanted a great defensive lineman to play at "100-meter speed," we had to relieve him often, even during the course of an opponent's drive. He had to know there was no need to coast, no need, while he was out there on the playing field, to conserve his energies. Go all out, young man. We'll take you out for a play or two and let you catch your breath. Then get back in there and go all out again.

This meant that we would have to play our defensive linemen in relays. We adopted the term *in waves.* There were some reservations voiced by a number of the defensive coaches. They wanted their best players on the field all the time. They were concerned about whether we had enough solid depth on our defensive line to make such a radical gambit work. I agreed that we would have to populate our roster with more men at that position than had been our policy, but I also noted that young players such as Leon Seals and Jeff Wright had performed well when given their limited opportunities. I felt that they were ready for more action and that their play would have a positive impact on our overall defensive performance. Times have changed, I told our veteran coaches, and if you don't change with the times, I warned, the times are going to change you.

There were players, also, who didn't like the idea. Bruce Smith wanted to be on the field every down, and it is true that there was no one on our team (or any other team, either) who could go out there and match Bruce at his best. For him to be at his best, however, he needed to be fresh, I told him. Grudgingly, Bruce accepted the fact that this was how we were going to operate. Playing only "part time"—but he sure was the crest of "the wave" while he was in there—Bruce was able to stay fresh. For 18 years he played the most physically demanding position on a professional football team, and even though he wasn't out there for every snap, by the time he retired after the 2003 season, Bruce had sacked opponents' quarterbacks 200 times, the only player in the history of the NFL to have accomplished that.

Other veteran defensive linemen were also affected by our planned approach. Fred Smerlas, our starting nose tackle and a longtime fan favorite, was outspokenly upset when I told him about it. I had asked

Fred to come to my office where, because of the respect I had for him, I wanted to tell him what we were doing and why we were doing it. He was shocked. He viewed the move as a disingenuous tactic on my part to ease him out of the starting lineup in favor of young Jeff Wright. I told Fred that I did see a time when Jeff would be our starter and that was an additional reason why I wanted him to get more game experience. It all fit perfectly with the "waves" approach that we were going to utilize.

Fred was having none of that. He had always been straightforward, and so once again, with a disdain for careful phraseology, he expressed his feelings. To him, it was a humiliation. If that is what we had in store for him, he said, he'd prefer to go elsewhere.

I was now faced with either backing off from employing an approach to defense that I felt we needed or going ahead with it and having a disgruntled and vocal team leader. The first option was out of the question, but the alternative would have led to the second coming of the Bickering Bills. As we continued our discussion, it became apparent to me that the only remedy was the one that Fred had suggested. It was time for him to continue his playing career elsewhere. Fred and the Bills parted company, and he went on to play for a few more years with the 49ers and the Patriots.[1]

Jeff Wright, entering his third NFL season, stepped in as our starting nose tackle, and he exceeded all expectations. What really helped him to play at a near frenzied tempo while he was in the game was knowing that he'd be given those necessary breathers. That next wave was rolling out onto the field to help keep him from getting overheated. We were able to afford that relief—credit John Butler and his unmatchable crew of scouts—because in the 10th round we drafted a nose tackle out of UCLA named Mike Lodish. Mike showed up ready to play, and that gave us a big boost along our defensive line.

There were other men, also, in that 1990 draft who helped us become better on defense than we had been the year before. Linebacker Marvcus Patton, also out of UCLA, was an eighth-rounder who made the final cut. His kicking game contributions and his ability to learn our defensive schemes quickly were welcome surprises. Our No. 1 pick in

---

1. Several years later when he returned to Buffalo for a sad event—the funeral of former teammate, Dean Prater, who had died in a tragic accident—Fred approached me, and by the nature of the conversation we had, I could tell that he held no lingering animosity toward me. He reminisced about all the good times he had enjoyed during his playing days in Buffalo. It is appropriate that he retains those fond memories, because the fans in Buffalo will always remember Fred. His name is proudly displayed on the front of the upper deck in Ralph Wilson Stadium on The Buffalo Bills Wall of Fame.

that year's draft was cornerback James Williams. Teams were finding that they could no longer get the job done with the old standard of just two cornerbacks. As the offenses became jazzier, you needed more good pass coverage defenders on the other side of the ball. In many situations teams were putting three, or even four, cornerbacks on the field at one time. The addition of James gave us greater flexibility and made our defenses less predictable.

We didn't neglect our offense, either, and there were some additions to that unit that would help to make us even more potent than we had been. In the second round we drafted a bruising fullback, Carwell Gardner, and for the next several years he functioned as the perfect backfield companion to Thurman Thomas. Carwell was a devastating blocker, as big and as aggressive as any linebacker who might get in his way as he led Thurman through the holes being ripped open by our ever-improving offensive line. The steady infusion of good young talent into the usually anonymous group of linemen is one of the reasons why they kept getting better. In the third round of the 1990 draft we selected Glenn Parker from the University of Arizona, and for the next seven seasons, he was one of the key reasons our offense performed as well as it did. He was dependable, and he was really smart. I'll tell you how smart he was. On our plane trips, while all his teammates were playing cards, listening to music, or staring at the television screen, Glenn was sitting there quietly *reading*—a *book* even.

There was another, at the time unnoticed, newcomer to our team. He was a running back. So what! We already had Thurman, didn't we? There is no reason to get excited about anyone else playing that position, is there? Yes, there is. There is no place on the football team that requires depth more than that spot. It is the position that is the most vulnerable to injuries, and it is also one where it is essential to provide a break for a relatively smaller man who is taking a merciless pounding, play after play, from an angry mob of behemoths. The Packers had decided to release running back Kenneth Davis, and when his name appeared on the waiver wire, Bob Ferguson fell down three times running down the hall to tell me about it. We claimed him, and Kenny became a Buffalo Bill. Why the Packers had chosen to part company with Kenny I will never know. He was in tremendous physical condition, he was bright, he had been a high draft choice, he was responsive to coaching, he was quick, balanced, tough, and energetic, and—the man could play! Courtesy of Green Bay we had now been able to add to our team both Kenneth Davis and James Lofton. When I was a young lad growing up in Chicago, I, like all other enthusiastic Bears fans, had viewed the hated the Packers with contempt. Now, I was really beginning to develop a fuzzy feeling in my heart for those accommodating cheeseheads.

♦♦♦♦♦♦♦♦

It was early September 1990. The ardors of training camp were over. The preseason schedule was behind us. The trauma I always experienced when making those final cuts was behind me. The makeup of our squad had been determined. In six days we would open the season, before a sellout crowd, at home, against division rival Indianapolis. It was time for our coaching staff to put the final touches on our game plan.

On Monday, we held a light workout, and we concluded it by executing a snappy rehearsal of our two-minute offense. It is something every team practices every week. Jim Kelly was as sharp in that drill as he had been in the fourth quarter of our season finale in Cleveland eight months earlier. Andre Reed, James Lofton, and Don Beebe ran their routes with a crispness that assured me that they were ready to play for keeps. The timing on our screen passes was textbook perfect. Kent Hull at center made the complicated line blocking calls flawlessly, despite the time restrictions imposed on him by the hurry-up nature of the drill. It was fun. We had a good time.

That night at our staff planning meeting, offensive coordinator Ted Marchibroda asked me a question.

"Marv, Tom [Bresnahan, our offensive line coach] and I have been talking about this. What would you think about our *opening* the game this Sunday by using our two-minute offense?"

Several of the other coaches in the room looked at Ted as if they believed he had forgotten to take his medication. I was stunned, too, but for a different reason, because as I had walked off the practice field earlier that day after seeing how effectively we had executed that drill, a similar thought had invaded my consciousness. I didn't dwell on it then, however, but it appeared now that, thanks to Duffy Daugherty (not to mention Jim Kelly) we *had,* indeed, learned something from losing on that wintry day along the lakefront in Cleveland.

"Let's talk about it," I said, thereby causing those other coaches to shift their solicitous glances from Ted over to me.

Talk about it we did. Far into the night and all during the next day we plotted our strategy. It meant that we would begin the game with three wide receivers and just one running back. On those plays where our quarterback would be under center, Pete Metzelaars, the best blocking tight end, would line up at his position. When we elected to go from the shotgun, we planned to send Keith McKeller into the game in order to use his speed in what was obviously a pass-oriented formation. Our shorthand designation for that alignment was "the K-Gun."

Opening day arrived. We kicked off to the Colts, and after a few plays we forced them to punt. We huddled up to call our first play. That was the last time we went back into the huddle on our initial possession until prior to kicking the extra point; the whirlwind minute and a half, 75-yard drive had culminated in a touchdown. On the Colts' next possession our defense forced a punt. This time we sent out the K-Gun, and again we zipped down the field against their befuddled defenders. It took us almost two minutes to go flying into the end zone once again. Midway through the first quarter we led 14-0.

We stopped them for a third time, but when we took over we went one, two, three, and out. Our defensive unit had to go back out onto the field once again after too short a rest. They surrendered a lot of yards this time, and they had to stay out on the field for a long time. They stiffened enough so that the Colts were forced to settle for a field goal, but I now knew that we had to maintain ball possession or else our defense would not have time to regroup. It was time for us to come out of our no-huddle mode for a while or suffer the consequences of an exhausted defense. We switched to a grind-it-out, clock-consuming style of play. The Colts struggled to adapt to our sharp switch in offensive style, and when we capped our drive with a field goal of our own, we regained a 14-point lead.

With that bit of a respite, our defense played well, limiting the Colts to a touchdown late in the game. We spent the rest of the game alternating those fast-paced no-huddle forays with our more conservative time devouring formations. The Colts hung on gamely, but we added three more field goals and chalked up a comfortable 26-10 win. Our no-huddle offense, judiciously applied, had helped us dominate our opponent. We felt good about it, but we still had a lot to learn about its merits—*and* its shortcomings.

One week later, we were provided with an unpleasant exposure to a number of those shortcomings. There are almost always times during a game when your opponent succeeds in stopping you, and then there are also those occasions when, for a variety of reasons, your offense doesn't click. In either situation you must then turn to your defense to get the ball back so that you can launch a more successful attack.

After dazzling the Colts with our K-Gun innovations on opening Sunday, we took the show on the road. We headed down to Miami, who, along with us, were one of the co-favorites to win the AFC East championship. After that game there were no *co-favorites* anymore.

Miami beat us resoundingly 30-7. What was even more disheartening, however, was how devastatingly destructive our no-huddle tactics had been—not to our opponents, but to ourselves.

Miami had taken the opening kickoff, and in the late summer Florida heat, quarterback Dan Marino engineered a six and a half-minute drive. We kept them out of our end zone, and they had to settle for a field goal. The Dolphins led 3-0, but—look out, guys—here comes that rapid-fire no-huddle scoring machine! In 45 seconds, due to a dropped pass on third down, our offense was off the field, and our sweat-soaked defenders were back out there. So were Marino and his teammates. Another six-minute drive led to another Miami score (this time, a touchdown). We now trailed 10-0.

We were going to catch up fast. That was, until, after getting two first downs and being on the field for little more than a minute, we fumbled. Our defensive players hadn't even had time to screw off the caps from their bottles of Gatorade before being sent out into that 97-degree subtropical oven. The only thing hotter than the air temperature that day was Marino. Soon it was 17-0.

By that time we were really straining, and the pattern that had been set early in the game prevailed throughout. Our defensive players were already exhausted, and we had to slow it up on offense or our defensive stalwarts might have been in the hospital suffering from heat stroke. The Dolphins stayed in control all afternoon, while all we could muster for the day was our lone seven-pointer.

How our players and coaches reacted immediately after that disaster in Miami turned out to be a pivotal moment for the Bills. The defense did not moan about how our offense had bombed, nor did our offense remonstrate about how our defense had *gotten* bombed. No one (except me, that is) questioned my decision to run the no-huddle. "I can do better, and I will," was the mantra espoused by every player and coach in the room. And what I really liked is that they meant it.

I had often told our players that it was amazing what a team could accomplish when no one cares who gets the credit, and soon I would learn that there was a flip side to that pronouncement because I also discovered that it is equally amazing what a team can accomplish when no one is looking for someone to blame. That is the reason why, in this particular account, I did not mention the name of the player who dropped that third down pass or who fumbled on the next series.

I'd like to believe that that off-season course in Teamwork 101 taught by Professor Levy had contributed to this healthy new attitude, and perhaps it did. It would have been meaningless, however, had it not been for the quality of character that marked the men on that team.

Leaders such as Kent Hull, Darryl Talley, Jim Kelly, Frank Reich, Carlton Bailey, and so many others (I could read off our full roster here) are the ones who made it all work.

So much for the morale factor. How about something even more identifiable? How about playing better? We had a lot of reassessing to do, and whatever it was we decided, we had to have it ready in just seven days because we would be on the road again facing another tough division opponent—the Jets. Question number one for us was whether we should abandon the no-huddle "gimmick" (as one media critic described it). And the answer was—*No!*

It was a big gamble to stay with it, but during the next 48 hours Ted, Tom, and I made some momentous decisions. We cut way back on the number of plays in our no-huddle game plan. Doing this allowed us to get a far higher number of repetitions in practice for the plays on the abbreviated list. It simplified the split-second line calls that Kent had to communicate to the other men along the offensive line. They needed to get that information, assimilate it, and then put it into action in far less time than was normal.

Our list of selections became limited to the point where there was no need for us to slow things down by getting in the quarterback's ear via the headset. Not only was that cackling headset a distraction, it was an encumbrance that served to slow down our intentions. With just five or six plays to call, Jim knew exactly which one he wanted. On rare occasions when Jim felt the need for guidance, he would merely point his finger at Ted, and Ted would then send in a play. Swashbuckling Jim loved operating this way. He exuded confidence, and that confidence spilled over onto his teammates.

Helping further to keep it simple and freer from error was our starting count. With infrequent exception we always snapped the ball on the first "hut" after Jim had called the play. As a result, we were rarely guilty of false starts, the penalty that so often has been an offensive drive killer. Wait a minute, here! Didn't that make us too predictable? Couldn't their defense now anticipate the ball being snapped and thereby takeoff just as quickly as our offensive linemen? Believe me, they had bigger problems. They had to get reassembled after every play as we rushed to the line and prepared to snap the ball on our next play. Their defensive signal caller had to get the message from his bench telling him what defense to call. Then he had to call it. Then they had to break their huddle. After that, their free safety had to convey the pass coverage nuances to the secondary. Then they had to line up. There were many occasions when the other team had to use one of their precious timeouts to allow themselves time to regroup.

Also, please remember that I said we always snapped it on the first "hut" *with infrequent exception.* Jim and Frank became masters at sensing when any of the opponent's defensive linemen had dug in with the intention of exploding out of his stance on our first "hut." A code word, used when the play was called, tipped off our players that the snap would be on the second "hut." I would guess that about 80 percent of the time when we employed that tactic our opponents jumped offside. Even when they didn't, they'd better not try to guess when the ball would be put into play.

One additional benefit from this hurry-up, no-nonsense style was that our opponents could not substitute. They couldn't make the change of personnel normally called for by the down and yardage situation. They were also unable to relieve a weary player. If they had tried to make such a substitution while our drive was sizzling along, they'd wind up with too many men on the field or they'd be unable to make their defensive call and get lined up.

There also was a surprise bonanza that we realized as a result of our hurry-up style and the reduction in plays in our playbook. Practice zipped by. We had to practice as we played—quick, quick, quick! With fewer plays to learn, there were fewer mistakes being made, and thus, far less need for coaches to bellow out their most often heard utterance at practice, "Run that play over again, and this time do it right!"

Kent was the pacesetter for this rapid and rhythmic activity, and our players came to love it. The drudgery that so often was part of a long, slog-through-it practice evaporated. The increased level of concentration became so contagious that even our defensive players found themselves practicing their assignments in a similar manner. We covered only what we had to, and as we became ever more adept at implementing this approach, we reduced by almost half the amount of time we were spending on the field. The shorter practices left our players feeling more refreshed and more buoyant as game day drew closer. There was also increased time available for our coaches to plan and for the players to go to the weight room or to the film room. As a result, the learning process had been enhanced even further.

There were a lot of advantages. What then were its disadvantages? The obvious one was that this approach put added pressure on our defense. If we failed to get a first down after taking possession of the ball, our defensive players had to return to the game in a matter of seconds. Even when we might move the ball swiftly down the field and put points on the board, it all happened with lightning speed. Because of this approach, in every closely contested game we played, our time of possession was far less than that of our opponent. I could certainly understand it if our defensive players and coaches came to feel that an unfair burden had been thrust upon them.

But no one ever complained. True, I had explained to all defensive players and coaches that we would require heroic exhibitions of stamina if we were going to succeed, but it was *their* willingness to sacrifice that was responsible for making our hurry-up style of offense prevail.

One of the arguments I had called upon in seeking to convince our defenders how potent our no-huddle could be was asking them to visualize themselves in the shoes of our opponents. Imagine the stress, the uncertainty, and the unrelenting tempo and disorder to which they were being exposed. By the looks of empathy for those unfortunates that I detected on the faces of our kindly linebackers and defensive linemen, I believe that my plea for sympathy helped them to less grudgingly accept their roles.

During most of the years when we ran our no-huddle offense, our defensive staff was composed of coordinator Walt Corey, defensive backfield coach Dick Roach, defensive line coach Dan Sekanovich, and linebacker coaches Chuck Lester and Ted Cottrell. There couldn't have been better teachers or a more loyal group of men anywhere. They worked under extremely difficult circumstances, and even on those rare days when our offense sputtered, their coaching abilities and inspirational leadership kept us in the game.

There was one noteworthy difference between our no-huddle offense and the standard two-minute drill style of attack, and that variation would fall definitely in the category of "disadvantages." Late in the game when a team goes to its desperation two-minute offense, they intend to use all four downs, if necessary, to keep the chains moving. Our no-huddle offense, of course, was being employed in that stage of the game when you either pick up a first down in *three plays* or punt. Now that is a big difference!

We also had a cluster of plays that were not applicable to our no-huddle or K-Gun formations. These were executed from a tough two-back formation. Often we would include two hard-blocking tight ends in the grouping. This was a grind-it-out, time-consuming tactic. Whenever we had been able to take a commanding lead, we would shift down into this gear. Make the clock run; keep the other team's offense off of the field; provide a respite for our own defenders. In these games the time of possession was equal. Our defense loved it when we got the big leads that allowed us to go into this mode. Hey! So did I!

We also used our sturdy two-back sets at unpredictable times during the game. Why? So that our opponents could not direct all their attention toward getting ready for our no-huddle. It also kept them from experiencing the comfort that comes from knowing exactly what they would contend with on Sunday.

That was our plan. If it worked—brilliant! If it didn't—uh oh!

Still smarting from our defeat in Miami, we came barging into the Meadowlands eager to face the Jets. We had begun the practice week in a noticeably less enthusiastic frame of mind. The torrid weather conditions in Miami had taken their toll on our players, and when we returned to Buffalo, there was news that an unusually warm spell was expected to invade western New York and linger throughout the week. On the steaming practice field, just one day after our thrashing by the Dolphins, our players' concentration was abominable. They appeared to be lethargic and dispirited. Now I was steaming, but not from the hot weather. When I finally brought the drills to a halt, I told the players that we would all gather in the team meeting room just as soon as they had showered. This was the first time that I had called a team meeting *after* practice since taking over as coach of the team. I felt it was time to tell them another story from a time long gone.

I took them back to World War I, to June 1918, where 25 miles outside of Paris, France, the German army was advancing relentlessly toward that French capital city. The U.S. Fourth Marine Brigade, of which my father had been a member, was sent to meet the enemy in what would be known as the Battle of Belleau Wood. I told our players how, after the first three days of the conflict, the marines, despite having sustained heavy casualties, had halted the Germans' forward progress. And then I told them how the dog-tired marines, after just one day of rest, were ordered to attack, across an exposed field of wheat, the enemy forces that were now entrenched several hundred yards away.

The surviving marines—tired, bloodied, and shaken—were hardly able to believe that they were now being directed to make what appeared to be a forlorn counterattack. It was then, as their doubts were most evident, that the commanding officer of my father's unit, Colonel "Hard John" Hughes, stood up and shouted to the leathernecks, "When it's too tough for them, it's just right for us!" Then Colonel Hughes commanded, "Follow me!" whereupon he sprinted out into the wheat field. The marines all followed, and the battle that was to turn the tide of World War I ensued.

I allowed the message to sink in for a few moments, and then I said to our players, "When we practice on Wednesday, it is going the be hotter than hell, but I'm going to go out there concentrating 100 percent.

After practice I'm going to run three miles faster than I've run it in the last five years. And if you guys give anything less than all you are capable of giving, you'll just be showing me that 'when it's too tough for you, it's just right for me!'" Then I dismissed the meeting.

Wednesday's practice was the best one of the year. The nature of our newly instituted no-huddle practice structure undoubtedly had a lot to do with the improvement, but I also hoped that my story recounting the Battle of Belleau Wood contributed to the metamorphosis.

Our game against the Jets was rife with similarities to the one we had played just one week earlier in Miami. It was against a strong division foe. It was in their backyard, another road game for us. It was played in very warm weather. For the second week we would be gambling, in the face of stern questioning by fans and media. In Miami, we had lost the game 30-7, and this time in the Meadowlands, the final score was exactly the same. But there was one big difference. This time we had the 30, they had the seven. The Jets were left breathless as our hurry-up offense kept them reeling. Then late in the game, we went to our grind-it-out power game. Before the day was over, Thurman had rushed for 214 yards. This was an offense, that because of the threat of the forward pass and because Jim didn't give a damn about his own statistics, was able to strike the perfect balance between the running and the passing games. In those games where we were successful in exploding for an early lead, we were also able to keep our defense rested while chewing up huge chunks of time. Overnight the nation's fans and media became enamored with the Bills' startling new K-Gun attack. But—could we keep it up?

We played Denver next. We didn't put 30 points on the board against the Broncos. We had to settle for 29, but that was enough for us to win again. Then we posted 38 while defeating the powerful Raiders. We kept it up, week after week, to a rising and deafening crescendo from our fans in Rich Stadium. The year before, the Bills, for the first time, had drawn more than 80,000 fans to a game. Now, in 1990, we would exceed that number on three occasions. The wins kept coming, and the scores kept mounting while Jim led our no-huddle devastators as they gained ever-increasing confidence and rhythm.

The closest we came to having our string of victories interrupted was after we had won three in a row. In a second meeting of the season against the Jets, at home, we had to mount a last-ditch drive. It took an improvised play to resuscitate us, and it was almost as amusing as it was harrowing. It also helped to highlight why we often practiced some outlandish maneuver during the week.

At our practices every Monday and every Saturday, I would conclude our drills by working on some special and unusual situation. It might be years before it might actually come up in a game, but I felt that, if and when it did, our players would at least have, at some time, been exposed to the methods for handling such surprises. On the Saturday before our second game against the Jets, we devoted a couple of minutes to working on our *scramble drill.* This involved rehearsing those instances when our quarterback, upon dropping back to pass, was flushed out of the protective pocket and would begin to scramble about desperately seeking to find an open receiver. His moves, of course, were unpredictable, and so we would occasionally practice having our receivers, who were down the field, mirror his breaks and changes of direction so that they would be in his line of vision.

As we ran our scramble drill on the eve of our game against the Jets, Jim finally delivered a line drive strike to fullback Jamie Mueller in the end zone. The ball bounced off Jamie's chest onto the ground. As I struck my forehead with the heel of my hand, all the players had a chance to good-naturedly rib one of their teammates.

But that was yesterday. There were now 19 seconds left in our game against the Jets, and we trailed by a score of 27-23. Jim had led us on a long drive, and we were at their 10-yard line, facing fourth and 10. Jim faded back to pass; no one was open. He broke out to his left, then to his right, and then back left once again. Even from the sidelines, I could see Jim's eyes widen as he spotted an open teammate running parallel to him in the end zone. He drilled the ball right at—oh, no!—Jamie. Jamie clutched it to chest and fell to the ground in firm possession of the winning touchdown. We won 30-27. Our streak was alive.

The day after that game, in order to underline how important those special situations drills were, I had our players execute that good old scramble drill one more time. Jim put on quite a performance. He must have changed direction a dozen times before letting the ball fly. It went straight to Jamie, and—he dropped it. In the locker room afterward I asked Jamie if he really dropped it or if he was just pulling my leg, but he pleaded the Fifth Amendment. I guess I'll never know.

Our winning run continued. We beat Cleveland and Arizona and then shut out the Patriots for our eighth consecutive victory—the longest winning streak recorded by the Bills since they joined the NFL.

All good things must come to an end (as I once read in a book of trite sayings), and so did that string of victories. On the last Sunday in November we journeyed to Houston, and there we dropped a 27-24 squeaker to the Oilers. We bounced right back the following week at home by beating the Eagles 30-23. It was in this game, a full year after he had joined our team, that we began to realize what a momentous addition to our squad James Lofton had become. During the previous year and a half our pass receiving load had fallen almost solely on the shoulders of Andre Reed. In that period of time Andre had, on nine separate occasions, exceeded 100 receiving yards a game. Against the Eagles it was James who had the breakout game, as he posted 174 yards. We now had two scary threats lining up outside, and young Don Beebe was on the brink of becoming our third.

After coasting to a win against Indianapolis and edging the Giants in a hard, close battle, we had won 11 of our last 12 games, but—do you know what?—we *still* hadn't clinched the AFC East Division championship. And there was one good reason. It was the Dolphins.

We sure had played well, but so had they. After taking us apart 30-7 on the second weekend of the season, they had a superb season-long performance, resulting in the two teams being deadlocked for the division lead when they came to Buffalo late in December. The winner of this game would walk off the field with the AFC East Division title *and* with the top seed in the AFC playoffs rankings. The loser would still make the playoffs, but it would be as a wild card entry. This one was in Buffalo, and it was in winter. Advantage Buffalo—and winner Buffalo. It wasn't easy (it never was against Miami), but we won the game and the division championship. The final score was 24-14. Let the playoffs begin! Hey, why not? We had a bye in the first round.

While we rested, the Dolphins, because of their wild-card status, had to play on the road during the first week of the playoffs. They won their game, and they advanced to the next round. They were the only wild-card team that survived that initial weekend, and they now had to face us, the top-seeded AFC team. I would just as soon have declined the honor in favor of meeting any of the other playoff participants. But as you know, the rules are the rules.

It was mid-January, and it was cold. There was a mix of snow and sleet swirling down onto that hardy assemblage of Bills fans (not to mention the players and the coaches). The wind was picking up. Conditions were such that it didn't appear as if there would be much offense in this game. Are you kidding me? This was Kelly versus Marino. By the time the snow had settled, the two teams had combined to score the most points recorded in a regulation-time playoff game.

We were just a minute and a half into the game when Jim completed a 40-yard touchdown aerial to Andre, and by early in the second quarter we had extended our lead to 20-3. You may think that was a rather comfortable situation, but being aware of the weapons Miami had, we knew better.

Unfortunately, they proved our knowledge to be accurate when, early in the fourth quarter, Marino connected on one of the three touchdown passes he threw that day, and Miami closed to within three points—30-27.

It was then that we put the game away. A touchdown run by Thurman, followed by our recovery of a fumble forced by kicking teams ace Hal Garner on our ensuing kickoff, plus another Jim-to-Andre scoring toss moved us ahead 44-27 before the Dolphins scored their last touchdown in the dying moments of the game. Our offensive fireworks had been impressive. We had gained a total of almost 500 yards. Thurman had rushed 32 times for 117 yards and two touchdowns. Andre had 122 receiving yards to go along with his two touchdown catches, while James ratcheted up 149 yards and one touchdown. The Dolphins, too, had kept the chains moving by gaining 430 yards on their way to scoring their 34 points. It had been an exciting day—especially because we were the ones who had won the game.

For the second time in three years we were in the AFC Championship game. This time, however, it would be played in Orchard Park before 80,324 fans, the largest crowd, up to that time, to ever witness a Bills home game. They were crazy. I had to be there, but they didn't, and the weather conditions on that day were severe enough to scare away Admiral Richard Byrd.[2]

By the time the pregame warmup (it should have been renamed "coldup") for our AFC Championship game against the Raiders was over, my fingers and toes were already frostbitten. My six layers of thermal underwear had failed their task miserably. Compared to this day's weather, that from the previous week was like a day at the beach. The wind bit into your skin like a knife, the mercury continued to plunge, the snow blew sideways, icicles hung from the upper deck, and our fans howled with glee.

As our team huddled along the sideline just prior to trotting out onto the field for the opening kickoff, I could actually see pain on their faces. It was then that our linebacker Darryl Talley asked me if he could say something to his teammates. "Sh-Sh-Sh-Sure. G-G-G-Go ahead," I chattered. When Darryl spoke, he repeated a one-sentence message that had been delivered for the first time more than 72 years earlier by another man intent on helping to lead his comrades to victory.

2. For those of you who direct your leisure time primarily toward the search for vacations to tropical paradises, it is probably necessary for me to explain that Admiral Richard Byrd led the world's first successful exploration of the North Pole.

"When it's too tough for them, it's just right for us!" Darryl barked.

Then our kickoff coverage team sprinted out onto the field, and the Bills kept on sprinting all afternoon long. Thurman rushed for 138 yards. The two former Packers, Kenneth Davis and James Lofton, also played starring roles. Kenny scored three times on power runs, while James racked up 113 yards and a touchdown on pass receptions. We gained more than 500 yards in total offense, but the most impressive statistic in that game was posted by our defense. They intercepted six passes, two of them by Darryl. He returned one of those pickoffs 27 yards for a touchdown. Free safety Mark Kelso got one, too, giving him a total of four interceptions in playoff games, a Bills team record.

We won the game—*51-3*. For the first time in the team's history, we were going to the Super Bowl.

Yes, you *can* teach an old dog new tricks! The nature of our victory over the Raiders taught me a new lesson about our no-huddle offense. Or was it about our defense? Whatever. What I did learn was that when our swift strike attack was successful in scoring early in the game, especially if we did it twice, our opponents immediately became one-dimensional in their offensive efforts to catch back up. They felt the need to score quickly in order to get back into contention. That meant they were going to throw the ball, and we knew it. They were now predictable, and our defensive coaches and players drooled at the prospects that opened up for us. These were the situations that greatly increased our chances for forcing turnovers. The six interceptions by our defense in our victory over the Raiders serve as the perfect example of that assertion.

You can bandy statistics about in many exotic ways, but there is only one that overwhelmingly and consistently correlates with winning, and that is the takeaway/giveaway ratio. During my years with the Bills, we played in 19 playoff games. We won 11 of those games, and in not one of those victories did our opponent have more takeaways than we did. In the eight games we lost, we did not win the takeaway/giveaway battle once. Our cumulative TA/GA ratio in the playoff games we won was +20. In those we lost it was -19. All these numbers may be boring, but winning isn't.

I have already recounted, in the first chapter of this book, the final heart-stopping seconds of our 20-19 loss to the Giants in Super Bowl XXV. I reviewed, as well, the agonies we experienced in the immediate aftermath of that crushing defeat.

Some analysts have felt the Giants' large bulge in time of possession (approximately 40 1/2 minutes to our 19 1/2 minutes) indicated a dominance not reflected by the final score. Not so. In many of the close games we had played, there were similar disparities. Our no-huddle, remember, was on and off the field in a hurry regardless of whether we had moved the ball successfully. It was tight all the way.

Five times during the game, the lead changed hands (it came within a whisker of being *six,* darn it!). Total yardage figures were remarkably alike in that they accumulated 386 yards to our 371. The leading ball carrier in the game was Thurman, who piled up 135 yards on just 15 carries. That included a 31-yard touchdown sprint early in the fourth quarter that put us ahead 19-17. Had we won the contest, Thurman undoubtedly would have been selected as the game's Most Valuable Player.

Yes, it was close, but they had won the battle that was headlined in the newspapers the next day as "A Game for the Ages," and that it was. There was nothing we could do about that loss now, but there was a lot we could do about the future. It was time for us to turn our attention in that direction.

CHAPTER 31

We're Going Back to the Super Bowl

What do you do after you've *lost* the Super Bowl? Do you give up? Do you retire? Do you say, "Oh, what's the use?" Do you blame others? The Bills didn't so any of those things. What then did we do? There was a five-step formula I adopted to help us get back on track:

1. ALLOW YOURSELF SOME TIME TO MOURN. You don't just shrug it off. You've worked too hard to say that it really isn't important. It is realistic to expect that you are going to hurt for a while. Just don't continue to lie in the fetal position too long.
2. OWN UP. Recognize and admit what it was you could have done better. Doing that will help you zero in on proper remedies.
3. RECOGNIZE THE GOOD. Acknowledge what a splendid group of people it was with whom you worked. Shine the spotlight on all the positive qualities that exist within your organization. Highlight reasons for optimism while still being realistic about what can be improved.
4. MAKE A PLAN. This is the "what are you going to do about it?" part of the project. Exactly how are we going to get better? How are we going to deal with obstacles that need to be overcome?
5. GO TO WORK ON THAT PLAN. A brilliant idea is a job half done.[1]

---

1. That statement was first spoken by Ralph Waldo Emerson. I don't know what team he played for, but he sure was right.

Our concentration in the 1991 draft was directed toward defense. Our first-round pick, from the University of Illinois, was defensive back Henry Jones, and in the second round we selected a defensive end from North Dakota State, Phil Hansen. Neither Henry nor Phil broke into our starting lineup as rookies, but it wouldn't be long until they would become two of the most dominant players in the NFL. In the ninth round we added Mark Maddox, a linebacker from Northern Michigan, who, besides his sterling kicking teams contributions, would see a lot of action on defense.

The draft was over. It was time for training camp to begin. What would the state of mind of our players be coming into the new season after their Super Bowl loss? That was my biggest concern. I needn't have worried. They were eager and ready to go.

We came roaring into the season, looking even more potent than we had the year before. After our first five games, our record was 5-0, and two of those victories had been on the road. We were scoring an average of more than 32 points a game. In four of those games Jim Kelly had thrown for more than 300 yards while completing 12 of those tosses for touchdowns. Andre Reed, James Lofton, Thurman Thomas, and Don Beebe had all turned in 100-plus-yard receiving performances. Thurman had also rushed for more than 100 yards in three of those outings. Our no-huddle offense was becoming more difficult for other teams to slow down as we refined it. As our opponents came to more fully understand what it was they would be facing, we found that rather than their gaining confidence by virtue of that knowledge, they developed a fear of the arsenal that they were about to face in the coming battle.

I think at this stage we began to believe that no one could stop us. Enter a game in the NFL too convinced that this is true, and you'll find out in a hurry how skewed your vision was. In our sixth game of the season we journeyed to Kansas City, where the Chiefs dismantled us 33-6. What rankled me the most was how cavalier we had been about protecting the football. Turnover after turnover we presented to the Chiefs. They were a strong team, but I remained aware of how much our ineptness that day had contributed to giving them the win. I blamed myself for having allowed our players to approach a game in such a state of mind. I knew one thing for sure: We were going to pay attention during the coming week to protecting the football *and* on taking it away from our opponent. The heck with those Xs and Os.

We devoted large segments of our practice time that coming week to all aspects of the takeaway/giveaway battle, and then, at our Saturday meeting at the team hotel before our game against the Colts, after going over the game plan, I once again reached back into the pages of history in an effort to capture the attention of our players.

I walked over to the blackboard, which, up until that time, I had left unused. I picked up the chalk, and then, silently and slowly, I wrote:

Adolf Hitler
Hermann Goering
Heinrich Himmler
Joseph Goebbels

When I turned back to face the players I noticed several of them checking their scouting reports to see if they had overlooked the names of some Colts backup players.

"Do any of you know who these men were?" I asked.

No hands were raised, although I did learn later from offensive guard Mitch Frerotte that the guy sitting next to him thought they might be the members of Germany's Olympic mile relay team. Because no one responded, I told them that during World War II and the years leading up to it, these men had been leaders in the infamous Nazi party. I spoke of the many atrocities of which these men and their malevolent followers had been guilty. Once again, I could read on the faces of our players that look of "what in the hell does this have to do with tackling Eric Dickerson tomorrow?" There was only one person in the room who was actually taking notes, and that was our team psychiatrist.

Nevertheless, I persisted, by telling them of the disdain with which those four villainous tyrants were viewed by members of the allied armed forces who were sent into battle against them. I referred specifically to the soldiers in the renowned British Eighth Army who had fought and won the tide-turning Battle of El Alamein in the desert sands of North Africa. These heroic warriors, I continued to explain, had composed a bawdy (and perhaps somewhat vulgar) little ballad that helped them express their contempt for that quartet of scoundrels whose names I had written on the blackboard. The words that they employed had been crafted by the men who sang them, but the melody was borrowed from a popular tune of the day, which we all know as "The Bridge over the River Kwai." Without the benefit of accompaniment, I launched into their song:

Hitler—has got just one ball;
Goering—has two, but they are small.
Himmler—is somewhat similar,
But "Go-Balls" has no balls at all!

When I finished, I remained silent for just a few moments.

"In tomorrow's game," I growled, "there will be *just one ball.* When we've got it, hang onto it! When they've got, take it away from them! Meeting dismissed."

The next day, in Orchard Park's Rich Stadium, our Bills roared to a 42-6 victory over the Colts. Both Thurman and Kenneth Davis rushed for more than 100 yards during the game. Kenny did it on just nine carries. We didn't fumble once, and we didn't throw any interceptions, either. I can't tell you how many takeaways we got from them until I get my computer repaired.

We kept on rolling, putting together our second five-game winning streak of the season. During this run we burned out a lot of scoreboard lights averaging 35 points a game. In four of those five games Thurman surpassed the 100-yard rushing mark, while James and Andre kept going past that figure in pass receiving yardage. In our 35-16 trimming of the Bengals, James recorded 220 yards in receptions. That is still the all-time third highest total in one game for a Bills receiver.

Our fourth and fifth victories in that string were achieved on the road, first at Green Bay and then on a Monday night in Miami. Then, for the third straight week we had to play an away game, this time in Foxboro, Massachusetts, against the Patriots.[2] In New England we lost our second game of the year when the Patriots inflicted a 16-13 loss on us. Oh, well, at least we had a home game the following Sunday before having to go on the road for the next two games. That meant that late in the season we had a five-week span in which four of our games were away from home.

It was now early December, and even with a 10-2 record, we still had not clinched our division championship. We did it, notching a hard-fought 24-13 victory against the Jets. With three games remaining in the regular season, there were still hurdles we had to surmount if we were to secure the coveted home field advantage, and so we prepared to take our weary team back on the road for the next two weekends.

The first trip would be to the West Coast. There we would be meeting the strong and revenge-minded (remember last season's 51-3 AFC championship loss that they had endured) Raiders. We won, but—believe me—it wasn't as easy as had it had been the year before. This time we came away with a 30-27 win in overtime. Then it was on to Indianapolis where, at last, by virtue of a 35-7 triumph, we assured ourselves of being at home for all playoff games.

---

2. Wait a minute. Let me get this straight. Three weeks in row we have to travel, and the final trip comes after a short week because of a Monday nighter the week before? Who makes up these damn schedules, anyway? During my 12 years of coaching the Bills we were to play 17 Monday night games, 14 of them were away from home! Go figure.

What a season it had been so far! One year earlier, our Bills had set an all-time single-season team scoring record as our no-huddle maniacs posted 428 points. Now, just one year later, we shattered that mark again, posting 458 points. No Buffalo team has ever matched that—before or since. If you think our players were maniacs, let me tell you about our fans. Six times during the 1991 season more than 80,000 of them were in attendance. There were 80,366 of our partisans there the day we beat the Bears 35-20 (Papa Halas would have been happy with the crowd, but *not* with the outcome). That throng established an all-time high for a Bills home game.

There was an even more remarkable attendance figure that underscores the devotion exhibited by our fans, because it was in 1991 that they set a single season in-stadium attendance record that has never been equaled. It wasn't just a Bills record, mind you. It is an *NFL* record. Just think of what it might have been if the weather was good!

In 1991, our explosive offense led the league in scoring and in total yardage, gaining more yards than any team in Bills history. We had achieved a great balance between the run and the pass. We led the league in rushing, while finishing fourth in passing. On 11 occasions Thurman had rushed for more than 100 yards in a game, and his cohort at the position, Kenneth Davis, also did it twice. Between Andre, Thurman, James, and Don there had been 11 times when someone had more than 100 yards in pass receptions during the game.

Credit Jim Kelly for helping us to strike this winning balance. He called most of the plays out there on the field of play, and there has never been a more unselfish signal caller than Jim. Once we got a comfortable lead, he kept it on the ground. When the situation called for a run, that's what he called, too. Jim did enjoy many outstanding days, and if ever an opponent tried to overplay defending against our running attack, he'd scorch them in a hurry. At the beginning of most games, when we sought to stampede our opponent in our quick-strike mode, he was masterful. And there is no one I have ever coached who was any better when it came to coping with the unexpected or an adverse turn of events.

During the 1991 season, Jim had some magic days. He was over 300 yards passing on numerous occasions. One Sunday early in the season against the Steelers, just a few miles from his hometown of East Brady, Pennsylvania, he threw for six touchdowns while leading his team to a 52-34 victory.

Even when it involves a star like Jim, however, there are incidents that can illustrate how fickle some fans can be. It was only a few weeks after Jim's big day versus the Steelers that he came out gunning once again. This time we were playing the Bengals, and we were at home. In the first quarter of that game Jim "completed" three passes. Trouble is all of them were to Bengals defenders. And then I heard some catcalls and booing come from a small contingent of painted faces in the stands.

"Get that jerk outta there," one of them bellowed as our offensive players came to the sidelines after the third of those errant aerials.

Of course, I didn't comply with that gentleman's delicate plea. By the time it was all over, Jim had led our team to a 35-16 win.[3]

All of those impressive stats were fine, but they wouldn't mean a darn thing if we didn't now translate them into effective weapons of mass destruction as we entered the playoff fray.

The first week we had a bye, and then, refreshed, we prepared to host the Chiefs. That was the same team that, after our whirlwind start at the beginning of the season, had drubbed us 33-6 back at Arrowhead Stadium early in October. It was now early in January, and we were in Orchard Park. The result was as different as the venue. This time we had complete command right from the outset.

Less than one minute into the game Jim hit Andre on a 25-yard touchdown pass. A few minutes later, it was Jim to Andre again on a 52-yard scoring connection. Scott Norwood added a field goal. Then Jim drilled another touchdown pass, this time to James Lofton. It was early in the second quarter, and we had taken a 24-0 lead. By late in the fourth quarter we were on top 37-7, and we coasted to a 37-14 victory.

That night we celebrated, and then, in the early morning darkness the next day our coaches reported for work as we began the game planning for the AFC championship game against the Broncos.

This one promised to have plenty of fireworks. Two of the most prolific scoring machines in the NFL were poised to churn out the points. Jim was going head to head with John Elway. It doesn't get any better than that. Fathers told their young sons to go to the restroom before the kickoff because if they had to make that trip during the game, they'd be sure to miss seeing two or three electrifying touchdowns. Also, I wondered how those poor officials were going to be able to keep up with this impending track meet?

3. That grandstand quarterback had better numbers on the afternoon, however, than Jim had. While Jim had completed only five touchdown passes, that guy offering advice put away nine beers by the time the final gun sounded. At least that's what Ed Stillwell, our director of security, reported.

Let me take you forward now to late in the third quarter of that game. The score is 0-0. What?! That's right, *0-0.* Bor-r-r-r-ing, you may be thinking. Allow me to differ. In my 47 years of coaching, this game has to rank among the most exciting five of my career. Every snap was drama.

We played our best defensive game of the year, and as the beginning of the fourth quarter drew near, we had the Broncos backed up deep in their territory. Elway dropped back to pass, and our front line of Bruce Smith, Jeff Wright, and Leon Seals came storming in at him. He had lured them well, because he was setting them up for a screen pass. At the last moment Jeff read it. He fell off just enough so that he was able to deflect Elway's throw into the hands of our linebacker, Carlton Bailey. Carlton grabbed it at the 11-yard line and sprinted into the end zone. Neither offense had scored a point as yet, but nevertheless we had taken a 7-0 lead.

The defensive struggle resumed, and with only four minutes left to play in the game, Scott booted a 44-yard field goal. We were now in front 10-0, and things were looking very rosy for us. Oh, yeah! That was, until the Broncos took the next kickoff and marched 85 yards in eight plays. They scored the game's only offensive touchdown with just 1:43 remaining. All we had to do now to wrap up the game was recover the onside kickoff everyone knew they going to attempt. They kicked. We all scrambled. And—*they recovered it!*

On their first play from scrimmage they threw into the flat to their running back, who caught it and then sprinted up the field toward our goal line. On every team there are some quiet, conscientious, gentlemanly types of fellows about whom you don't hear a lot because they are not self-promoters. The public doesn't get to know much about them, but their teammates do, and their teammates like and respect them. One of the many on our team who fit that description was a modest, hard-working cornerback named Kirby Jackson. Kirby made the play that day that saved the game for us. He applied a jarring tackle that dislodged the ball from the grasp of the Denver player who had caught the pass, and then Kirby recovered the loose pigskin. We ran out the clock, and we won 10-7.

We had a lot of stars on our team, but on that January day in Buffalo it was the relative unknowns such as Kirby Jackson plus those eighth- and ninth-round draft choices from 1988, Jeff and Carlton, who provided the heroics. Scott, less than a year removed from his fateful miss in Super Bowl XXV, had stepped up and kicked that 44-yard field goal with under four minutes left to play, thereby affording us the margin of victory.

We were going back to the Super Bowl!

In Super Bowl XXVI we met the NFC champion Washington Redskins at the HHH (for Hubert H. Humphrey) Metrodome in Minneapolis. Our performance that day, unfortunately, served to add yet another "H." This one, I am sorry to say, stands for "Humiliated." After a scoreless first quarter, the Redskins scored 17 unanswered points before the halftime break. Just 16 seconds into the third quarter, they extended their lead to 24-0 by returning an interception. It was one of five turnovers that we committed.

The turnovers had made us fall behind. Because we were behind, we became more predictable in our need to try to catch up. Too early in the game we had to abandon striking that balance between the run and the pass that had sustained us during the long season. Now we were in the position where we had to force the pass, and when that happens, the likelihood of committing more turnovers increases.

Finally, we put some points on the board, closing the margin to 24-10, but our shoddy ball protection woes continued, and the Redskins scored another touchdown plus two more field goals. With six minutes left they led 37-10. At least we didn't quit. Jim hit tight end Pete Metzelaars on a short touchdown pass. We followed that with an onside kick that our incomparable special teamer, Steve Tasker, recovered. Then, with just four minutes remaining, Jim drilled another scoring strike, this one to Don Beebe. It was now 37-24. Once again we called for an onside kick.

I thought that Steve recovered that one, too, but the officials ruled that we had touched the ball before it had gone the required 10 yards as specified by the rules. Our last-gasp attempt at pulling off a miraculous comeback had come up short. It was over. Our quest for redemption had gone unfulfilled.

It had been a noble effort on the part of our players. After losing a Super Bowl they had rededicated themselves to doing all that it takes to get back there again. In NFL history only two other teams, Dallas in 1972 and Minnesota in 1975, had ever fought their way back to play again the next year after having lost a Super Bowl. No team had ever done it after experiencing *two* consecutive defeats.

Perhaps it was time to acknowledge that we gave it our best shot, but it just didn't work out. We tried; we tried hard, but it wasn't meant to be. Let it go, already!

Not the Buffalo Bills!

CHAPTER 32

Four Scores and Seven Minutes Ago

Upon entering my seventh season as Bills head coach, I was cognizant of many changes that had taken place since I had first walked into the team meeting room in midseason of 1986. Our team had gone from being a perennial doormat to becoming the best in the AFC. We had instituted a style of offense that captivated football fans in Buffalo and throughout the country. We had made some startling personnel moves, and we had seen many of our draft choices (including several obscure lower-round selections) blossom into Pro Bowl-caliber performers.

What you aren't aware of when you are mired down in the day-to-day details is how much change is constantly taking place. The NFL Players' Association had been aggressive in their dealings with management, and as a result, the initial repercussions from free agency were beginning to be felt.

Now that the 1992 season was about to begin, I realized that a number of familiar faces were no longer in our locker room. Starting safeties Leonard Smith and Dwight Drane had departed after the 1991 campaign, but first-round draft choice Henry Jones was ready to step in. We had traded defensive end Leon Seals, a starter in both Super Bowl appearances, to the Patriots. Replacing him would be Phil Hansen, whom we had picked in 1991 in the second round. What a star he turned out to be. We had seen an injury end the career of rock-hard fullback Jamie Mueller after the 1990 season, but young Carwell Gardner took over.

There were other key departures, as well, but we kept finding and developing just the right guys to help us continue to play at a championship level. Perhaps the most startling move we made during the off season happened only because of a unique free agency opportunity. Our director of pro personnel, Bob Ferguson, always kept an up-to-date list by position and rank of every player in the NFL. I also assigned each assistant coach on our staff to maintain his own evaluations on every NFL player at the position for which that coach was responsible.

On the day that the Buccaneers announced their place kicker, Steve Christie, was a free agent, Bob and Bruce DeHaven, who had done such an outstanding job coaching our kicking teams, appeared at my office door simultaneously.

"Let me guess why you are here," I intoned, affecting my best Johnny Carson imitation, before they said a word.

"Coach," they both chimed in unison, "Steve Christie is the best damn kicker in the whole damn league!"

"I know that," I responded. "Let's go see Bill Polian."

We all traipsed down the hall to Bill's office, and when we got there, I asked him if he knew who Steve Christie was.

"Best damn kicker in the whole damn league," he answered.

"Bill, do you think we ought to look into this a little bit more?" I ventured.

"I've already called his agent," Bill said. Upon noting my look of surprise, Bill elaborated, "He'd love to come here. He knows about the tremendous attention we pay to the kicking game, and that excites him. Also, his home is just across the bridge in Canada, and that adds to the appeal. And, oh yeah, Marv, he's one of those overachievers from the College of William and Mary that you always keep telling me about. Are you interested in bringing him aboard?"

Now came the tough part. If we were to sign Steve, it meant that we would have to release Scott Norwood. There was no question, however, that during the previous few seasons Steve had been the best young NFL kicker and that his finest years were still ahead of him. In addition to his accuracy on field goals, Steve also had a far stronger leg on kickoffs, and that is a factor that is too often overlooked. The right decision was easy to see and easy to describe, but implementing it from an emotional standpoint was painful.

I once read a quotation by Martin Luther King, Jr. that went as follows: "Some decisions are made because they make good sense politically. Some are made because they are the popular thing to do, and some are made because they are the right thing to do. Whenever the first or second reason comes in conflict with the third one," he had said, "do the *right* thing!" Signing Steve was the right thing for the Bills to do, and so we did it. When we had to bid farewell to Scott, he was able to know that he left with the respect and affection of everyone in Buffalo.

Steve joined punter Chris Mohr, whom we had signed one year earlier, and together they formed the best kicking duo in the NFL for the next nine years. By the time Steve left the Bills after the 2000 season, he was the team's all-time leading scorer with 1,011 points. Scott, with 670 points, was second on that list.

It isn't just changes in player personnel that occur as the years pass by that must be dealt with. Adding to the constant readjustments are changes in the coaching staff. Once the proper mix of instructors is in place, the head coach must also remain aware that there will be turnover among that august group. In order to stay prepared for those eventualities, I maintained a file containing detailed information about prospective coaching candidates.

At the annual orientation meetings that I would conduct for the men who worked as college personnel scouts for the Bills, I would always instruct them to bring back reports not only on the player prospects but also on all members of the coaching staffs at the various colleges they visited. Also, I personally evaluated the work of other NFL coaches, and from those observations I maintained a constantly updated list of men I would like to bring aboard in the event a vacancy developed on our staff.

There were three general criteria I felt to be important when selecting an assistant coach. First was his work ethic. I wasn't interested in men who were *willing* to work hard; we wanted guys who *wanted* to work hard, who had a love of the game and a love of their jobs. Secondly, they had to be excellent teachers. They had to be able to convey that knowledge to our players in a manner that resulted in those players applying it with confidence and with effect. Finally, they had to be able to work well with others on the coaching staff and within the whole organization. Those autocratic types who went strutting around as if they knew it all were destroyers of unity and morale. I wasn't looking for wimps, but there is huge difference between saying, "That's a dumbass thing to say" as opposed to "I don't agree with you."

After the 1991 season our offensive coordinator, Ted Marchibroda, was offered the head coaching job with the Colts. His work with us had been outstanding, and although I hated to see him go, I was at the same time elated to see that he was being so justifiably rewarded. I wished my friend, Ted, good luck (except when the Colts played the Bills, that is) and began my search for our new offensive coordinator.

I took five steps down the hall, and I found him. Without hesitation, I promoted offensive line coach Tom Bresnahan. He handled this new responsibility while continuing to tutor the offensive line. That was just a carryover from how Ted had operated when he had coached the quarterbacks while also serving as our offensive coordinator. With Ted's departure, we also needed a new quarterbacks coach, and so I brought in Jim Shofner, a respected and highly recommended veteran NFL coach.

After that 1991 season our offensive staff continued to undergo considerable fine-tuning. Just a year earlier I had added Don Lawrence, a former member of my Chiefs contingent, and the coaching job he did in preparing our tight ends was superb. Elijah Pitts stayed on, continuing to work effectively with our running backs. Elijah had been offered a head coaching position with one of the teams in the newborn NFL Europe, but he wanted to stay. I added to his title the designation of assistant head coach.

There was still one more offensive staff consideration that had to be addressed. We had an opening for a new wide receivers coach, and I had my eye on a young fellow who I felt had all the desirable qualities, Charlie Joiner. During the latter years of his Hall of Fame playing career with the Chargers, Charlie had told me how much he wanted to coach. I kept a close eye on him, and when he finally hung up his cleats, he secured some coaching assignments. I studied his work closely, and I was impressed. The timing was right, and I hired him. I never regretted it.

That was a lot of restructuring, but even with all those new men in place, we kept right on humming. They were the right men.

Eager to renew its quest, our team took off at full steam once again in 1992. We won our opener against the Rams 40-7. One week later, we journeyed to the Bay Area for our first road game of the year. In this one we faced the powerful 49ers, and it was a thriller. It was another classic duel of classy quarterbacks—Jim Kelly versus Joe Montana. There was a host of other stars and future Hall of Famers on the field that day also, but even with receivers such as Jerry Rice, Andre Reed, and James Lofton cavorting about on the beaten-up sod at Candlestick Park, the hero of the day was our under-appreciated tight end, Pete Metzelaars. Pete had more than 100 yards in receptions that afternoon, and it was his fine catch and subsequent stirring run that led to our fourth-quarter winning touchdown as we nipped the 49ers 34-31.

It had been a day for offense. Jim threw for more than 400 yards and three touchdowns, while Andre led all receivers with 144 yards on 10 catches. Neither team could really stop the other, and as a result there wasn't a single punt by either team in the entire game.

After playing the Colts and the Patriots, we had won four straight, and we were averaging more than 38 points a game. Next, archrival Miami came to town, and that was the end of our winning streak. Before 80,368 fans, still the largest crowd to ever attend a Bills home game (it topped by *two* people the number that had seen us play the

Bears one year earlier), we bombed. The Dolphins enjoyed a pleasant trip home as they were able to celebrate their 37-10 victory.

The spell had been broken, and that was driven home even more forcefully the next week when the Raiders shut us down 20-3. By this time we were struggling, and then an inordinate series of injuries added to our problems. Both Thurman and Andre were hurting, and although they tried to play, neither one was able to perform up to his full capabilities. We pulled ourselves together for a while, and although we barely got by on a few occasions, we were able to string together victories in our next five games. The highlight came when we gained vengeance on the Dolphins by beating them down in Miami 26-20. Don Beebe had by this time emerged as a polished young veteran, and in four of those five games he surpassed 100 yards in receptions. With Thurman trying to play while banged up, Kenneth Davis answered the call. In one game against the Falcons, Kenny stepped in and set the pace for us by rushing for 181 yards on 20 carries as we downed the Falcons 41-14.

We were able to overcome a number of injuries through the middle part of that 1992 season, but as they continued to occur on both sides of the ball, we found our ranks becoming too thin. As some wise coach once commented, "It's great to have depth—until you have to use it." I knew what he meant.

Following that five-game winning streak, we lost two straight. Then we inched by with victories in our next two games. We entered our final week of the season with a 10-5 record, and we needed to win that last game on the road in Houston in order to repeat as the AFC East Division champions for the third year in a row. Win or lose, we would be in the playoffs, but gaining the home-field advantage during that elimination process was always a prime objective.

There were additional obstacles that added to our discomfiture. The Oilers needed to win the game if they were to make the playoffs as a wild-card entry, and so their motivation was at a high level. In recent weeks they had been playing superbly, and quarterback Warren Moon was running their Run and Shoot offense just the way their coaching staff had envisioned it. And worst of all, our physical readiness to compete had never been more suspect. In addition to a long list of others on the shelf, we learned that both Cornelius Bennett and Jim Kelly had joined that group of wounded. Neither one would be able to take the field for that crucial game down in Houston. Things had gotten so bad that I asked team owner Ralph Wilson if he'd like to suit up for the game, but he wanted too big a contract.

It was no contest. The Oilers cruised to a 27-3 victory, and we limped home. There'd be no first-round bye this year. Beaten up, and with a perilous road that we'd need to traverse in order to get there, we would have to win three consecutive games on three consecutive weekends beginning the next Sunday if we were to make it back to the Super Bowl. The last two of those games would come in the home stadiums of division-winning teams. In so doing, they had earned the coveted right not to travel.

The first game, at least, would be at Rich Stadium, since our wild-card record had been one win better than the wild-card opponent we would be facing. Trouble was that that team was on a tear, and they were healthy, while we were gasping for air and would still be without the services of Jim, Cornelius, and many others. The first team we had to play on the first Sunday of the new year was the one that had just taken us apart—the red-hot Oilers.

We knew all week long that Jim and Cornelius would not be active for the game, but midway through the first quarter, which was closely contested, we were dealt another staggering blow. Thurman had to leave the field, and our team doctors told me that he would not be able to return for the rest of the game. Even I pulled a calf muscle running along the sidelines, but they taped me up, and I was able to continue shouting borderline obscenities at the officials (as if what was happening to us out there was their fault). At the end of the first quarter we trailed 7-3. And then Moon really went to work.

By the time that excruciating half had ended, Warren had completed 19 of his 22 pass attempts for 218 yards and four touchdowns. We headed off the field at halftime trailing 28-3, and our fans were exiting the stadium faster than our Super Bowl hopes were vanishing from our locker room.

There weren't a lot of disconcerting adjustments that we needed to make. We just had to play better, but with a load of backup players in the lineup that was one of those "easier said than done" solutions. My comments directed to our full squad before sending them back out for the second half were brief.

"You are two-time defending AFC champions," I said. "When you walk off that field after 30 more minutes of football, don't let anyone ever be able to say that you laid down, that you quit. Be able to walk off with your heads held high, knowing that you fought until the final tick has gone off the game clock."

Then I walked over to Frank Reich's locker where he was sitting with quarterbacks coach Jim Shofner while they discussed plans for the second half. Frank looked up at me almost apologetically, and I felt the need to say something encouraging to him.

"Frank," I said, "they tell me that you were the quarterback at the University of Maryland and that you led your team to the greatest comeback victory in collegiate football history. Well, today you are going to lead us to the greatest comeback win in the history of professional football."

Quietly, with tightened lips, Frank nodded his head.

As we were marching back up the tunnel on our way out to begin the second half, Jim Shofner fell in beside me and said, "Marv, the greatest comeback ever recorded in NFL play was from a 28-point deficit. I know; I played in that game. We're down by only 25."

"Aw, Frank doesn't know that," I countered. What difference did it make, I thought. No one would ever remember a throwaway remark like that.

At least we got to receive the kickoff to begin the second half. Maybe we could put together some kind of drive, one that might even result in a score. That is exactly what happened. We picked up a first down, and on the next play we connected on a pass that went for a touchdown. The problem was that the "connection" was with Houston's strong safety, Bubba McDowell, who returned that interception 58 yards for yet another Oilers touchdown. The score was now 35-3. Another 10,000 Bills fans headed for the parking lot.

On the next kickoff it appeared as if matters were about to become even worse. Houston's kickoff man, Al Del Greco, tried to line drive his kick so that it would bounce around deep in our territory, but the ball flew straight at Steve Tasker, who was lined up as a member of our front five at the restraining line just 10 yards away. The ball hit Steve and then ricocheted directly back at the horde of Houston coverage men. They all dove for the loose pigskin, and so did Steve. There were 12 men seeking eagerly to gain possession, 11 Oilers and Steve. Steve is the guy who came up with it. He will never cease to amaze me.

Guess what? We finally put together a glimmer of offense. It took us 10 plays and six minutes to go 50 yards, but we capped it off with our first touchdown of the day when Kenneth Davis banged it into the end zone from the one-yard line. The score was now 35-10. Big deal! So what? Now it was our turn to kick off and put the ball back into the hands of Moon and his scoring machine.

The heck with that. I was deep into my "what have we got to lose?" mental state, and so I ordered a surprise onside kick. Steve Christie nursed the ball forward 10 yards, and then both he and our "eat you alive" coverage man, Mark Pike, streaked in pursuit after it. Mark laid a block on the nearest Houston player that gave even me a toothache, and in the scramble that ensued Steve came up with the ball. Three plays later,

Frank hit a speeding Don Beebe on a pass-plus-run-after-the-catch gem that went 38 yards for another Bills touchdown. Make that 35-17.

Our defense was now rested and inspired. It was one, two, three, and out for Houston on their next offensive series, and we actually forced them to punt for the first time in the game. We took over at our own 40-yard line. Bang! Bang! Bang! In three plays we moved it down to their 26, and from there Frank zipped a dart into the Oilers' end zone, where Andre pulled it for the score. 35-24! This was getting to be fun. I noticed the flow of patrons in the stands had now reversed directions. People were pouring back *in!*

We still had a long way to go, but almost immediately after our next kickoff Henry Jones snatched the first of two game-changing interceptions that would occur on that never-to-be-forgotten day. He picked it off at their 38-yard line and brought it back to the 23. We moved it to the 18, and there we were faced a fourth and five. Do we attempt a field goal or do we take our chances and try to pick up a first down? These are decisions to be made only by the head coach. You only have about 10 seconds in which to make up your mind because more than half of the 40-second allotment that you have between plays must be used to get proper personnel onto the field, to get the play called, to break the huddle, to get lined up, and to get the ball into play.

Frank had been pointing at himself, a signal that meant he had in mind a play that he felt had an excellent chance of succeeding. At the same time, I heard several of our coaches screaming into my earphones that we ought to kick the field goal. If we made that three-pointer, we would move to within eight points of tying the game, but something inside of me desired more than that. I didn't want to have to score twice (and then have to add a difficult two-point conversion, as well) in order to *tie the game.* I wanted two scores to result in our taking the lead. I decided to go for it, and so I pointed back at Frank, a gesture that served as his instruction to go ahead and call his play from scrimmage.

Benjamin Franklin, writing in *Poor Richard's Almanac,* had once observed, "People make their most important decisions with their hearts, not their heads." I determined that if we picked up that first down, I'd write him a thank-you note.

Frank called his play, took the snap, and dropped back to pass. He hit Andre cutting across the middle of the field, and Andre, after gathering it in at the eight-yard line, sprinted on into the end zone for the second time in the last two and a half minutes.

"Four scores and seven minutes ago" we had been losing 35-3. It was now 35-31, but we were still behind as the third quarter came to a close.

The defenses on both teams stiffened, and time was running inexorably off the clock. We were down to six minutes left to play, when we forced the Oilers to punt for just the second time during that long afternoon. We had possession once again, but we were backed up on our 26-yard line. We moved quickly down the field running our no-huddle offense, and we reached their 40-yard line, where we had a third-and-10 situation. Speaking into my headset to Jim Shofner, who was signaling plays out to Frank, I told Jim that we would use all four downs. There would be no fourth-down punt, I said, even if we came up short on third down.

Knowing this, and anticipating that Houston would be expecting a pass on our third-and-long situation, Jim called for a passing formation, but instead of throwing the ball, he called a running play. Kenny, subbing for the injured Thurman, bolted through the line for a 12-yard gain. The drive stayed alive. Two plays later, it was—let's hear it again—Frank to Andre. This one was a 17-yard touchdown strike. The Bills had taken a 38-35 lead. There were three minutes left to play. Believe me, the game wasn't over!

The Oilers came roaring back. They crammed 12 plays into the next two minutes and 45 seconds. They kept moving the chains, and they kept drawing closer and closer to our goal line. There were under 20 seconds left to play, and they were at our 25-yard line. Moon faded back for another pass attempt. Barreling in from our defensive left end position came second-year man Phil Hansen, who had played at an intensity level rarely seen even in the NFL. As he leapt into the air in his attempt to block Moon's throw, a Houston blocker attacked his legs and sent him on a twisting somersault that culminated with Phil landing on the ground in jarring fashion flat on his back. Houston had been setting up a screen pass to our left, which they now threw out to their star running back, Lorenzo White.

White caught the perfectly thrown ball and with three big offensive linemen arrayed in front of him, he headed upfield for what appeared to be an unimpeded path to the touchdown that would break our hearts. He was speeding toward the goal line when a human missile hurled itself from behind at White's ankles, tripped him up, and sent him sprawling to the turf eight yards short of the end zone. It was Phil, who, the instant he had hit the ground, had bounced up and gave frantic (and seemingly hopeless) chase. Many moments in that historic game have been recounted in the years that followed, but I will always remember that if we had not had a man at that position with the fiber and character qualities of Phil Hansen, we wouldn't have won that game.

We still hadn't won it at that exact moment, either. With just a few seconds remaining, Houston kicked a field goal. The score was tied 38-38. The game went into overtime.

Houston won the toss, and, of course, they elected to receive. All they really had to do then was advance the ball into position to kick a game-winning field goal, and, given the way they had been moving the ball, I am sure that any impartial fan (that's an oxymoron) would have felt that the odds favored the Oilers.

At least we covered the kickoff like a rootin' tootin' Bills team ought to cover it, and they had to start their drive from deep in their territory. On their third play from scrimmage, it was now our *right* defensive end, Bruce Smith, who applied heated pressure on Moon. Moon had to unload quickly, and when the ball was airborne, cornerback Nate Odomes sent the now repacked stadium crowd into a frenzy by picking it off and returning it to Houston's 20-yard line.

We ran the ball twice, getting six yards closer to their goalposts while maneuvering so that it came to rest in the middle of the field. A hush fell over the stadium as we sent our field goal team onto the field, and then Steve Christie, "the best damn kicker in the whole damn league," split the uprights. We had done it. We had come back from a 32-point deficit to win in overtime 41-38. We had just registered the greatest comeback victory in NFL history, and we had done it with a battered group of men as courageous as any who had ever played the game.

Can you believe that winning that game was the *easy part* of our task? We still had to win two more, in a row, on the road, against teams that had won their division championships. But that could wait. Let our team and the people in Buffalo celebrate for just one day at least.

In our raucous locker room after the game, the excitement finally abated, and when it did, Frank sauntered toward me. I could tell as he approached that there was something he wished to say.

"Hey, Coach," he said, "when you spoke to me at halftime and told me that I was going to lead the greatest comeback in pro football history, I knew that we were behind by only 25 points. That's why I threw the interception that they returned for a touchdown on our first series in the second half. I was just trying to follow your instructions about all that comeback stuff, you know."

"Frank," I countered, "I'm going to tell you an even bigger lie. I believe you."

Those of us who were down on the field that magic day will never forget it, and neither will the great fans in Buffalo. Even today, whenever I am recognized by some Bills fans, they always recount their memories of that game. The strange thing is that, although there were about

80,000 people who filed in, then out, then back into the stadium again, I have met at least 500,000 who have told me that they were in attendance. You would think, also, that out of a group that large I might meet someone who didn't say to me, "I am *the* No. 1 Bills fan of all time." You'd think, wouldn't you, that from among that many people there must be someone, somewhere, who is the No. 2 fan?

Once before, on the day after a game, I had posted on the bulletin board located at the entry of our team meeting room a poem that had significant application to the events that had happened the day before. That was the one about Sir Andrew, and I had displayed it in the hopes that it would help motivate our players to rebound from the loss we had just suffered in Super Bowl XXV.

On the Monday after "Comeback Sunday," I determined that it was once again time for some poetry. The selection that I now tacked onto the bulletin board had been originally composed by Edgar A. Guest but had been shared with me by a former college coach. I placed it there because it served as an appropriate tribute to every player on our team. It read as follows:

Somebody said that it couldn't be done
But he with a chuckle replied
That "maybe it couldn't," but he would be one
Who wouldn't say so till he tried.
So he buckled right in with the trace of a grin
Never doubting or thinking to quit it.
And he started to sing as he tackled that thing
That couldn't be done, and he did it!

We got started on the "hard part" by traveling to Three Rivers Stadium the next weekend, where we met the rested Steelers. Jim was still not healed from his sprained knee, and so Frank started once again. Once again, he had to apply his come-from-behind charisma. This time, however, we had fallen behind by only three points. The Steelers scored on Gary Anderson's first-quarter field goal to take a 3-0 lead.

Those were the only points they got all day, as our defense turned in its finest performance of the year. We held the Steelers to just 240 yards total offense, and we sacked their quarterback, Neil O'Donnell, seven times, including one where Bruce Smith forced a fumble that Phil Hansen recovered. That one set up our first touchdown, and it came with less that two minutes remaining before the end of the first half. We went to the locker room nursing a 7-3 lead.

Our defense kept up its mounting pressure, while on offense we played an atypical, close-to-the-vest-style that served our purpose well on that day. We didn't turn the ball over once, while forcing three takeaways from the Steelers. Our drives were long and time-consuming. Kenny, handling most of the ball carrying for a still hampered Thurman, picked up 107 yards rushing, while fullback Carwell Gardner added several tough-yardage carries including a put-the-game-away touchdown late in the fourth quarter. By the time the game was over, we had run the ball 39 times.

Frank threw only 26 passes in the game for a modest 160 yards, but two of them were for touchdowns and none of them was intercepted. It wasn't as exciting as it had been the week before, but I loved the result. We won 24-3.

After the game, the Steelers' fine coach, Bill Cowher, upon meeting me at midfield and extending his gracious congratulations, said, "Marv, I believe that this year you guys are the team of destiny."

They were kind words, and I longed for them to be true, but there was still a long and arduous road we'd have to navigate before finding out if they were.

For the third straight year we would be playing in the AFC championship. This one, however, wouldn't be at home like the two previous ones. This time we had to travel. Not only that, we would be making that trip to Miami in order to face the division champion Dolphins for the right to play in the Super Bowl.

♦♦♦♦♦♦♦♦

Jim was healthy and raring to go for this one. Cornelius was back in the lineup, and Thurman, too, was close to 100 percent recovered. Besides that, our defense was really playing well. Great performances by that unit and by our kicking teams had sustained us at a time when our offense had been riddled with injuries. Our defensive players had answered the challenge, and so had our defensive coaches. We had added Dan Sekanovich as our defensive line coach before the start of the 1992 season, and that resulted in a notably improved level of performance by the men in that front line of defense.

Ironically, Dan had been a member of the Dolphins' coaching staff the previous season and for several years prior to that. When I learned that his contract had expired, I moved quickly in my efforts to convince him to join us in Buffalo, knowing him from when he was a member of my Alouettes staff. Talk about a great sales job. I had just sold a man on moving himself and his family from Miami's sun-washed beaches to Buffalo's soot-laden snowdrifts. Is anyone in the market for a used car?

As we were going through the pregame warmup for our game against the Dolphins, however, I wondered if I had done Dan an injustice by having wrapped him up before Miami had had a chance to re-sign him. In each of the previous two years he had seen the Bills make that Super Bowl trip by nosing out his Dolphins. Now, in 1992, when he was no longer a member of their staff, it was Miami who was favored to eliminate us on their way to the Super Bowl. Was Dan destined to always be standing on the wrong sideline?

Even with the return of all our offensive weapons, our defense continued to assert its superiority. They held the Dan Marino-led Dolphins to 276 total yards (only 33 of them on the ground) during the game, much of it coming late in the contest after we had taken a 26-3 lead. Besides picking off two interceptions, our defenders also forced four Miami fumbles.

The Dolphins did a good job of taking away our quick-tempo, quick-strike long passing game, and Jim, calling his own plays in confidence-inspiring fashion, did a magnificent job of adjusting to those tactics. Against a "stop the deep pass"-oriented defense, he slowed things down and kept the ball on the ground. We ran 48 times, racking up 182 yards rushing. Thurman and Kenny collaborated for 157 of those yards on 39 carries. I believe that the mental fine-tuning required from our center Kent Hull in calling our line blocking schemes went beyond the capabilities of even Albert Einstein. Not only that, Dr. Einstein couldn't long snap as well as Kent could.

With our deep passing game throttled, Jim did not try to force it. He called running plays, and when passes were called for, he threw underneath their coverage, hitting our running backs and tight ends on 12 of 17 passes. A lot of drives, using this conservative approach, didn't get us into the Miami end zone, but they ate up the clock and did wonders for my blood pressure by keeping Marino off the field. Thurman scored one of our touchdowns in that game, and Kenny scored the other one, but what really kept us in command was knowing that when our drives stalled in Miami territory we could call upon Steve, "the best damn kicker in the whole damn league." Steve kicked five field goals, tying an NFL postseason record.

We won 29-10. The Bills (*and* Dan Sekanovich) were heading to Pasadena to play the Cowboys in Super Bowl XXVII.

There was one overriding reason, I felt, why we had been so successful on our three-game march through the playoffs. In every one of those games we had won the takeaway/giveaway battle. We had surrendered the ball on just three occasions while grabbing a combined total of 10 interceptions and forced fumbles from the other teams. If we could keep that up we would become Super Bowl champions.

That is exactly the way we started out. On the first series of the game, our defense kept the Cowboys from making a first down, and when they attempted to punt to us, guess who came roaring in to block that kick? If your answer was Steve Tasker, you are eligible to audition for an appearance on *Jeopardy*. A few plays later Thurman scored on a two-yard run, and we had jumped out to a 7-0 lead just five minutes into the game. And then we embarked on the worst case of self-destruction that I was to experience during my 47 years as a coach.

An interception in our territory by Dallas safety James Washington set up a Troy Aikman-to-Jay Novacek touchdown pass late in the first quarter. The score was tied. They kicked off to us, and *15 seconds later,* Dallas defender Charles Haley forced us to fumble. The Cowboys' Jimmie Jones picked it up on our two-yard line and scooted into the end zone. Two turnovers = two Dallas touchdowns = Dallas 14, Buffalo 7.

Matters got even worse in the second quarter. Not only did we keep losing possession of the ball, we also lost the services of Jim who, while suffering one of the four sacks they inflicted on us, was injured midway through period. He would not be able to return to the game. Late in that same quarter, after Steve Christie got us back on the scoreboard with a field goal, the Cowboys converted two more of our ball-possession miscues into touchdowns. At the half they had extended their lead to 28-10. By adding a field goal in the third period, they inched ahead even more, but on the last play of that quarter, Frank Reich connected with Don Beebe on a 40-yard touchdown pass. Entering the final period we were down 31-17, and despite all the blundering we had done, our comeback kids still had a fighting chance.

It wasn't that we couldn't move the ball, it was just that we kept shooting ourselves in the foot. During the game, we gained a respectable 362 yards, with sizeable contributions from both our running and passing attacks. Andre was the game's leading receiver with 152 yards on eight catches. Thurman and Kenny combined to gain 105 yards on the ground in 26 carries, but those numbers don't mean anything because during that 60 minutes of nightmarish football, we gave up four interceptions and five of eight fumbles.

If you think it was bad up until now, take an anxiety pill, and I'll tell you about the fourth quarter. In a span of two minutes and 33 seconds, Dallas, courtesy of the benevolent Bills, scored three more touchdowns. People who were able to count that fast relayed the information that the Cowboys were now yippee-yi-yo-ky-aying on a 52-17 ride toward the postgame awards platform. In the dying seconds of the game, we managed to bumble into committing one more turnover, and—do you know something?—this one was good for us. That's right!

The game was just about over, but we were going to play hard until the final gun sounded. We had a semblance of a drive going when Frank was sacked and lost possession of the ball. Dallas defensive lineman Leon Lett picked it up at the Cowboys' 36-yard line, and he took off, unmolested, toward our end zone. It looked like clear sailing for Lett as he dashed toward fulfillment of a lineman's fantasy. Way down at the Dallas five-yard line, Don Beebe, who had been running his deep route pass pattern, hesitated not an instant. He took off in pursuit.

To the sound of rousing cheers from the Dallas fans, Lett zipped past our five-yard line, and then with one hand, he thrust the ball high into the air in preparation for his triumphant entry into the promised land. One foot from the goal line stripe, Don, at the end of his own tormented 95-yard dash, swiped at the ball, knocking it out of Lett's grasp and out the back of the end zone. It was a touchback, giving us possession of the ball for the fleeting and meaningless few seconds that remained in the game.

Don's actions that day had absolutely no effect on the outcome of that game. With or without Lett's score, we still would have been routed. What Don had done in that moment when he took off in pursuit had not required a "decision." It was a reflection of his character, and in reacting without hesitation as he had, he was also saying to the world that this is how the character of this team—"not just me, but my teammates, also"—has allowed us to persist. And continue to persist we will!

We hadn't won the game, but maybe we won something even bigger than a football game. We would be back!

A few hours after the game, I was sitting next to Bill Polian as we rode the team bus back to our hotel. We had a brief conversation in which we reviewed the strategic planning we had addressed two weeks earlier as we had prepared for our trip to the Super Bowl. When we both realized that those sessions had really solved nothing, Bill and I retreated silently into our own thoughts. While we sat there listening to the hum of the bus's tires as we rolled along the L.A. freeway, Bill suddenly turned to me and spoke some words of simple wisdom.

"You know, Marv," he said, "the only thing that really counts is what you do once the ball is kicked off."

No wonder I like that guy so much.

There was another much more compelling issue involving Bill that was foremost in my mind, and just before returning to our respective rooms at our hotel, I said to him, "Bill, the first thing in the morning I am going to speak again to Ralph about you." He knew what I meant.

Way back before the 1992 season had begun, Bill and Ralph had gotten into an argument. Bill was an individual with a quick temper, and he would often become very animated when venting his emotions. Almost always, I learned, Bill's anger came while he was defending someone in our organization who was being criticized by someone else. I never did know the source of the disagreement that Bill had had with Ralph, but I did know that it was not the first time in talking with Ralph that he had given passionate expression to his feelings.

Ralph had reacted by telling Bill that because they apparently could not get along to their mutual satisfaction, he felt it was best to terminate Bill's employment with the Bills. After the initial shock he experienced upon hearing that news, Bill accepted Ralph's decision, and they entered discussions regarding the terms of the splitup. The season was just about to begin, however, and such an upheaval at that moment would have had adverse implications for everyone involved. Also, Bill's children had just started their school year, and uprooting them at that precise time would prove to be disruptive.

Ralph and Bill agreed that they would not make the termination effective until the end of the season. In the meantime, Bill would continue to function as general manager. They agreed that there would be no public disclosure of their agreement, although they did inform me about it with the proviso that I keep that information confidential.

At our hotel the morning after our loss to the Cowboys, I telephoned Ralph. When I asked if I might be able to speak with him, he told me to come on up to his room now. I walked down the hallway rehearsing how I would present the thoughts that had kept me awake much of the previous night. After exchanging some pleasantries, he asked me what was on my mind.

"I came to talk about Bill Polian," I said, and I could tell from the expression on Ralph's face that he wasn't surprised about my reason for having asked to see him. To the best of my oratorical ability I proceeded to extol all the qualities that Bill possessed. I reminded Ralph about

how knowledgeable and thorough Bill was. I pointed to his honesty and integrity, to the high level of morale that Bill had instilled at One Bills Drive, and to the respect he had earned from everyone in our organization and throughout the NFL. His sense of humor was infectious, I said, and his loyalty to us all—including his loyalty to Ralph—was unquestioned. I went on, highlighting many of Bill's other attributes, and Ralph listened carefully to all I had to say without interrupting me. When I finally finished speaking, Ralph did not seem to need any time to gather his thoughts before responding.

"Marv, I agree with everything you have had to say about Bill," he said, "but the two of us just do not get along. I am sorry if it disappoints you, but I am going forward with my decision to replace him."

I did regret that my intervention had not elicited the reaction that I so deeply desired, but, as always, I knew that from Ralph you were going to get a straight and honest expression of his feelings.

Bill's departure from the Bills was about to become a reality. I knew he would land on his feet, and so I need not have worried about my good friend's future.[1]

I wondered, however, what it would like for me. Bill would be the ultimate tough act to follow. Where could they possibly find anyone to replace him? Could there possibly be another person with whom I could work so cooperatively and who was so competent that he would earn my true personal and professional respect?

I'd find that out later, I guessed. In the meantime there were big challenges that were up to me to handle. As I dwelled on those thoughts during our flight back to Buffalo, something else dawned on me. Earlier that day, when I had gone in to plead with the team owner on behalf of another person in our organization, my own credentials showed that I had been the coach whose team just lost the Super Bowl *52-17!* I'm lucky that I wasn't the guy about to be shown to the door.

---

1. Bill went on to serve several years as the general manager of the then-expansion franchise Carolina Panthers and as general manager of the Indianapolis Colts. Both teams saw their fortunes soar under his stewardship, and I've lost count, already, of how many times he has been named as the recipient of the NFL's Executive of the Year award.

CHAPTER 33

The Dream Goes On

In early 1993, Bill Polian's departure from the Bills was but one of several administrative personnel changes that took place in our front office. Bob Ferguson ("Fergy" to everyone who knows him), the man responsible for scouting all players who were already playing pro football, was lured to Denver, where he became the Broncos' general manager. Ed Stillwell, our director of security and a good friend of Bill's, was so distressed over Bill's dismissal that he elected to move up his planned retirement. Another of Bill's close friends, Steve Champlin, our outstanding director of stadium operations, left also, knowing that he would be among the first that Bill would seek to hire upon taking over a job with another team.

And then I learned about another crucial vacancy that was about take place, and this one didn't bother me at all. John Butler would no longer be our director of scouting and player personnel. The reason I greeted that news with such relish was because John was the man whom Ralph Wilson, after reviewing a field of candidates, had decided to employ as our new general manager.

John had some big shoes to fill, and he would have been the first person to acknowledge that. At first, there were many who would question if he could measure up, but I wasn't one of them. I knew that Ralph had landed the best man available and that John's work over time (and overtime work, too!) would serve as proof of that. Doggone if I wasn't right once again.

John moved quickly to help reestablish continuity and continued the practices that had led us to Super Bowls. From his own staff of scouts, he elevated Dwight Adams to fill the position that John was vacating and he selected A.J. Smith to take over the responsibilities and the title of director of pro personnel.

The rising tide of player free agency also came washing through our ranks. When you have been a good team, one with several young, but proven, veterans, and one with good and recognized depth, it became impossible to keep that group together. The primary reason for that was because, in the just forged player/management agreement that had granted free agency to the players, it was also established that there would be a salary cap, which applied equally to every team in the NFL. This kept any one team from outspending all others in a manner that allowed that team to consistently enlist all the stars while the others all floundered in their vain efforts to stay in contention.

The process had caught up to us now. As players' contracts expired and came due for renewal, we could not pay them all what they could command on the market and still be able to come in under the newly instituted salary cap. If we paid the big bucks to Bruce Smith, Jim Kelly, Thurman Thomas, Andre Reed, Cornelius Bennett, Kent Hull, Jim Ritcher, and many others at key positions, we just would not be able to compete financially for players on our own roster whom other teams in the league, which did not have our salary cap constraints, were pursuing aggressively. What a dilemma!

After the 1992 season we had to wave painful goodbyes to talented and high character players such as linebacker Shane Conlan, defensive back Kirby Jackson, defensive lineman Mike Lodish, and starting offensive left tackle Will Wolford. It appeared as if time was finally catching up to James Lofton, also, and when we were unable to fit him in under our salary cap, we had to watch as the Eagles lured him away with a contract we couldn't match.

Fortunately, a solid draft from the year before afforded us some excellent replacements. Our first pick in that 1992 draft, offensive tackle John Fina, was exceptionally bright and athletic, and he was ready to step in as a starter replacing Will Wolford. He would be a fixture at the Bills' left tackle position for the next nine years. From that 1992 draft, we also received bolstering from defensive backs Kurt Schulz and Matt Darby, from linebacker Keith Goganious, tight end Nate Turner, and wide receiver/special teamer Chris Walsh. It was a good draft, and we had needed it.

Although we were not able to go after a lot of players in the free agent market, we were able to sign one new man, wide receiver Billy Brooks, who had been with the Colts. He was the perfect fit, helping us to fill the spot vacated when James Lofton left. In Billy we added a veteran player who was smart and talented. His leadership by example was another of his many attributes, and his contributions helped us continue to be among the best teams in the NFL.

It was now early September 1993. All that off-season activity was about to move off stage. It was opening day, and we kicked off to the Patriots. Let the games begin.

We beat the Patriots 38-14, and the week after that we enjoyed an even more meaningful victory, a 13-10 win over the Cowboys, the team that had embarrassed us in the Super Bowl eight months earlier. We did it in Dallas, too, and that added spice to the taste of vengeance we savored. I know that's not nice, but at least it's the truth.

Even with some unsettling changes in personnel on and off of the field, we were embarked again on another season of exciting and—more importantly—winning football. It wasn't perfect. We had a few down moments, too. Miami beat us in Orchard Park, bringing a quick halt to our season-opening two-game winning streak. (We got even late in the year, when we went down there and won 47-34 in another one of those Jim Kelly versus Dan Marino ping-pong acts.) In midseason, just about the time we thought no one could stop our no-huddle attack, Pittsburgh inflicted a 23-0 awakening on us. It was the first time the Bills had been shut out since 1985. Then on successive weekends late in November and early in December we lost first in Kansas City to the Chiefs 23-7 and then at home to the Raiders 25-24.

Sounds pretty bad, doesn't it? Four lousy losses! Cheer up, Bills fans. We won the other *12* regular-season games! We won our division. We had the best record in the AFC. We had home field all the way throughout the playoffs. And, get this! The three teams that had defeated us in the three previous Super Bowls had all been on our schedule, and we had beaten all three of them. Besides our 13-10 early-season win in Dallas, we downed the Giants 17-14, and then we trimmed the Redskins 24-10. Frankly, I would have preferred not having to seek revenge, but given the circumstances, it was pretty sweet anyway.

It was time for the playoffs to begin, and after a first-round bye, we played host to one of the teams that had taken our number during the regular season. The Raiders, 25-24 victors over us in Rich Stadium just six weeks earlier, were back in town.

Our earlier-season game against the Raiders had been a really tight one, and so was this rematch. The lead changed hands six times during that harrowing afternoon. You couldn't predict anything in this one except the January weather. The thermometer was at exactly zero degrees at kickoff, but the temperature cooled off a bit as the afternoon wore on. The mercury may have fallen, but the tension and the excitement rose with every snap of the ball. Midway into the second quarter we took a 6-3 lead, but running back Napoleon McCallum capped off two offensive thrusts by the Raiders with short touchdown runs, and we trailed 17-6 with just a minute left to play in the first half.

That was when I heard Jim say to his teammates on the sidelines, "If we don't get our butts in gear, we aren't going to win this damn game."

Then he went back out onto the field and took just four plays to spearhead a 76-yard touchdown drive that concluded with Thurman scoring on an eight-yard run a few seconds before time expired. At half-time, we trailed 17-13.

We began the second half with another long march, and this one, too, ended with a touchdown when Jim connected on a 25-yard completion to Billy Brooks. We had moved in front 19-17, but when our ensuing PAT attempt was blocked, my irate screams could be heard even above the din from the crowd. Throughout the second half our defense managed, with the exception of one play, to shut down the Raiders' attack, and when Steve Christie kicked a field goal with less than a minute remaining in the third quarter, we bumped our precarious lead up to 22-17.

In the entire second half our defenders surrendered, just one first down to the Raiders, but what a first down that was! When we kicked off after Steve's successful field goal attempt, on the first play from scrimmage, from their 14-yard line, Raiders quarterback Jeff Hostetler hit wide receiver Tim Brown on an 86-yard touchdown pass. *That* was their one first down. So much for our lead. They, too, missed the extra point, but going into the fourth quarter we trailed 23-22.

Once again our Hall of Fame-bound quarterback rose to the occasion. Nine plays and 71 yards later, we scored, for the second time that day, on a Jim-to-Billy aerial. This one covered 22 yards. We even made the PAT. Then our defense continued their stingy ways, shutting the Raiders down. We clung to our hard-earned lead, and we won 29-23. We kept doing it the hard way, but—*we kept doing it!*

For the fourth year in a row (five out of the last six) we'd be playing for the AFC Championship. To get there we had beaten the Raiders, a team that had defeated us during the regular season. Now we'd have to face another opponent who had beaten us. Not only that, it would be against a team that somewhere in the deep distant—but not forgotten—past had fired me. It would be the Chiefs versus the Bills. It would be outdoors at Rich Stadium in the middle of January. It would be for the right to go to the Super Bowl. Where else would you rather be?!?

Although there was a mixture of drizzle and snow falling when the Bills and Chiefs took the field, the air temperature stood at a torrid 29 degrees at kickoff. Our defense, which had played so well the week before, would have to face an offense led by Chiefs stars such as Marcus Allen and Joe Montana. We appeared to be meeting that challenge, and at the end of the third quarter we were clinging to a tenuous 20-13 lead.

One week earlier it had been our passing attack that had won it in the clutch, but that was then, and this was now. In this game, Jim had a modest 160 yards throwing the ball, but there were no interceptions and no sacks. With a one-touchdown lead, we did what we were doing best all that afternoon. We ran the ball. And then we ran the ball. And then—(you get the idea). We had 46 rushing plays in that game for a total of 229 yards on the ground. Thurman had 33 carries for 186 yards. (The week before against the Raiders, Thurman had had to leave the game because of a concussion, and there had been some doubt up until midweek whether he would get clearance to play. After he turned in this performance, I inquired of our team doctors whether it would be okay to give Thurman a good ding on the noggin as part of his warmup for every game. The doctor said he'd get back to me on that one, but I never heard back from him.)

A time-consuming, 79-yard fourth-quarter drive set up a field goal. That made it 23-13 and gave us a little additional breathing space. Then we ground it out some more with Thurman and Kenneth Davis boring the television audience while delighting me as they chewed up the clock and the yards before Thurman punched in a touchdown from one yard out. Our valiant defenders had kept us in control throughout the game by limiting the Raiders to just 52 yards rushing while sacking their quarterbacks four times and picking off a couple of interceptions. We were in complete charge now 30-13, and that's the way it finished.

It had been a monumental struggle, but we had persisted, against almost insurmountable odds, in our quest for that Super Bowl title that had so tantalizingly eluded us. We were going back. For the fourth year in a row! Can you believe it?

♦♦♦♦♦♦♦♦

Super Bowl XVIII was played at the Georgia Dome in Atlanta, and, just as it had been the year before in Super Bowl XXVII, it was the Bills versus the Cowboys. Early in the first quarter, Dallas placekicker Eddie Murray booted a 41-yard field goal. We retaliated on our next possession, and when Steve Christie made one from 54 yards out (a Super Bowl record) we were tied 3-3. The field goal battle continued as Murray connected on another one later in the firstt. It was now 6-3. Undaunted, we then put together a

17-play drive that covered 80 yards and took us almost seven minutes to complete. We finally got to our destination when Thurman scored on a four-yard run early in the second quarter, and we inched ahead 10-6.

With less than a minute remaining until halftime, Nate Odomes picked off a Troy Aikman pass—our only takeaway of the day. Nate's interception set the stage, a few seconds later, for Steve's second field goal. We began the third quarter with a 13-6 lead, but less than one minute into that period, we were struck by the same plague that had destroyed our Super Bowl hopes one year earlier. In what I believe was the most demoralizing moment of his great career, Thurman, on a carry into the line, was stripped of the ball at our 46-yard line. Dallas safety James Washington picked it up and brought it back for the touchdown that tied the game 13-13.

Then, all the clichés that coaches utter and that inspire rolled eyes by fans and media made their truths known. "Run and stop the run." "You gotta win the turnover battle." "Defense wins games." "The team that throws the most wins the least." "Control the clock by knowing when to slow up," and "____________________," (I'll let you avid football fans fill in the blanks).

After tying the game, Dallas was able to execute all of those "simple, but not easy" precepts. Despite our efforts to do the same, we did not match them. They stopped our running attack and forced us, particularly later in the game, to go almost exclusively to the air in our vain attempts to play catch-up. We wound up throwing the ball 50 times and for more passing yardage than they did, but so what? They kept us to under 100 yards on the ground, while their great running back, Emmitt Smith, on his way to becoming the game's MVP, gained 132 yards on 30 carries. And when it came to the takeaway/giveaway ratio, we didn't get the job done. We had Nate's interception late in the first half, and it had led to a three-pointer for us, but as I pointed out, that was the only time we separated them from the ball. Dallas forced three turnovers in the game, including that huge pendulum-swinger at the beginning of the second half.

Emmitt's performance in that game included a 15-yard go-ahead touchdown jaunt toward the end of the third quarter and a put-the-game-away one-yard score in the fourth. His second touchdown upped their lead to 27-13, and then Murray added another field goal near the end of the game. The final score was Dallas 30, Buffalo 13.

You don't get used to losing. You don't just accept it. This loss hurt as badly as any of the others. We would go through that period of mourning. We would own up. We would recognize the good. We would make a plan. And we would go back to work just as hard and with as much dedication as we always had.

We would never surrender.

CHAPTER 34

Never Give In. Never Give In. Never! Never! Never!

—Winston Churchill

During the next four years our teams would continue to compete as doggedly as we had during the four Super Bowl years we had just finished. Our goal remained the same, and so did the effort put forth by everyone within the Bills organization. What was different now, however, was the swiftness with which free agency and, in some instances, the advancing age of our star players, was taking its toll on our ability to sustain the consistency of play that had been a trademark of our teams.

After the 1993 season, our two starting cornerbacks, Nate Odomes and James Williams, departed via free agency. Also, time seemed to be running out on free safety Mark Kelso, and because of salary cap restraints we had to let him go. He was one of the many quiet guys on a team where others got the headlines, but without whom we could not have won those repeated AFC titles. There were so many of them. I wish I could name them all now, but if I tried I'm sure I'd miss several. My gratitude to those "unknown soldiers" of the gridiron is greater by far than my ability to express it.

Our draft from the previous year had given us some good defensive backs such as Kurt Schulz and Matt Darby, and now, in the 1994 draft, we used our first-round pick to select Jeff Burris, a Notre Dame defensive back. Not only did Jeff play the position well, but he provided us with an excellent kick return threat. Linebackers Sam Rogers (second round) and Marlo Perry (third round) were two others in that 1994 draft who would eventually make solid contributions to the Bills.

What an awakening that 1994 season was. Our fans had come to believe that winning was automatic, and when we started out with victories in three of our first four games, they must have thought it would be more of the same. Then we suffered our second loss of the season. Then we won one. Then we lost one. Then we won one more. Then we lost *two!* "What in the devil is going on around here?!?" those fans wanted to know. Then we won again by defeating the Packers 29-20 on a day when Andre Reed set a team record by catching 15 passes for 191 yards. We followed that with a (you guessed it) loss, before continuing the roller coaster ride by beating Miami on the road 42-31 (Now that looks more like the Buffalo Bills I used to know). With just three games remaining, our record stood at a rather mediocre 7-6. We were in danger of not making the playoffs for the first time in seven years.

In those last three weekends, we erased all doubts about our playoff worthiness. We lost them all. In the final game of the season, we fell to the Colts 10-9. Not only were we out of the playoffs, but we had finished with a losing 7-9 record. I could begin my brief off-season vacation much earlier that I had in many years, and I *hated* that.

At our wrap-it-up press conference, one of the writers from *The Buffalo News,* who had been extremely critical of many of my coaching decisions and of me personally, asked me if I had given any thought, now that we had blundered through an embarrassing losing season, to retiring so that "someone younger with fresh ideas and enthusiasm" could come in and revitalize the team's sagging fortunes. I glared for a moment at that out-of-shape scribe, waved away the haze of smoke from his cigarette, and then told him that I intended to keep on coaching the Bills. I emphasized my resolve by reciting some spontaneously composed verse that earned for me the title of "Poet Laureate of the Locker Room." I prefaced those lines by telling him that, although my 70th birthday was approaching:

I can still out-run ya;
I can still out-fun ya;
I can still out-fight ya;
And I can even out-write ya!

♦♦♦♦♦♦♦♦

"If you don't change with the times, the times are going to change you," was a snippet of knowledge that I frequently bestowed upon my coaching staff, and it was time for me to heed my own advice. The personnel changes had become more swift and more disruptive than at any time in NFL history. How to cope with that upheaval and formulate a strategy for dealing with how to put together your roster consumed the attention (and the energies) of Ralph Wilson, John Butler, director of finance Jeff Littman, and me.

In taking the steps we had needed to take in order to retain the services of many star players whose contracts were up for renewal (and of some of the budding young standout prospects we had determined to keep aboard), we had to make numerous sacrifices. The player departures that had occurred after the 1993 season had hurt, but it was after the 1994 season that we really began to get bludgeoned. Compounding all the free agent/salary cap implications were the additions of two expansion teams, the Jacksonville Jaguars and the Carolina Panthers. They were to begin play in 1995, and so, immediately upon the conclusion of the 1994 season, they were fully involved in acquiring player personnel. Because they had no players under contract, they could enter the competition with more salary cap room available to them than Bill Gates and Aristotle Onassis combined.

The Panthers moved quickly by jumping at the opportunity to hire Bill Polian as their general manager, and in true panther fashion, Bill was ready to pounce, too. Before anyone was able to yell, "Look out!" Carolina signed wide receiver Don Beebe, tight end Pete Metzelaars, and quarterback Frank Reich. We took a blow at running back, too, because age had finally brought an end to Kenneth Davis's playing days. On defense we lost two of our finest veteran starters, also, when the intricacies of contract structuring made it impossible to retain linebacker Darryl Talley or nose tackle Jeff Wright.

Strained by salary cap restrictions, we had to venture cautiously into the market for experienced players. Other than one signing, we had no other notable free agent additions to our team following our disappointing record in 1994. All indications were that things would get even worse in 1995. Wait a minute here. We are talking about the ever-resilient Bills, aren't we?

That one free agent acquisition was another John Butler coup. Outside linebacker Bryce Paup of the Packers was the one player we had in our sights, and John signed him. I was really learning to love Green Bay, because once again, a former Packers player, just like James Lofton and Kenneth Davis, came rumbling into Buffalo and made us a far better team. Winter weather must really have been invigorating for those fellows. In his first year with us, Bryce, a blitzing linebacker extraordinaire, led the league with 17 1/2 sacks. Twice he was selected as the AFC Player of the Week, and he was an overwhelming Pro Bowl choice.

With so many players now departing Buffalo because we could not afford to keep them, we were beginning to see a swifter turnover of personnel from year to year. This also meant that more of our draftees would have opportunities to fill those newly created openings on our roster. We had 11 choices available to us in the 1995 draft, and *10* of those men made it through the final cutdown. Unprecedented!

Ruben Brown, an offensive guard, was our first choice, and he developed swiftly into a perennial Pro Bowler. Two fine defensive cornerbacks, Marlon Kerner and Kenny Irvin, joined recent-year high draft choices Jeff Burris and Thomas Smith to help us relieve the devastation from our losses of Kirby Jackson, Nate Odomes, and James Williams during the two previous off-season raids on our defense. We picked up two linebackers, Damien Covington (third round) and John Holecek (fifth round), both of whom exhibited surprisingly strong early indications of becoming excellent NFL players. There were others in that draft class who helped to make it the most deeply talented that I had the good fortune to acquire during my days in Buffalo.

We also signed a young graduating collegian out of Canada named Tim Tindale. Tim, a running back, had been the recipient of the Canadian version of the Heisman Trophy, and there has never been anyone who possessed more grit and toughness than that young man. He was an excellent short-yardage ball carrier, and he became a kick coverer in the mold of Steve Tasker and Mark Pike. He quickly won the respect and admiration of all his teammates.

It was time to find out if we would continue to fade away, or if there was any substance to all that talk about how resilient we were going to be. On opening day in Denver, the Broncos whipped us 22-7, and there were a lot of the Bills fans and media already bemoaning our demise. If there was a large contingent of people in Buffalo who believed that was true, the Bills players and coaches were not among them. We began immediately to answer any "put up or shut up" doubts that existed. We did that by winning our next five games in a row.

We still had challenges ahead, but first I had to come face to face with an opponent tougher than any I had ever met during my 45 years of coaching on the football field. A few days before training camp, I received a telephone call from our team internist, Joseph Armenia. He told me that he had some concern about the score of my PSA test that had been administered as part of my yearly physical. When I told Dr. Armenia that I didn't know the PSA from the college board SAT exams, he explained that the PSA was a procedure used to detect prostate cancer. He suggested that I have a biopsy to determine whether there actually was cancer present. The biopsy verified that there was.

I was stunned. I felt great. There had been no symptoms. I had always thought that cancer was something that happened to *other* people. How serious was it? How far had it advanced? Was it life-threatening? I had decisions to make. Training camp was just about to begin. Could there possibly be some way to delay treatment until the season was over? Since I had begun coaching back at St. Louis Country Day School 45 years earlier, I had never missed a single day of work. I didn't want to now, either.

The several options for treatment were explained to me, and I decided to rely on surgery because that was the one way, I was advised, to find out with certainty if the cancer was confined to the prostate gland or whether it had spread. I asked Dr. Robert Huben of the Roswell Park Cancer Institute in Buffalo, who would be performing my surgery, if it was feasible for me to wait until after the season before going forward with the operation. He told me that although there just was a small risk in delaying, it was not a "no risk" situation.

Other than my family, I informed only John Butler about the news, and I allowed a month to pass while I was at training camp before I told Ralph. I explained to him that Dr. Huben had advised me about the "small risk, but not no risk" considerations, and that I was willing to go through the season before having the planned surgery.

Ralph got out of his chair, walked over to me, stuck a forefinger into my chest, and said, "You're not waiting. Make the arrangements to have it taken care of as soon as possible." When he detected a trace of hesitancy on my part, he added, "That's an order."

The surgery was scheduled to take place on the Tuesday after our sixth game, and on that Monday, after informing our players at our team meeting and the members of the media later that day about my condition, I checked in at the hospital. I told them all that Elijah Pitts, our assistant head coach, would be in charge until I returned. I had asked Dr. Huben how long it would be before I might be able to resume my coaching duties, and he told me that, if all went well, the usual time required was about six to eight weeks. He did mention that he had one previous patient who had made it back to work after just four weeks. I told the doctor that I was going to try to break the record.

My surgery, thanks to that magnificent Dr. Huben and all the people at the Roswell Park Cancer Institute, was successful, and I was blessed to learn that the cancer had not spread. News such as that is not something anyone should ever take as routine. That was driven home to me in tragic fashion, just a day or two later. I was still in the hospital at the start of my recuperation process. I was walking, as instructed,

up and down the hallways, and while feeling uplifted by the sense of recovery that I was already experiencing, I was stopped for a moment by a melancholy, relatively young man standing outside the room next to mine. He had recognized me, and he told me that, like every other person in Buffalo, he and all his family were Bills fans.

After we had conversed for a short while, I asked him if he was visiting someone there, and he informed me that his wife was a patient in the room outside of which he was standing. When I inquired about how she was doing, his answer stunned me.

"She's not going to make it," he said, and I could hear the tears in his voice. That is when I returned to my room, where I found myself also unable to keep from crying.

Two days later, I was able to return home, where I embarked on as vigorous a rehab program as my body could tolerate. At first, that wasn't very much, and although I acknowledge that some pain and discomfort attended such efforts, I am convinced that one of the greatest agents in a person's growing old is their unwillingness after a debilitating injury or illness to battle back. By not doing so they increase the devastating effects wrought by any recent attack on their health.

More painful for me by far than the exercises I had undertaken was having to sit at home knowing that the season was flying along without me. When I had gone into the hospital, we had just come off of a five-game winning streak, but four of those games had been played at Rich Stadium. Now the team had to go on the road for the next three weekends. And here I was, sitting home in my pajamas and watching those games on television. If you think that was tough on me, think about poor Frannie who had to listen to my screamed advice on every play. I even tried to coach the characters who appeared in the commercials.

I sat there at home and watched as our winning ways came to an abrupt halt with consecutive losses, one in New England and another in Miami. Those really hurt because they were both division foes, and that had unfavorable implications for our playoff hopes. Add to that an injury to Andre that would plague him all season long, and our prospects dimmed still more. But to the rescue came Billy Brooks, who stepped into the lineup and contributed three 100-plus-yard receiving performances. It turned out to be quite a year for Billy. By season's end he had scored 11 touchdowns on pass receptions. That is still a Bills single-season record.

For the third week I had to watch the Bills on television, and for the third week they had to play the game out of town against a division opponent, the Colts. We managed to eke out a 16-10 win, but I couldn't stand it any longer. On Monday, I reported back to work after three weeks' recovery. I guess I broke the previous record of four weeks.

There is no feeling quite as good as "normal." How exciting it was to be back at work as we began preparations to host the Falcons. On that coming Sunday I would once again be able to walk up that tunnel and out into packed and boisterous Rich Stadium. The emotion I experienced the most on that day was gratitude toward all of those people who had made it possible for me to do again what I so loved and enjoyed. I was a fortunate man, indeed, and I must never forget it.

I was back, but Andre Reed and Thurman Thomas were both on the shelf for this game. Football is too tough a game to expect that you can avoid injuries, and so I had often told our players and coaches that, while it is desirable to remain injury-free, it is more realistic to realize that *overcoming* injuries is what you must truly be able to do. With Thurman and Andre on the sidelines there were others who showed up that day. Billy grabbed seven of Jim Kelly's throws for 101 yards, and rookie running back Darick Holmes, our last choice in the draft, gained 100 yards rushing on 23 carries while subbing for Thurman. We won 23-17.

We battled our way through the season, and by the next to last weekend, our record stood at 9-5. Tied with us in our division were the Dolphins, who had beaten us when we had met earlier in the season. Now they were coming to Orchard Park, and the convoluted formula used to determine playoff structure dictated that the winner of this game would capture the AFC East Division title. This time it wasn't our passing game that took center stage. We wanted to run the clock and keep the ball out of the hands of Dan Marino. When you want to run the clock, you've got to run the ball. We did. Thurman carried it 35 times for 148 yards, and it was just enough to allow us to emerge with a 23-20 victory. The Bills were back on top.

Miami won its final game of the season the following weekend, and in doing that, the Dolphins earned the final wild-card spot in the playoffs. Because our division-winning record was not as good as those of the other AFC division winners, we did not get a first-round bye; we would play the wild-card team. For the second time in three weeks it would be the Bills versus the Dolphins in Orchard Park.

If you think we ran the ball a lot in our late-season win against Miami, you should have been there on December 30, 1995. We had planned to run, but then when Andre had to exit early in the game, we became committed even more to calling on our infantry. We ran it 52 times for 341 yards (an AFC postseason record). Thurman had 25 carries for 158 yards. It was the sixth time in his career that he had surpassed the 100-yard rushing mark in the playoffs. Rookie running back Darick Holmes added 87 yards on 15 carries.

We dominated the game from the beginning and went to the locker room at halftime with a 24-0 lead. Because of Andre's injury, special teams ace Steve Tasker got to see some action at wide receiver, and as he always does, he sparkled. By halftime, Steve had five catches for 108 yards, including a 37-yard touchdown. No wonder Jim was always bugging me to play Steve as a wideout. I just couldn't allow the best-ever kicking teams player to forfeit his main role. Steve didn't get any more catches in the second half, because all we did was run the ball. Even Steve's kicking teams cohort, Tim Tindale, got into the act. He rushed the ball four times for 68 yards, including a 41-yard touchdown romp in the fourth quarter. After Tim's score we led 37-14.

With just two minutes left in the game, Miami scored a touchdown and added a two-point conversion to close out the day's fireworks. We had won 37-22. It had been the ninth consecutive home win in the playoffs since I had come to coach the Bills. So much for looking back on history. Now it was time to look forward to traveling to Three Rivers Stadium to face the Steelers in the second round of the playoffs.

You don't always just breeze through the playoffs. If I had had any doubts about that (which I didn't), they would have been dispelled when I received a call late on the Friday night before our scheduled departure for Pittsburgh. It was from Dr. Armenia. I liked and respected Dr. Armenia, but I did not like receiving a call from him the night before a team trip. I was pretty sure he wasn't calling to tell me that he thought we ought to use our zone blitz package against the Steelers in long-yardage situations. I wish I had been wrong, but I wasn't.

"Marv, I'm calling to let you know that Bruce Smith has a severe case of the flu," he stated.

"Will we have to limit in any way the number of reps he gets in the game?" I asked hopefully.

"He's got a 104-degree temperature," the doctor said.

"Do you think it might let up a little bit by the second half?" I tried again, but I knew where this was heading.

"He's definitely out of the game," Dr. Armenia told me. "He'll be all right in five or six days, but he needs to stay in bed, and he needs close medical supervision."

If you think Bruce wasn't feeling well, wait until I tell you how sick I was upon receiving that news.

This was another game in which a devastating running attack was the instrument employed in gaining the ultimate victory. The problem, however, was that it was the other team doing all that running. With Bruce not able to play, we had lost a great player, and we suffered by having to take the field with a thinned-out number of defensive linemen. The Steelers ran the ball 43 times for 147 yards, and they kept our battered front-line defenders on the field for more than 38 minutes. Even though early in the fourth quarter our valiant never-say-die Bills rallied from a 26-7 deficit by closing the margin to 26-21, our exhausted defense was unable to stop the Steelers when they renewed their ground assault. They answered our "we're-back-in-the-game-now" touchdown by marching 76 yards in nine plays while ticking six precious minutes off of the game clock. That score widened their lead to 33-21 with about four minutes remaining to be played, and when we turned the ball over on our 23-yard line on the next possession, they proceeded to grind away for another touchdown. The game ended, and the Steelers won 40-21.

This time it was my turn to congratulate Pittsburgh's coach, Bill Cowher, and to wish him luck the following weekend when they would be playing for the AFC championship. They did go on to win. The Steelers ended up heading to the Super Bowl. We were heading home.

There came to me one contemplative moment early in the summer of 1996, while musing through our media guide, when I became sharply aware of how drastically the makeup of our roster had changed as the years were now were flying by. The ever-tightening constraints of free agency had made it impossible once again to "keep them all." With heavy hearts we watched as Cornelius Bennett moved on, enticed by a lucrative contract offer from the Falcons that we could not match. Of the players who had been with us when we won our first division championship on "the day they tore the goalposts down"[1] back in 1988, only seven still wore our uniform: Kent Hull, Jim Kelly, Mark Pike, Andre Reed, Bruce Smith, Steve Tasker, and Thurman Thomas.

There had been others who would come and then go, sometimes because of the free agency complications and sometimes because their skills had finally succumbed to the advancing years. After the 1995 season, we could not come up with the type of contract Billy Brooks mer-

1. Again, for those too young to remember and for those steeped in nostalgia, this was a poignant line from the song presented so captivatingly during the 1960s by a popular quartet called The Four Freshmen. The title of that composition was "We Will Have These Moments to Remember."

ited, but there were other teams whose salary cap constraints allowed them to spirit him away. We also saw the end of playing days arrive for our outstanding long snapper, Adam Lingner. You rarely hear much about those guys until they foul up. That is exactly why you never heard much about Adam. He never fouled up. Upon his retirement, the Bills' marketing director hired Adam immediately, and he went to work for the team in that new capacity. He never fouled up there, either.

As I have already noted, our player losses were often offset by the addition of new blood, and in preparing for the 1996 season, we made some acquisitions that were vital in helping us to retain the style, the effort, the attitude, and the character that had become so emblematic of the Bills. At wide receiver, we brought in Quinn Early, formerly of the Chargers, and he stepped right in to fill the void that had been created as a result of Billy Brooks's departure. A year earlier, upon losing linebacker Darryl Talley, we had signed Bryce Paup, and now as Cornelius was leaving for Atlanta, we were able to sign another highly regarded linebacker from the NFC Central Division. This one wasn't even from Green Bay. This time it was Chris Spielman from the Lions.

Where did John Butler and A.J. Smith keep coming up with these guys? I truly doubt if there has ever been anyone who played in the NFL with a work ethic that could equal Chris Spielman's. It was so intense that it even got me angry. No matter how early I might show up at the stadium, Chris was already there, either working in the weight room or watching opponents' game tapes. Not only that—and this part *did not* get me angry—the guy could really tackle!

In 1995 we had shown that our team could fight its way back and win the division crown after having failed the year before to even make the playoffs for the first time in seven seasons. We had posted a 10-6 record, and that was a mark that we would repeat again in 1996. That was sufficient to gain us a playoff berth, but it wasn't good enough to allow us to repeat as division champions. The Patriots, with an 11-5 record, claimed that distinction.

One of the Patriots' five losses occurred in our home stadium early in the season. It was—as I just wrote—"early" in the season, and it also was "Early" (Quinn, that is) who made it happen. Late in the fourth quarter, with the score tied 10-10, we were backed up deep in our territory. Our plight was even worse than that because we faced a third-and-17 situation. It was highly likely that the Patriots would be in a deep zone defense, one that would help them take away the long pass and limit any thrown underneath to a modest gain. Then it would be fourth down, and we'd have to punt.

Jim called for a screen pass, and as we lined up and he began to yell out his cadence, we could see a horde of New England players creeping up closer and closer to the line of scrimmage. It was apparent that they were about to execute an all-out blitz, and that was exactly what we didn't want to see given our play selection. While our linemen would be running toward the sidelines to set up that screen of blockers for the man who would catch the ball, leaving Jim almost completely unprotected, an assigned Patriots player would be shadowing Thurman, our intended receiver, and be standing right there with him when the ball was released. A screen pass was designed for use against zone defenses, not against man-to-man coverages, and most of all, *not* against a blitz. We saw an impending interception or possible sack/fumble/New England touchdown in the making. So did Jim and wide receiver Quinn Early.

When the ball was snapped, Quinn did not sprint deep along the sidelines as he was supposed to do on screen passes. Instead, he took two quick steps forward, and then he broke with surprising nimbleness on a route toward the middle of the field, which had been denuded of defenders when all the blitzing Patriots secondary players came pouring in. Jim read Quinn's adjusted pattern, and he unloaded the ball to him at once. Quinn then snatched it out of the air and raced almost 80 yards for the game-winning touchdown. The maneuver they had executed is called *sight adjustment,* and it is one that teams practice to cope with blitzes, but it is seldom performed as smoothly as Jim and Quinn did when we defeated the Patriots 17-10.

There were other highs and there were lows, also, just like every football season. Naturally, I prefer remembering the more pleasant events, and one of those took place at the Meadowlands when we played the Jets. The Jets scored three touchdowns in that game (one of them they followed by adding a two-point conversion), while we were able to get into the end zone only once. Funny thing is—*we* won the game. Wait a minute here! Are you beginning to question your mathematical skills? Or—worse yet—*mine?* Please relax. There is an explanation. We won the game 25-22, and, in addition to the one touchdown that we registered, Steve Christie kicked six field goals. You probably suspect it already, but that is a Bills single-game record.

In our happy locker room after the game, to the accompaniment of "Hooray for Steve," he was awarded the game ball. I stopped by to congratulate him, but not wanting him to get too big a head, I reminded Steve that in the 52-17 loss to the Cowboys in the Super Bowl a few years earlier, we would have won 53-52 if he had just kicked 12 more field goals. That brought him back down to earth.

Later in the season, when we played the Jets again, this time back in Buffalo, we won more convincingly. The final score was 35-10, but what is noteworthy about that day's triumph is that once again, because of injuries to our starters, Steve Tasker was called upon to play wide receiver. He contributed six catches for 160 yards in helping us to notch that win. It was the most yardage gained in a single game by any of our receivers during that entire season. Jim was knocking on my office door again early the next morning, but he should have known that I still wasn't going to take Steve off of those kicking teams in order to do something so pedestrian as catching touchdown passes.

It wasn't all forward passing for us, remember. Proof of that was illustrated by our midseason 38-13 trouncing of the Redskins. In that one, Thurman rushed 23 times for 107 yards, and his relief man, Darick Holmes, piled up another 127 yards on 22 carries.

So far, all I've reminisced about have been the games that had happy endings. We had our share of losses and disappointments, too. That is why it was New England rather than Buffalo who came away with the division title. In our second game of the season against the Patriots—this one played in Foxboro—we dropped a keenly contested 28-25 decision to them. Had we won that game, we would also have beaten them out for the division championship. But we didn't.

Injuries always take a toll, but one of the most unsettling injury situations I had to deal with continued to visit us throughout most of the 1996 season. Despite a variety of recurring bumps, bruises, sprains, strains, headaches, and assorted other Tylenol-devouring ailments, Jim Kelly, the toughest SOB to ever take a snap from center, kept trying to function. There were some games when he did not get medical clearance to play, and there were others when he limped out onto the field and gave it his best before limping, even more pronouncedly, into the training room after the game was over. Despite it all, he played pretty darn well, but often we would not know until well into the week whether Jim could play. In some instances, Todd Collins, whom we had drafted in the second round out of the University of Michigan just one year earlier, would have to replace Jim while the game was in progress because of Jim's physical inability to continue.

The only benefit that could be derived from all that uncertainty was found in the opportunity it provided for Todd, Jim's heir apparent at quarterback, to gain some valuable game preparation and game action. Todd responded well. In one early-season start at home, he threw for 309 yards and the winning touchdown in leading us to a 16-13 win over the Colts. Late in the year, we played the Colts again, in Indianapolis. In this game, Todd and Quinn hooked up on a 95-yard touchdown pass, the longest ever by a Bills duo. That was the only touchdown we scored all day, and we lost the game in overtime 13-10.

With Jim hurting badly, we found ourselves struggling to stay in the playoff hunt. On the final Sunday of the season, we came home after having experienced a gut-wrenching 16-14 Monday night loss in Miami, when Steve Christie's last-second 48-yard field goal attempt struck the right upright and then bounced back onto the field. We would now have to meet the Chiefs, and we had to win that game in order to qualify for the playoffs. Jim was still sore, but he played anyway. And we won 20-9. For the eighth time in the last nine years we would be still in the fight as the playoffs were about to begin. We were a wild-card team with the best wild-card record, and so we would be hosting the Jaguars.

♦♦♦♦♦♦♦♦

Do you like exciting football? If your answer was in the affirmative, you should have been at Rich Stadium in December 1996 when the Bills and the Jaguars squared off in the first round of the playoffs. If you are a Bills fan and you enjoy the games *only* when your team comes out on top, then maybe you would have been better off attending a lecture on medieval rug weaving. At least you would have stayed warm.

Early in the first quarter, Thurman scored on a touchdown pass from Jim. It was Thurman's 19th touchdown in postseason play, and it established a new NFL playoffs record. We led 7-0. They intercepted a pass and returned it for a touchdown. It was 7-7. We capped off a 10-play, 68-yard drive when Thurman (him again?) barged in from two yards out. We were back on top 14-7. Jacksonville's Mike Hollis then kicked a field goal. It's now 14-10—and we were still in the first quarter!

Things then slowed down a little, until late in the second stanza when Jaguars running back Natrone Means gave them their first lead of the day by racing 30 yards for a touchdown. The scoreboard: Jacksonville 17, Buffalo 14. Steve Christie answered with a 33-yard field goal two minutes later. It was now halftime, and the count read 17-17.

Third quarter. Steve. Field goal. Buffalo 20-17. Still third quarter. Mike Hollis. Field goal. Tied 20-20. The ball changed hands a few times, but now, early in the fourth quarter, Jacksonville was on the march when our linebacker, David White, deflected a pass attempt by Jacksonville quarterback Mark Brunell. Cornerback Jeff Burris gathered it in and sprinted the length of the field to the delight of more than 70,000 Bills fans (not to mention a handful of coaches, as well). We took the lead again 27-20.

But it was not meant to be. Jacksonville retaliated with a 10-play, 65-yard drive that culminated with a two-yard Brunell-to-Jimmy Smith touchdown toss. It's tied again 27-27. Now we were moving the ball, and we got as far as the Jaguars' 42-yard line, where we lost the second of the two fumbles we committed during the game. The Jags moved into our territory, and Hollis's 45-yard field goal attempt in the dying minutes of the game (and, I might add, in the dying moments of our season) smacked into the right upright and then it bounced on through. They took the lead 30-27, and when we were unable to muster any last-second desperate heroics, that was the way it ended. After nine consecutive playoff victories at home, covering a period of nine years, our fans finally filed quietly out of Rich Stadium. Our season was over, and so was theirs.

In the season's aftermath there would be other sad moments for this proud team and this proud city. I knew it was coming, but that didn't lessen the emotional jolts I suffered when two of Buffalo's most beloved players *and citizens* announced their retirements. The two men most responsible, ever since the beginning of that decade, for having successfully steered our seemingly helter-skelter no-huddle express toward opponents' end zones, felt that the time had arrived for them to bid adieu. Center and team co-captain Kent Hull would no longer be snapping the ball to his quarterback, and neither would his quarterback and team co-captain, Jim Kelly, be there to take it. Never again will there be another center/quarterback combination to equal that one. I am so lucky, so blessed, to have been their coach.

Jim and Kent would not be with us when we kicked off to begin the 1997 season, and neither would seven-year starter Glenn Parker, one of those underappreciated offensive linemen who do so much and about whom you hear so little. We had seen many good men depart, but we had seen others join us, and I knew that they would continue to fight with the same unswerving dedication as had been displayed by those whom they were replacing. We weren't as deep as we had been; we weren't as experienced, either, and we probably weren't as talented. But despite all obstacles, we would carry on. We would never give in!

And so back to work I went, with just as much enthusiasm as I had brought to my job 40 years before when I had been named as the new head coach at the University of New Mexico. On that day in 1957, I had been 32 years old, making me the youngest major college head coach in the nation at that time. As I prepared for the upcoming 1997 season, I found out that only the venerable George Halas had still been coaching in the NFL at age 72. That is how old I would be once the season was launched. But I sure didn't feel it.

I remember the 1997 season as one of new faces and decimation in our ranks. Todd Collins, beginning his third season in the league, was our new quarterback. Dusty Zeigler, a sixth-round pick out of Notre

Dame one year earlier, took over at the vacated center position where Kent had starred for so many years. Andre and Quinn returned to give us two solid wide receivers, and they were backed up by our 1996 first-round pick, Eric Moulds, who was still a year or two away from emerging as a premier player at that spot. There were new faces all along the offensive line and at tight end, and our offense was not as potent as it had been. As a result, we scored fewer points during that 1997 season than any Bills team had totaled since 1985.

It was because of our defense and our kicking teams that we were able to stay competitive. We still had Bruce Smith and Phil Hansen up front, and they were joined by massive free agent nose tackle Ted Washington and some capable rookies such as Sean Moran and Shawn Price. Our secondary had been a strong point for us, and they were now experienced, as well. But what I really felt good about was knowing that, despite the losses over the years of linebackers such as Shane Conlan, Darryl Talley, and Cornelius Bennett, we had restored strength to the position by adding free agents like Bryce Paup and Chris Spielman. From recent drafts, fellows such as Sam Rogers, Marlo Perry, Damien Covington, and John Holecek provided promise and good special teams help.

We opened the season at home against the Vikings. I should say that the *Vikings* opened the season, because we never got untracked. We bumbled around and handed them a 34-13 gift-wrapped win. And then we had to go on the road to play the Jets. I said earlier that we would never give in, and we didn't. We came away from the Meadowlands with a win by downing the Jets 28-22. The on-again/off-again trend that was to prevail for us until shortly after midseason resumed when we lost the following week in Kansas City 22-16. We were now 1-2, but at least the next game would be at home, where we were scheduled to face the Colts.

At halftime we trailed 26-0, and I hadn't heard that many boos since the Cubs committed four errors in the ninth inning against the Pirates back in 1939. Didn't I say that *we would never give in?* Okay, are you ready for this? We won 37-35! Do you believe me now? It was the *third* greatest comeback in NFL history.

That was the way the season continued to unfold. The team wasn't a powerhouse, but no one could take us for granted, either. That is until we got hit by a "tornado." Day after day, someone else was injured and declared out for the season. We went into some games with absolutely no one backing up starters at as many as five positions. I found myself at practices concentrating only on wanting to get through them without sending someone else off on a cart. It became impossible to structure a meaningful game plan.

After our ninth game of the year, a 9-6 victory over the Dolphins, our record was 5-4, but I learned in the locker room afterward that linebacker John Holecek, who had emerged as a true force on our defense, had torn the anterior cruciate ligament in his knee. He would join a host of teammates on the out-for-the-season injured reserve list.

Practice was becoming a torment for me, and for the first time in 47 years, I wasn't having any fun out there. For the first time in my life, I was "getting through work." And then matters became worse. Much worse! Another young linebacker, Damien Covington, who had been showing such remarkable natural talent that we all believed we had uncovered a unique future star, went down. But his wasn't just your "usual" injury. I and those on the practice field that day all commented later that we had never seen an injured player who was in such apparent and extreme pain. Besides tearing internal ligaments and other tissue inside his knee, we learned later that there had been severe damage done to some nerves in his knee and leg. Damien was never able to play football again, and that happy-natured, friendly young man was never able to walk without exhibiting some lingering effects of the injury that ended his promising professional football career.

We were bringing players in off the streets in a desperate and inadequate effort to be able to show up on game day. Our preparation wasn't for opponents any more; it was more like the early stages of training camp. We lost our next three games in a row. We were 5-7 and realistically eliminated from any playoff possibilities, but somehow we came home from a two-game road trip, and we managed to scratch and claw our way to a 20-10 victory over the Jets. We had won that game, but I learned a couple of days later that we had *lost* something far more important than a single football game.

Chris Spielman had suffered a serious neck injury in the game. With great concern we monitored his condition, staying in almost constant contact with our medical staff. At last we learned the breathtakingly good news that Chris would recover and that he would not be afflicted with any permanent paralysis or disability. But, the doctors cautioned, there had been enough damage to and weakening of the vertebrae in his neck and spine so that he should never play football again. The career of the most ardent player I had ever known was over. I was stunned, not as much by what I knew I would be losing as a coach, but by how devastating this news had to be for Chris. Fortunately, Chris, among his many attributes, is an optimist. After his initial shock and disappointment, he gave thanks that he could walk, erect as always, out of the locker room and into the joys of the years that lay ahead for him, his wife, Stephanie, and his children. I remember No. 54 fondly.

Three games remained to be played in this nerve-shattering (and body-shattering) season, and two of them were on the road. Home or away, it didn't make much difference. We fell to the Bears in Chicago 20-3. At home the following week against Jacksonville, we fought hard, but we lost again 20-14. And then, we finished that dismal year with a trip to Green Bay, where we were defeated 31-21 by the Packers.

Although that loss in Green Bay had no impact at all on our playoff aspirations or even on our ability to salvage a winning record, there had been a special incentive that I and all the players on our team, had for wanting to win it. We had all hoped to be able, in the locker room after the game, to make a joyous presentation of the game ball to Steve Tasker. On Friday, the day before we traveled to Green Bay, Steve had made public his decision to retire.

When the gun sounded signifying the end of the final game of our 1997 season, it also heralded the conclusion of playing days for a man who could never really be adequately replaced. All the players and coaches in the NFL knew that, and it is best recognized by noting that when the Pro Bowl teams were voted upon every year, there was *only one* hard-core special teams player selected from each conference. Year after year in the AFC it was Steve Tasker. He was the conference choice seven times (six of them in consecutive years). In 1992, he was named the Most Valuable Player in the Pro Bowl. If the Board of Selectors for the Pro Football Hall of Fame really believes that the kicking game is vitally important (that's why they call it *foot*ball, isn't it?), they will, for the first time since the inception of that hallowed institution, designate for induction the greatest kicking teams performer the NFL will ever know. If that doesn't happen, they ought to investigate the balloting to see if there were any hanging chads.

Our loss in Green Bay did not provide the finish we had hoped for, but, at last, the most miserable of all seasons I had ever coached was over. We had lost six of our last seven games, and our overall record was a depressing 6-10. It was the poorest won-lost mark we had posted since I had come to Buffalo. I had seen so many of the great young players whom I have had the good fortune to coach grow old. I had seen the depletions in our ranks because of inroads from free agency. I had been there as the warriors I had come to know, and come to view with so much admiration, knew that it was time to lay down their shields and retire. And during this past year especially, I had witnessed, almost on a daily basis, injuries so severe that I experienced, with writhing empathy, the pain that they were enduring.

For the first time in 47 years, I was happy that the football season was over. For the first time, I was truly weary. And, to my stunned surprise, for the first time, I heard my subconscious ask me a question that I never thought it would utter: "Do you really want to keep doing this?"

CHAPTER 35

Farewell to Buffalo

During the next 48 hours as the question—*Do you really want to keep doing this?*—kept repeating itself in my head, I realized that it was demanding an answer. I knew that had that question ever been asked of me at the conclusion of any football season before this one, I would have shot back the quickest "of course I do," imaginable. It bothered me that I was allowing myself now to ponder over whether I should continue to coach. That delay in brushing such "nonsense" aside had to be part of the answer my mind was formulating. My gosh, I was actually thinking about it!

Did I finally and really want to get a full night's sleep? Wouldn't it be delightful to be on vacations, where my mind (as well as my body) could enjoy a stroll down the Champs-Elysées or through Trafalgar Square without dwelling on whether we should emphasize left or right kickoff returns in our opener against the 49ers? Did more leisurely and romantic dinners out with Frannie seem alluring? Would a respite from what I remembered most about the season that just ended—the terrible toll that injuries had taken on our team and on men I cared so deeply about—refresh me in both mind and spirit? The answers to all of these question kept coming up "yes."

Every year, during the week following the end of the football season, John Butler and I would travel to either Detroit or down to Ralph Wilson's vacation home in Florida in order to meet for several days with Ralph. While a variety of subjects would be on the agenda, the main thrust of our attention was directed toward plans for the future. These were always tremendously productive sessions, and the three of us always left the meetings feeling we were enlightened and geared up to work cohesively toward implementing our off-season strategies.

On our first day in Florida after the 1997 season, while we talked, during the breaks for a pleasant evening dinner, and again after I returned to my room at night, I continued to experience the same doubts about whether I should continue to coach. The next day, I surprised even myself when, almost involuntarily, I heard myself say, "Ralph, perhaps the time has come for you to bring in a new head coach for the Bills."

"I'm not going to do that, Marv," he responded immediately. "Now let's get on with discussing some of these salary cap problems that we are going to have to deal with."

I dropped the subject, and we all went back to work, although I did notice John shoot a querulous glance in my direction.

I didn't mention it again at that meeting, but when I returned to my room to freshen up before dinner, I realized that my feelings hadn't changed. At the meal that night, I waited for what I felt was an appropriate opening, took a deep breath, and then said to Ralph that I had spoken earnestly earlier that day when I had suggested that he bring in a new coach. After some discussion of the matter, Ralph told me that neither of us should do anything for the time being.

"Wait until after you return to Buffalo. Think about it some more, and then we'll talk further," he said.

We left the matter there, and on the flight back to Buffalo, John urged me to not act too quickly. He reassured me of how much he felt it was in the best interests of all of us and of the Bills for me to remain head coach. This wasn't the general manager talking to me. It was a good friend.

There was, however, a momentum building inside of me, and I felt it accelerate once I had articulated some of my pent-up sentiments. When I returned to Buffalo, I told Frannie of my conversations with Ralph and John, and she too wondered if I truly felt this way or if I was being hasty. Back at our offices the next day, John continued his efforts to dissuade me from taking the final step. Our football season had now been over for one full week, and it was time for me to "do it or don't do it!" I could tell that I wasn't going to turn back. I had initiated the subject, and once emboldened, I felt a compulsion to see it through. I told John, and then I called Ralph to inform him of my decision. On two occasions Ralph had tried to talk me out of it, and understandably, he wasn't going to do it a third time.

On December 31, 1997, just 11 days after our final game of the season, the Bills held a press conference at which I announced my retirement. Ralph, John, and all of our coaches, scouts, and players were there. So were all the people in the Bills' organization who had been instrumental in making my years there so enjoyable. I thanked them all, but I can't recall anything I said because I was too busy trying to control my emotions.

I had done it. And for three months it felt great. And then I began to wonder. Had I, as Frannie had cautioned, been too hasty?

On New Year's Day I came back to my stadium office in order to remove my important papers and memorabilia. It was a holiday, and no one else was there. After I was done, I decided to take a contemplative walk through the eerily quiet, empty facility. On the corridor walls were pictures. Some were of star players. Some were team photographs. Some were action shots of stirring moments in Bills history. I stopped, and I studied them. Some of the players had been gone for several years. Some had been with us only fleetingly. Some had come to training camp where they had tried but couldn't make the team. There also was the team picture of our 1987 group, the one that had filled in so enthusiastically for just three weeks during the player's strike that year.

As I stood there gazing at all those different people from different backgrounds, possessing varying levels of talent, each with his own individual personality, there was one thing that struck me hard about all of them. Those faces that stared back at me off of the hallway walls were a testament to the commitment that Bill Polian, John, and I had made when we resolved to bring only men with solid character onto our team. There wasn't a "look-at-me" showboat among them. There were no choreographed end zone dancers who thought they were cute but really weren't. In fact, I don't recall seeing even one backward baseball cap wearer up there.[1] I never saw or heard any of our players indulge in degrading displays of blatant self-aggrandizement. All I saw were men who, if they wanted to brag, would have been justified in boasting, "I came to play."

I was no longer coaching, but there was still plenty for me to do. I was in good health and better shape than most people 30 years younger. I was able to devote time to my physical workouts, and I enjoyed that opportunity to perspire guilt-free. I could now pursue some activities and embark on some of the travels that had seemed so appealing, and they were. I had time to study French and Spanish, just for the fun of it. Frannie managed to goad me into acquiring some computer skills, and I even learned how to spell e-mail. How about that? And finally, there was time to really sit down and read.

There were speaking opportunities, plus several NFL radio and television gigs that helped to fill my days. How gratifying it was to sit in

1. That is probably the ultimate unoriginal look anyone could ever adopt. Whenever I see one of those guys, I am inclined to deduct 10 points off of his IQ score. Put the bill of the cap sideways, and you can take off another five points. Diagonally sideways, and it's minus another 1.75.

a broadcast booth or a television studio and pontificate. It's a good thing that I found all those reasons to get out of the house. It preserved Frannie's sanity, *and* it got me out of doing that which I detested most—household chores. It wasn't that I was lazy. I vehemently deny any such allegations. It's just that I am so totally inept when it comes to such matters. Frannie probably summarized it best when she once commented to me, "You not only do not know how to fix it, you don't even know who to call." She should have been a coach.

The leisure life was refreshing, and after a while, I felt rejuvenated. And then I began to miss coaching football. There were a few opportunities for me to join teams as a consultant, but that isn't "coaching football." Besides, when I put myself mentally back into the shoes of the head coach, I could think of no greater way for him to be distracted and undercut than operating under the encumbering overseeing of a "second guesser," regardless of how well intentioned that person might be.

The urge to coach again continued to grow, and, after a year or two away, when I made that desire known to a few owners whose teams had head coaching vacancies, I was served a dish that was difficult for me to swallow. Even though I was prepared, experienced, healthy, motivated, and ready for action, there was a reticence to consider me because of my age. The owner I appreciated the most is one who actually came out and told me that that was the only reason he did not want to hire me. He pointed out that he was 20 years younger than I was and that he knew he didn't possess the energy required for keeping up with the demands that would be placed on a head coach. Perhaps he didn't, but I did. More than 40 years earlier I had been told I was too young. The man who said that was wrong. Now, I was too old, and those who said that are just as wrong.

I am convinced that none of those owners is guilty of seeking to discriminate, but they have succumbed to believing society's one still acceptable stereotype, the one that categorizes a person's capabilities not by their functional age, but by their *chronological* age. I could coach for another 10 years, at least, and maybe some owner who wants to win a Super Bowl as much as I do will afford us both that opportunity. If not, I will continue to relish the experiences I had as a coach, and I will continue to follow the exciting game that has brought me so much joy.

♦♦♦♦♦♦♦♦

Even though it wasn't coaching, my involvement with football remained close. Preparing for my radio and TV activities kept me in constant contact with the people in the game, and it was during a

January 2001 television assignment in Tampa that I received news that would ensure that my association with the NFL would become eternal. I had some free time, and so, as my wife, my daughter, and I sat in our hotel room watching ESPN the day before Super Bowl XXXV, the executive director of the Pro Football Hall of Fame, John Bankert, came to the microphone in order to announce the names of the men who had been selected for induction later that year.

Seven envelopes lay on the podium, and John's magnificent sense of measured timing, as he sliced each one open, then, while nodding his head, read it to himself, could have earned him an Academy Award nomination. Slowly, he rolled off the first name. The three of us waited as he repeated that procedure a second time, and then a third time. He opened the fourth envelope, and when he announced "Marv Levy," my daughter, Kimberly, let out a scream as she executed a vertical jump that, had she been draft-eligible, would have assured her of going no lower than the third round. She then began a trampoline act on the bed that caused me concern about whether she might bang her head on the ceiling, and so I told her to put on the souvenir Bills helmet I had brought along for donation to a charity autograph signing event later that afternoon.

A few minutes later, we boarded the hotel elevator on our way to the Convention Center where a press conference introducing the new inductees was to be held. One of the other newly announced members, former Dolphins linebacker Nick Buoniconti, was standing in the elevator grinning at me. Next to Nick stood the man who had been his coach, the great Don Shula. When I greeted those two legendary figures, I thought that this isn't an elevator I'm entering; this has to be the vestibule of the Hall of Fame itself.

As I had just about finished walking down the long corridor at the Convention Center on my way to the auditorium where the press conference was to take place, I heard some rapid footsteps accompanied by the shouting of my name. There were Bill Polian and Steve Tasker racing after me. When they arrived (it was a dead heat), I was overwhelmed by the glee they poured forth while congratulating me. As we stood there talking, Larry Felser, the sports editor of the *Buffalo News,* also stopped by, and he asked me who would be my presenter at the official ceremonies. That is when I turned to my friend, Bill, and asked, "What are you doing the first week in August?"

"I'll be there," he said with a smile.

On August 3 I sat on the platform in Canton, Ohio, along with the other members of the Class of 2001: Nick Buoniconti, Mike Munchak, Jackie Slater, Lynn Swann, Ron Yary, and Jack Youngblood. Someone had asked me if it was exciting to be inducted into the Pro Football Hall of Fame, and my honest answer was that if you are not thrilled upon receiving that honor, you don't deserve to have it accorded. Members from classes as far back as 30 years before were in attendance, and on their faces I could still see reflected the shining pride that they must have exhibited when they were there for their inductions.

(One year later, I would be there again, this time as the presenter for Jim Kelly as he entered the Hall of Fame along with the other men in the Class of 2002. I was just as much aglow about that ceremony as I had been a year earlier when Bill presented me. I am looking forward to being there again in the coming years when so many of those deserving Bills players put on that golden jacket in celebration of their inclusion into that special fraternity.)

Mark Twain once apologized for delivering a long speech by noting that he hadn't had sufficient time to prepare a short one. I know what he meant. On the steps of the Pro Football Hall of Fame, each inductee, when he is introduced, is allotted only eight minutes to speak. In that short period of time it was impossible for me to be able to thank all those who had been so important to me during my lifetime, and it was just as difficult for me to convey all the emotions I felt on that memorable day. I do recall some of the sentiments I expressed, and without trying to cover them all, I will revisit just a few of the remarks I made on that hot summer day when I was surrounded by football greats *and* by great football fans.

I started out, "It has been a long trip from the corner of 71st Street Stony Island Avenue on the South Side of Chicago to Canton, Ohio. It has taken me 76 years, but in the words of that old song, 'I wouldn't have missed it for the world' because on every step of this joyous journey I have been accompanied by some remarkable companions." I went on to mention that if it had not been for their love, abilities, and counsel I would not be standing "Right here! Right now!"

"When I first walked out onto the practice field as a high school assistant football coach exactly a half century ago next month," I continued, "men like Jim Thorpe, Red Grange, Bronko Nagurski, Sid Luckman, and Marion Motley were already mythical gods. They still are, and I walk this ground with great reverence for them and for all who reside here. Never did I dream that someday I might be invited to share these same lodgings with them."

When I reached that point in my remarks where I expressed my love for all the members of my family—my wife, Frannie; my daughter, Kimberly; my sister, Marilyn; and my former wife, Dorothy—I noted that they were all girls. And then I went on say, "Someone once commented, given my enthrallment with this game, that it is a shame that I never had a son. He was wrong," I declared. "Don't tell me that I never

had a son. I've had thousands of them, of every size, shape, color, faith, and temperament—and I love them, every one! And because of them, I still hear echoes from those sounds that glorify this game.

"I hear the cheers of the crowd as Thurman or Andre goes hurtling into the end zone, or as 'Bruce! Bruce! Bruce!' sacks yet another quarterback. I hear the grunts and collisions out on the field on play. I hear Jim Kelly calling cadence at the line of scrimmage. I hear Kent Hull's confident Southern drawl as he relays our lineblocking schemes to his teammates up front. I hear the thundering footsteps of young men as they streak down the field to cover a kickoff. No one ever did it better than two men who are here today—Steve Tasker and Mark Pike.

"And I still hear the distant strains of college fight songs: 'Cheer, Cheer for old Notre Dame'; 'The Sturdy Golden Bear'; 'Roll Alabama'; 'Ten Thousand Men of Harvard'; 'On Brave Old Army Team.'

"And even now, I hear words spoken more than 50 years ago by a man whose memory I cherish. He was my basketball coach and my track coach at Coe College. His name was Harris Lamb, and I will close my remarks to you now by repeating what he said to me and to my teammates so many years ago:

'To know the game is great.
To play the game is greater.
But to love the game is the greatest of them all.'

"Harris, my dear friend, I have truly loved this game. And I love everyone who has shared this passion with me. Thank you all for enriching my life."

EPILOGUE

That extended weekend in Canton, Ohio, when I was inducted into the Pro Football Hall of Fame, had been a hectic, event-filled four days, and I recall that as it drew to its close, I was as weary as I might have been after a playoff game on the road in Miami. I actually looked forward to the peaceful quiet that I would find aboard our late-night flight back home. After I settled into my seat next to my wife, Frannie, she kept humming and singing softly the words from that song to which I had referred during my remarks two days earlier: "I wouldn't have missed it for the world."

Her happy tune mixed with the quickening thrust of the plane's engines as we accelerated along the runway, and the harmony from those two sounds provided a perfect lullaby. I began to doze off as we became airborne and headed for sweet home Chicago. The voices of my daughter, Kimberly, and my sister, Marilyn (still celebrating in the row behind us), and the hazy recall of the pride and the sense of affection I had experienced as I had looked out into the audience upon the faces of former players and coaching associates joined the other pleasant images that eased into my fluttering consciousness, but the recurring theme, "I wouldn't have missed it for the world," pervaded.

As we soared higher into the blackness of the night sky, the caresses from those words continued, and then they expanded, nudging to life dormant memories. For 47 years, in scenes similar to this one, I had sat on an airplane heading home after a football game. Some we had won, and some we had lost. My recollection of the details from most of those games had become as faded as the yellowed newspaper clippings that had captured the excitement and the deeds that had seemed so important on autumn afternoons long ago. There were a few, however, that would remain in my mind's eye always, as sharp and as clear as they had been on the day we had played. There had been moments of unbridled exhilaration and other times when we knew only crushing disappointment. It had been 47 years with young men who had learned to push themselves to levels of effort they had once believed they were incapable of reaching.

The visages of these young men appeared to me now. Sometimes they gazed at me through swirling snow, sometimes through pelting rain or sleet, sometimes as rivulets of perspiration streaked the dirt on their faces while they labored under a searing sun in suffocating humidity. And still the words, "I wouldn't have missed it for the world," coursed through my mind. Deep down in my subconscious a thought shouldered its way through the panoply and gripped me with one of those rare and pure moments of revelation. It wasn't just today; it was always. It wasn't just a song; it was truth. As I drifted more deeply into slumber I embraced that truth: *I wouldn't have missed it for the world!*